Monaca aka Phillipsburg

Beaver County River Town

Volume I of II

by Sandy Davis

Volume I   Table of Contents

FORWARD

The entire time I was relaxing, reading, and researching information for this book, there was a song that kept going through my head.   It is from an old classic rock and roll song from 1970 that was on the charts when I was much younger. Joni Mitchell wrote, composed, and originally recorded the song "Big Yellow Taxi."   Her words and thoughts could not ring louder in my mind. Part of the chorus in the song says....

> *"Don't it always seem to go*
> *That you don't know what you got 'til it's gone*
> *They paved paradise, and put up a parking lot"*

In the fall of 1911, S. A. Batchelor wrote a quite lengthy article on Monaca; he went into great detail on many of the features of the town.   The fact that he called Monaca "the South Side Metropolis" and went on to say "a typical Western Pennsylvania industrial city of considerable size and importance," is amusing to me.   It is amusing only because in my mind, it was a false statement. It just didn't seem truthful since I never saw Monaca through a businessman's eyes, but instead saw it as this small, homey, and friendly place. Through the eyes of a young person, there was no "industry," nor did "considerable size" factor in since I could easily cover several square blocks of the town in what seemed like a minute, getting to say hello to many, gathering penny candy, picking up a lemonade, soda, or a donut from a local store on the way.

Monaca was like a very big family and as a child, if you were doing something wrong, you seldom got away with it because you had so many *parents* right there keeping an eye on you.   If you needed any help or needed anything at all, someone was within calling distance and ready to give assistance.   A far cry from being thought of as an industrial city of considerable size indeed !   From the businessmen's eyes and the providers of families, I am sure that Monaca was seen as being somewhat different.   It was a place for growth, a perfectly located site with potential and promise of prospering.   This type of thinking and prospective of Monaca is what I am sure S. A. Batchelor is referencing in his writing.   The pride of his connection with Monaca is also evident; but then that same pride exuded from any one of the residents from the head of household on the way to a job, a housewife if you stopped her while she shopped in one of the many businesses in town, to neighbors engaged in conversation. That is what made Monaca – Monaca !

Please sit back and enjoy reading and seeing how the past is blended into the here and now of 2016 as you read what I have accumulated, assembled, and juxtaposed.   Sandy

ACKNOWLEDGMENTS

"We must find time to stop and thank the people who make a difference in our lives." -John F. Kennedy

I want to personally thank the following persons for all the patience and time they extended to me while I was doing the researching and collecting information and pictures for this book.   They all shared personal memories, pictures, and/or special information with me.

Richard Temple for his contributions

Cindy and Craig Stuehling

Randy Ball

Nickolas Mandalakas

Georgia Davis

Borough of Monaca

Center Township

The Beaver County Historical Research and Landmarks Foundation for their vast collections and archived materials.

The Beaver Area Heritage Foundation

To all the libraries and other historical locations and organizations for being so willing to share and aid in my research.

A very personal expression of gratitude goes out to a special person I now consider my friend - Ellen Glasser. Without hesitation, she allowed me to pick her brain for many, many of the businesses, items, locations, and names of businesses, owners, and individuals.   If she was not sure of something, she went to one of her two sisters - Amy Coombs and Alice Phillis, so they also receive a special thank you. Additionally, Ellen provided me with many resources for this book and spent many, many hours helping proofread the material with me.

I am so grateful to have such good people in my life.

"The best kind of people are the ones that come into your life and make you see the sun where you once saw clouds. The people that believe in you so much, you start to believe in you too. The people that love you, simply for being you. The once in a lifetime kind of people." -Anonymous

INTRODUCTION

In each of the different categories/sections of this book, I have included as many facts, notes, explanations, ads, and pictures of buildings as I could find for each.   The businesses listed under any specific category are loosely listed by 'type' of business and most likely not in any chronologically and/or alphabetical order.   Please let it be known that I in no way make the claim that within my books you find ALL the businesses or people that were at one time or another located in Phillipsburg or Monaca.   I have tried to the best of my ability and resources to locate and list as many businesses and people as possible though. No business or person was excluded on purpose!   With that being said, I do admit that the newer and most recent businesses will not be as well represented, nor was attention centered on them. My goal was to find older or former businesses and show how the area moved forward.

There are many individual sections or categories in this book to follow where I have broken down the different types of shops, storerooms, business, industries, mills, and trades that were and are found in Monaca. Along with the listings of all these, I have included specific facts and information, as well as the addresses and former owners of the business (when known).

To explain what you will find within each category and/or section....   If there was any information on a business, then I included as much as possible within each category.

First will be listed......

Business name and any known address(es)

Right under the name will be.....

Year or multiple listing of years I found information for being in business.
Not every individual year is listed, just a random or variety of years where
 information was found to verify the business.

Under any years will be .....

Miscellaneous information about the business, the owner(s) if known, and
all other pertinent details.

And lastly.....

If there was a picture available, it is included along with a sampling of any
advertisements found for the business.

Readers will find many references to Phillipsburg, Moon, Monaca, Colona, Center, and Potter. This is because they all gravitate and mesh together during the course of time, yet each has also stood proudly alone. History books tend to state that Moon became Center Township, which is truthful for the most part, but a bit misleading.   There is a bit more to this statement. Moon Township was indeed the parent township for Center, but also other communities were formed from Moon: Raccoon Township in 1837, Phillipsburg Borough in 1840 (now Monaca), Potter Township in 1912, as well as Center Township in 1914.   In 1932, the remaining upper portion of Moon Township, between the Borough of Monaca and Center Township became annexed to Monaca.

I will also take this time to apologize for all misspellings and possible errors in the information in this publication. Everything was read, reread, cross referenced, and doubled checked to the best of my ability – but I am only human.   Speaking of references, there is a complete list of all resources at the end of Volume II.   By listing all at the end of the book, I felt this made the book flow more easily rather than have it cluttered with multiple specific references with each business or entry.   I found the majority of my information from endless hours of reading historical publications and archived newspapers spanning over more than a hundred years. Regarding newspaper publications, those specific dates and pages of where the information was extracted are not listed in this book, just the names and time frames for each of the papers; again, this was done to streamline the list of reference information.

While I strive for accuracy in the factual content, I cannot offer any guarantee of accuracy. Names have been entered and spelled as they were found in articles and/or documents.   Readers will notice many variations of all names, but I did not feel comfortable altering any spellings from the original findings.   Information is provided "as is" without warranty of any kind, either expressed or implied. Information could include technical inaccuracies or errors of omission. Opinions and commentary are those of myself or others who made them and do not necessarily represent the views of anyone else.   It is not my intention to usurp any copyright holders' rights but only to promote the older material as purely educational.   I do not bear any responsibility for any consequences resulting from the use of this or any other information provided.

LIFE, INFORMATION, HISTORY and LOCATION - Phillipsburg / Monaca, PA

Early life in the Phillipsburg/Monaca area......

During the eighteenth and early part of the nineteenth centuries, what is now the Ohio Valley was mainly considered farm land with some areas yet unsettled; the cities growing from what started as mere frontier towns. Even Pittsburgh was but a handful of log houses with very few brick and stone structures and maybe a half dozen stores in the 1700s. The people from the Phillipsburg and Moon Township areas were of German, Swiss, Irish, and Scotch backgrounds yet were predominantly English speaking, or very willing to learn the language. Families were usually quite large due to being needed/ used to work on the family farms, in the homes, or apprenticed with a trade or business; also remember that the mortality rate, especially for infants, was high during this time period.

A typical family in the area lived in log cabins or what was then quite practical and simpler houses. Very early homes were also windowless since window glass was not made in Pittsburgh until 1797. Very small homes usually only had one fireplace; larger homes had a fireplace in almost every room. Most households used wooden utensils at first and later metal. Foods in a common home consisted of bread, meat, homegrown vegetables and fruit, and homemade whiskey was everywhere. Clothing was most likely made from homespun woolens and linen since cotton was considered a luxury and wasn't generally available in this area until after 1790. As merchants began to be more numerous and the ability to travel to Pittsburgh became easier, luxuries such as teas, coffee, spices and a variety of clothing became easier to obtain.

The first settlers to the area relied on trapping, hunting, limited Indian trading, and agriculture as the source for income and building the economy. Horses, cattle, sheep, pigs, and poultry also became great economical assets. By 1800, grist mills, brickyards, glasshouses, boatyards, breweries, and tanneries were being added as business investments. They strengthened the economy, too. Although work and building the economy were important, social life of the people was also important. Unlike many affluent areas, Phillipsburg and Moon Township were not 'society' driven areas, yet it was still obvious the former military officers and professional men were "at the top" and the men who performed more menial labor were "toward the bottom"; women were definitely considered second class citizens, as was "homemaking" for the occupation. Entertainment was fairly simple with drinking, dancing, card playing, and parties at home being the most popular. Men would meet in the taverns or blacksmith shops to exchange stories or for daily talks to solve the world's problems.

Health was an ongoing problem before modern medicines and most of all, identifying the causes of some illnesses. The low-lying and swampy areas bred malaria (no one knowing at the time that mosquitoes were the culprit). Other more common ailments suffered were small pox, cholera, typhoid fever, tuberculosis, and vitamin deficiency related diseases; all being treated at first with common home remedies. As doctors, as well as the knowledge of these ailments, became more common, so did the curing of the diseases.

Information of Phillipsburg / Monaca...........

When I begin to give more detailed information on the history of Phillipsburg, I will be mentioning the names Count Maximilian deLeon, Bernhard Müller, Father (George) Rapp, and/or Frederick Rapp. I want to take the time prior to the basic history to give you some important background regarding these persons; specifically this history on Bernhard Müller aka Count Maximillian deLeon. It is not the usual "he came, he built, he left"; it is rather the truthful and not so pleasant background on him.

For as long as I could read and cared to listen to the adults talk about Monaca's early history, it has always been about how Bernhard Müller, or as he named himself and was better known, Count Maximilian deLeon, was the first to bring a group of people to settle in Phillipsburg. In later years, after finding I had ancestors who were paid employees of the Harmony Society at Old Economy in Ambridge and then another ancestor that actually was one who religiously helped influence Father Rapp, I looked deeper into the Harmony Society and Father Rapp. (That ancestor was Jacob Bohem.) In the process, I found very interesting information about Mr. Bernhard Müller.

Perhaps, sharing more on Bernhard will give a better understanding to why he did not stay long in Phillipsburg. It will also explain why the majority of the persons who followed him to Economy and then Phillipsburg (Monaca) did not continue to travel nor follow him when he moved on to another state. There are many books and publications on the Harmonists of Economy and in my genealogy research, general research, and now my research on Monaca, I will now share what I found regarding Count deLeon.

Bernhard Müller

Bernhard Müller was born in Germany in 1788. To avoid religious persecution, like so many others, he came to America. He gave himself quite a few fictitious "titles" and names including Archduke Maximillian von Este, Proli, Maximilian, Count Maximilian, Count Maximilian deLeon, and Count deLeon. In 1829, Müller wrote to the Harmony Society, as well as numerous leaders in Europe and other communes in the United States claiming that he was the prophet "Lion of Judah" and was in possession of the Philosopher's stone. He also made claim that he and his followers were the true Philadelphians*. Since the Harmonists and Father Rapp were deeply religious people, they took Müller at his word and honestly thought he was the hopeful sign they were waiting for. The Harmonists invited Müller to join them in their latest settlement of Old Economy in Ambridge. In 1831, he arrived with about 40 other people and settled in. This was a short lived situation because it did not take long for Father George Rapp and the majority of the original Harmonists (known as Rappites) to see Müller for his true colors.

Even though for several years all the people of Economy lived together peacefully, and Father Rapp's community was seemingly again becoming solidly settled in, the utopia would soon be turned into a battleground. It is repeatedly stated and printed that Müller and some others left Economy and moved, settling in Phillipsburg because of the mere fact of not agreeing to the practice of celibacy. While it is a true statement to say they left Economy and moved to Phillipsburg, celibacy was not the exclusive reason at all. Bernhard Müller, then using the name Count Maximilian deLeon, did not move to Economy to live in harmony in the community, but rather had the intentions to steal away many of the Harmonists to start his own utopia, as well as obtaining a great financial security.

Müller proved to be a faker and through his teaching of strange doctrines, caused dissension; some writings also state he was discovered to be "a selfish, deceitful imposter." In many of Müller's long, angry speeches of criticism and/or accusations, he began to cause much dissatisfaction with the society's strict doctrines, with the Rappites, as well as with Father Rapp. With many of the Harmonists being so dissatisfied, the cognitive dissonance, and no signs of Müller conforming, Father Rapp decided that Müller must leave. Müller showed no concern since he thought he would be able to win over the majority of the community and therefore take over. In March, 1832, the Harmonists held a vote and by a two to one margin, they declared their loyalty to Father Rapp. After this vote, Maximilian/ Müller and his now approximate 250 followers agreed to leave Economy and go to find their own settlement. Müller's then followers were 'convinced' that Father Rapp had influenced his original people to reject Müller; when in reality, it was Müller's followers that were being mislead. They gathered their belongings, took the negotiated settlement of $105,000 and moved down river and settled in what became called Phillipsburg, now Monaca.

It did not take long for Müller to seemingly squander the amount of money they had received. In one publication, it was stated that Bernhard Müller aka Count Maximilian deLeon was an impostor and actually absconded with the greater part of that $105,000 payment. Whether he withheld monies or it was squandered by the whole community, the end result was the same --- the community was out of money. Rather than provide an explanation to his followers as to why they were out of money, Müller convinced them that they were due more money and were going to go to Economy and seize it by force.

Father Rapp heard about Müller's plans to attack and therefore prepared a defense. The Harmonites were for all intents and purposes a passive group of people, but would rise to the occasion when they were threatened. A Harmonist militia waited in the woods to ambush Müller's men. Müller's followers marched on Economy and headed for the Great House but before they could break in, they were pelted with stones and bricks, and doused with hot water thrown by the Harmonist women from a window above the entrance. The Müllerites fled the Great

House and headed for the Economy hotel, which was owned by the Harmonists of Economy village; the intent was to steal valuables.   This also failed because the Harmonist men who had been hiding and waiting in the woods drove them from the hotel.   It has been written that the Müllerites were marched out of town while a small band played *The Rogue's March*.   After this defeat, Müller and many of his followers again packed up their belongings, left Phillipsburg, and headed for Louisiana by flatboat on the river.   Müller died the next year.   Those that followed Count deLeon most likely found a disastrous end to the utopia he promised to them.   There were quite a few original followers of Maximilian who made the decision to remain in Phillipsburg. Whether they saw Müller for his true self, and decided to stop supporting him, or whether they were disgruntled with being faced with yet another move or perhaps they may have been just plain satisfied with living in Phillipsburg and wanted to settle there, will probably never be known.

So, that is some of the accumulated information I have found on who the true Maximilian Count deLeon was and how it was not as simple as his leaving Economy with some followers, starting up the new community of Phillipsburg, finding all their money was spent, and moving to Louisiana. It was quite a bit more dramatic and intense and full of deception and even some violence for people who were known for living in peace and harmony. Until 1831 when Bernard Müller showed up and caused such a schism, the Harmony Society of Economy was prospering. After Economy rid itself of Müller, it did come back, and the original Rappites prospered and lasted until the end of the nineteenth century.   With the practice of celibacy, it is no wonder that as the members of the community began to age, workers retired, and not having a new generation to replace them, that by about 1905, the once thriving community all but dissolved.

> *Philadelphians does not refer to people of Pennsylvania or other American areas, in this instance,
> it refers to people in the Bible book Revelations which references "Philadelphia" – Smyrna is an ancient
> city, known today as Izmir (Turkey) and Philadelphia share the distinction of receiving nothing but praise
> from Christ.   This is why modern Protestant churches sometimes use "Philadelphia" as a component in
> the local church's name as a way of emphasizing its faithfulness.*

Count deLeon

Now that you have a short tutorial about the persons credited with being the first to begin the settlement known as Phillipsburg, you will understand why I will only casually be mentioning deLeon's name. Giving him any type of praise to me would be unfair.   The reader will find repeated mention and see the names of the persons who remained and continue to settle Phillipsburg / Monaca, though, since they were the ones who actually did permanently settle and develop what is now known as Monaca, Pennsylvania.

*** *** *** *** ***

History on Phillipsburg / Monaca.................

Phillipsburg, situated on a level plateau, consists of a long narrow strip of ground parallel with the Ohio River. It was described by one old-timer as "a quaint German village placidly dozing in the sunshine, ferried only into the big round world." This scenic area, containing approximate 330 original acres was in what was first known as Smith Township from 1769 and then "Appetite." There are hundreds and hundreds of adjoining acres in any direction you look. There was the former Hog Island to the NW in the Ohio River, with another 100 acres and about two and a half miles included in, yet beyond Appetite, all lying along the Ohio River. All this acreage has one thing in common – the advantage of slack water and providing over a thousand acres of the best sites for manufacturing purposes in Western Pennsylvania. The Phillipsburg area was primarily bordered by the Moon Township land.

> *Fun fact: I found one pamphlet that stated Moon Township is said to have been given the name "moon" from a physical characteristic of the Ohio River, being the Ohio River makes a distinctive bend in the immediate area. When drawn and/or viewed on a map, it resembles a crescent shape, being the same as one formed by the moon during one of its many phases.........tah dah.......Moon Township.*

The status of borough was achieved in 1840. There was also a very large amount of land that immediately adjoined Monaca and was situated just above Monaca. This area was pulled from the original Moon Township land and officially became annexed to Monaca in the December 1931; it contained enough acreage of its own to be a city of the first class. The Monaca Heights Land Company, Allaire Land Company, Colona Land Company, and Freedom Oil Works held a large portion of acreage in Monaca Heights and Colona Heights. Along with these main companies, there were several other quite financially influential men who were stockholders in the same land. Some of these were Col. Schoemaker (vice president of the P & LE railroad), A. M. Jenkinson (the cigar man), L.A. Robinson, C.D. Armstrong, Henry Cooper (state senator), J.B. Finley (pres. of Colonial Steel Co), Charles Brown, F. B. Nimick, T. H. Childs, James H. Welch, and H. C. Fry. These men, along with some others, had combined fortunes totaling millions of dollars. It is said that all of these companies and individuals agreed that the land in Monaca would only be sold or given to manufacturers of such importance that would assure the building of a city on Monaca Heights. The heights had fire departments, schools, parks and recreational areas, many individual business and companies, and many residents, each with their own strong skills and trades. Did these men of yesterday consider the area its own city? Maybe, but as the land companies began to subdivide lots, building and selling homes, and this newly annexed area grew rapidly. It was a part of the Borough of Monaca and rather than becoming its own city, it became the Fourth and Fifth Wards of the Boro.

From its very beginning back in the late 1700s as a plot of land, it grew into a wonderfully prosperous and noted town and area. In about 1910, Monaca was considered but a village and had less than 400 inhabitants. The 1920 census came in with 1,400 and in 1930 it was at 2,008; 1940 brought credit of 3,376 residents, almost a 60% increase. If Monaca had been credited with the population of Monaca Heights and Colona area, the total population would have been 5,350, giving it a ranking of 4th in size among the Beaver County towns at that time.

Monaca is one of the few towns of the county which can trace the origins of its existence back to the Indian times. There are many publications that delve into the early history of Phillipsburg and Monaca. I, too, will touch on this subject and give the basic details so if this is the first you have decided to read information on Monaca, you will have some information. Unlike others, I am not going to be as detailed in the type of Indians from the area or go into lengthy explanations. I will be giving enough enlightenment to keep the romance of the story of the area without being repetitious with easily found information.

Another interesting fact with Monaca is that it has always had the distinction of being a borough free of debt or not being horribly indebted with extreme taxation of its residents. Going back to 1911, Monaca was enjoying paved avenues and streets, the completion of its sewerage system, and had a water works system in place; yet it was a borough free from debt and having some $25,000 in its treasury. This was an accomplishment that few surrounding towns could boast of.

Over the years, the many industries of Monaca have been very diversified. There were numerous smaller, more personal businesses. Some of the bigger and prosperous industries were the Colonial Steel Co., Opalite Tile Co., U. S. Sanitary Co., Pittsburgh Tube Mill, Colona Mfg Co., Pittsburgh Tool-Steel-Wire Mill, American Glass Specialty Co., Phoenix Glass Co., Welsh-Bright Co., and many, many others. All gave employment to hundreds, then thousands of employees; each employee either had a home or was anxious to find housing in Monaca.   Living so closely to their places of employment would mean less time in travel and less expense in finding rides on the ferries, street cars, buses, and railroad.   The wear and tear, cost of gasoline, and parking of an automobile came into play later.

With the desire to extend traveling distances and all the growth of factories, industries, and manufacturing companies in Monaca, the Pennsylvania and Lake Erie Railroad found the area to be most attractive for building a new track through the town.   The P & L E Railroad brought even more growth to Monaca and vicinity in 1877, opening a new world of travel also.   Prior to the P & L E railroad, the people of the Monaca area only had access to the outside world by traveling the Brodhead Road into Moon Township and other areas, or accessing the other side of the river using ferry boats.   The railroad not only brought more employment to Monaca with jobs directly connected to the railroad, but it brought more interest in companies to make Monaca their home and therefore increased local employment once again.   Many individuals found that with the ease in finding many means of transportation more convenient and affordable, they could easily also find employment outside the Borough of Monaca.   Residents found they could now explore a new wheel of interest while continuing to enjoy their homes already established and settled in; yet begin to broaden their travels and all the places of business and amusement since they became easier to access.   They could still have the personalized and smaller familiar home life, businesses, their churches, and friends remain the same.

Yet another means to broaden the areas of travel for Monaca residents came when the pedestrian/vehicular suspension bridge was built over the Ohio River between Monaca and Rochester in 1895.   The Beaver Valley Traction Company extended their line from Rochester to Monaca across this bridge bringing in street cars, too.

> *FUN FACT – The original bridges were made of wooden planks.   There would be large wooden barrels filled with water and randomly kept sitting along a bridge.   They were needed to dowse any fires that were started when a cigar or cigarette was dropped by a careless pedestrian.   With the barrels of water sitting right on the bridge, fires were not only easily extinguished, but much more rapidly.   Without the water being readily available right there on the bridge, then to assembly the volunteer firemen, horses, wagons, etc. could take much longer time and more of a bridge could be damaged.*

Today, it is very unusual to find an unpaved, tar and chipped, dirt road in any given area; but this was more of the norm back when Monaca was first developing and growing. Sidewalks consisted of wooden planking.   Eventually all the streets and then sidewalks were paved - not with concrete or asphalt as you find today, but in the early 1900s, paving was done with bricks. Many of these brick streets and alleys have been paved over with asphalt today (2015), but some towns still maintain and have retained their brick alleys and roadways.   They are something to appreciate when you consider the quantity of bricks, the time, amount of energy, patience, and talents involved in laying miles and miles and MILES of brick streets.   When you think about it, some of those brick streets and sidewalks were laid at least 100 years ago and are still in very good condition; yet we sit in traffic for great amounts of time nowadays while crews tear up and replace worn asphalt or concrete that has only been in place a fraction of the age of the brick ones.

Just as interesting and appreciated, should be the same time and energies that went into erecting all the buildings, most still standing today; as well as the early completion of the water lines and sewerage systems.   There were no large flat bed trucks to deliver materials, no backhoes, no bulldozers, no huge dump trucks, or cement mixers back then – it was all done by horse and wagon and the sweat and muscles of individual men working together.

With the residency growing, Monaca found its need for banks and places of depository, as well as places for people to obtain credit and loans for building new or bigger businesses and houses.   Along with the population growth and more business springing up, also came the many diverse places of worship in Monaca.   From the late 1800s to the early 1900s, people could choose between attending churches of different faiths – Methodist, Lutheran (English, German, Slovak), Baptist, Presbyterian, and Roman Catholic.   Monaca still has many churches today (2016).

Many persons today do not give it a second thought when they need an article of clothing, pair of boots, shoes, jewelry, lace, hats, a new lawnmower, a chair, curtains, or even a shovel or garden tool.   They hop in their car or go on line and buy what they want from one of many businesses or companies available to them.   I was reared in the very end of the era when people still made almost everything locally or at home; and most importantly, usually it was made by hand or in a quite small business.   Oh, there were still places to go to buy items that were needed since no one in the family or community had the knowledge, skill, or resources to make all things or items. This makes sense because not everyone was a master of all trades; plus, as former tradesmen were aging or dying off, there was no one left to replace them.

I grew up not knowing of places that were called a "business" or "company"; nor were they just somewhere that merely sold things.   Instead, we would go to what was most likely called a "shop" or it had an individual's name sake attached to where you would …. go to the meat shop (would have been Mateer Bros. Meat Market), go to the bakery (would mean Klingseisen Bakery), or take your shoes to Chris's (meant Chris' Shoe Repair Shop).   A shop was someplace that not only had items that you would purchase or a specific service, but the majority of the time it was the very place where that item was also handmade or the service was performed. Each shop had a personality, just like their proprietors.

There were "chains of usage" in a village or area.   What do I mean – well….. one good example of this chain of usage would be: People wanted to buy meat and would go to a butcher or meat market.   The butchers were most likely the ones that slaughtered the animal, cleaned and skinned the animal, and then processed/cut the meat.   Most areas had what was called a tanner.   They purchased hides from the butchers and would work their magic on the leather to make it workable so once the local shoemakers purchased the leather, they could apply the skills of their trade and make shoes and/or boots or other leather items.   Some shoemakers not only made custom ordered footwear, but would assemble numerous sizes and styles of shoes and then local merchants would purchase them and sell in their stores.   Shoes were not simply discarded if the soles would wear or a seam would lose its strength; shoemakers were also masters at making repairs as needed.   Some farmers who raised animals and fowl and were also considered butchers; they didn't have their own meat/poultry shop, so they would sell items to the markets or shops that did sell it.   So…….meats, hides, poultry, feathers came from a butcher -- hides went to the tanners and then to the shoemakers, the meats to the markets, the feathers went to pillow and quilt makers………… a chain of usage.

Furniture was also made by hand; many of the wagons and buggies were made locally as well as the farming implements. Farmers would raise sheep for their wool which would be sheared and either sold to individuals or to woolen mills and shops that worked, carded, and spun the wool. Most women would do the working, carding, and spinning of the wool themselves and then weave or knit items of clothing or blankets as needed.   Homemakers would also purchase cotton, flax, and linen, then use looms to weave it into material to make clothing and other items. Lace was made by tatting and/or bobbin lacing.   There were women who would sell their hand-woven cloth or lace to a seamstress or milliner who would hand sew it all into articles of clothing and hats for those who could afford that luxury.

The route to finding a less time consuming method of obtaining clothing, shoes, furniture, home goods, and foods brought about usage of machine made goods.   Even though machines making goods started to meet the supply and demand much more easily, it also meant that the high grade and excellence of the hand-made goods was compromised.   People of today are starting to realize that the quickest and cheapest articles purchased are often the most expensive – why ----- well, when you come down to it, these items do not last as long nor wear as well and people have to purchase the same items more often.   In most cases, many of the newer mass produced products lack or fail to show any true artistic beauty.

In earlier years, people used to take better care of articles and items they owned because the amount of time and effort put into making or obtaining them was totally appreciated since it was not as simple as putting out some cash like we tend to do today.   There was a sincere pride that not only went into making items to be used personally, but for all those that would be used by other persons.   There was a definite quality to the work when it was handmade and the maker did his best knowing his name was going to be attached to the articles or items. This is something that machines and assembly line work just do not have today – no real form of pride or concern. If a business person provided a service or specialty skill, then it was also very common for them to have an apprentice or two that was being taught that trade, too. The traits and quality of work of all apprentices was closely monitored because again, the owner's name was personally attached to all items as well as how trained an apprentice would become. As you look through all the different shops, markets, and livelihoods of the persons of Monaca, I wanted you to appreciate what went into each storeroom, especially in the earlier years.   The majority of the people who were entrepreneurs did not just sell things; they were the individuals who built, produced, sewed, cooked, and/or made what was in their shop or home.

Phillipsburg / Monaca

Prior to settlers, land grants, patents, or deeds, the first persons to live on and settle the land are now known native Indians. Monaca is shortened from the name of Monacatootha, who was an Oneida warrior chief and a representative of the Iroquois Confederacy who met with George Washington during his visit to Logstown in 1753. The American colonists gave the name "Delaware" to the Lenni Lenape native Indians who were the most populous nation found in Pennsylvania. They mostly populated the present day New Jersey and eastern Pennsylvania areas, but after their communities were greatly weakened by intertribal conflicts, newly introduced diseases, and violent conflicts with Europeans, they moved west into the upper Ohio River basin. They were pushed even further west, and in the 1860s, the U.S. government eventually sent them to Indian Territory (now in Oklahoma and surrounding territory).

There are some publications that state that from 1769, a 330 acre tract of land, now part of the Borough of Monaca, was first recorded by colonists under the name of Smith Township and this same tract of land was surveyed by William L. Lungan who gave the property the name Appetite. The *History of Beaver County* written by Joseph H. Bausman in 1904 states and displays information with Monaca's original area coming out of the then Washington County's Robinson Township; with Smith Township being laid out on the other side of Raccoon Creek. I would have to believe that by doing an extensive research of warrants, surveys, and deeds, it could be determined whether the area that became known as Appetite/ Phillipsburg/ Monaca was originally situated in Smith or Robinson Township of Washington County. I have chosen, at this time, not to make verification of this information the center of my researching, but to rather only present the conflicting information at this time.

On Sep 5, 1787, Appetite was purchased through a Commonwealth of Pennsylvania patent for 42 pounds, 7 shillings and 6 pence by Ephraim Blaine, who was the grandfather of American statesman James G. Blaine.

On Jun 17, 1801, Blaine sold Appetite; it was purchased by Robert Callender, who died in 1802 and willed the land to John Wilkens, Jr., George Wallace, and Alexander Addison. These three men, as trustees of Callender's will, sold the land yet again, and divided the property as Robert's will so stated. Dec 29, 1804, Appetite was purchased by John Niblow. John retained title to the land until Aug 1813.

Aug 1, 1813, it was sold again to Frances Helveti, a Polish nobleman who was exiled from his native country and immigrated to America and is said to be the first white colonial settler of Appetite. Helveti purchased Appetite with the desire to raise and breed Merino sheep for their wool. He had some problems with this business and financial planning proved unsuccessful. Helveti became indebted to George Rapp which led to the property being auctioned at a public sale.

On Aug 30, 1821, the property of Appetite was sold by the sheriff of Beaver County, James Lyon, and purchased by Frederick Rapp, George Rapp's adopted son. (Frederick was in charge of finances and eventually became head of Economy after George Rapp's death.) At the time of the sheriff's sale, it is described in the deed that there were "two log houses, one kitchen, one large sheep house, shingle-roofed, and one cabin-roofed stable and about 84 acres cleared, 16 acres of which are in meadow."

About the same time, there was a steamboat yard beginning business along the shore line. The actual origins of the town are dated about 1822 when Phillips and Graham, established their very large, successful steamboat yard and boat building business along the river. The name of Phillipsburg came about for Stephen Phillips of this boat building firm. They continued the business at this site until into the 1830s. Once again, Appetite was sold, by Steven Phillips. The original 330 acres of land had been continuing to develop into a small community by this time under the name of Phillipsburg.

On Jul 21, 1832, Count Maximilian deLeon and his followers purchased about 800 acres of land which included the previously named Appetite acreage. They promptly developed and began adding on to the already small community and referenced it as New Philadelphia; calling themselves the New Philadelphia Society. They constructed 50 houses, a hotel, factories, and a stone church; with all being held in common, yet also living in family units. This new community and the New Philadelphia Society only existed for a very short period of time, 17 months to be exact. Once deLeon and most of his followers left the area by flatboat for Louisiana, New Philadelphia was dropped and the name Phillipsburg was once again used.

In 1834, Phillips and Graham, having plied their trade in Monaca since 1822, decided to move their business further up river to what is now Freedom and transferred their tract of land to Adam Schule and Anthony Knapper. By 1834, what started as a plot of land called Appetite was beginning a gradual division of lots which is very small in comparison to the several thousand lots that exist in 2015.

There were no books or information recorded for the first 40 or so years as to the definite governing body of Phillipsburg. On Apr 12, 1880, the first Town Council was organized and the following were selected as the officers of the Town Council: William Wagner-President, R.G. Onstott-Secty and Treas, John Buchanan-Solicitor, Christine Erbeck-Burgess, and members Jacob Bucheit, E.R. Frank, Henry Volhardt, W. J. Porter, and Samuel Bickerstaff. By 1890, the Town Council was quite busy and had started to improve the streets by grading them and then laying the sidewalks.   The Borough of Monaca had spent thousands of dollars for the improvements in the streets, adding sewers, building a new municipal building, enlarging the water plant and adding many improvements to the distributing system of the water plant as well as extensions.   In 1848 the Water Cure Sanitarium was established when several of the larger buildings erected and owned by the New Philadelphia Society were purchased by Dr. Edward Acker who used hydrotherapy to perform medical treatment. It was considered the first hospital in Beaver County.   There was a brief time in the mid 1800s where the name of Water Cure was applied to Phillipsburg and the post office, but this name was not used for any length of time. Water Cure sanitarium was operated successively by Dr. Edward Acker, Dr. Baetiz, and a man named Cimotti.

In 1865, Rev. William G. Taylor came to Phillipsburg and not only took on the task of starting up the Soldiers' Orphan School, one of the first schools of its kind in Pennsylvania, but Rev. Taylor funded the majority of the expense in starting this school.   Dr. Taylor also supplied much of the furnishings and a multitude of other necessaries to make it a top notch school.   The school flourished well until a fire destroyed the main building in 1876 while Rev. Taylor was out of town.   Due to the damage, expense, and time frame to rebuild, it was decided to close the school.

With confusion developing over the name of Phillipsburg since there was another town in Pennsylvania that had the same name, the town's name was decidedly changed on March 21, 1892, to Monacatootha after the Native American Oneida Chief Monacatootha who supported George Washington during the war and served as a representative of the Iroquois Confederacy.   Monacatootha became known as just Monaca from usage of an abbreviation of the name the Pennsylvania and Lake Erie Railroad used on railroad passes and tickets.   Evidently the complete name of Monacatootha did not fit on these passes and tickets, so it was abbreviated to Monaca.

Speaking of railroads --- The first Pittsburgh & Lake Erie railroad locomotive came into the borough in 1877. With the railroad now accessing the area, industry in town began to rapidly expand. For a quiet, smaller, and somewhat dormant town, Monaca was about to see major changes beginning with the population growing, as well as more construction of homes and many new manufacturing plants and businesses coming in.   Although the railroad did mean growth and modernization to the borough, it also meant that finally the southern portion of Beaver County could now have much easier access to the northern portions of the county and other areas outside the county.

The population of Monaca did indeed steadily increase over of the years -- 1877 had 400 people, 1890 showed 1494 persons, up again in 1910 to 3376, and in 1900 there were 2008 people.   In the year 1931 Moon Township was annexed to the Borough of Monaca which increased the population by 2,200. This annexation made for the addition of the Fourth and Fifth Wards and gave Monaca approximately two square miles of additional area.   By 1950 the total population was at 7415.

On Nov 24, 1914, due to a dispute among Moon Township residents, the court decreed that the larger, more sparsely populated, southern section of Moon become Center Township. It was not until December 1932 that the remaining smaller, northern portion of Moon became annexed to Monaca, now more commonly known as Monaca Heights. Although within the boundaries of the Borough of Monaca, Colona was at one time considered a village of its own; there is still reference to Colona businesses, residents, and Colona Heights. Center Township has areas that still go down to the Ohio River with the dividing lines of properties sometimes appearing to be quite "gray" especially in historic references in and around the area being called Colona.   When Monaca had their 1940 Centennial, 1965 Quasquicentennial, and 1990 Sesquicentennial celebrations, many references to Moon /Center Township and Potter Township people, businesses, and places of interest are made and seem tied with each other's areas.   Other than the normal disputes all settlements experienced, the friendly and community feeling between Monaca, Center, and Potter businesses and residents has existed since the beginning of historic facts being collected.   They are all very important and diverse areas in their own rights, but yet also seem joined at the hip in many other ways.

PHILLIPSBURG BLOCK HOUSE

Blockhouse of Phillipsburg – 1780

The word *blockhouse* is most likely from the German word "blochaus" which means "a house which blocks a pass." Blockhouses were fairly unique to America as they were mainly used on the frontier to give the settlers protections and a means to defend themselves from Native American Indian attacks. Blockhouses were commonly a single structure, each being designed solely for a particular area and for short-term usage as a garrison. Blockhouses came in many shapes and forms and were constructed out of many different materials.

Prior to the signing of the Fort McIntosh Treaty of 1785, Indians in the area were known to make random raids on the area settlers. Some of the killing by the Indians was purposeful where they made the first move; but when they came in to just do their raiding, they were shot at, so they fought back. The initial raids are reported to not be so much for the killing of the "white man" as it was to obtain some food items and mainly materials for making tools and clothing.

> *Fun fact: Many times you read or see where Indians would raid an area and*
> *smash all the barrels and other containers.   They did not usually do this to be*
> *flat out destructive; nor to simply access the contents. If obtaining food had*
> *been the case, they would have left the barrels and containers in tact so the*
> *contents could be easily transported.   Instead, the reason for smashing these*
> *items was to break the metal hoops or other metal hinges and clasps loose so they*
> *could retrieve just the metal and then repurpose this already worked metal*
> *into arrow heads, other implements or tools, and even used some in jewelry.*

This blockhouse was located in the vicinity of the current St. John The Baptist Church.   Past practice of erecting a block-house in other areas was to have it easily accessible to the majority of the people, as well as it being situated more in an open area with full view of the surrounding grounds making it hard for attackers to hide or sneak up to the blockhouse.

ORIGINAL MONACA LAND GRANT

ORIGINAL MONACA LAND GRANT

THE SUPREME EXECUTIVE COUNCIL OF THE COMMONWEALTH OF PENNSYLVANIA

To whom these presents shall come Greetings:

Know ye that in consideration of the Sum of Forty two pounds seven Shillings and six pence lawful Money paid by Ephraim Blaine Esq., into the Receiver General's Office of the Commonwealth there is granted by the said Commonwealth until the said Ephraim Blaine, a Tract of Land called "Appetite".

Situated on the river Ohio opposite the Mouth of Big Beaver Creek in Washington County. Beginning at a White Walnut Tree on the Bank of Said River thence by Vacant Land South Forty Degrees West ninety perch to a Block Oak North Sixty-Three Degrees, West two hundred and fifty-six perchs to an Ash Tree, and North eighty-one degrees, West, One hundred and twelve, perch to a Black Oak on the Bank of said River thence up the same five hundred and twenty-two perchs to the place of Beginning Containing Three hundred and thirty Acres and allowance of Six Per Cent for roads, etc. With the appertanences (Which said Tract contains in pursuant of an application No. 3671 entered the 25. July 1769 by William A. Langen who by deed dated October 1769 conveyed the same to the said Ephraim Blaine for whom a Warrant of Acceptance issued the first day September Instant).

To have and to hold the same Tract or Parcel of Land with the appertenances unto the said Ephraim Blaine, his Heirs, to the use of the same Ephraim Blaine his Heirs and Assigns for ever free and clear of all Restrictions and Reservations as to Minus Royalties, Quit Rents or otherwise excepting and reserving only the fifth part of all Gold and Silver Ore for the Use of the Commonwealth to be delivered at the Pit Mouth clear of all charges.

In witness whereof The Honorable Biddle Esq., Vice President of the Supreme Executive Council, hath hereto set his hand and caused the State Seal to be hereto affixed in Council this fifth day of September in the year of our Lord One Thousand and seven hundred and eighty-seven and of the Commonwealth the twelfth.

—Attest James Trimble for John Armstrong, Secty.

PUBLIC NOTICE

The undersigned, members of the New Philadelphia Society at Phillipsburg, in the county of Beaver and commonwealth of Pennsylvania, have been authorized by said society to give public notice of the dissolution of their partnership. The public will therefore take notice that the partnership heretofore existing in Phillipsburg aforesaid, and transacting business under the title of the New Philadelphia Society, has this day been dissolved by mutual consent. All persons having claims against said partnership are hereby requested to present the same for settlement; and those indebted to said company are required to make payment to Abner Lacock, Stephen Phillips and Adam Schule, who are fully authorized to settle and adjust the accounts of said partnership.

Given under our hands this 10th day of August, A.D., 1833.
Maximilian deLeon,
Samuel G. Goentgen,
John A. Zickwolf,
Jacob Wagner,
John Schaefer,
Anthony Knapper.

MONACATOOTHA (MON-ahkah-TOO-thuh)
aka
Scarouayda (SKAR-roh-ah-dee)

Anyone remotely familiar with the town of Monaca has probably heard the tradition of the name being a shortened version of an Indian name Monacatootha. I wanted to do just a bit more research on this Indian to possibly determine why the name of this particular Indian came to be chosen and what the story and history was with him. Before I delve deeper into the Native American known as Monacatootha, I feel it is important to divulge a bit more general information on how and why many more local areas and towns received their names; concentrating on why Native American names came to be used.

Many years ago, as communities, towns, and cities were being formed and established, residents were also choosing names for the same. Many times the names were drawn from old world locations, classic established and sometimes ancient towns, and depending on the time period, choosing a word or two to represent a specific meaning. Some popular names relating to war times, anti-slavery feelings, and even town founders were also very often chosen. A particular location, condition, view, or landmark often came into play with the final decision of a name, too. This same thinking and decision making was used to name streets and roadways. As for what became Monaca, the decisions to chose the first names of Water Cure and Phillipsburg is fairly clear --- Water Cure came from the well known health facility of the same name and Phillipsburg was used to recognize and more or less give respect to Stephen Phillips' for his efforts helping develop the area along with his popular boat business. Even though I found no absolute documentation as to the one person who recommended Monacatootha, I did find multiple sources of information to formulate my own theory.

My theory stems from the general premise above, along with the fact that many names of towns and cities developed or came from those chosen by one of the railroad companies. How do railroad companies come into the picture with the name of a town you ask. Well..... The railroad companies were often the owners of the land alongside the train tracks; this was done to help encourage the railroad to build their railroads through a certain area. The railroad would then try to establish a depot on this land, doing so about every 15 to 20 miles making easier access for farmers. In many, many cases, it didn't take long for these depots to become the center of activity in any given community, and often becoming very important if not the center of a town or city. When developing schedules and printing tickets, the railroads found it becoming extremely more common for so many duplicate names of cities and areas. This in turn made it difficult for railroad companies to properly identify/associate some of their depot stops on the schedules and tickets. (A perfect example is Phillipsburg – there was another Phillipsburg in Pennsylvania; two other examples would be multiple usage of names like Freedom and Liberty.) To resolve this growing problem, the railroad companies started their practice of using names associated with Native Americans for their depots regardless of what the name of the city or community was. The railroad companies chose to use names of tribes from the area and many more times a noted chief or leader known to frequent the area; this gave the railroad companies a much bigger pool of names to chose from than the ones being used by most settlers. This practice removed all doubt for the railroad companies and conductors and it streamlined deciphering schedules and tickets of the railroads, too. Little did the railroad companies realize at the time that by using a name associated with Native Americans, it actually was going to be giving some historical value to the first land owners, or to a tribe /nation, or even a leader/chief.

> *Fact: There were about 175,000 American Indians in the northeastern and Great Lakes regions of North America during the beginning of the French and Indian War. Even though all these had very similar lifestyles, they made up different nations and each of those spoke different languages, had different beliefs, and wore different styles of clothing. Anthropologists of today often times group all these nations together and call them the Eastern Woodland American Indians.*

Beaver County, like all others, has its fair share of towns and communities whose names come from those chosen by a railroad company; just a couple for example - Aliquippa, Chippewa, Beaver, and especially for this book – Monaca. While there is a great deal of truth to the fact that in Beaver County alone, several of the names assigned to local communities and towns did come from a Native American person or tribe or nation, it does not always mean that any specific native person or tribe was personally associated with or actually resided in its namesake.   However, it does mean that more times than not, the Nation/Tribe/person was known to frequent, travel through, or have some type of connection.   I have a statement included within the Entertainment section with Aliquippa Park regarding how the city of Aliquippa received its name from the P & LE RR.   The town of Beaver seems to have its name from the river adjacent to it. I did not find proof to indicate whether the railroad named its depot after the river or the town or if the town took on the name of the depot.   The Beaver County site has a very good explanation for Beaver and the formation of its name – "*The Delawares called the stream Amockwi-sipu, or literally, "beaver stream." They gave this name to the creek because of its being a favorite home of the beaver."* "*......the Indian names of Sawkunk and Shingoe's Town, later by the English as "the old French town." Later it was called McIntosh, from the fort there and the town that was created by legislative action was called Beaver."*   I likewise did not do extensive research on Chippewa, so no proof is here as to whether it was a railroad decision or residence who first chose the name.   The Beaver County Historical Research and Landmarks Foundation states – "*Chippewa Township was formed in January 1816 when the Beaver County Court divided South Beaver Township and Ohio Township into four townships. One township was called Adams for Dr. Samuel Adams. The township name soon changed to Chippewa, which comes from the Indian word Chipwayanwok, meaning tailskins."*

> *Fun fact: During many of the early years, most Americans placed women "below" men, not giving them any "powers" or authority in affairs and men owned the land/homes, voted, held offices, etc. The American Indians had a completely different mindset than the general American population.   Leaders would reach different levels of status because of their skills and wisdom, regardless of their sex.   An example of this would be to use a better known woman, Queen Aliquippa; she held considerable political power.   Even Monacatootha/Scarouady said "It is no new thing to take women into our councils, particularly amongst the Senecas."*

In accordance with all previously said.................Monacatootha was the name chosen by the Pittsburgh and Lake Erie Railroad for their scheduled stop at the depot in what is now known as *Monaca*.   The original name was quite lengthy and railroad tickets and schedules didn't always have sufficient space for the entire name, so it was shortened and found printed on tickets as "Monaca."   With the confusion increasing between two Pennsylvania towns being named Phillipsburg, this shortened version of Monacatootha was obviously chosen to be officially adopted by the borough, hence the current name.   Now to some history of the namesake of Monaca - the actual Native American, Monacatootha.

Scaroudy, Scarroyaday, Scaroyaday, Scarouady, Scruniyatha (*side of the sky*) was also known by the English as the second Half King and by the Delawares as Monacatuatha, Monakaduto, Monacatoocha, Monacatootha (*great arrow*).   Scarouady/Monacatootha was born in about 1700; he died in 1757/58 in Lancaster, PA while attending a treaty.   The pronunciations of his name were "SKAR-roh-ah-dee" and/or "MON-ahkah-TOO-thuh." George Washington always called him Monacatootha.   He was an Oneida Iroquois and like many other leaders was often called half-king.   The Iroquois recognized him to represent them among the Shawnee and to have oversight of the Shawnee in the Ohio territory.

Illustration of Scarouady, NPS

Fact: Monacatootha was reported to have bow-and-arrow tattoos on each cheek; more research also found statements of his body having many tattoos indicating his warrior status, including a tomahawk on his chest.   When not wearing the more common English clothing, his more traditional appearance was described as "elegant, regal." He had a wild head of gray-black hair that puffed out of his split hawk-feather headdress.   He was also known to wear a bear claw necklace, fur mantle, and deerskin leggings adorned with floral beadwork – as Indian attire went, he was a masterpiece of imperial majesty.   He was noted for always having a tightlipped scowl.   He was said to be the same age as Tanacharison but somehow was able to maintain a more vigorous presence.

Scaroudy/Monacatootha was known as a famous warrior and chief; he is said to have participated in 31 battles, killed 7 warriors, and took 11 captives. He disagreed with many of the Iroquois who did not want to take sides in the French and Indian War; saying "You can't live in the woods and be neutral." He thought the best way for the Iroquois to maintain their way of life would be to side with the British; with the aid of William Johnson, he worked to keep the Shawnee and the Lenape on the side of the British, too. This thinking made him most noted for siding with the British and also his attempting to sway the Delaware Indians to also side with the British. Scarouady even met with officials of Pennsylvania and Virginia in 1753 to try and convince them to take action against the French. When the situation became so bad in 1754, Scarouady moved to Aughwick just to escape the French. Also in 1754, Monacatootha tried to get warriors to fight with Washington at Fort Necessity; he was not successful in this quest.

In reading through multiple histories of the French and Indian War happenings, I want to point out that there were multiple mentions of both Scarouady/Monacatootha and another Native American known as Tanaghrisson (tan-ah-GRIS-suhn). The Iroquois sent two vice-regents Tanacharison/the Half King, and Scarouady/Monacatootha, his successor, to rule over subjugated tribes in Pennsylvania. The Half King ruled over the Delawares and Mohicans of the Ohio Valley; he took residence at Logstown, on the north bank of the Ohio, about eighteen miles below Pittsburgh. Scarouady/ Monacatootha ruled over the Shawnees of the Ohio Valley and also had his residence at Logstown. Tanacharison and Scarouady took up their duties as vice-regents in the year 1747.

It is purposeful to include some information on Tanaghrisson before continuing with the information on Scarouady/ Monacatootha. I have included some direct copy of information provided by the National Park Service in their teaching guide of the French and Indian War because it best summarizes the majority of his information.

Tanaghrisson was also known by several names, including Dcanaghrison, Johoncrissa, Tanhisson, Thanayicson, and Tanarecco; he was born about 1700 and died in 1754. He was referred to in many writings as "the half-king" which can often confuse him with many other half-kings of the Ohio territory, including Monacatootha. They both disliked the encroachment of the French into the area. Tanaghrison was said to be a Seneca by birth. "When Tanaghrison was a child the French and their American Indian allies captured him. He was taken from his American Indian family. Later on, to express his dislike of the French, he was said to state that the French boiled and ate his father." "As a grown man, he was chosen by the Iroquois to lead all the American Indians in the Ohio River Valley." By 1749, he was recognized the dominant figure in the area of the *Forks of the Ohio*. "The British almost always referenced or called him the *Half King*." He was called the Half King because he did not have entire sovereignty, only an over-lord of the Iroquois or Six Nations. He lived in the area of the *Forks of the Ohio*, taking residence at different times at Logstown or Sauconk (Shingas's Town/Beaver, PA).

He is known mostly because he sided with the British. "As early as 1752, he told the Virginians that they should build a "strong house" at the Forks of the Ohio." Unfortunately, when they came to build the fort, they found the French had already done so. "In 1753, he went with George Washington to the French fort. He was very important in helping Washington deliver his messages. The next year, he met Washington again. He sent word that French soldiers were camped near Washington's camp at the Great Meadows. In the morning, Washington and the Half King surrounded the French camp. A fight broke out. The Half King saw that Ensign Jumonville was wounded. He said, "Thou art not yet dead, my father." Then he raised his tomahawk and killed him. This act was a symbol of the Half King's feelings. He wanted the French to leave the area. Washington asked the Half King to fight with him at Fort Necessity. He decided not to. Later, he said that Washington "would never listen to them"."

"He moved to central Pennsylvania when the French took control of the Forks of the Ohio. The French and Indian War was just starting when he died. However, his actions helped start the war." He died in 1754 of pneumonia in the area now known as Harrisburg. Tanacharison, the Half King, was described as being very strong in diplomacy, but not so as a leader on the battlefield.

Repeatedly I found writings state that little is known of his early life, or of his physical appearance, but the NPS had this illustration of him by Fred Threlfall so I wanted to share. From this illustration, it appears the artist may have found a description of him. If this is true, then whether all the time or periodically, Tanacharison also seems to have worn English styled clothing.

He was succeeded by Monacatootha/Scarouady.

Fun fact: The colonists and interpreters were accustomed only to imperial titles, thus the reason such titles as "King" or "Queen" being attached to various American Indians. While these titles were only meant to express how powerful or important various American Indians were, the Indians themselves had no such titles as "King" or "Queen." These titles seemed to be attached to various Indians especially in Pittsburgh area history. Ex. King Beaver, Queen Aliquippa, Half King Tancharison.

Those that held the status of being called king, queen, or chief didn't have any of the power or wealth like the European monarchs. Instead the chief "could neither make war nor peace, leagues nor treaties." Also, very much unlike monarchs, they hunted for their living just like the other citizens, they followed the suggestions of their council, and the "will" of their community. A chief was the worker of the people; no one would have followed a chief that was the only member of the community to live a certain lifestyle.

The status of chief was maintained as long as he/she remained strong and had the support of his/her people, which was established as long as the people continued to prosper.

So, back to Monacatootha.

When the Half King (Tanaghrisson) died, Scarouady/Monacatootha, being one of his closest associates, became the next leader in the Ohio River Valley. He was said to have had excellent oratory skills. After stepping into the position of vice-regent in the Ohio Valley, he then met General Braddock, whom he did not like, but agreed to fight with the British. In 1755, there were only eight American Indians who went with Braddock; two of those eight were Scarouady and his son. During this march, Scarouady's son was out scouting and some nervous British soldiers saw him, thought he was working with the French, shot and killed him. "The General displayed great sorrow for the unfortunate occurrence and after due expressions of sympathy and donations caused the body to be buried in the honors of war at the next encampment....." (This occurred in what is now Irwin, PA and is indicated by a historical marker.) Trying to make peace for this horrible murder, Braddock himself presided at the funeral; but from then on Scarouady referenced Braddock as "a bad man" and said that Braddock "looked upon us as dogs." He still continued to side with the British until his own death though.

They may not have been from the specific namesake towns, but definitely from the general area, so it is no wonder that the Pittsburgh & Lake Erie Railroad Company chose two noted American Indians when they chose the names of Aliquippa and Monacatootha. I did not find any commemorative areas or towns for Tanacharison, the Half King; but it is nice to know that at least one of the "half kings" - Monacatootha aka Scarouady - can be remembered if people take the time to learn of his history and also are reminded that many, many years ago, the railroads noted his importance even if the name of Monaca is a shortened version of one of his names.

HOUSES and BUILDINGS ON THE MOVE

Throughout this book you will read many statements of a structural house or a business storeroom being moved to a new location.   Property and lots were at a premium and once someone owned land, he was seldom in any hurry to give up that ownership.   Buildings, houses, or storerooms were also a valued possession.   BUT the union of a specific building on a specific lot was not always set in stone.   I wanted to point this out so the readers know it is not an error when you read of a building or house being moved; it was quite a common practice and absolutely not exclusive to just Monaca.   In current times, a person or business must usually own the actual property that a structure is erected upon.   But, back in the earlier days, it was considered normal procedure for property to be owned by one person and a building on that same property being owned by a completely different person.

   Example:

Mr. A would purchase some property and usually erect a building upon that property. Then Mr. A would decide to sell – he might sell both the building and property or he might just sell the building.   If Mr. A only sold the building, then when Mr. B made the purchase, he would only own the building and not the property it was sitting on.   Mr. B would most likely pay some type of rent or occupancy fees to Mr. A who still owned the property.   Another scenario ……. Mr. A may have only purchased the property and then let Mr. B erect his own building and once again receive an occupancy fee from Mr. B.   When it came to the building or house being moved – that occurred if Mr. B bought his own plot of land and would then move his current building to that location.   Or if Mr. A decided to erect his own building or not renew the occupancy to Mr. B, then Mr. B would have to vacate the property which meant he either razed his building and took the loss, or paid to have it moved to another lot.

All this was quite interesting and I was very surprised to see how many buildings and houses were actually moved around throughout town over the years.   This picture shows a house being moved by a truck and some type of platform.   During the 1800s and earlier 1900s, structures were moved by using teams of horses and large flat wagons.

This house moving happened during the end of Mar 1955.   Note the man standing on the porch roof in front of the one window.

> *Fun fact: This house was moved with all of the furniture, belongings, and fixtures*
> *in place inside.   I guess the phrase 'lock, stock, and barrel' applies here.*

This particular house was moved from Atlantic Avenue (near Ninth Street) to a lot / property on the river side of Atlantic Avenue (in 2015 it is at 711 Atlantic Avenue).   In this picture, the house has already rounded the corner from Ninth Street and is on Atlantic Avenue heading toward the Monaca Water Plant and its new location.   The article that displayed this move stated Mrs. Luther Saunders and children Buddy and Janie watch as their home is moved a block and a half to its new location.   The property this home was sitting on was owned by the Socony-Vacuum Oil Company and the house needed to be moved so the company could use the property to expand and make improvements to their service station that was located on an adjacent lot.

BUILDINGS

The Ark
Bank Building aka Bank Hall
Batchelor Building
Batchelor Furniture Store Building
Barnett Building
Bartell Building
Carey Building
Chess Club Building
deLeon house
Dietrich Building
Dixon building
Eagles Building aka Hamilton
Eberhardt Building
Eckert Building
The Gazebo
Hahn Building
Hamilton aka Eagle Building
Harbison Building
Keystone Block Building
Knapper Building
Koehler Property
Landis Building
Lay Building
Leary Building
Lindsay Building
Mateer Building
Municipal Building aka Public Hall aka City Hall aka Boro Building
Sadler Building
Schaefer House
Singer Hall
Sparling Building
Stein Building
Jacob Strawick Building
Sullivan Building
Wagner Home
Zigerelli Block Building

BUILDINGS

The Ark

The "Ark" was definitely first located on the triangle shaped lot between Fifth and Sixth Streets which is the present day (2016) location of the Monaca Roll of Honor monument.   The triangular lot was formerly called the "Band Stand Lot" because this is where a beautiful gazebo-type band stand was erected in the mid to late 1880s.   The Ark was erected in the late 1830s or earlier in the 1840s.   On the 1876 map of Phillipsburg, it was listed as the public school house.   The triangle lot shows no buildings on the "Band Stand Lot" on the 1900 map of Monaca indicating that the Ark was moved prior to 1900.

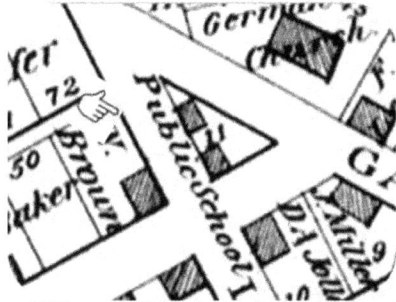

from 1876 map of Phillipsburg (with school marked)

from 1900 map of Monaca (no school)

Further research finds that "Noah's Ark" School was one of the first school houses built soon after the founding of the community.   It was a frame building and had been the very first original school.   Remember previously where I stated how buildings were moved here and there?   Well the Ark is an example of the manner in which buildings were moved around town.

The ark building was moved from the lot between Fifth and Sixth Streets to a lot on the 900 block Pennsylvania Avenue.   The building, along with an adjoining vacant lot was between 900 Pennsylvania Avenue and the Municipal Building. There was a 1919 article that said the Ark was located on Pennsylvania Avenue, owned by Henry C. Weirich, a local baker; it also stated it was a 2 storey frame structure lined with brick.   It was erected more in the late 1830s or in the 1840s; served as a church, school house, a restaurant, laundry, and residence.   From other references and articles, I have deduced it must have been moved/relocated from the triangle lot to what was about 920 Pennsylvania Avenue because the theatre building was erected at 922 Pennsylvania Avenue. The description of the properties involved with the new theatre were that it would be adjacent to the Municipal Building on one side and the theatre was to be erected beside it; this involved razing one of the oldest buildings in Monaca, known as the Ark.

In conclusion, from all published information, the Ark had quite a few former owners ....
-    -Formerly located on triangular lot between Fifth and Sixth Streets.
-    -Was a two storey frame structure lined with brick – built on its original lot in the 1840s.
-    -Was moved to approximately what would have been 920 Pennsylvania Avenue.
-    -Over the years the ark served as a school house, a church, a restaurant, a laundry place, and
        residence.
-    -1919 - Purchased by the Monaca National Bank.
        They were then at 829 Pennsylvania Ave and planned on erecting a new building there, but ended
        up purchasing and putting up their building the corner of Tenth Street and Pennsylvania Ave, so
        they never did tear it down but apparently sold it to W. J. Mellon.
        W.J maintained the building and had various businesses occupy it. (See article further.)
-    -May 1926 - Louis Stoll was erecting a new theatre/amusement house on property he purchased
        between the Monaca Theatre (which was at about 918 Pennsylvania Ave) and the
        Municipal building on Pennsylvania Ave.   The Monaca National Bank owned the
        property and it was one large vacant lot that was adjacent the municipal building and
        another lot beside it that had a two storey frame building on it that was said to be one of
        the oldest structures in Monaca – the Ark.   The Ark property adjoined the current
        Monaca Theatre property which was owned by the W. J. Mellon heirs.   The ark was
        occupied as a Chinese laundry (being run by Ping Fong) and dwelling until a few days

prior to May 7th.   The 2 storey Ark was scheduled to be razed at once, followed by clearing the site for the new theatre.   The adjoining Monaca Theatre was to be remodeled by the Mellon heirs and converted into a mercantile building.   The construction of the new theatre was to start at once.

I am sorry to say that hard as I tried, in all the older pictures of buildings and streets of Monaca, no pictures were found of the Ark on its original lot or of the building as it stood when it was a restaurant.

OLDEST BUILDING IS SOLD TO BANK

One of the oldest buildings in Monaca, known as the "ark," located in Pennsylvania avenue between Ninth and Tenth streets, and occupied by Mrs. Mary A. Hackett as a restaurant and residence, has been sold by Henry C. Weirich, a local baker, to the Monaca National bank. The consideration was $5000. The deal includes a vacant lot adjoining the above property on the north side and the municipal building is on the south side. The Monaca bank has plans prepared for what promises to be one of the finest bank buildings in this section to be erected on the site, and the plans have been submitted to the board of directors of the bank for approval. It is expected to have the building completed by the middle of summer. The building known as the "ark" was formerly located on the public park in Fifth street. It is a two-story frame structure lined with brick. It is said to have been erected seventy or more years ago, served as a church, schoolhouse and residence. Some of the older residents of Monaca attended church, Sunday school and public school in the building when mere boys.

●●●

Jun 1919

Bank Building   aka   Bank Hall   aka   Business Block - located at 308-310 Ninth Street
It was built with the original idea of it being called the "Opera House block building."

It was newly constructed and completed as of May 24, 1901 and is still standing.   This building was a multipurpose building when constructed.   Without going to find legal paper work, I have no definite company name or individual's name attached to the purchase of the original property or construction of the actual building.   I do know this 3 storey building was purchased in Sep 1945 by William V. Campbell and I also have the information of when town council approved the original construction.

Sep 24, 1900, it was approved by Council to erect a new business building with the front facing Ninth Street and adjoining the Hotel Monaca building.   It would be a three storey building constructed of iron, brick, and stone. The basement would contain three storerooms, a room for dynamo, engine, and heating apparatus, and three cellars.   The first (street level) floor would contain three large storerooms (18 x 70) – the second floor a stage and large auditorium – the third floor a lodge room (55 x 57), necessary anterooms, and closets.   The second floor stage/auditorium/theatre was described as being one of the coziest little play houses found in Western PA.   It had two entrances – one from Ninth Street and one from the side of the building.   This auditorium on the second floor was used for many events over the years once the building was opened.
The building still stands in 2016. The top of the building had large painted marquees over the years; one being *Citizen's National Bank* and the next being *Campbell / Mayflower moving*.   Citizens National Bank had a corner section of the building for its offices from 1901 until about 1929; thus the referencing of the building as the bank building or bank hall.

Despite the majority of references to the bank building or bank hall being to this Citizen's Nat'l Bank former building, it was still found that a few could be referenced as either one of two buildings -- the other building being the former Monaca National Bank building on the corner of Tenth Street and Pennsylvania Avenue.   It depended totally on the usage, event, person, type of group, and/or the references, but the majority of references were indeed to the building on Ninth Street.

Some examples and reference to confusion of "which" bank building..............

- In 1912 and 1914 and 1929 there was a lodge room for the Daughters of Liberty in the bank building – from this information, I would determine they were in the Opera House on Ninth Street.
- In 1923 the American Legion had their post in the basement area of the bank building – it was just renovated for the Legion; had reception room/parlor, bowling alley, rifle range, card and pool room, and other equipment and conveniences for the Legion. Again, this would indicate Ninth Street since it had a separate entrance to the basement entrance that the other did not.
- In 1929 there is an ad for an apartment for rent in the 'bank building' and it gives the address of the former Monaca Nat'l Bank building on Tenth Street/Pennsylvania Avenue.
- 1932 there is a statement saying just "bank building apartments" – that would indicate the former Monaca Nat'l Bank building because the old Citizen's Bank building did not house apartments.
- Charles Sweet's pool room and restaurant – basement of the bank building ..... this is referencing Ninth Street where there were outside stairs to this business.

View of the building from Ninth Street.......

former Opera House / Citizen's Bank Building   former Hotel Monaca building

View of the building from the intersection of Ninth Street and Pennsylvania Avenue....

Note the marquee on the top of the building The Citizen's National Bank.

This is a view of the side of the building from Pennsylvania Avenue in 2015.

Note the marque with *Campbell Moving and Storage* on the left and *Mayflower* on the right.

Entrance doors from Ninth Street. These doors opened to a large stairway that led to the 2nd floor auditorium/theatre area.

This is the stairway just inside the Ninth Street entrance. To the left at the top of these stairs is the doorway into the auditorium/theatre entrance.

This is a picture of the stairway continuing on up from the landing at the 2nd floor. They are approximately half as wide as the main stairway and lead to the third floor area. There is a door to the left at the top of the stairway which gave entrance to the former lodge/meeting room areas.

There was an entrance from the left side of the building which led to another stairway. That side stairway would have been a secondary entrance and led to both the second and third floors. All of these stairs have been removed with only a slight outline or marking of the former staircases visible on the original walls of the building.

There are no available older pictures of the former auditorium/theatre area on the second floor. All of the second and third floor areas have been converted over the years into large open areas for storage purposes. Current pictures of the area would not have done justice or given the proper proportional view of how very large the area each of the upper floors really are; nor would a current picture have reflected the height of the ceilings. From being fortuntate to have personally viewed both the second and third floors, I can say with assurance they both would have been quite impressive when decorated and used as originally intended - as an auditorium/theatre and lodge/meeting areas.

Batchelor Building - 1026 Pennsylvania Avenue
There were two buildings that had the name "Batchelor" attached to them. One was the Batchelor Furniture storeroom building and for several years, also was referenced as Batchelor's Undertaking business. Then when the Batchelors built an adjoining building, it was called the Batchelor Building. The furniture store/undertaking business building did have some apartments, but did not have any other businesses so it was most often than not referenced as the *furniture store*. The newer adjoining building though was the one referenced as the Batchelor Building. It had numerous businesses and offices housed in it over the years, as well as the post office for a few years. Once I became familiar with more of the businesses, it was much easier to distinguish which building was being referenced. Below is the information on the adjoining structure erected beside the Batchelor furniture building.

The light gray Indiana limestone building is located at 1026 Pennsylvania Avenue. It is a two storey structure, the front being trimmed with antique marble. It had a "Grennell sprinkling system" installed. The new post office was going to be moved into this building and there were all metal fixtures installed in that area of the building, along with oak finish. The United States Post-office Department signed a 10 year lease on the space in Feb 1930. In Aug 1930, the post office and a large storeroom were on the first floor, and several modern suites were on the second floor. These suites were initially offices in 1930 of Dr. Harry T. Ellsworth-Dentist, Robert E. McCreary and John Prather-attorneys, Dr. John A. Riedel-Optometrist, Miss Ann Grater-Beauty Specialist.

Batchelor Bldg -1026 Pennsylvania Avenue   Batchelor Furniture Bldg

Batchelor Furniture Store Building – 1028 Pennsylvania Avenue
There is much more information on the Batchelor Furniture business in the Hardware section.
The first storeroom was located on lower Pennsylvania Avenue in 1896. It was a frame, partial one storey building with parts that were two stories. There was either a two storey business building or private residency beside it at that time. They then erected a "modern building" in 1902. This building was located at 1020-1024 Pennsylvania Avenue. It was a three storey brick building, erected and owned by Alonzo S. Batchelor, Frank M. Batchelor, and C. C. Aughenbaugh.
In 1930 the Batchelor Brothers had an additional new two storey building erected – 1026 Pennsylvania Avenue. This building adjoined their current building; it was nearing completion the end of Jul 1930. (See previous description.)

Fun fact (or eerie fact, depending on your view): The Batchelor Bros. were not only into the furniture business, they were also in the business of undertaking. Before purchasing and building their funeral home at the corner of Atlantic and Tenth Street, the brothers conducted their undertaking business from the 2ⁿᵈ floor of their 3 storey furniture building on Pennsylvania Avenue. I find it eerie to think of someone being excited about shopping for new living room furniture while there would be embalming going on just one floor up.

Now the question remains – when the Batchelor building was referenced in the past, was it for the 1896 building, the 3 storey brick building at 1020 Pennsylvania Avenue, or the 2 storey stone facade building at 1026 Pennsylvania Avenue, beside the 3 storey building ?   Depending on the details of information found, I determined that the majority of the time, the referencing was to the #1026 building – not always, just the majority of the time.

Barnett Building   aka   Morris Barnett Building - between 900 and 916 Pennsylvania Avenue
This building was the site of his business.   Most references would have been to this location;
but just for general knowledge - Morris and Davis had a business on Pennsylvania and Eighth Street in 1900s.   (He also had a new dwelling on Pacific Avenue that was their home.)

Bartel Building – on Pennsylvania Avenue
E. S. Levy of Beaver Falls moved his pool table and fixtures into the large store room and opened up a pool and billiard parlor (1903) but this information did not lead me to find exactly where on Pennsylvania Avenue.

Carey Building - 899 Pennsylvania Avenue
Even though the site was the location of prior business, the Carey family had ownership and the area was referenced to them many years after the family no longer conducted business or lived at this location.   It was even called "Carey's Corner."

from early 1900s

from 2015

Chess Club Building – Pennsylvania Avenue, near Sixth Street
This building was erected by the Chess Club in about 1901.
The club sold the building in Feb/Mar 1907 and contemplated erecting a smaller club house
            elsewhere in the future.
        (Mar 1907) John and James Mateer purchased this club house and lot – they intended to move
            the building to a lot they owned on Pennsylvania Avenue, near Eleventh Street.
        Evidently, the Mateers never moved the building because........

        (Jun 1907) a number of men organized a social club and leased the building, "fitting it up in
            fine style."   By Jul 1907 – the men who leased the Monaca Chess Club Building named
            their organization the Belmont Club and were planning to elect officers.

After they sold their first building, The Chess Club used the Lay Building on the corner of Indiana Avenue and Eighth Street for a period of time.

deLeon House – corner of Atlantic Avenue and Fifth Street - 500 -504 Atlantic Avenue
When it was built, it had 4 large rooms, thick walls and was the home of the man who called himself Count Maximillian deLeon – Bernard Müller.   This building is still standing.

The Beaver County Historical Research and Landmarks Foundation placed a plaque at the site of this building which is still standing in Monaca (as of 2016).   The plaque reads:

"Founded 1832 by dissident members of the Harmony Society of Economy, Pennsylvania.   The house on this corner was the home of the society leader Count Maximilian deLeon and is believed to be the oldest house in Monaca."

Courtesy BCHR&LF

Dietrich Building –   815 - 817 Pennsylvania Avenue
The Dietrich brothers had their business in this building - Dietrich's Plumbing & Heating.   It is still standing today.

2015

Dixon Building - 1133 Pennsylvania Avenue
William L. Dixon owned multiple properties in Monaca and began businesses in the late 1800s. Oscar L. Dixon also owned multiple properties in Monaca.   I do not know which "Dixon" they referred to or named the building for. In a few articles and or ads, there were comments of this structure being formerly Dom's Shoe Repair on Pennsylvania Avenue.   Dom Yaccopino had his shoe repair storeroom at 1133 Pennsylvania Avenue (2015-Bluewater Cleaning Service).   This is a 3 storey brick building, so I am sure there was space in the upper stories to rent.

Dixon building   Dixon building

Eberhardt Building – There were two references to the Eberhardt Building – one was at 1127 Pennsylvania Avenue and the other was at a building on Pennsylvania Avenue and Eighth Street.

Eckert Building - there were a few buildings built by Chas. Eckert

> One was erected in Jan 1907 in 1100 block on Pennsylvania Avenue –it was between Pugh's
>> Hardware and Leary Bros. store (#1107).
>
> Another one was referenced at __?__ Pennsylvania Avenue............
>> Was considered new in Oct 1903. Stone work on the building was started Apr 23, 1903.   Brick
>> work on the building commenced May 23, 1903.   F. L. Wilson & Co. moved their office to the 2nd
>> floor of this building (in 1903).
>
> The Club had a few rooms in the Eckert building– each was well furnished; included in
>> them, a library and piano.   (in 1911)
>
> Attorney Charles R. Eckert – came to Pittsburgh as infant – s/o Henry and Charlotte Eckert.
>
> His home was at the top of Eckert Road (Fourth Ward); Charles moved to Beaver and had his law
>> office there with Mr. Sohn.

No specific name of this building – The large frame house at Fourth Street and Pennsylvania Avenue.
> This house was torn down in the late 1930s to make room for a service station.   It was owned
> by Christian Erbeck who married Phillipine Wagner.   Christian lived in Moon and was a farmer
> and butcher, then just followed farming.

The Gazebo – triangle lot between Fifth and Sixth Street

It was erected after the "Ark" was moved from that site and used for dances.   I have no dates for when this gazebo existed, but on a 1900 map, there is no type of building or structure indicated on the map.

This indicates it was either built and removed by 1900, or not yet erected.

Hahn Building – unknown location

Leonard Hahn – b 1823; immigrated to America with parents and joined the Economite Society; he married Katherine Scheid.   The "Society" had a law stating that any person unmarried must remain so or sever his membership, so.......

> Leonard left the Society and came to Phillipsburg.

Hamilton Building   aka "hotel building"

> Or   **Eagle Building** –   corner of Pennsylvania Avenue and Twelfth Street

Many ads for the Monaca Wallpaper Co. say "across from Eagle Bldg." The Monaca Wallpaper Co. was located at 1140 Pennsylvania Avenue in 1940.   The very large, 3 storey brick building that sits at the corner of Pennsylvania Avenue and Twelfth Street was the Hamilton Hotel, built by S. D. Hamilton in 1903.   I have not ascertained exact dates, but the building was eventually purchased by the Monaca Aerie for a new lodge home.   So, there are references to the hotel building, to the Hamilton building, and to the Eagle building – all being one and the same. See Hotel section for a picture of the building and more information.

Harbison Building – (Harbison "home" was at 901 Pennsylvania Avenue)

> Owned by J. H. Harbison.   Started brick work on new building Jun 11, 1903.
>
> Large plate glass fronts to the building in Sept 1903.
>> Glass fronts done by Ackerman & Jepson – the Hardware dealers.
>
> The Harbison's home was at Pennsylvania and Ninth Street.... 901 Pennsylvania Avenue.
>> They had been in this home from at least 1900, when George and his wife, a nephew,
>> his father-in-law and mother-in-law, and a boarder all lived on Pennsylvania Avenue –

somewhere near Carey's corner by the census – it must have been a fair sized home with all those residents. (901 Pennsylvania Avenue became: the Dairy Queen, Snowy White, Greenry, and finally Laundry Centre.)

George J. Harbison (a local contractor) and his wife had moved to the corner of Indiana and Tenth Street in 1930, evidenced when the Dinsmores were moving into it Jun 14, 1930. I do not know where the Harbisons moved to; they were in their 70s by 1932.

1943 – there was a two storey brick business, an apartment building, and two other dwellings on Pennsylvania and Ninth Street called the *Harbison property* and sold to Dan J. Nicely (self employed contractor).   George had the contract to many buildings in Monaca: 1926, buff brick, stone trim, 2 storey Monaca Nat'l Bank building, in 1909, the William Fisher house on 1200 block of Atlantic Avenue. So.....it was difficult to find proof of addresses of all these buildings and which exactly would have been called the "Harbison Building." There was also an ad to rent 2 sleeping rooms to gentlemen at 901 Pennsylvania Avenue.

Feb 4, 1944 – ad to sell 5 rooms of household furnishing and fully equipped beauty shop – AND, purchaser of furnishings could also rent the house.

Feb 22, 1944 –ad…. bedroom sets were being sold & studio couch, dishes, pans, etc.

The Dairy Queen building was built in 1975 on 3 lots and to do this, two buildings had to be \torn down – one being the Harbison's former home.   (Sobel's at 903 Pennsylvania had to be another.)

a glimpse of the Harbison building - this is at the corner Ninth St/Penna Ave

a partial view of the same Harbison Building looking from Pennsylvania Avenue

Keystone Block Building - 1012–1018 Pennsylvania Avenue

This building is still standing (2016), beside the former Batchelor's Furniture store building on the left and the Municipal Building on the right.   There is a "keystone" marker at the top of the building with the date of 1903, the year construction of the building was completed.

The brick layers commenced work on the Keystone Improvement Company's new building on Pennsylvania Avenue on Jul 8, 1903.   There was a 3 week delay waiting for joists to arrive and to be laid.

The address of businesses varies for this building – 1012, 1014, 1016, and 1018.

It was often just referred to as the Keystone Building.

Contractors were informed to submit bids in Feb 25, 1903 to Earl Bros. architects on Pennsylvania Avenue for the *Keystone Improvement Company of Monaca*'s building; there was no mention of who was hiring contractors, who owned the property, and who actually was awarded the contract.

Oct 1903 – the tile had been laid in the vestibules.   Fire escapes were erected on the Keystone building in early Dec 1906.

I believe this structure was strictly built as an investment venture – to obtain rents as an income.
It was owned by Henry Wischerman of Beaver Falls in Mar 1930.
There were a multitude of businesses located in this building over the years, not to mention the number of tenants in the apartments on the upper floors.
The building was not without its own problems. There was a fire in Mar 1930 that resulted in over $10,000 in damages, which was quite the sum in 1930. Flames damaged current businesses - at that time.......A & P store, Monaca Wallpaper, the post office, and a recreation room in the basement. The flames did not spread to the second floor, the location of Dr. Todd's dental business and apartments, nor to the third floor apartments.
The building was owned by Dr. Ray E. and Ruth Jane Reppert of Beaver in 1966.

| Keystone bldg | Keystone bldg | the keystone on top of bldg   "1903" |

Knapper Building – 111 Fourth Street

Fourth Street is where the Knapper Grocery business was, but there were also references to Knappers at 403 Pennsylvania Avenue. Either one of these locations or both of these could have been referenced/called the Knapper Building. Both buildings have been razed.

111 Fourth Street would be about where the end of the Monacatootha Apartments building now sits – the end closest to Atlantic Avenue.

The 403 Pennsylvania Avenue would have been at the end of the wall of the cemetery as you first come into Monaca.

Koehler Property – Paulus Koehler owned it - was this only where the Hotel Monaca was built
or was it another building since he owned several properties and lived at 826 Washington Avenue -right beside the hotel building ?

Landis Building – __?__ Pennsylvania Avenue
Had storerooms for rent in 1904 – John Frank opened a shoe repair shop in the Landis Building, formerly occupied by J. A. Schaffer.

Lay Building (1882) – corner of Eighth Street and Indiana Avenue – 800-804 Indiana Avenue
This building was one and the same built and owned by George Lay.   Most references to this building simply called it the Lay Building; then I found a few articles that spilled the beans.   This article stated that school taught in the city building by Miss Emma Andrews in Sep 1903 was transferred on Sep 28, 1903, from there to the "George Lay Building, corner of Eighth Street and Indiana Avenue."   It went on to state that it was fitted with an additional room and both Miss Andrews and Miss Dale Bowser taught classes there.

Over the years this building was also home to a hotel and restaurant owned by George Lay. The Chess Club had the building as their "home"; as well as the Charles Brown business.

On the drawing below, it appears to be a boxier building, but when viewed in person, it is actually a longer, rectangular shaped two storey frame building, facing Indiana Avenue. It was still standing (2016) -- currently subdivided into apartments.

George Lay came to Phillipsburg with Maximillian and he married Mary Baker.   He was a carpenter by trade.   The former Lay's home was right beside the 'Lay building' at 810 Indiana Avenue; this home is also still standing (2016).

The pointer indicates the Lay Building, with the Lay home to the left of it.

Leary Building – could have been one of a few locations - – first located in lower Pennsylvania Avenue (near Fifth Street), then 1107 Pennsylvania Avenue in 1911, then 1032 Pennsylvania Avenue and
in 1925, at 1100 Pennsylvania Avenue.   I do not know why so many various addresses were attached to the *Leary Building*.

Lindsay Building – unknown location
There were a few references in newspaper articles in 1931 to this building, but I found nothing further on it.

Municipal Building aka Public Hall aka City Hall – 928 Pennsylvania Avenue
There is a separate history, pictures, and information on the Municipal Building in Volume II; but there is one of the earlier pictures of it with the Mateer Building.   (The Mateer Building was located next door.)

Mateer Building – 1000 Pennsylvania Avenue
Their store was located at 1000 Pennsylvania Avenue, but the Mateer brothers purchased many buildings throughout town.   An educated guess would say all references were made to this storeroom at 1000 Pennsylvania Avenue since they were there for so many years; but I have no proof of this theory.

Reader Building – 1129 Pennsylvania Avenue
James M. Reader started a butcher shop/meat market in the building in the 1800s.   This is most likely why it was from then on referenced as the Reader Building.   In 2015/16 the building was renovated and is currently the Monaca Draft House.

Sarah Radler Building – 1213 Pennsylvania Avenue

Schaefer House or Shaffer House – 609 Pennsylvania Avenue (corner of Sixth and
Pennsylvania Avenue)
I found that the Schaefer family lived at 609 Pennsylvania Avenue.   Jacob Friedrick Schaefer/Shaefer/Shaffer was born in 1801, immigrated to America and was with the Harmony Society when they were in Butler County.   He learned the trades of carpentry, weaving, dyeing, and machinery; practicing the trade of carpentry in 1850 while living in Monaca.   In Economy, he was known for dyed silk which today still holds its brilliant color (2016).   He became one of the trustees of the New Philadelphia Society, one of the first three members of town council, one of

the first school directors, and was active in helping build Monaca. He was also the manager of the first mill in Phillipsburg. Jacob married Catherine Christine Staiger. It is no wonder that his house would be referenced as a notable site in Monaca. 609 Pennsylvania Avenue was the same address of the former site of Monaca / Graeser's Auto building and the current site of the Monaca Public Library (corner of Sixth and Pennsylvania Avenue).

Shaffer's house would have sat where indicated by arrow.

Singer Hall - unknown address
Singer's Society Hall was on Monaca Heights prior to 1910.

Sparling Building - 390 Sixth Street
Sparling Building which became the Morris Service Station - Corner of Sixth Street and Pennsylvania Avenue
> There was the Sparling family's home on Pennsylvania and Sixth Street in 1904.
> W. Sparling was proprietor of "The Only Drug Store" in 1903.
> Fred Patton, the jeweler, moved from the Sparling bldg in 1903 to the Keystone block bldg.

> The Only Drug Store was originally on the corner of Sixth Street and Pennsylvania Avenue, then moved to the Keystone Building in late 1903 – W. A. Sparling was the druggist.
> There was the Sparling family's home on Pennsylvania and Sixth Street in 1904, so this tells me that Mr. Sparling conducted business out of his home in the early 1900s. I do not find the Sparling family on the census in Monaca in 1910 or after, they may have moved elsewhere. This would have left the home/building on the corner of Pennsylvania and Sixth available and referenced as the Sparling Building. The house was evidently a nice sized home because there was Mr. and Mrs. Sparling, their two teenage daughters, a teenage niece, and Fred Patton (Jeweler) boarding with them, too. I deduce that the Sparling's moved from the area by 1903 and the home was sold because........
> Not only did the Only Drug Store move in 1903 – but Fred Patton, the jeweler, moved from the Sparling Building in 1903 to the Keystone Block Building.
> Then, like many other mysteries, specific details were revealed ....
> Feb 1904 – the Sparling building was stated as being at the corner of Sixth Street and Pennsylvania Avenue – E. W. Nelson was the proprietor of the shooting gallery and bowling alley in the *Sparling Building* at that time.
> C.C. Noss of Rochester purchased this property because an article stated that he exchanged the old Sparling drug store building – corner of Sixth Street and Pennsylvania Avenue for a 37 acre farm in May 1912.

Stein Building – about 1128 Pennsylvania Avenue
> This was adjacent to the United 5 & 10 store building.

Jacob Strawick Building – corner of Ninth Street and Washington Avenue
> It was occupied by Frank Gray – Poultry and egg dealer in Jan 1901.

Sullivan Building – __?__ Pennsylvania Avenue (corner Pennsylvania Avenue and Eighth Street)
In 1902 - 1906, there was the Hunter & Sullivan produce market in the building.   Eventually that same year, Peter Sullivan bought the business and had his own Produce Market in this building.   It became known as the Sullivan Building for many years later.   No known exact address except the corner of Pennsylvania Avenue and Eighth Street.

Wagner Home – 319 Eighth Street
   Wilhelmina Wagner married Howard Shanks – had a sister Josephine Wagner, too.
   #319 on Eighth Street was closer to Maple Alley than to Pennsylvania Avenue.   There were most likely some buildings or homes that faced Pennsylvania Avenue from that corner of Eighth Street; and there were either a few small buildings or open lots, because on the census, the next home with any occupancy in 1930 was the house at #434 Eighth Street.   I believe the true address is 314 Eighth Street. The census said *NINTH STREET* in 1920 -?- (Census takers were not perfect !)
   The First Ward school house was across the street from the Wagner house and there was an ice cream parlor and skating rink close by, too.

(faces Eighth Street)

Zigercal / Zigerelli Block Building

I am very sure that this building was located at 1308 Pennsylvania Avenue; it was built by
   Joseph Zigercal/Zigerelli in 1909.
Joseph's son, John F. had his own building at 1414 Pennsylvania Avenue, too.
This building was used by striking Sanitary workers until they moved to their own building near 15th St (1912).
Also John F. had his barber shop here, then the next businesses at the address were
   a hardware and a confectionery store in 1950s.
1308 Pennsylvania Avenue is now (2016) empty/boarded up; 1414 Pennsylvania Avenue houses
   the Flesh Mechanic business.

1308 Pennsylvania Avenue

1414 Pennsylvania Avenue

***   ***   ***   ***   ***
***   ***   ***

Locations

Allaire
Colona
Colonial Steel Homes
Michael Wall/Wahl Plan
Dockter Heights
Monaca Heights
Eckert Plan
Citizens Improvement Co.
John S. Griffiths Plan
Stephen Phillips Homes / Apartments
Baker's Landing
Welsh / Welch Plan
Josephtown
Bellowsville
Kobuta

LOCATIONS
with VIEWS and PICTURES

Photo courtesy Beaver County Historical Research and Landmarks Foundation
Typical homestead in Monaca in mid 1830s

While I was going through so many of the old newspapers and articles researching information on Monaca, I found that it was a very common practice as early as the 1800s to reference a location or meeting place as being in or by a building that was given a specific name.   Snippet example – "moved his fixtures into the large storeroom in the Bartel building."   From finding and reading such information, I could easily obtain a date of such a move, the name of the owner, and usually the name of the business, but was totally lost as to its exact location.   Sometimes it would say Eckert building on Pennsylvania Avenue, bank building, or Markey's old house and with further research, I could usually obtain an avenue, street, or general placement of the building.   This explains why I previously went to the extent of defining all the specific buildings; but again, that still did not always help me locate the exact address of the business or person.

I also discovered with doing all the researching, it was obvious that in earlier years and even to some extent in current times, you definitely had to be born and raised in an immediate area or would have to know and be led by a native resident of the area to help you navigate and locate any specific address or location.   This situation was (and to this day) not exclusive to just Monaca, since I am sure all settled areas were and are the same; with locals referencing buildings and homes and land areas rather than roads, house numbers, and routes.   We are creatures of habit by nature.

The reason for my statements in the last paragraph is to stress how difficult it was to get from point A to point B by a local's directions.   You would most likely be told to go two doors down from the Burry cottage; or to see John at the Hamilton building; drive on past Baker's Landing; or you could buy it at Ridge Market in Fifth Ward.   All these would be foreign locations to a non-Monaca resident.   To an out-of-towner, it was most likely an adventure since the names of the streets had been given one name in the 1800s and by 1900 were all changed.   People seeking directions were told to go here or there with locals using and referencing former owners or a former business. They would be indicating an area or location that had been given a nickname by the locals, something a visitor would not know.   The Borough of Monaca itself had its own variety of names: Smith Township, Moon Township, Appetite, Phillipsburg, Water Cure, Monacatootha, and Monaca.   Throw into the mix that it was also annexed and had a quite flexible line that connected to Center Township and Colona; you may have needed to know where Dockter's Heights, Monaca Heights, Skeeter Hill, Allaire area, Colona Heights, Fourth-Fifth-Second-Third-First Wards were all located, too.

Being more stubborn by nature, I wanted to find as many of the addresses of buildings, streets/roads, and businesses; this almost became an obsession for me.   Making the determination of the addresses of the majority of the buildings and now obsolete roads mentioned in my research proved to be a task in itself.   I believe I have determined many of these, while others are still a mystery.   Although the buildings or locations I have included are not a complete and thorough listing, I have tried to include as many as possible. I also apologize for errors in my reasoning and if any of the address are incorrect.   Trying to find any persons or documentations to absolutely verify some of my theories and deductions proved fruitless. I totally recognize there are still mysteries yet to be solidly solved. Oh, I have my suspicions and personal conclusions, but that does not mean they are correct, just logical in my own mind; therefore I omitted quite a few. I did include all information as it was found or could be proven and included all where applicable. Readers will find that any affirmed information that was found is embodied were applicable. A large majority of locations for business, buildings, and people included in this book are verified regarding specific addresses since I did find and confirm those via publications, tax listings, and newspaper articles.

In this section, I will try to give some information on a few of the various areas that have been used when referencing the Borough of Monaca.   I have not by any means listed all of them.

As stated previously, the borough of Monaca is situated on a level plateau parallel with the Ohio River.   The larger area of acreage in the Borough of Monaca is located primarily above the town of Monaca, now known as Monaca and Colona Heights. This area was officially annexed to Monaca in Dec 1931 from Moon Township.   In 1940, a vast amount of acreage in the hill top area above Monaca was held by the Allaire Land Company, the Colona Land Company, the Freedom Oil Works, and a few others; stock holders whose combined fortunes equal millions of dollars.

Allaire

The Allaire Land Company began as early as October 1901 with sewer and water systems being done as early as 1901; and then the company was active again in September 14, 1911.   The plat map for the Allaire housing area was dated Sep 1901. This map shows there was to be a "Moon Street" that ran fairly parallel to and connected onto Elkhorn Street, but there is no such street nowadays. This map also showed over 854 lots laid out in the plan.

In Nov 1901, under Monaca News in The Beaver Times, I found that the excavation for the foundations for the frame dwelling and storeroom which Mrs. Jane Lawson was having erected in "the new town of Allaire" near the twenty one new houses that were under construction by the Allaire Land Company, had been completed.

and ….

The excavating had been completed for the ten new houses recently contracted for the Allaire Land Company. They had been built on the lots laid out "on the top of the hill."   All the other houses built by the Allaire Company had been erected along the foot of the hill, near the new plant of the Colonia Steel Company.

Property on Jackson Street (directly behind the Fifth Ward School) was donated to the Borough of Monaca in 1936 by the Allaire Land Co.   It was partially cleared and used as a park with improvements made in Apr 1964.   It was donated to the Borough with the stipulation that it would not be used for anything other than recreation or park use.   The first work on the area was done by the W.P.A. with the help of some interested citizens in 1936.
Fast forward to 1984, the waterslides opened and had a 34 foot vertical drop into a 'landing pool'.
The slides were built by a Coraopolis based Water Adventure, Inc. and were the beginning operators of the slides. The borough maintained ownership of the property.   Water Slides of Monaca took over the lease of the slides in 1999.   Waterslides at Allaire Park aka John A. Antoline Park were closed in 2002 and dismantled in Aug 2005. They fell victim to one) a property dispute between the borough and the owner of the adjoining property; two) the abandonment by the most recent operator – the Aliquippa based Water Slides of Monaca, Inc.

Colona

Colonial Land Company – Sep 14, 1911

All property handled by the Colonial Land Company was close to the Colonial Steel plant with some being located in the Monaca Heights area.

> H. C. Fry, the Rochester glass manufacturer was chairman of the board of directors controlling the Colonial Land Company in 1912.
>
> Gilbert Trumpeter was a representative of the Colonial Land Company in 1902 and Oct 1919.
>
> Henry C. Cooper, Charles Armstrong, and Frank M. Main of Pittsburgh were directors of the Colonial Land Company in late 1920.

A 1901 Monaca news item stated that..........One of the most valuable deeds ever placed on record in Beaver Court House was the one done on Aug 7, 1901, from Henry C. Fry to the Colonial Land Company. It was for $300,000 worth of property in the South Monaca vicinity and compromised seven different pieces of ground. It was a gigantic deal and one that only a man with Fry's push and business ability would have undertaken to execute. It was understood that his profit in the transaction is a "snug sum."

Its land's location was in the Third Ward of the Borough. It included certain portions of Cascade Street and was called *Plan of Colona, PA.* It included land north from the P&LERR, west by the Pgh Tool Steel Wire Co., south by Colonial Avenue, and east by land of Mont D. Youtes.

In 1912, the Trumpeter real estate dealer showed 400 acres of land owned by the Colonial Land Company. H. C. Fry, the Rochester glass manufacturer was chairman of the board of directors controlling the Colonial Land Company. The unnamed interested party of the 400 acres was planning to use 100 acres for manufacturing purposes and 300 acres to be divided into town lots. After the plan fell through, the Colonial Land Company was considering plans to divide a 150 acre tract into 1 and 5 acre plots to be sold in the near future.

> Mr. Gilbert Trumpeter has entered the employ of the Colonial Land company, and will quit the gardening business. He will shortly move to the old Eckert homestead, which is located convenient to the lots at Colonia, which he will have for sale.　　　　　Feb 1902

Thomas Jackson had land at South Monaca which became part of the Colonial Land Company.

In 1906 and 1907 for sure, there was a long flight of steps going down Colona hill from Colona. These steps ended by the roadway which was not paved at that time. The mud at this point in the roadway would become quite deep and most times be almost impassable.

Colona – was considered a village of its own.
> They formed their own volunteer fire department – Colonial Hose Company.
>
> The Colonial Steel Company donated the lot and building and located fire plugs at proper intersections for fire use.
>
> The Colonial Hose Company became known as the Monaca Fifth Ward Vol. Fire Dept.
>
> The Colona Heights School was a frame school building.
>
> The Colona railroad depot was built and later moved to Fourteenth Street (see Railroad section).

Colona was considered a separate suburb of Monaca. 1899/1900 – the town of Colona came into existence and was recognized as Colona in 1900/1901. It received its name from the association with the Colonial Steel Company. This community had all the designs to be an outstanding "town'" of its own. There were many homes, most built after Colonial designs and were mainly occupied by the better class of employees and heads of departments of the Colonial Steel Company. There was a very nice brick church, their own fire department, a hotel, sewers, excellent water supply and electric lighting; many social organizations claimed Colona as their home base, too. The roads were in excellent condition, too. Colona also had a railroad depot of its own. Also note - some of the area once referred to as "Colona" was later attached to parts of what became Center Township.

The area of Colona included the houses up on the hill of Monaca.   It was always called Colona until Monaca took over the area from Moon Township in the 1930s; then this area became known as Monaca Heights.   There are many ties to the original Colona name still found and noted in 2015; some of those are Colona Heights, Colona Hill, Colonial Street, Colona Heights School, and Colonial Arms Apartments.

The Volunteer Fire Department was once called Colona VFD. It was formed in 1903.   This same company was also referred to as The Colonial Hose Company.   It is now referred to as Monaca's No 5 VFD.   The Colonial Steel Company donated the lot and building and located fire plugs at proper intersections for fire use.

Colonial Steel Homes

There was a section of homes in Colona that were erected by the Colonial Steel Company to aid in the housing of workers that the company hired to work for them. The first of August 1901, Colonial Steel secured bids for the erection of 20 five room frame houses to be built on the Jackson farm which was near the steel plant.   Each house was built to be about 36 x 16 feet in size. Most of these housed immigrants who came to the area to find work in the local industries; in the August 1901 paper, it stated "A number of foreigners, who will be employed at the Colonial Steel company's plant, arrived in town yesterday."   Colonial Steel sold and rented these homes only to their workers.   In Dec of 1922, The Colonial Land Co. had submitted another plan for 15 building lots along Beaver Avenue.

In Apr 1912 The Colonial Land Co. had submitted a plan of farm lots. The land was subdivided into approximately 140 lots.   By 1918, about 15 more lots were added to the plan bring the total homes considered within this plan to be about 155.

I have included an aerial view of a portion of the Colona/Colonial Heights area on Monaca Heights.   In the background is the Colonial Steel Division of The Alloys Steel Company and then the Ohio River.   To the right is the extension of Beaver Avenue which turns into the Monaca-Aliquippa Boulevard.   Between the houses and the plant is a hillside.

**Colona, Home of
Colonial Steel Co.
Adjoins Monaca and is
Really a Part of the
Borough---It May Be
Annexed.**

Monaca's population would be increased several hundred if adjoining property were annexed. Colona, the home of the immense Colonial Steel Mills, several stones' throw from the south borough line, is really part of the borough, although it is not included in the census. A large settlement of laborers, mostly foreigners, live in Colona and are employed at the mills. The town is a stop for trains on the Pittsburg & Lake Erie railroad. The heights surrounding Monaca have provided home sites for many. They are not included in the census.

Sep 1911

These are a few of the row of homes that were built for workers – they are located on Beaver Road, across the road from the former Colonial Steel plant at the end of Monaca.

1953

These are the homes built on the hill top adjacent to the plant.
Many of the streets in the area were named after a boss from Colona Steel Co.

Fun fact:
In the Financial section of this book, you will find more information on CAMMAR; but I wanted
to make mention of it here being it is applicable to the areas.

The CAMMAR Co. started in 1901 as a combination of Colonial and Allaire Land Companies and
was joined by the Moon Township Land Company. They were in business through 1990.

The CAMMAR name came from all three of these companies:
C - Colona   A - Allaire   M - Moon Twp   M - Monaca   A – Aliquippa   R - Rochester

Michael Wall/Wahl Plan

I found a few indications that this was located somewhere on Pennsylvania Avenue about 1903.   Then I found a legal ad for a sheriff's sale stating that the property at 1100 Pennsylvania Avenue in the Wall/Wahl plan was being put up for sale.   So............in 1902, Michael Wall/Wahl laid out lots specifically at and around 1100 Pennsylvania Avenue.   There is mention of the George Bartel confectionery building being located here.   George Bartel had moved to Florida by 1932, so the Wall/Wahl plan had to have been in place prior to the early 1930s, too.   It appears that Michael Wall/Wahl purchased a plot of lots and then began to sell them off or built his own structures and rented them out for monthly incomes.   Wahl Street still runs between 1120 and 1116 Pennsylvania Avenue.

Dockter Heights

Fred Dockter and family lived here in fall of 1908.   It was located on Monaca Heights.   In many directories or in directions or location guides, it would list it as "east of Sixth Street."

Monaca Heights

Monaca Heights is situated above Monaca proper.   It was accessed by residents in the earlier years by climbing stairs up the hill and then a roadway was made.   Many directories give direction or description of Monaca Heights as being "north of Fourteenth St. Extension."

Monaca Heights Land Improvement Company.
        This company was formed to purchase land and lots in the annexed portion of the Borough of Monaca – Monaca Heights.   The company owned land in the area of Bechtel Street /Allen Avenue/Alder Alley and others.   In 1979 the properties were referenced to be in the Fifth Ward.   They either erected and sold homes on lots, or they just sold lots to individuals and gave them the burden of building.   To-date, I have not found the individuals, firms, or businesses which made up the Monaca Heights Land Improvement Company.   In 1979 and 1983, there were sales of properties on Monaca Heights and the deeds and descriptions of the properties would include the wording "in the Monaca Heights Land Improvement Company lots."
        As early as 1902, there is mention of about 35 lots being purchased in the Welch Plan by the Monaca Heights Land Improvement Company for the purpose of building houses.   There were some sheriff sales of real estate over the years that also referenced the company and would have "aka Welch Plan" in parentheses.   McKay Bros. completed the water system on Monaca Heights the first of August, 1907.   This system was installed for domestic purposes for the benefit of the residents on the hill.   A well was drilled and a tower erected fifty feet high.   A gasoline engine was also installed at the plant.
        There is one of the more popular streets called Marshall Road.   The area was once farmland, but then subdivided and became private lots and homes of many people.

View of Monaca Heights in c 1890 to 1920.   BCHR&LF

Eckert Plan

Charles Eckert made a plan of lots that were situated in what was still Moon Township in Jul 1910. These multiple lots were laid out in an area around Dockter Avenue, Charles Street, Bechtel Street and Welch Avenue.

Citizens Improvement Co.

This company was formed very early on in the history of Monaca. I have no starting or ending date for this company other than I found in 1893 A. M. Johnson was the President and H. J. Speyer was the Secretary and Treasurer. This company laid out a plan of lots in what is now the Monaca Heights area with all lots in and around McClellan Street, Kay Avenue, McCoy Avenue, Speyer Avenue, Johnson Avenue, and Bechtel Street.

John S. Griffiths Plan of Lots

In May of 1926, John S. Griffiths laid out a plan of lots; they were located on Monaca Heights. These 90+ lots were in the area of Elmira Street, Chestnut Street, Linden Street, and Dockter Avenue.

Stephen Phillips Homes / Apartments

Monaca Borough has a former WWII Housing Development plan of homes – the Stephen Phillips Homes / Apartments on Cascade Road, Monaca Heights. These homes were built to help house the workers needed at the local mills and factories that were "war plants." (See Kobuta for more housing information.) Given the pre- and post-WWII housing shortages, many such plans of homes were developed. These plans and projects were sold off to private companies that managed them as profitable rental properties; but many more were transferred to local housing authorities or municipal and county agencies. These actions helped to supply Federal public housing for many families. Stephen Phillips Homes was a 100 unit housing development plan that was constructed in 1942 for use as public housing. This housing plan was known to many of the Monaca residents and especially those living in the plan as simply "The Project."

In the spring of 2009, the housing Authority received a grant under the "American Recovery & Reinvestment Act (ARRA) of 2009" to assist in beginning the conversion of the 100 unit plan into 71 modern and accessible units. Current residents at that time were shifted into vacant units as work was completed on their particular units and then they were moved back into their newly rehabilitated units.

The Stephen Phillips Homes are currently managed by the Housing Authority of the County of Beaver and consists of 13 one bedroom units, 48 two bedroom units, and 10 three bedroom units.

Baker's Landing

This was an area that was considered part of Moon Township which actually later was included in Center Township, yet many references called it the south area of Monaca.

Where the street name should go on the census sheets in 1900, 1910, it would have "Baker's Landing." There were several families who called this area home and had their dwellings located there; to name a few........... Homer, Allen, and Hiram Craig – David Wilson – Mrs. Mary King - William Bowers – Henry Pink – Emil Vogt – Frederick Shively – John Brooks – Cain – Daniels – Keherar – Larkins – and of course, John Baker. Baker's Landing was even the name of the post office of parts of Moon Township in the very early 1900s, referenced as being adjacent to the borough. There was also a Baker's Yard mentioned in some articles which without further researching, one can presume it was located within the same area as Baker's Landing.

There is the Baker Cemetery located behind the current Metco (2015) plant. This indicates that this was definitely where at least a portion of the Baker's property was, with Baker's Landing not far from this area of what is now Monaca. Portions of this same surrounding area was referenced as Colona. So without a surveyor's notes, specific areas of what was or is actually Center Township property or what part was annexed to Monaca, one thing is certain, this whole area went by many names and was given more than one nickname from time to time.

Welsh/Welch Plan

James H. Welch owned extensive land in the area above Monaca actually being in Moon Township.   This area was referenced as in Monaca Heights, Monaca, Moon Township, and even some land in what became Center Township.   Moon Township, Monaca Heights, and Center Township boundaries just seemed to blend together until there were the divisions made with Fourth and Fifth Ward areas.   Lots from this plan in Monaca Heights were being sold as early as 1902.   This was a very large section of the heights since it is said there were 256 of the Welch Plan lots already sold from this plan by the first of Mar 1903.

This plan came from land purchased by James H. Welch – the proprietor and general manager of the Welsh-Bright Fire Brick Co. at the north end of Monaca.   His home was described as being on the hillside above the town and it gave an excellent view of the surroundings; the estate was called "Welchmont."   Welchmont was actually not located within the Welch Plan, but instead was in the portion of Moon Township that became Center Township – nowadays known as the Sylvan Crest area.   James obviously owned quite a bit of real estate.   Until as late as Nov 1916, there were extensions to the J. H. Welch Plan being made; these lots were all in the area from about Bechtel Street, to include Elm Street, Walnut Street, Welch Avenue, Taylor Avenue and extended to Beech Street.   There was a school house in this plan in 1903 and 1904. Prof. Joseph Thomas was the teacher at that time.   It was reported to have been very overcrowded.   This information tells me that this was the Fourth Ward School since some of the mentions of homes in the Welch Plan were located with the area of the Fourth Ward.

Apr 1904

IDEAL SITES FOR HOMES AVAILABLE IN MONACA HGHTS.

Welsh Plan Of Lots Conveniently Located In Section Above Southside Town

No section of Beaver County has received more attention in the way of improvement with Federal aid during the past four years than the Fourth Ward of Monaca, known as Monaca Heights. This plateau has been recognized as an ideal home site for many years. While lower levels are often blanketed in fog, it is sparkling in the morning sunlight and ringing with the song of birds.

Its soil of rich loam, responding to the long hours of sunlight, has always been a joy to those interested in gardens. The freshness of the air is nature's best tonic. Since this section has been admitted to Monaca Borough; the extension of sewers and water lines has brought the completion of domestic conveniences and now that bus service is about to be installed, the community will enjoy all the accommodations of modern urban life. The James H. Welsh plan of lots is so conveniently located as to be within easy walking distance from schools, churches, railroad station and either the business or industrial section of Monaca. With splendid concrete and macadam connections to the district's highways all points of the county are easily reached. When all these advantages are considered, one does not wonder that Federal agencies found this a worthwhile investment for the government funds and the individual seeking a home will also be impressed with its economic advantages.

1937

*** *** *** *** ***

Miscellaneous information

There was one more item I wanted to include in this section.   There really is no street or specific area involved, there is no address per say, nor is there a permanent building, but..........

In 1912, I found a resident living in an unusual location and "home."

Vernor and Elsie Grater had their residency and address listed as "boat house."   Using the surrounding addresses, it was located near the Monaca Bridge.   Vernor was listed as a *laborer*, so did his occupation keep them close to the river, was there no housing available, or was this a case of just a true love of the water ?

*** *** *** *** ***

For general interest, here are a few areas outside the Monaca Borough........

There are three other locations that may interest the readers.   Throughout this book, there may be mention of a few locations or a few post offices that may sound foreign; therefore I have included a bit of information to clarify and satisfy any curiosity.   All three of the following were very close to each other in proximity, yet were also considered quite individual.   They were once located in what is now a massive earth moving project, just across the Center Township and Potter Township lines as you come off the Beaver Valley Expressway/ 376.   If you were or are at all familiar with various 'land marks' in Beaver County, then the former ARCO, St. Joe Lead, Koppers, Horsehead plants and the current BASF plant may stir a memory or two.   These were all located in the exact area or adjacent to what was once called and known as three distinctly different small communities - Josephtown   Bellowsville   Kobuta.

Josephtown

St. Joseph Lead Company, located along Frankfort Road/Rte 18 once had the address of "Josephtown" associated with it. From all historical topo maps I could locate, it appears it was considered to be between the Beaver Valley Expressway / Rte 376 and the former Pleasant Drive, along Frankfort Road.   It was not uncommon in the 1930s and 1940s to find reference to the P & L E railroad and other transportation to state "between Monaca to Josephtown."

There was once a post office located at the St. Joseph Lead Company, but it was short lived (1931-1933) and then discontinued.   In 1938 and 1939 St. Joseph Company presented Potter Township with a school building they erected; the school was appropriately called "St. Joe School Building."   This school had two classrooms, a storage room, a heater room, and a small kitchen, and was supplied with well water.   They also constructed a nice play area on the school grounds.   This school was built in the area of the former Horsehead plant's scales.   It was used as a community center for several years, then was turned over to the plant and was used by Beaver County for special education classes.

With no post office, no railroad station, no signs that it ever really existed on modern maps, people still referred to it as Josephtown.   Almost sixty years later, it seemed to have faded off into just memories.   There was a 2000 report by the Raccoon Creek Watershed Association discussing watersheds and other topics and it made a reference to Raccoon Creek stating "...until it discharges into the Ohio River near Josephtown in Beaver County."

St. Joe Lead Company would have been the area once called Josephtown in Potter Township.   Note the Vanport Expressway bridge in the top right corner of the next picture.

Bellowsville

Bellowsville was considered a small community of its own, having a post office from 1874 to 1902. It was formed/founded by Samuel Maxwell, a county industrialist who died in the early 1900s. Maxwell's old home was left standing along the old Narrows Road, but had become quite run down and overgrown with weeds and vines. Ferry Street, Vanport, is where the ferry would come from and go to Bellowsville. From historic topo maps I located, it appears that Bellowsville was located within the area between the Beaver Valley Expressway/Rte 376, almost to Poorhouse Run Creek, from the Ohio River to the railroad tracks (not going as far as Frankfort Road or the Josephtown area). Many references to it are made along with Josephtown, so it is clear that these were close to each other, yet considered separate and of their own area. In 1900, I located some references to about 275, maybe 300 people with an address indicating they lived in Bellowsville.

Just a very short distance up the Ohio River from Bellowsville (heading toward Monaca) along the shore of the Ohio River was a place known as Rag Run (where the Rag Run Creek emptied into the Ohio). It was also the site of a local ferry that would travel down the short distance to Bellowsville. Many references state that the County Home (Poor Farm as it was often referenced) was situated close to the Ohio River and between the two small, now defunct, towns/communities of Bellowsville and Josephtown. Those buildings and grounds are now also gone and unrecognizable with the current land moving project going on in Potter Township.

Fun Fact:

In the late 1890s, Theodore Hostetter and his wife purchased several hundred acres of property and had a mansion erected. Theodore was the son of David Hostetter, both accumulating fortunes in the manufacturing of "bitters." The property was located within the area of where the Nova Chemical plant was built. In 1900, Theodore and Allene (Tew) lived here with their daughter Greta and son Theodore AND had a maid, two cooks, a chamber maid, two butlers, and a governor living in the house with them.

Just on the other side of the Potter Bridge (which was at that time a covered bridge), if you made a quick right turn, you would be on a tree lined road/drive that led up to the massive mansion. Both Mr. and Mrs. Hostetter enjoyed horses and they had almost two dozen sorrel horses and up to forty horses in all for gaming and breeding. Theodore was a lover of polo and had a polo field in place on his property as well as golf courses and quarters for hunting dogs. In addition to the mansion and polo field, they had three barns for the many horses and another large house as well as a care taker's house. It is said Mr. Hostetter purchased the first motor car in the area and everyone thoroughly enjoyed riding in it except Mrs. Hostetter because it scared her horses.

The house itself was huge and contained 25 bedrooms, a large drawing room and a beautiful banquet hall. As stated, Theodore was in the bitters manufacturing business with his father and both had become millionaires. The Hostetter mansion and grounds were merely a summer and vacationing home for the family and guests. There was eventually a docking area added to the property along the Ohio River and the family and their many guests could then easily access the estate by boat rather than traveling the road ways.

Unfortunately Theodore died of pneumonia in 1902 and the house was eventually said to have been under the control of a Pittsburgh bank and was rented out. In July 1932, Mr. and Mrs. Edward Martine from Indiana Avenue, Monaca, moved to the Hostetter house; whether they had the entire house to themselves or only rented a portion of the home is unknown. It was also said that J. C. Davis was an occupant of the house in 1926 or 1936. The house had a caretaker in 1936, Mr. Robert Strock; both Robert and his wife lived in the house at that time. An article stated that an adopted girl of the Strobucks "had a bit of the arson bug in her" and went upstairs in one of the mansion's bedrooms and set fire to the place. This happened in mid August 1936; the house caught fire and burned completely to the ground.

It is also said that prior to the Hostetters owning the mansion, the property once held a horse racing track built by David and Sam Collins; it was operated as a training track for six or seven years with no commercial races being held. It is also long standing folklore that the author Mary Roberts Rinehart, author of the book The Circular Staircase, used the Hostetter House as the setting for her book. If this is true, she was most likely inspired by the actual circular staircase in the home.

So...............Bellowsville, Potter Township, and the Monaca area had a millionaire living there many years ago.

Hostetter home – sat on several hundred acres, had barns, polo field, <u>25 bedrooms</u>.   It was made of red wood and also had one board from every state in the union in its construction.

Kobuta

Located along Frankfort Road/ Rte 18.   Kobuta was an unincorporated community that was located in Potter Township.   Local lore states that the name Kobuta is said to have been a combination of Koppers and butadiene (an ingredient used by Koppers Co. to produce synthetic rubber......see War section).   Kobuta has disappeared from modern maps, but is still reflected within a few business names.   The building of the Koppers United plant began about Apr 1943.   With the construction of the Koppers plant and its operation that started in late 1942, there was the need for many men.   As the Koppers plant was first being erected and into the early days of its operations, the unincorporated community of Kobuta was already being formed.   The workers of the plant were living in two smaller communities at the time – Kobuta Village – the trailer camp, and Camp Beaver – the barracks area at the plant; these were necessitated due to housing facilities in the being sparse.   The trailer camp was for the workers with families and the barracks (mere huts) were for bachelors or men who came to work without bringing their families.   Kobuta Homes, as it was called, was constructed by the Public Housing Administration, acting for the Federal government, and were specifically built for the housing of families and individuals engaged in vital war work; this being exactly what the workers at Koppers United were considered to be doing.

November 26, 1943, the Beaver County Housing Authority, Koppers United Company, the Housing Architects of Beaver County, County Commissioners and other prominent county people were present for a dedication ceremony of the community building at the Kobuta Homes. It was the second largest war housing project in Beaver County. (Van Buren Homes, Vanport, was the largest.) It consisted of 300 dwellings and housed employees of the Koppers plant. (In 1946, forty-eight units were transferred elsewhere for veterans' housing.) Ground was to be broken in the very near future for a project school; classes were held in the community building until such time as the school was completed.   References were made into the 1950s for addresses to residents living within these homes as Kobuta Homes.

There was a Navy physician that spent several days at the Village vaccinating all who asked for it and who would attend to other matters.   Victory gardens were cultivated along the bank of the Ohio River by the village residents.   The entire grounds were fenced and patrolled 24 hours a day by the Koppers plant police force.   The children living at the Village had a playground set up for them.   There were about 65 to 70 children who attended classes at Potter Township grade school and about 10 others went to Monaca High School.

Eventually there was also a smaller hotel built at 427 Frankfort Road, located across the road from Koppers named Kobuta Hotel. There were also two other former well known watering holes/tap rooms/bars for the plant workers along Frankfort Road that should be mentioned – The Red Rooster Inn/Tavern and the Midway Bar. (See Restaurant and Bar section for more information on both of these businesses.) Even before all the reconstruction of the area by the giant land moving equipment, almost every thread of evidence of the former Bellowsville, Josephtown, or Kobuta community's had already disappeared.

1943 view of a section of Kobuta Homes / community.

Since it was directly connected to the government and the war effort, coupled with the vital nature of the product Koppers United Company used (butadiene and styrene) for their production of synthetic rubber, it goes without saying that the plant was well-guarded against sabotage. The guard force was organized shortly after construction of the plant was started in Jul 1942. The guards had a genuine arsenal of weapons and ammunition. There was also a rifle range and pistol range on site; also a well-equipped guard force in place under the jurisdiction of the Third Service Command, Fourth District, Military Police, U.S. Army.

In October 1952 there were approximately 114 families living in the war housing project of the Kobuta community. They were all notified that they must now vacate their apartments and living quarters by 1953. The land that the community was located on had been leased by a company that planned to dredge the site for sand and gravel. When the Kobuta Homes and the community were first constructed in 1942/1943, it was to have the normal life of seven years. Although there were 114 families living in Kobuta in 1952, there were actually 233 family units that were still located there but scheduled to be demolished.

1944 aerial view of Kobuta showing the plant in upper portion of pictures and the housing plan (trailer area and barracks) in lower portion.

Photos courtesy of the Beaver County Historical Research and Landmarks Foundation

Shell moved in with their land moving equipment and none of the former area is as it once was ! I only included one picture to show how the entire area of the former Bellowsville, Josephtown, and Kobuta sites came to be totally changed; how it all looked in 2014/2015.   The company continues to 'move the earth' with the views changing monthly, sometimes even weekly, depending on the amount of hours workers man the equipment.

This aerial view is looking at the whole area (the river would be at the bottom and out of the picture).   The Expressway and Center Township are to the left; Raccoon Creek and Potter Township would be to the right.   To anyone not familiar with the former area, there are no more recognizable landmarks to know where Bellowsville, Josephtown, Kobuta, the Beaver County Home, Horsehead, Kobuta, St. Joe Lead, Kobuta Hotel, Midway Bar, etc. ever were. Former hillsides have been flattened and other new hillsides created, all former vegetation was stripped, roadways have been eliminated and new ones created, small dips and valleys have been filled in …..etc. In Jun 2016, it was reported that there will definitely be a cracker plant erected on this property within the next few years.

Also affected with all these changes were the roads.   Route 18 / Frankfort Road was greatly altered, and all of the remaining traces of Narrows Road have been removed.   See "Narrows Road" further in the next section.

*** *** *** *** ***
*** *** ***

STREETS / AVENUES / ROADS

Street Names – prior to and after 1900

General Information on
Streets, Avenues, and Roads

Dead Streets, Avenues, Roads

Street Names – Prior to and after 1900

Research and review of old deeds and maps led me to find one of the most entertaining facts about Monaca – the street names. When Phillipsburg was first settled, there were completely different names of the most common streets and avenues you will find today. I was not even certain that I was researching the correct people or area when I first started because I was finding Garden Street or Factory Street or Third Street. Then I finally dug out my magnifying glass and reviewed the 1876 atlas of Phillipsburg; low and behold, there were all the "odd" street names that I was finding.

I have not seen that anyone else pointed out all the different names of the streets and avenues, so I thought I would include them here for those who will find it as interesting as I did.

Prior to 1900	After 1900
	(These all run parallel to the river.)
FACTORY STREET	PENNSYLVANIA AVENUE EXT, coming into Monaca under RR bridges to large curve
FOURTH STREET	PENNSYLVANIA AVENUE
THIRD STREET	WASHINGTON AVENUE
SECOND STREET	INDIANA AVENUE
FIRST STREET	ATLANTIC AVENUE (from 9th Street to 6th Street – waterworks) Property was altered between 1876 and now in the area that now has a round stone structure where Sixth Street and Atlantic meet, just above the Water Works.
OHIO STREET	ATLANTIC AVENUE EXT (from 6th St to newer boat dock area)

(These run from river to main street, perpendicular to river.)

HANOVER STREET	FOURTH STREET
GARDEN STREET	FIFTH STREET
LACOCK STREET	SIXTH STREET
HIGH STREET	EIGHTH STREET
PHILIP STREET	NINTH STREET

(sometimes also called "Bridge Street")

Phillipsburg had what appeared to be some alleys throughout and between the above streets, but I did not find names for any of them.

From what was PHILIP STREET (Ninth Street) and on toward the end of town (heading toward Aliquippa) was farm land and/or large plots of land owned by individuals. There was a roadway that lead to all the properties which appears to be an extension of the FOURTH STREET (Pennsylvania Avenue), but it was not named. There were also a few smaller roadways that went between some of the properties; they were unnamed also.

General Information on Streets, Avenues, and Roads

There were many interesting items and bits of information I found while doing the research on Monaca. One thing I would like to point out or clarify is that in the early 1900s, there were several mentions of the streets being paved or a sidewalk being laid. During these early years, it was not concrete or asphalt that was used; all the paving and laying of the roadways, streets, alleys, and sidewalks was done with bricks. These bricks were put into place brick by brick by persons and/or crews from companies hired specifically for that chore/job. As with Monaca, there are still quite a few towns where you will find brick sidewalks or streets still being used and the surface is entirely of brick; most have been layered over with asphalt though. So as you read certain bits of information throughout this book about the streets being paved, note the dates because that may help to clarify if the paving was done with bricks or if the use of asphalt was in play.

One of the remaining older brick sidewalks of Monaca.

An example of a brick street.

By 1907, Monaca was one of the few boroughs in Beaver County that had no paved streets. By 1911, thirty-three thousand dollars had been spent in paving, with the credit going to George V. Mullen who spearheaded an ordinance providing for the first paving laid in Monaca. Just another reminder: this paving was not asphalt or concrete, but rather of locally made bricks.

Streets   Avenues   Roads

Tenth, Eleventh, Twelfth, Thirteenth, Fifteenth, Sixteenth, and Seventeenth Streets were added and there were homes built within these blocks, too, but they were not all mapped out to exactly as they appear in 2016. There was also a Fourteenth Street. Fourteenth Street does not run through town like other streets. It begins at Pennsylvania Avenue and appears to have crossed the RR tracks and led to places across the tracks and on up the hill side.

When looking over the maps of Monaca in current times, one may notice that there is no Seventh Street. This street was absorbed when the 1980 revitalization project took over in Monaca when Phoenix purchased massive amounts of lots. Seventh Street never went through the main part of town from Pennsylvania to the river. Much of the Pacific Avenue disappeared during the same revitalization project, as well as former business and residents. This same project involved removal of many of the homes and businesses of surrounding alleys and along Pennsylvania Avenue between Sixth Street and Ninth Street; all due to the borough's giving permission to the Phoenix Glass Company to expand.

Ever hear of Thorne Alley ?   Well, after looking long and hard, I found it. Thorne Alley is by the old Potter building, near Slush Puppy and Johnstone Supply; it runs from Pennsylvania Avenue and goes toward the railroad tracks.

None of the maps show Apple Alley, but I have my own conclusion of where it is –
         Runs from Pennsylvania Avenue, beginning alongside Harper's Styling and goes all the way to Atlantic Avenue.   There are articles in the newspaper stating the council took actions on different situations involving Apple Alley; one stated "on Pennsylvania Avenue between Apple Alley and Eighth Street."

Fourteenth and Fifteenth streets
I could not locate any documentation or ordinances to explain why or how Fourteenth Street hill actually became Fourteenth Street.
Why would I mention this you may be thinking – well............

If you never noticed, as you come from Pennsylvania Avenue past the old railroad depot, and cross the railroad tracks, there is a road/street almost straight ahead of you (a little to your left) that also goes up the hill and has about a dozen homes along it.   It is known as Fourteenth Street Extension.

Instead of going up this extension street, stay to the left, around the bend onto Beaver Avenue, and you will come to a "T" in the road – to the right goes up what is now called Fourteenth Street hill or you can go straight to the stop sign. If you go straight to the stop sign and make a left into what appears to be a drive or entrance to an open lot, you would be on what is labeled as a continuation of Fifteenth Street.

To back up what I am saying, if you start on the opposite side of the railroad tracks and turn onto Fifteenth Street from Pennsylvania Avenue heading toward the railroad tracks and look through the bushes across the tracks, you can see why I say it would be logical that Fifteenth Street would have easily gone straight up the hill.   It is confusing to me as to why the hill going up to Monaca Heights was not named Fifteenth Street Hill since it is obviously more of a continuance of Fifteenth Street than that of Fourteenth Street.   Just saying............

The Pretzel Path (people path)
This extends on the left a little way up from the bottom of Fourteenth Street Hill where it intersects with Beaver Avenue and goes on up through the woods, then running almost parallel to Eckert Road, coming out onto the property of the former high school at the far end of the ball field by the Central Valley Middle School.   It is not a roadway, but rather a foot path.

I 376
Not part of Monaca – but for general information.......
The Beaver Valley Expressway (Interstate 376) opened from the Vanport Bridge to the Greater Pittsburgh Airport the end of June 1971.   Construction of the bridge over the Ohio River in Vanport began in 1966 and opened in 1967.   On Nov 20, 2003, there was heavy rain that caused flooding down the Ohio River causing 20 barges to break away.   The Vanport Bridge, along with three other nearby bridges were closed. Inspection crews found no serious damage was caused.

*** *** *** *** ***

Defunct Streets, Avenues, Roads

I am most certain this is not a complete listing, but rather, it just contains quite a bit of information found on streets, avenues, alleys, and roads that were removed or eliminated by the borough.

This was an alley way that ran beside the First Ward School from Pennsylvania Avenue to Pacific Avenue.

1919
Colonial Avenue – The first of Oct 1919, the Pittsburgh Tool Steel Wire company and the Colonial Land Company asked Council to open Colonial Avenue from Fourteenth to Twenty-First Street. This avenue paralleled the P & L E railroad right of way and was open about 500 feet between Sixteenth and Twenty-first Streets. The Pgh Tool company opened a bridge leading to their plant in about 1913. The public was using this bridge quite regularly to go from Monaca to Monaca Heights.
Council was going to prepare data for consideration.

1925
Phillipsburg Road - In 1925 there was a road that went through the old J & L Steel mill site from Monaca to the South Heights; it was called Phillipsburg Road. It was given to J & L by Aliquippa, which in turn was given the land that is now Rte 51.

1930
P & LE railroad had plans drawn showing a proposal for the borough to vacate certain portions of Factory Street and Atlantic Avenue extension, near the Welch-Bright Company brick yard. This vacated property would be exchanged for property owned by the railroad. The railroad needed this property to construct a new spur track from Monaca to St. Joseph Lead Co.

1931
Arroyo Avenue - This avenue was in the Colonial Land Company Plan extending from Beaver Avenue, in a southerly direction to the estate of Gilbert Trumpeter.

1933
Baldwin Lane – was laid out and named in mid 1860. It was vacated by an ordinance approved by the Borough of Monaca in February 1933. It was sometimes called a part of Twenty-first Street. It was about 33 feet wide, began closer to the Ohio River, and was one hundred fifteen and five tenths perches long (equal to 1,905.75 feet -- - 1 perch=16.5 feet).

1941

An unnamed alley along the right of way of the Pittsburgh and Lake Erie railroad near Beaver Road was vacated by Monaca Council. The alley with the exception of about 70 feet was unused at the time of the vacating. There is one house on the corner of Beaver Avenue and this alley and then 2 houses are still situated on a small portion of this alley.

1964

Ninth Street - 82 feet of Ninth Street Extension, at the entrance to Phoenix Glass Co. was officially vacated on May 19, 1964. In Jul 1964, the portion of Ninth Street from Pacific Avenue to the Phoenix Glass Co. was vacated. The borough approved this action with the firm donating 20 feet of the area to provide access to Hemlock Alley (which dead ends at the plant).

1971

Keiber Street – 10 feet wide and was an extension from Ninth Street that went up in an easterly direction about 122.6 feet. Was a dead end.

Seventeenth Street went all the way to the railroad tracks at one time.

Twenty-first Street
The Monaca Borough officially vacated Twenty-first Street from the Ohio River to Pennsylvania Avenue at their March 15, 1933 meeting. This action was taken to enable the Pittsburgh Tube Company to construct an addition to its plant.
It crossed over and intersected with Pennsylvania Avenue. Once located where the old iron bridge and current overpass of the tracks is at the end of town by Metcon (2015).

It appears that there was a street crossing similar to what still exists at Fourteenth Street (2015). It was decided that due to many serious accidents that were occurring in the area of Twenty-first Street and the crossing of the P & LE railroad tracks, an "overpass" with the highway and steel truss bridge should be constructed. This overpass / viaduct would also provide the opportunity to extend the street car line of service.

There was a viaduct* constructed by the State Department of Highways spanning the P & LE railroad crossing near Twenty-first Street in Monaca. It opened the first of July 1938 and constructed as a project of the Federal grade crossing elimination plan. The work on this project was started in June 1937, was a federal aid project, and provided 410 men employment throughout the process.
   *a long bridge like structure, typically a series of arches, carrying a road or railroad
    across a valley or other low ground.

This project was a 44 foot concrete span of highway leading from the Aliquippa-Monaca road near Colona. It was constructed across the railroad tracks on a banked curve and then a gradual grade leading to the end of Pennsylvania Avenue. It also included a steel truss bridge, 189 feet long. The bridge and steel truss bridge stood at that site for over 73 years, then between 2011 and 2015, they were both torn down. A new viaduct was constructed just to the side of the original. When completed, the old steel truss bridge and original viaduct were removed.

Twenty-first Street was not completely taken off the map with the construction of the viaduct. Proof........In Oct 1975, the P & LE railroad was doing repairs at the Fourteenth Street crossing and Twenty-first Street was referenced and directly tied to the overpass at the end of town..... "Traffic will be detoured via Pennsylvania and Beaver avenues over the Twenty-first Street overpass located near the Pittsburgh Tube Co." In 1982, there was a Wilson's Garage at Twenty-first Street and Pennsylvania Avenue. This street was still referenced in March 1991 when it was announced that fire hydrants would be flushed between Fifteenth Street and Twenty-First Street.

Original photos by Lucy Schaly

Little Beaver Historical Society   Monaca - looking NW - 1938

On the top of the bridge, you could see that the Fort Pitt Bridge Works constructed this bridge.
They are working on completing the viaduct and laying the tracks for the street car in this picture.
This would have been the area of the Twenty-first Street in Monaca with the original roadway crossing over the railroad tracks (that are under this bridge) in the same manner as at Fourteenth Street/Beaver Avenue. This overpass was built to eliminate crossing the existing railroad tracks at this site for two reasons: there had been numerous serious accidents at this crossing and there was a need to lay street car tracks on the roadway.
By raising the roadway it especially solved the problem of interfering with the current railroad tracks since the street car tracks could not be laid directly "into" the railroad tracks; passing over the railroad tracks provided the needed extension of the street car route. (The mill you see through the bridge would be Pittsburgh Tube.)

Twelfth Street to Pacific Avenue -(1919)

This strip of property was not an official street or avenue, but was being used daily as a shortcut to access the P & LE railroad depot. The property was not owned by the borough, but rather by the Mitchell Lumber Company. To alleviate the public usage of this property, they wanted to create an extension of Twelfth Street which involved a 40 x 100 feet section of the current Mitchell Lumber Company. Twelfth Street originally only ran from Atlantic Avenue to Pennsylvania Avenue. For some reason, Mr. Mitchell would not sell the plot of land, yet agreed to the borough condemning it, which they did. That strip of property of the Mitchell Lumber Company was turned into more of Twelfth Street which is still the section that passes beside the current Monaca Cornet Band Room building and the former Penn Super business from Pennsylvania Avenue to Pacific Avenue.

River Street   aka   Saw Mill

This roadway was first known as Sall Mill because it provided access to an actual saw mill that was located along the road near the pump house.   This mill was owned by Baldwin & Baldwin (Frank D. Baldwin of Washington Avenue and Irwin Baldwin of Indiana Avenue) who were also dealers in coal, stone, lime, cement, brick, contracting & hauling. Once the saw mill was no longer located there, it became better known as just River Street.

Jun 1930, the Borough passed Ordinance No. 295 that allowed for the widening and extending of Saw Mill or River Street in the Borough of Monaca.   This section of the street was between Ninth Street and Sixth Street area, between the Ohio River and the end of the properties of the land owners along that stretch of Atlantic Avenue.   It referenced lots 15 through 24 being involved in the process of condemning that strip of property under the power of eminent domain for the use of the roadway. They wanted this roadway improved, widened, and extended for use in securing a better water supply for the borough and for municipal wharf purposes.   I have to believe that the depth of the river and spreading of its waters onto the shorelines is one reason we do not see this roadway today.

1900 lithographic view of the area where Saw Mill or River Road would have been (along river bank).

Narrows Road

Repeatedly I found information on a roadway called the Narrows Road, yet I could not absolutely locate such a road or any remains of it. Of course this process was halted dead in its tracks with all the current land moving and reshaping of the property in Potter Township, since this is a main area of where the roadway was located.   I have included all this information regarding Narrows Road in this book because though this road was mainly identified with being in Moon/Center and Potter Township, it seemed that Monaca officials were called upon to make the decisions with this roadway.

Here are some snippets from older publications related to this road:

1903 - there was an old shack that stood along the Narrows.
1906 - "A force of men are at work putting the river road, known as the Narrows in good condition,
        a slide having occurred there a few days ago."
1907 – "The work of repairing the river road, commonly known as the Narrows is progressing rapidly
        and when completed the road will be in first class condition. John P. Potter is doing the work."

All this is what peaked my interest in trying to locate the road.   At first I was leaning toward it being a roadway that may have been renamed and that we're all driving upon the former road known as the Narrows more frequently than not. But as I dug further into more information, I can almost guarantee that this road way was located right along the shore of the Ohio River.

It would have started in the area of Potter Township known as Bellowsville (by the former site of the Beaver County Home, later more familiar landmarks would be the Midway Bar, St. Joseph Lead/ Horsehead Corp.) and led traffic to and past the Beaver County Home, continuing between the steep embankments and the Ohio River, then ending in Monaca.   It would have continued down along the Ohio River bank and came into Monaca by the P & L E railroad bridge. It was the decision of the State Highway Department to move and relocate the roadway further inland making it more useful to a larger population.

In the 1911 cropped picture of the demolition of the old Ohio River railroad bridge(see further), you can see what appears to be a roadway just above the shoreline along the river bank.   This is where I believe the Narrows Road was.

(A full version of this picture is available in the Railroad section and Map section.)

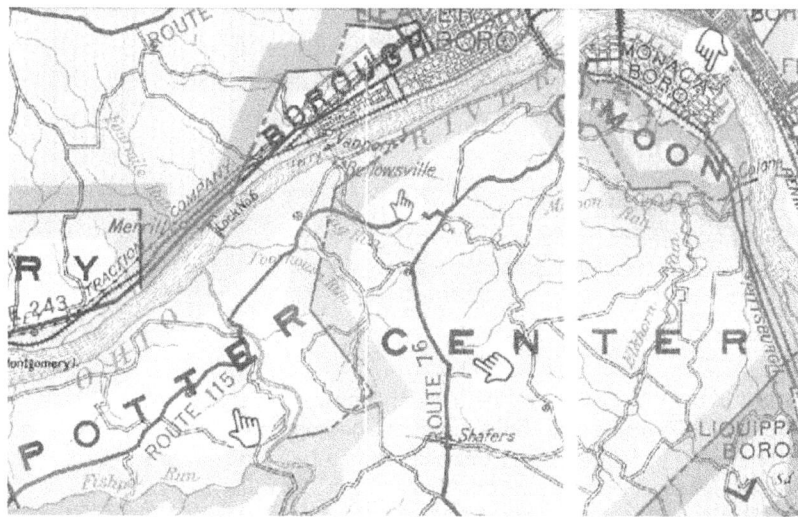

1926

This map shows the old Rte 115 which was renamed Rte 18; that stretch of Rte 18 that passes through Potter Township is called Frankfort Road.   There is also a Rte 76 listed and it was renamed Rte 51; now most often being called Brodhead Road.

This map is mainly to just show the location of Bellowsville and the area going to Monaca in 1926, the Narrows Road is not indicated.

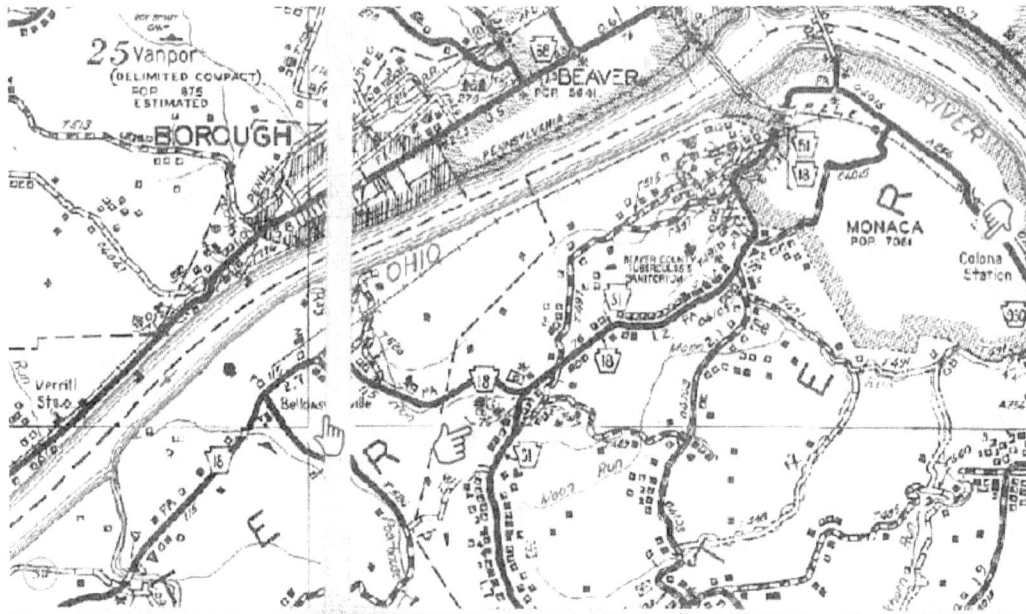

1941   This map shows the renamed Rtes 18 and 51
(Note – Bellowsville is still listed on this map.......as is the Colona Station in Monaca.)

Again, the Narrows is not listed on this map, it was simply included for additional viewing.

The roadway along the bottom of the hill, just above the bank of the river is defined above.
This photo is looking toward Potter Township and Midland and the photographer would be
standing on the P & LE RR bridge.   (A full version of this picture may be found in the Railroad
section – it shows the older/first RR bridge being torn down.)

Coming from the Potter bridge, heading toward the Beaver Valley Mall................ The roadway to the left
is the old Rte 18/Frankfort Road; it went past the Midway & toward the location of the former Beaver
County Home.

The roadway that was the exit/entrance to the Midway Bar was listed as old Rte 18.
Once you turned off Frankfort to go to the Midway, there were a couple homes to the right. The road
continued on past those houses and would have lead down to the Poor Farm/County Home.

This photo was taken looking OVER the side of the expressway bridge and facing toward Potter. The
Ohio River is on the right of the photo. A bit of the former roadway can still be seen in the left/middle of
the picture.

This photo is looking OVER the other side of the expressway bridge facing toward Monaca with the Ohio River on the
left of the photo - part of the road can be seen here, too.

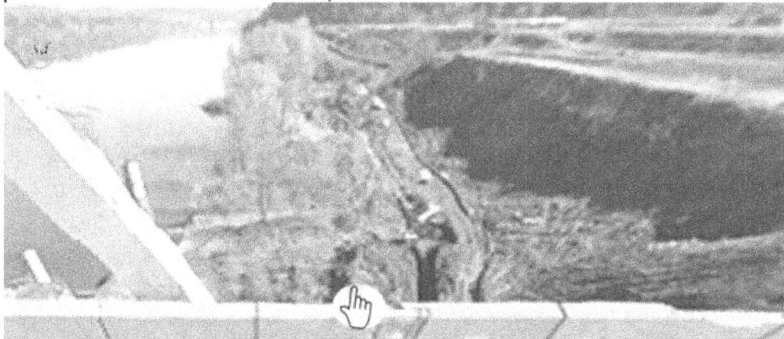

The Narrows Road never was further developed. A portion of the old Frankfort Road in the area was called "the
Middle Road" and/or "Stone Quarry" as it met up with "Route 76" which became Brodhead Road including the hill
going down past the lower entrance of Penn State. I have condensed quite a few articles to give as much
information on locating the Narrows as I could find. Once you read all the information, you will see why I came up
with these conclusions. It is a fact that Narrows Road did indeed go along the river's shore line. It was level and
void of all the hills on the other roadways. It was totally abandoned when St. Joe Lead Co. came to Potter
Township; a single track railroad was built in almost the same location as the old Narrows Road. Looking from
River Road in Beaver to across the river, you once had a fair view of where the roadway was once located.

Oct 1914 -   The South Side Good Roads Club was also involved in the success of having the paved road between Monaca and Aliquippa.   It was a five year project to attain the approval and success in the project.   The base of the road was concrete and overlaid with brick; this continued over a two and one half mile length of roadway. Once this section of roadway was paved, with the exception of a small section between Woodlawn and South Heights, there would be an improved highway all the way from Monaca to Pittsburgh. (None of this has to do with the Narrows road, it just shows how active the club was in the area.)   The article went on to say......
With the success the Good Roads Club had seeing this road work being completed, they turned their attention to the Narrows road way.

Voters decided not to allow the county commissioners to remove the County Home as was planned. With the Home remaining at its location, the Good Roads Club took up a campaign to improve the highway between Monaca and the Home.   The commissioners wanted to move the Home since there were times it was inaccessible during very rainy weather or in the winter. The Club wanted a new road made for travel to the Home instead. The Club stated that the main route of travel to the Home was the Narrows Road which ran along the Ohio River's shore. They went on to say this road was bad in two ways – one, it was not kept up and two, it was subject to frequent landslides in the winter.   To eliminate the possibilities of landslides, the Club proposed having another road made as the accepted route to the Poor Farm. They wanted the Red Gate Road (a nickname for Old Brodhead Road) to be that new road, with it running from Monaca to the Israel Wagner and Hodgkinson farms.   Using Red Gate would be no longer a route to the Home by this road and there would be no landslides as occurred on the Narrows Road. (From this information, it shows how portions of Brodhead moved from being on what is now North Branch Road to the portion of roadway that goes past Center Stage and on down past Penn State.)

At a Monaca Women's Club meeting, Frank Batchelor, President of Council, spoke on various topics, one being securing a highway from Monaca to Washington which involved the relocation of Rte 115 and the Narrows.   He stated that with the growing industrial activity at Shippingport and the splendid town sites in the vicinity of Bellowsville a new roadway was imperative.   He led all in attendance at this meeting to believe that it was better to keep the location of the highway along the Narrows as opposed to doing as the state proposed with building a road down through a deep valley from the North Branch Church. (But we all know that road down through the deep valley did indeed occur, coming from the intersection of 18 & 51 and turned into Frankfort Road.)

Between 1914 and 1924, it appears that the state road department won the battle of moving (eliminating) the roadway once referred to as the Narrows Road.

Jul 1924 - The topic of the Narrows Road needing resurfaced in 1924 with Monaca Council wanting to have the state improve it, found that the state considered it no longer their property since they considered the roadway relocated.   Why didn't Monaca seem to know of this move ?
The Borough of Monaca was going to communicate with the State Highway Department in Harrisburg to find out where the road was moved.   In 1924, the road ran from Bellowsville (Potter Township) to Monaca – entered Monaca on one of its principal streets.   It was found that in some manner, this road had been relocated and instead of going to Monaca, it then went from Bellowsville to a point on the Brodhead Road near the North Branch Church or Simon Field School - at least 3 miles, if not more, from Monaca. (intersection of 18 & 51)   Council wanted to know how and why this change in the road was made.   Monaca needed this information before they could take any actions on the borough's responsibility of any portion of improving the road; they found the move came about because the portion of the road called the Narrows in the borough of Monaca was in such bad shape and the location of it made it impossible to safely improve and maintain.

Dec 1924 - A committee of citizens of Potter, Raccoon, and Center Townships attended a regular Monaca town council meeting to discuss the Narrows Road.   The committee wanted Rte 115 (Frankfort Road to the Narrows Road) to run from Bellowsville on what was known both as the "Middle Road" and "Stone Quarry Road" so it would join Rte 76 (Rte 51/Brodhead Road) at what was known as the Red Gate (Brodhead Rd) a half mile from Monaca. Council deferred action.

Jan 1925 - An engineer of the State Highway Department was going to hold a conference with the Beaver County Commissioners to discuss the Narrows Road. The majority of the commissioners favored the improvement of the Narrows Road if it could be done at a price that did not exceed the cost of the improvement of the Hill Road (could have been the name of roadway coming past Toys R US - 2016). They felt that the improvement of the Narrows would open up one of the prettiest drives in Western Pennsylvania, it would give access to several clay and coal mines, and provide one of the finest bathing beaches along the Ohio River. It would also furnish a direct route to the proposed Beaver power plant of the Duquesne Light Company at Shippingport.

The proposed Hill Road would leave Rte No 115 (became Rte 18/Frankfort Road in Potter) at a point southeast of Bellowsville and would connect with Rte No 76 (Brodhead Road) for a direct route to either Woodlawn or Monaca. It was decided in favor of the Narrows Road being built below the present roadway at a very reasonable price. The business men of Rochester, Monaca, Freedom, and Beaver were interested in the improvement of the Narrows Road; it was claimed that Woodlawn and Pittsburgh interests favored the roadway over the hill.

In answer to the question Monaca Council had as to where, why, how the change came about – the Narrows Road was originally selected as a part of Rte No 115 to be completed to Monaca, but was later changed in a survey of the highway department to connect with Rte No 76 (Brodhead Road) a few miles southeast of Monaca. With all the concerns presented at this January 1924 meeting, it was decided that the State Highway Department would resurvey the Narrows Road before any further decisions were made.

Feb 1925 - The highway engineers, county commissioner, and officials of the Beaver Valley and Duquesne Light Company all met and (in the rain) drove their automobiles to the junction of improved Rte 76 with the proposed North Branch Road, which was planned to connect to Rte 76 with Rte 115 one mile southeast of Bellowsville. From that point, the delegation inspected the North Branch route and the Middles Quarries Road (Stone Quarry Road) which was also proposed as a substitute for the Narrows Road and the North Branch Road. They then inspected the actual Narrows Road from the County Home (in Potter Township/Bellowsville) to Monaca. They found that other than a few fallen trees from a recent storm, the road was in good condition. It was determined that it would not be affected by any high water of the river and although the cliffs look imposing, they were flatter than a 2 to 1 slope and therefore not hazardous to road building by reason of slides. The representatives for the State Highway Department promised to give the question of the road to be improved consideration and make a report later; so once again, a decision was delayed.

With all this information of landslides, rising waters of the Ohio, etc., it is concluded that the Narrows road was a separate portion of roadway from what is now all of Frankfort Road coming from Potter Township and joining up with the old portion of Brodhead Road in the area of the current intersection of 18 and Brodhead Road (formerly Rte 18 & 51 intersection). If you were familiar with the area in Potter Township by the former Kobuta Hotel and Midway Bar and Grill, there was a roadway that cut off Frankfort Road and ran parallel to Frankfort going past the Midway building and toward where the county home was located. I believe that this would have connected to what was the end portion of the original Narrows Road which would have trailed along between the Ohio River and hillside leading to the river.

The survey of the Highway Department showed the elimination of the Narrows Road and they opted to straighten out Rte 115/Rte 18 and constructed a new roadway from that point straight up the hill to the 18/51 intersection.

Mar 1930 - The county commissioners were talking of taking over the Narrows Road from Monaca to Independence school house in Potter Township along the bank of the Ohio River. It is obvious that these talks did not come out as (I am sure) Monaca Council would have liked since the Narrows Road did not become a state road and was never improved by the state, but instead was transferred to the P & L E railroad so construction of a spur track to the new St. Joseph Lead Co. could be completed.

Oct 1930 - Once it was known that the state had transferred the Narrows Road area to the P & L E railroad, action of the Monaca council was taken to retain a right of way along the Narrows Road, so in the future if the road was needed there would be a right of way on which to build.

Dec 1930   -   It was reiterated by council once again how there was a need for a highway to replace the Narrows Road along the Ohio River.   Council president, Frank M. Batchelor was confident that another roadway would be built by the railroad company once they completed the new tracks, which were under way.   It was the understanding that the railroad would take this action once their project was complete.

Apr 1938 -   Monaca Council once again tried to have the P & LE railroad build the Narrows Road, asking the County Commissioners to cooperate in the manner.   They stated that several years ago the right-of- way of the old Narrows Road was taken to build a spur railroad line from Monaca to the St. Joseph Lead Company Plant and it was understood at that time that in return for the right-of-way, the railroad company would eventually construct a new road adjacent to the spur line.   Eight years later, this still had not occurred.

        So...... it was Apr 1938 and Rtes 115 and 76 had become Rtes 18 and 51 respectively; Bellowsville's post office had closed; Monaca residents and businessmen had numerous meeting and discussions; the State Highway Department was involved; and the P & L E railroad was even involved, yet there was still no improvement or construction to the Narrows Road.   If it were a contest, then the State won with their plan of redirecting the roadway.   Rte 115/18 came from the Potter Bridge that crosses Raccoon Creek, then went straighter right through some hilly areas and up the hill to meet up with Rte 51, which went on down and came into Monaca to meet up with Pennsylvania Avenue Extension.   North Branch Road was left out of the mix as was Simon Field Road and both became their own roadway.   Whether the Narrows was still used being treated as a private roadway and maintained by the railroad, individuals and/or businessmen is unknown.   But it was no longer listed or shown on any maps as of 1926 or after the 1941 map I located.   Up until 2014, prior to all the land moving that occurred, you could look over either side of the Vanport Bridge of the Beaver Valley Expressway, on the Center/Potter Township side and see some signs of the former Narrows Road visible.

*** *** *** *** ***
*** *** ***

VIEWS and PICTURES of MONACA

Former and current views.......

Views of Streets

Views and Pictures of Monaca

Specific buildings

Aerial Views

Map of former Moon Township, Beaver County and Phillipsburg

Wards

Views of Streets

Photo courtesy Monaca Borough

The building on the right side of this photo was the Adam Huff homestead; it sat on and beside the site of the buildings of the Soldiers Orphans' School. There is a full picture of the Huff house in the Furniture section. The Orphans' School buildings were razed, as was the Huff house for the construction of the water pollution plant. The gas station on left corner was Paul & Ted's Super Service (#404 Pennsylvania Avenue). The gas station was razed, as were both houses in the above picture. The German Lutheran cemetery is between the former location of the house on the left and the tunnel.

This view is without the Huff's house (right) or gas station (left). In this photo the roadway is still 2 lane and is still curving to the left.
This section of street was called Factory Street – it became Pennsylvania Avenue (Ext).
Note the road leading out through the tunnel. This shows how the old Brodhead Road/ Rte 51 used to lead to turn to the left rather than going straight and up to the mall.
-to the left of the photos would have been former Fourth Street - now Pennsylvania Avenue.
-to the right of the photos would have been former Hanover Street – now Fourth Street.

Pennsylvania Avenue turns into Brodhead Road after being made into a 4 lane highway.
Construction on this project began Nov 1965.   Note how the roadway now goes to the
right after passing through the tunnel area instead of to the left.

Rte 51 changed routes in Center Township when a new section of Brodhead Road was constructed in the 1960s.
At one time, PA 18 joined with PA 51 in north Center Township*.   Both routes were shifted to a new four-lane
highway that replaced (now) Old Brodhead Road, a narrow, twisting, two-lane road. The new construction provided
easy access to the new Beaver Valley Mall and improved access (via PA 18) to the Beaver Valley Expressway.
"New" Brodhead Road rejoined the old road just outside Monaca and the new construction replaced the existing
road into Monaca. Brodhead Road lost its connection to Rte 51 and the road leading into Monaca is now only Rte
18.   Both Rte 51 and Rte 18 meet again in Monaca and cross the Ohio River to Rochester on the Monaca-
Rochester Bridge.

*The intersection in Center Township is now referenced as "intersection of 18 and Brodhead Road."

Little Beaver Historical Society
View of construction taking place on Pennsylvania Avenue Ext– arch 1903.
The top left of the picture is one of the Soldiers' Orphan's buildings. Between this bldg and the 2nd (upper) bridge in
the picture would have been the main building of the school that burned in 1876.

Little Beaver Historical Society
The P & L E RR awarded the contract for the building of the concrete arch under the new bridge between Monaca Borough and Moon Township to McKelvy & Hinds, general contractors of Pittsburgh who began work at once.

*** *** *** *** ***

Views and Pictures of Monaca

Views of Pacific Avenue.   The top picture is the first portion; the picture below continues from about where the car is parked/telephone pole above.   Both courtesy BCHR& LF

This complete row of houses along Pacific Avenue was razed during the revitalization and redevelopment done by Phoenix Glass.   Pacific Avenue now ends with #1105 – the 1000 or 900 and lower blocks of Pacific Avenue no longer exist.

Homes along Pacific Avenue and homes and business along Pennsylvania between Sixth and Ninth Streets were destined for a redevelopment plan.   All being demolished and families and businesses relocated.

The fire in July of 1978 destroyed most of the Phoenix Glass Co., now located a stone's throw in either direction from Pacific Avenue.   The first home along this section of Pacific Avenue was built in 1909 by the Nunziato family (changed to Nunzio).   Frank Nunzio operated a small bakery in the rear of his home, with bread being his specialty.   He made deliveries as far away as Midland and Ambridge.   Frank also had a general store at the front of the house.   Some of the families that were long time residents and had homes along this section of Pacific

Avenue over the years were Lamberto, Pacitti, Nunzio, Gales, Curtis, Trella, Winterow, ONeill, Marotti, Revay, DeFelice, Carper.   The homes were to be torn down in compliance with a redevelopment program; in place of these homes was built a new and expanded Phoenix Glass plant.

The redevelopment program didn't stop with Pacific Avenue, but also took all the homes and buildings along parts of Ninth Street and the entire 800 block along Pennsylvania Avenue.

All of the buildings in the next pictures were also razed in 1980 with the approved revitalization project by Phoenix Glass Company. These pictures are all small just to show how many buildings no longer exist; larger pictures are printed within the next few pages where I have made comparisons of "then and now" views of Monaca.

The following nine photos are courtesy Borough of Monaca, Beaver County Historical Research and Landmarks Foundation, or are personally taken by the author.

Ninth Street   Pennsylvania Avenue

This is looking down toward lower Pennsylvania Avenue from the intersection of Ninth Street.
        The 800 block of Pennsylvania Avenue (2016 - site of CVS building)
Left to right – are pictured:
Dr Doyle's record store -- then a private home (not in view) -- then 834 Pennsylvania Avenue, Dr. William Milliron's office/home -- beside his home, although you cannot see it, was the First Ward School; there is a tiny bit of the steeple visible.   (There are several full view pictures of this school under the Education section in Volume II.)
The long building with the windows was Kemmer Hardware Store until c1910.   (The original Kemmer Tin Shop-1893, was a quite smaller structure and adjacent on the right of this building.)

This is side view of Doyle Disco Den building with Ninth Street running left to right.

Corner view of Pennsylvania Avenue and Ninth Street.

The open space was the location of a service station and is now the location of the Mortgage Solutions building.   Also in this picture is a view of all the buildings located beside/behind 898 Pennsylvania Avenue. The building of Doyle Disco Den is the 2 storey building on the right in the picture. The First Ward School is to the left of the picture -- the steeple of the school and the back ½ of the school is visible.   All these buildings were located where the current CVS drug store now sits (2016).

Kemmer's former farm tools and hardware store and former tin shop next door
The school would have sat to the left of this picture

The former alleyway is on the left of of the building and the chain link fence belonged to the First Ward School property.

This is a continuation of the 800 and then goes into the 700 blocks of Pennsylvania Avenue. The building above on the left – was Kemmer's Tin Shop in 1893, then used by the Mitchell Bus Company, and then was Barbara's Beauty Shop. The next buildings were homes.

Eighth Street Extention was on opposite side of dark bldg
O'Keefe's Confectionery store would be along the row of buildings just past Eighth Street

View of Eighth Street Ext from Pennsylvania Avenue in 1940s/50s.

View in 2016 of where this same street would have been.

Eighth Street Ext   Legion bldg then Seventh Street (off picture)

From L to R --- the 3 storey building from the picture above – Eighth Street Ext – 798 Pennsylvania Avenue - then O'Keefe's -two unknown buildings/homes – the VFW building would have been next but is out of the picture.   Seventh Street went back toward the railroad tracks and ran beside the former VFW.

The above picture was taken on the right side of Pennsylvania Avenue looking down Pennsylvania Avenue toward Ninth Street; photographer was standing from about where Jim Harper's storeroom is now located (2016).

This is a 2016 view along Pennsylvania Avenue looking toward Ninth Street showing where all the buildings in the above pictures would have once stood.

Eighth Street   CVS   Phoenix plant

The photo below is from the early 1900s.   I believe that this photo would have been taken at the intersection of Ninth Street and Pennsylvania Avenue, looking down toward Tenth Street.   The steeple with the pointer on it appears to match the one that was on the top of the original Municipal Building.   Note in the photo all the older structures, trolley tracks, unpaved street, clothing, and a glimpse of the way of life in and about 1900.

Photo courtesy of Beaver County Historical Research and Landmarks Foundation

This picture is from the 1930s – note the street car tracks and look at the model of the cars.

Many of the buildings in this photo are still standing in 2016:

.....Starting with the small building on the left – it is the Bechtel Insurance building.
   The building with the lettering "IGNS" in view on the left - was Johnston flowers / is the La Piazza.
   The next building with the awning is now the White House.
   The next building became most recently the Fergy's Vape.
   The protruding building was torn down and a new building erected – it is the light gray block
       building beside Batchelor's former furniture store.
    Note the next 3 storey building on the left with what appears to be stripes on top with layers of brick work –
       this is the Batchelor Furniture building that is still standing; as is the next building with
       the Keystone on top.   All these buildings on the left can be viewed in the next more updated photo.

...... Starting on the right – I did not identify the building with the awning (It may be either the Enterprise
       Restaurant or the Levine & Bellan Grocery & Meat Market, they were both at the corner of
       Pennsylvania Avenue and Eleventh Street).
   The next building would have been the Presbyterian Church – you can see it's steeple above the first
       building. (there is a man walking directly in front of the church fence and property).
   All the remaining buildings on the right are not visible, but in 2016 this would be all be the site of
       the fountain/park area and then the post office.

The next picture is of the same view of Pennsylvania Avenue - looking from Eleventh Street down toward Tenth Street.   In the center of the pictures, off in the distance, you can see a building – this is the intersection of Ninth Street and Pennsylvania Avenue.   A pointer indicates what was the Carey building, and more recently, the Monaca Inn and currently P-Dub's.

This photograph has to be after 1971 and before 1986.

On the left is Bechtel Insurance and then Johnson Flowers.

Next is the White House Restaurant which opened in 1988 and it is not in this picture, nor is Isaly's which was still open in 1971.

The new post office was dedicated in Apr 1963 (on right side of Pennsylvania above – see pointer).

The George Washington school wasn't scheduled to be demolished until 1986.

So ....thus the conclusion that this picture is after 1971 but before 1986.

Times photo by Dan Stauffer

Aug 1990

View of Pennsylvania Avenue from the fountain plaza; to the right of the fountain would be the Post Office.   (Callaghan's Drug Store sign can still be seen.)

2013 view of the same section of Pennsylvania Avenue standing by the fountain plaza.

Batchelor Building   Batchelor Furniture   Keystone Bldg   Municipal bldg

A 2014 view of Pennsylvania Avenue looking from the fountain plaza down toward the Municipal building.

The glass windows on the left would have been the former site of Callaghan's Drug Store.

Post office and fountain plaza are just off to the left   Batchelor Bldg
                                                    (Batchelor Furniture storeroom would be to right-out of picture)

A different view looking from Tenth Street toward Eleventh Street – 2016.

1920s or 1930s view of 1100 block looking down Pennsylvania Avenue toward Tenth and Ninth Streets.

The buildings on the left (2016) are Main Street Barbers – Electric Garage Door Sales – Jiu-Jitsu Academy - Metro PCS (former United 5 & 10), then Wahl Street.   On the right side (2016) are an open lot between former Hamilton Hotel building (the building in the picture is no longer standing) – then Bluewater Cleaning - Monaca Draft House.   Note the steeple in the distance on the right – this was from the former Presbyterian Church that was at 1029 Pennsylvania Avenue. (Nowadays, the fountain and post office would be just past the former Presbyterian Church lot.)

This is the same view, but in 2016; looking down Pennsylvania Avenue toward downtown Monaca – post office & fountain in the distance – 1000 block, on the right side

1130 & 1128 Pennsylvania Ave.   1126 Pennsylvania Ave.(former 5&10   1129 & 1133 Pennsylvania Ave.

Pennsylvania Avenue looking up toward Twelfth Street   1920's   Photo courtesy B C H R & L F

On the right side of the picture is the P.H. Butler Grocery store (became former Monaca Men's and Boys' Store), then Wahl Street, then Margolis Department Store (became United 5 & 10).
In 2016, the Monaca Draft House would be about where the car is sitting on the left of the picture.

Monaca   Former   Former   Former   King Bvr Cigars
Draft House   5 & 10   Men's Store McNees
2016 View looking up Pennsylvania Avenue from about Eleventh Street, toward Wahl Street (right).

A 2016 view looking down Pennsylvania Avenue from Fourteenth Street (which is on bottom left).

| 1213 Pennsylvania | 1215 Pennsylvania | 1219 Pennsylvania |
| Formerly Balamut Electric Shop | now Bvr Valley Sheet Metal | former retail of Joe Setting |

2016 view of former storerooms on Pennsylvania Avenue.

former Mecklem Bros. Lumber site   1549 Pennsylvania

2016 view looking toward downtown on Pennsylvania Avenue from industrial area/Sixteenth and Seventeenth Streets.

Building in middle of picture was former post office, Ellsworth (dentist), McCreary/Prather attorneys, Riedel optometrist, and Miss Ann Grater beauty shop – now an insurance office

This is a 2016 view of Pennsylvania Avenue from Twelfth Street up Pennsylvania Avenue. The former Penn Super Market would have been to right of picture and the former Hamilton Hotel is directly behind photographer.

Thirteenth Street then Taormina's   this open area was former site of Groth Motor Sales

This photo is a view looking up Pennsylvania Avenue. Thirteenth Street is to the left in the photo – just past the trees. Twelfth Street is a short distance behind the photographer.

1965 photo – (Balamut Electric Shop was at 1213 Pennsylvania Avenue).
You are looking up Pennsylvania Avenue from about Twelfth Street toward Thirteenth Street.
These vintage cars were on parade for the Monaca Quasquicentennial.

Seventeenth Street to East Rochester/Monaca bridge

2016 View from southern end of Monaca toward downtown are at Seventeenth Street intersection of Pennsylvania Avenue.

Looking down Ninth Street from bridge.

Another 2015 view from the bridge at Atlantic Avenue down Ninth Street.
Phoenix plant in foreground and Monaca Heights on hill.

Entrance to finance bldg   P-Dub's   Laundry   Hair place
                                        Campbell's/old bank bldg and   old hotel

2016 view along Pennsylvania Avenue – looking toward the intersection of Pennsylvania Avenue and
Ninth Street (bridge toward right).

Laundromat   Hartley Hair   Red Wing Anthony's   Mortgage
                                                                                   Solutions

2016 view of intersection of Ninth Street and Pennsylvania Avenue.
   Ninth Street to bridge is to the left; CVS and entrance to Phoenix Plant is to the right.

Photo by Pete Sabella

1983 view along Pennsylvania Avenue – looking from corner of Ninth Street toward Tenth Street.

Laundry   Hartley Hair   Red Wing Shoes   Anthony's Place

2016 view along Pennsylvania – Ninth Street toward left, Tenth Street toward right.

Anthony's Place   Clip and Cuddle   former antique place   Deborah's Bridal Traditions   Gnu Tub   10th St

2016 view along Pennsylvania Avenue.
     The Municipal Bldg is to the right - across street from Gnu.
     Tenth Street is beside Gnu and then there is the former bank building (now Sakura Restaurant).

RR bridge   Fourth Street   (steeple of Lutheran Church in back ground)

2016 view of Pennsylvania from Sixth Street toward Fourth Street (and Pennsylvania Avenue Extension).

Parts of Phoenix glass plant   The old First Ward School would have sat

CVS is to far left (out of picture)   in this area   Legion to far right (out of picture)

2016 view along Pennsylvania Avenue – Ninth Street to the left - part of Monaca Heights on hill.

Extreme right of Phoenix   Approximately where Seventh Avenue would have been   Legion Bldg

Another view on Pennsylvania Avenue from across the street at the corner of Eighth Street and Pennsylvania Avenue. The hill above Legion would have been Welchmont aka Sylvan Crest area.

Parts of Phoenix Glass plant   there were houses and businesses along this side of street   Legion bldg
but all were torn down ____ to expand Phoenix

2016 view along Pennsylvania – across from Eighth Street area.   The hillside to the left of this photo is one edge of Monaca Heights.

Legion Bldg   Sixth Street   old RR station   Saxon Club

2016 view from Library parking lot across Pennsylvania Avenue toward more of Sixth Avenue.
Part of Monaca Heights on hill in foreground.

Former Graeser Bldg/now Library   CVS   Phoenix plant   Legion

View looking down Pennsylvania Avenue from Sixth Street toward Phoenix Glass Co.

*** *** *** *** ***
*** *** ***

Specific Buildings

This is a photo of a once familiar scene - a farm setting that was in Monaca prior to the whole area being made into a an actual town environment.

This farm above was located in the Seventeenth Street vicinity.   Photo courtesy BCHR&LF

Photo courtesy of Beaver County Historical Research and Landmarks Foundation

This was used as the first polling place in the borough Mar 1840.   It is said to have also been used as a seminary in 1834 under Rev. Ferdinand Winter and L. F. LeGollon was the manager of the seminary.   In 1840 William Stumm was owner of the building and it became Stumm's Tavern.

Carl F. Kaercher purchased the building in or about 1876 and his family lived here until c 1932.   It was also listed on tax records as being Shriner's Tavern.   The building is still standing; I am not sure exactly when, but as of 2015 it is divided into apartments.

Carl F. Kaercher b 1816; 399 Atlantic Avenue; married Kasia ___; children- Bertha K., Wilhelmena; the family was living in Monaca in 1880 and Carl was a grocer.

This was the former Wurburton / Lay house at the corner of Atlantic Avenue and Eighth Street. The left picture is how it originally looked when built in 1854; the one on the right is from 2016.

This is another example of one of the houses that was built in the 1800s and still standing in the 800 block of Atlantic Avenue.

Photo courtesy BCHR&LF

Most of the main and older buildings still standing in Monaca were erected in the late 1800s and early 1900s.   Here is an example of one of those older buildings - 1306 Pennsylvania Avenue.
There were many types of business in this building over the years – grocers, H & R Block.

FOR RENT—Spacious room for parties, club meetings, etc., afternoon or evening; well furnished; player piano and Victrola; conveniences for preparing and serving refreshments. Those interested call at 1306 Pennsylvania ave., Monaca. Bell phone 173-M.   8.25-30

1919

Across Fourth street from the former Huff house, in front of you after coming through the railroad viaduct, was another two storey home that is no longer standing.   It was at 139 Fourth Street (at the bend /corner of Fourth Street and Pennsylvania Avenue Ext).   It would have faced Pennsylvania Avenue Ext.   I do not know exactly when this house was built, but the structure of the building indicates it was most likely one of the original or very early homes of Phillipsburg.   I also do not when the building was razed or the reason, but the lot stands empty as of 2016.   If you look closely on the left of the picture, you will see the German Lutheran Church in the back ground.

BCHR&LF

I do not know the location or year of the photo below; it is definitely from the early 1900s by the clothing of the woman and child on the porch. If you look closely, you'll appreciate the early craftsmanship of the structure – the diamond shaped windows, the spindling on railing, the framing around the windows, ginger-breading along the house roof and 2nd floor porch roof, etc.   The windows in this building were almost as large as the doors.   Also note the access to the third floor with a bridge/ walkway.   It was a true three storey home because you can see there is a porch on the bottom level/floor.

Photo courtesy of Beaver County Historical Research and Landmarks Foundation

Guba Home

Another house that is no longer in existence was originally owned by Joseph M. and Marie Catherine (Schnobel) Guba. It was built for them in Phillipsburg in 1887. This house was located beside what is now the entrance to the Alloy plant, on the right, just past the rail road trestle on your way out of Monaca going toward Center Township. The house was sold, stripped of its siding, lighting fixtures and all other materials of value before purposely being burned to the ground about 2014.

Photos from Milestones / B C H R & L F

The following information on this homestead was obtained from an article in Milestones which is published by the Beaver County Historical Research and Landmarks Foundation.

James Park was hired to built the house for an agreed upon sum of $1,400. The frame was of hemlock and the interior woodwork was to be walnut. It was a six room home with five fireplaces that all had wood mantels. There was also an extension built on one side of the house which was later moved and connected to the back of the house. Joseph Guba didn't enjoy this home for long; he died in 1892, Mary Kate lived to be 52, dying in 1911. They had two children – Wilhelmina and Josephine. The girls continued to live in the home after their parents died. There was a barn and a pasture on the flat area by the road; a large portion of this area being taken when the roadway was straightened, moved and re constructed.

Josie married the widower Daniel Bracken "Brack" Winkle. He was considerably older than Josie and had a daughter from his first marriage that was almost as old as Josie. They lived in the home and had three children – Daniel, Frank, and Jean Louise shortly after their marriage – then had Martin W. much later when Brack was 61.

Josie kept the house and grounds in show place conditions. After Brack died in the 1930s, Josie and the children struggled, but remained in the house. In the 1950s, Josie sold the house and contents to their son Martin W. He never married, but supported Josie the rest of her life. Later in life, Martin had to have heart surgery and then went to live his last 16 years of life with his sister and family, still going to cut the grass at the house and check on things. The house, with no resident, fell victim to vandalism with oil paintings being slashed and many items being stolen. After Martin died, the remaining contents were sold at auction and the house was sold. Many of the items from the house are in various museums, including Mary Catherine's mourning clothes which are available to view at the Beaver County Historical Research and Landmarks Foundation which is housed in the Vicary Mansion in Freedom, Pa.

Aerial Views

Courtesy of Beaver County Historical Research and Landmarks Foundation

This photograph is from the 1900s – a view of Monaca taken from the hill above Monaca which would have been known as Welchmont and is now known as Sylvan Crest (2016).

The large building on the right side (with open area and the circular path) is the remaining building of the former Soldiers' Orphan School.   The Monaca sewage plant is located at this site (2016).

The previously mentioned Guba home is at the bottom-middle of this photograph.

The houses in the middle of the picture going from the former Orphan School bldg then toward the river indicate where Fourth Street is today; the Monacatootha Apartments now stand in this area.

This is a view of Rochester across the river; and the bridge to Bridgewater.

1840 view of Phillipsburg.

View of Monaca in 1890 – note there is no suspension bridge going to Rochester.

Looking down Ninth Street in Monaca in the early 1890s before the bridge to Rochester was built.

Early 1900 view of Monaca with the Thirteenth Street on the left side, Fourteenth Street in the center.

P & LE RR depot   Fourteenth Street

In 1900, Phillipsburg had become Monaca and was rapidly growing in population.

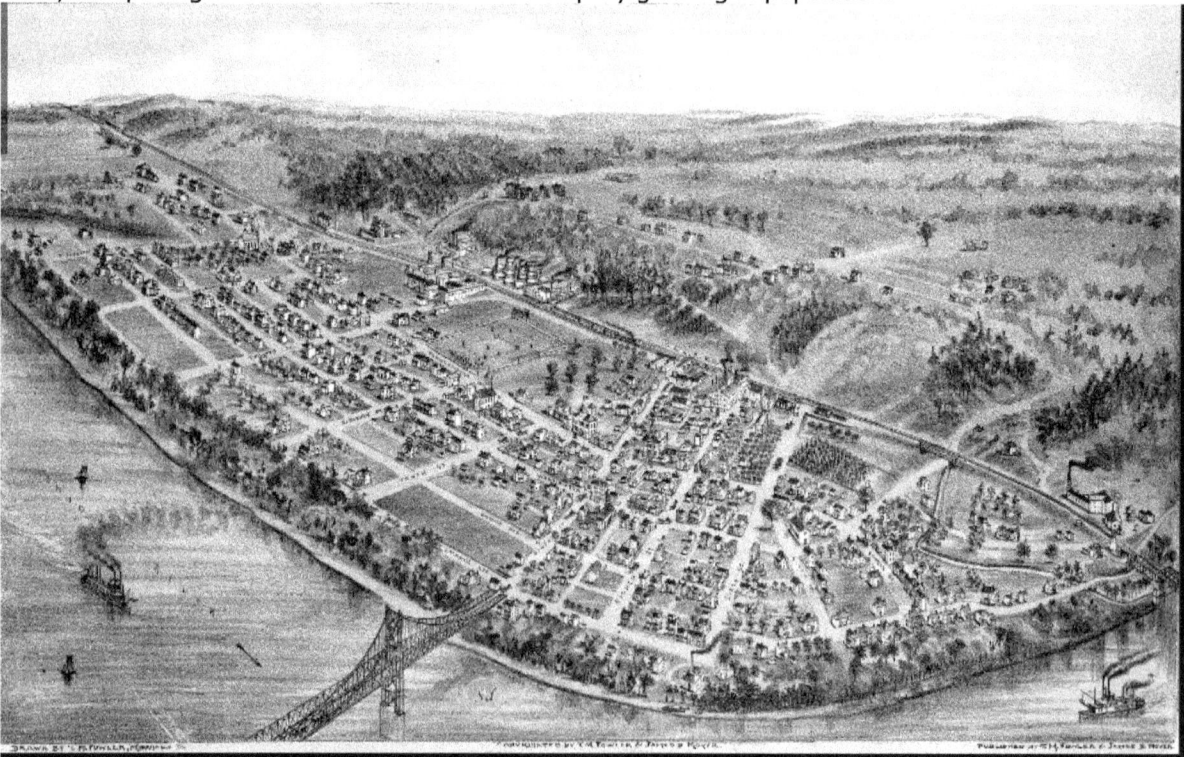

Drawn & published by T. M. Fowler & James B. Moyer

I used a magnifying glass for days and days after I received this map; I found so many things on it so interesting !   It still amazes me to really look at this and know it is not a photo, that it was all hand drawn.

1956 Aerial view of Monaca

***   ***   ***   ***   ***

Map of former Moon Township in Beaver County (became Monaca Borough and Center Township).

This 1876 image above is not clear enough to read and was captured ONLY to show the massive size of Moon Township to compare sizes of Phillipsburg (downtown Monaca), what would become the annexed portion of Monaca Heights, and Center Township.

- the Ohio River bordered Moon Township on the top and left side.
- Raccoon borders it on the bottom.
- Hopewell borders it on the majority of the right side, with Independence Township on the lower right side.

On the 1876 map, Philipsburg (Monaca downtown area) would be by the "E" and "R" in the word RIVER at the top left.

The annexed portion that became Monaca Heights is included, but not limited to the open area around the names John Eckert, R. Patterson, and Geo. Dockter.   The original map is very legible and has all the owners of the lands printed, as well as notes where schools, churches, etc. were located.   Again, I have included this map only for reflecting the location of Phillipsburg/Monaca to Moon Township.   Within the annexed area that became Monaca Heights, some of the names printed include John Eckert, R. Patterson, Geo. Dockter, and John Stewart.

This is a copy of a portion of the 1860 Beaver County Landowner Map. This copy may not be very clear, but Possibly you can make out some of the early settlers to the Phillipsburg immediate areas (and what became Center and Potter).

I have inserted a star where the general area of the annexed portion of Monaca was formed. This map was quite accurate for the time, but having true aerial views and advanced equipment now available makes inaccuracies more noticeable.

I have placed pointers at a few interesting things: the first is the Beaver County Poor Farm (on the left)—this location seems quite a bit *off* though since it was really just to the left of where the current expressway bridge is located)........... the next pointer is to show one of the ferry crossings; from Bellowsville to Vanport (the location of the current expressway bridge to Vanport); this is where the Poor Farm most likely was really located)..............the top pointer is the Monaca / Rochester ferry crossing (current location of Monaca-Rochester bridge).

*** *** *** *** ***

Although not extremely legible, here is a copy of the enlarged 1860 view of Phillipsburg without all the surrounding areas. I have put pointers in to mark a few things: on the left (by the "O" in Ohio) to show a ferry site – this is not indicated on the previous, larger 1860 map...........on the left/almost center is the site of Water Cure..........there is a pointer at the bottom to show the roadway out of town that now leads toward Center Township / the mall..........and lastly, the pointer on the right indicates what was called Fourth Street in 1860, but became Pennsylvania Avenue.   Missing is the site of the main ferry that crossed between Rochester and Monaca; it would have been located approximately in the area of the "I or V" in the word River.

*** *** *** *** ***

Wards

The first concept of dividing the town into wards was presented at one of the early school board meetings in 1876. This concept may have been introduced for the purposes of housing the students at that time. Over the years the Ward division in Monaca was continued for election purposes. There are a total of five Wards in Monaca as of 2016. Three were created prior to 1931 and the last two were created at the suggestion of Beaver County Court officials with Monaca Borough's annex of the Moon Township sector. A district, or in Monaca – Wards, makes it possible to have the same number of representatives per the amount of voting citizens in any given area. Redistricting is usually decided and enforced through the court house.

Over the years, the boundaries of Monaca's wards have changed. I am sure the boundaries and areas of Monaca's districts have changed since the land grant dated July 25, 1769, by William A. Lungen, who in the same year granted to Ephriam Blaine all his rights when he made said application for the grant.

In all my writings and researching, I can only go by references made during the year of the event or business. For most of the very early dates, I am fairly sure that the districts referenced as First, Second, and Third Wards in Monaca remained almost identical to the original as covered in the Pennsylvania Land Grant from 1787 to Ephriam Blaine. But as Monaca continued to grow, especially the Monaca Heights area, I lost track of where all the boundaries were for each Ward.

1931 – Fourth and Fifth Wards
If you are doing any genealogy research, you may come across references to different areas of Monaca that are not familiar to you. Did you know there was an area in the Fourth Ward known as Dockter Heights (the area around Bechtel Street and Speyer Ave., Cedar Alley, Palmer Alley, Johnson Ave., and Redwood Alley). There are other areas, also, amid the Fourth and Fifth Wards on Monaca Heights. You may read, find, or have someone reference Skeeter Hill; it was considered the area around of the Fourth Ward Fire Hall, Colona Heights (area around Blaine Road, Marshall Road, Elkhorn Street), Allaire Heights (the area around Jackson Ave., Hillview Dr., Summit Ave.).

In 1940 – this is how the Borough of Monaca was divided into Wards.

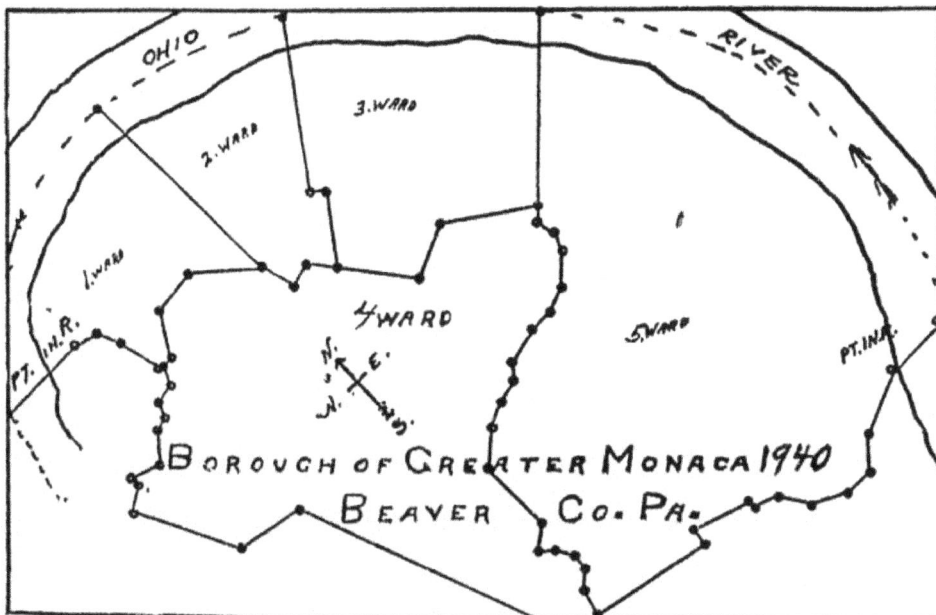

*** *** *** *** ***

*** *** ***

Clothing   and   Dry Goods

Millinery / Seamstress / Dressmaker

Tailors

Shoe Business   and   Shoemakers

Carpet makers and weavers

Cleaners

General   and   Miscellaneous Businesses

CLOTHING and DRY GOODS, SHOES, MILLINERY, SEAMSTRESS, DRESSMAKER, TAILORS, and CLEANERS

This section deals with the businesses and merchants that supplied many of the personal items used by people. These items and services included clothing, dry goods, altering and making of clothing items, shoemakers and shoe dealers, and cleaners of apparel items. I also included the general stores in this section. General stores would sell household items, stationary items, china, etc., and many times they often carried dry goods and personal items in their storerooms, too.

I listed several merely as *merchants* with no other explanation, type of business, or address of a storeroom. They are included here just to be sure that they are acknowledged as being involved with the history of Monaca. Being a *merchant* means they sold some type of product or goods and had a business and/or storeroom that brought them income. They knew exactly what they did, but would be referenced on census and in articles, for simplicity, as just *merchant* rather than a more specific description being provided. There were no newspapers or publications that gave me much information for the 1800s. I still managed to find a limited amount of information on some of these men and women; but usually nothing more than their name, year, and occupation since most times this came from the census enumeration sheets.

To start this section off I have to ask if you are familiar with "gum boots." Some may snickered at this word, as with some of the other old words. I actually knew what a gum boot was. When I owned a horse, it was necessary to have "mucking boots" or "gum boots" to use when you were cleaning the stall. When I saw these words in some of the ads and writings, I knew exactly what they were.

Gum boots are made of rubber, they are waterproof, flexible, and in the 1800s and early 1900s, quite UNstylish. Nowadays you may still find them for sale, but often referred to as rain boots or even still called galoshes. Many are now made from PVC or other plastics and not real rubber; plus they are quite stylish now since they come in many colors and designs. They look like gum boots, but they're just impersonating the real thing ☺ Another unfamiliar word nowadays, but used by many people in those earlier years was "poke." A poke was what a paper bag use to be called.

> Misses', gents' and children's rubbers and gum boots at Barnett's.
> ●●●●●●●

1907 ad

Now you can say you know what a "poke" is as well as what "gum boots" are.

CLOTHING and DRY GOODS

Michael Beckhert – dry good clerk
1860

————

R. Scheid & Co. - dry goods store – 1000 block on Pennsylvania Avenue
1892, 1900, 1902, 1903, 1904
     Mary Hahn and her sister Rosa Scheid were owners.
     Mary resided at the same address as the store.
     Rosa Scheid was on the 1892/93 Directory as a milliner.

R. SCHEID & CO.

Dry Goods, Notions, Trimmings.

Pennsylvania Avenue.   Monaca, Pa.

————

LeGoullon Dry Goods – Indiana Avenue and Fifth Street (in 1800s)
1831, 1860, 1870, 1894, 1900, 1902
     Started by Francis R. LeGoullon.
     He was one of the first residents in Phillipsburg, settling in 1831 – one year before the
          Economites arrived.
     He also was one of the first merchants, having a general merchandise and grocery store.
     Francis R. was b 1802 d 1879. He married Ernestine Louisa Hihne.
          Children: Augutus, Philip, Sophia, Gustavus, Lamartine, Henry & Monteldo(both died in infancy).
     Francis R. was the first burgess and justice of peace in Phillipsburg and was the manager of
          the seminary. He was also known for his excellent penmanship. He had the distinction
          of having written the first deed that was put on record in the Beaver County Court
          House.
     1870 – Francis R. was listed as "retired dry good merchant."
          Augustus married Mary Anna Daly.
          Gustavus was an apprentice to his father in – 1860. He married Dora Massey.
          Philip was a clerk in the store in 1860.
            He married Annie Anderson and they then lived in Pittsburgh.
          Lamartine LeGoullon was a clerk in dry goods store in 1870.
            He owned a grocery store in 1880. Still owned the store in 1900; his son Francis
            was working with him; married Clara Bott (who was a student at Thiel); they had
            5 children.
          Sophia Louisa married George Krober; after George died, she married Charles
            Maenner/Meaner.

————

Philip LeGoullon – General Store – Indiana Avenue and Fifth Street
1892, 1893

————

William F. Swansey – furnish goods store
1892, 1893

————

William J. Porter – dry goods store
1892, 1893

————

J. A. Schaeffer – Pennsylvania Avenue (Landis Building)
1904

————

Mrs. S. D. Howe – Dry goods and notions store - Pennsylvania Avenue
1907, 1908
      She sold her entire stock and quit the business in Nov 1908.
      Mr. and Mrs. S. D. Howe lived on Pennsylvania Avenue.

————

Anthony Knapper   aka   Bechtel Company   aka M. Bechtel & Co. - Hanover Street (now Fourth Street)
1837, 1841, 1850, 1870, 1892, 1893, 1921
      See the Grocery section for extended information on all three of these.
      From early maps, this building would have sat at about what is now 111 Fourth Street.
            Their home and the store would have been located just about where the drive into the
            parking lot beside the Monacatootha Apartments is now located (2016).
      Anthony listed himself as a *dry good merchant* in 1850, 1860, and then *retired dry good*
         merchant in 1870.
      George Bechtel was the only one listed in 1892 and 1893 on the Directory.

————

Maria Deveny - Notion Store – Colona
1910   She resided on Beaver Avenue.

————

William J. Johnston – General Merchandise - Pennsylvania Avenue
1898, 1903

————

Meany's Goods – Ninth Street – beside Whippo's Barber Shop (behind Carey's store)
1908, 1909, 1924, 1929
      Opened Nov 1, 1908.   Edwin Meany – owner (he lived in Rochester in 1920).   Merchant tailor.
      He had several notices of price cuts in "Gent's furnishing goods."
      Took over the R.C. Jones' Shoe Store (Penn) Nov 1, 1908 -- Store was located beside M. W.
      Carey's place and short distance west of Max Barnett's shoe store.
            In the *EAST LIVERPOOL REVIEW* on Thursday, May 23. 1929, there was a notice........ "STORE
ROBBERY SUSPECT HELD - MONACA, Pa. On Mar 13 Peter Vorcla held in jail here today pending a
hearing on a charge of breaking and entering and larceny following his arrest yesterday in connection with
the robbery of the E. B. Meany's tailor shop, Ninth Street, Mar 10. Clothing valued at $200 was taken. The
arrest was made when Meany recognized a pair of trousers carried by Anthony Marcella, who said he
bought them from Vorels. Most of the loot was found in Vorels's room, police said."
            Another article from 1906 in The Daily Times – "Ed. Meaney, Rural Free Delivery No. 3 carrier, had
the rear axle of his buggy break while driving near Colona yesterday. Nothing daunted Ed, unhitched his
horse and mounting the animal, finished his route."

————

A. D. Brown & Company - Unknown location
1908   Ladies clothing.

————

McClurg's stand - General Store   aka   The One Horse Cash Grocery (1898)
– corner of Pennsylvania and Twelfth Street
1898, 1900, 1903, 1904
Dry goods, flour, feed, notions, shoes, tin and granite ware.   Joseph R. McClurg was owner.
By Mar 1904, Joseph was no longer at his business because E. Hood took over the building and
the McClurgs moved to a house on Virginia Avenue.   He married Martha __and had 4 children.
Joseph had his occupation as "laborer, odd jobs" in 1910.   Jos. died between 1910 and 1920.   He was
also the Street Commissioner of Monaca in 1907.

J. R. McClurg,
DEALER IN
Dry Goods, Groceries, Boots, Shoes, Rubbers.
Cor. Twelfth St. and Pennsylvania Ave., MONACA, PA.   1900

———

J. C. Doutt & Company – Clothing Store - 1102 Pennsylvania Avenue
1909, 1910, 1926, 1928, 1929, 1931
John C. Doutt owner – they lived in Rochester in 1920, 1930.
Also had stores in Rochester and West Bridgewater.

CLEARANCE SALE
Twenty to Thirty Per Cent. Discount on Nearly
All Merchandise for Twelve Days.
Sale from Saturday, January 30th, Until Friday, February 12th.

Domestics	Embroideries and Laces
American and Simpson Prints at .... 5¢	We have just ----
Lancaster Ginghams at. .... 6¢	broider-
""essentials at.... ..... 7 1⁄2"	

Children's 25¢ Fleeced Hose at........... 19¢	one Hand Bags at ....37¢
Ladies' 25¢ Wool Hose at.............. 19¢	One lot of Hand Bags at..............19¢
Ladies' 35¢ Wool Hose at.............. 29¢	One lot of short length Dress Goods at about HALF
Ladies' 50¢ Wool Hose at.............. 39¢	PRICE.

We have received our Spring line of Long Cloths, India
Linens, Nainsooks, Persian Lawns, Batiste,
Percales and Ginghams.
Long Cloths from 10 to 25c.   India Linens 8½ to 30c.
Batiste from 25c to 75c.   Ginghams from 10c to 25c.

J. C. Doutt & Co.
Rochester   Monaca   West Bridgewater
                                                          1909

———

Leon Schnitzler/Schnitzer – 310 Ninth Street (Citizen's Bank Building)
1906, 1911, 1912
Clothier.   His store caught fire Jul 1, 1911 – it was contained to the clothing store and did not
damage the remainder of the building or any of the hotel next door.
He must have closed after this fire since a news article stated that Leon's former store
room was used as the Republican headquarters and social room in Oct 1912.

———

H. B. Bazell – clothing business – 1106 Pennsylvania Avenue
1922, 1928
In 1928, he was listed as an authorized represented to sell Richman's Clothes.

———

Leon Schmitzer – merchant in dry goods – unknown location
1920

———

A. F. Frances – dry good merchant – R.D. Monaca
1929

———

Gordon's Clothing Store – 308 Ninth Street
1900, 1911, 1912
>Reuben, Elias, Barney(Barach) all listed as proprietors of the Clothing Store on Pennsylvania and Ninth Street in 1900.   Barney was listed as residing on Washington Street in 1912.
>Closed by Apr 1912; they had counter cases, electric light globes up for sale.
>They were all sons of Michael and ___ Gordon.   Elias was married and living in Rochester by 1920– manufacturer of ladies' garments.

> For Sale—A three horse power electric spark gas engine, can be seen running; must be sold soon; complete, price $25.00. Inquire at Gordon's Dry Goods Store, Pennsylvania avenue and Ninth street, Monaca, Pa.

1911

Bell's Fashion Shoppe – 922 Pennsylvania Avenue (1928) –930 Pennsylvania Avenue (1929, 1943)
1928, 1929, 1943
>Ad in 1928 stated it was "on the car line at City Building stop," which places it in the Penn Theatre building.
>Owner – Bertha Mae Bell (this was "Miss" Bell – Bertha M.'s daughter).
>>Miss Bell married H. O. Allison in Jul 1928 and they eventually went to Michigan.

LOOK AT YOUR HAT—Who Else Has One Just Like It?

WE HAVE 'NDIVIDUAL MODELS   PRICED SAME AS ORDINARY HATS

Come In And Let Us Please You

BELL'S FASHION SHOPPE
MONACA

Pretty Dresses
—WELL MADE
—GOOD MATERIAL
—PRICED LOW
—STYLISH
—EXPRESSIVE
—CHARMING
—FITTED

New Line of Hats

Bell's Fashion Shoppe
COME TO MONACA AND BUY

1928

Fred Egermann's "The New Store" – Dry goods store
1917

DOLLAR DAY

Fred Egermann's
—MONACA—
"The New Store"

All 50c Goods Will Be Sold During The Dollar Day at 3 For $1.00

3 50c Ties for . . . .
3 50c Socks for . . . .
3 50c Caps for . . . .
3 50c Shirts for . . . .
3 50c Hockey Caps for . . .

$1

Fred Egermann's
⚜ New Store ⚜
MONACA, PA.

Feb 1917 ad

Samuel Weiner – merchant in clothing store – unknown location
1930

_____

Dorca's Style Shop – Pennsylvania Avenue
1960

     Owned by Henrietta (Thomas) Bell. She also owned and operated Bell's Economy Supermarket.
     Had an awning added to the front of the store in 1960.
     Henrietta married John H. Bell.

_____

Geo. J. Schmidt – corner of Pennsylvania Avenue and Twelfth Street
1904

     Took over McClurg's old stand.
     1906 - Was selling out at cost – dry goods, notions, shoes, tin and granite ware.

```
WHILE THEY LAST
Gloves sold at $1 00, now.....$  65
Gloves sold at    75, now.....   5
Gloves sold at    50, now.....  35
Gloves sold at    25, now.....  15
            UNDERWEAR
Men's, Ladies' and Children's
  Ribbed    Balbriggan    and
  fleece lined, sold at 50c now  35
Ladies' Hose, sold at 25c, now  20
Men's Socks, sold at 25c, now   20
Men's Shirts, sold at 50c, now  30
Men's Overalls sold at 50c,
  now.................           35
Shoes  sold at $2 00, now..... 1 50
Shoes  sold at  1 50, now..... 1 00
Shoes  sold at  1.25, now.....   90
Shoes  sold at  1 00 now.....    75
Felt Boots sold at $2 50 now.. 1 90
Extra gums sold at $1 25, now  1 00
Rubbers,  sold at   65, now     40
Rubbers,  sold at   40, now     25
Rubbers,  sold at   30, now     20
Rubbers,  sold at   15, now     10

GEO. J. SCHMIDT,
   Pennsylvania Avenue and
       Twelfth Street.
MONACA,  - -  PENN'A.
```

_____

Montgomery Dry Goods Store – 1102 Pennsylvania Avenue
1940, 1957, 1960

     M. E. Montgomery – owner.
     Was next to Bender's Drug Store (which was at 1106 Pennsylvania Avenue).

SUPER SPECIAL
Batiste and Crepe Gowns
Reg. $3.85 and $3.50 $2.69
MONTGOMERY
DRY GOODS STORE
Penna. Ave.   Monaca

Jul 1949

Children's School Dresses
"Cinderella" and "Kate Greenaway"
$1.95 to $4.95
MONTGOMERY
DRY GOODS STORE
Penna. Ave.   Monaca
(Next to Bender's Drug Store)

1949 ad

_____

Henry Finn's Dry Good Store   aka   Hyman and Henry Finn – Pennsylvania Avenue
1900 to 1910, 1917

His storeroom was located between Daniel Leary's 2 storey frame building/ novelty and wall paper
store on first floor...Leary's residency on 2nd floor and Heckman Bros. Hardware dealer's
business in adjoining bldg at 1030 Pennsylvania Avenue). This would put Finn's store in
the 1032 Pennsylvania Avenue area.

He went by Hyman and Henry Finn, too; started the business between 1900 and 1910 (in 1900 he
was listed with the occupation of *day labor* then in 1910 he was proprietor of a dry goods
store and storeroom).

It was a frame building with brick front.   Building belonged to Atty. Charles Eckert of Monaca Heights.

There was a fire in his storeroom in Jul 1917. Mr. Finn, his wife, and one month old son were
on the 2nd floor of the building in their apartment and their 4 year old son, David, was in
the storeroom on the first floor.   The boy accidently started the fire while playing with
matches. Everyone escaped; but the fire burned his business and damages were
sustained by the two adjacent buildings. (Leary's and Heckman Bros.).

Henry was married to Lillian __; they lived with their 7 children at the same location.

1910 – Lillian was listed as proprietor of a clothing store; Henry was a laborer; a daughter living with them
was a dressmaker.

1912 – Henry was hired as conductor on a street rail in Woodland.

1920 – Henry was 75 years old, Lillian was 54 and they rented at Washington Avenue.

1930 – Henry, Lillian, and a daughter were living in Pittsburgh. He was now 85 and
she was 64.   Henry died in the fall of 1931 at age 87.

*I also listed him below within the "notion businesses."

> For Sale—Dry goods and notion
> store, best location in Monaca. Will
> sell for $900.00 or invoice. Apply
> Mrs. H. Finn, opposite postoffice, Mo-
> naca, Pa.

1912 ad

———

Barnett's Dept Store –corner of Ninth Street and Pennsylvania Avenue and 809 Pennsylvania Avenue
1882 to 1922

Would have most likely been on the corner of Ninth Street and Pennsylvania Avenue -where
12 sided finance building stands (2016).

Established 1884.   The first of Apr 1922, there was "going out of business" ads.

Owned by Morris Barnett. Morris married Anna __, they lived at Indiana Avenue in
1902/03.   Morris was a very good business man; in 1906 he had large consignment tin
cups made with his name on them and he distributed them in the parks and public places
throughout the county.

Morris's son Harry opened a shoe store in the same building (in early 1906).

Morris had the exterior to his building newly painted and otherwise improved.

Had a big "26th anniversary" sale in Jul 1909.

1910 he joined in business with his son Max Barnett.
Family home was at the corner of Eighth Street and Indiana Avenue.

Moved to Rochester in 1914 (to the Campbell Bldg there).

1918 Max married and moved to Rochester.

Ad in the May 12 and Jul 10, 1917 paper said Morris Barnett would be closing out the Monaca store and to
come to the Rochester store on Brighton Avenue, Rochester – next to Grand 5 cent and 10 cent store.

Morris Barnett died in the fall of 1946, in his home in Pittsburgh.

Morris started in business in 1886 with "Jimmy" Davis at Pennsylvania and Eighth – a general
and confectionary store which was destroyed by fire in 1893.   In the same year, 1893, he built a
large two storey brick building on Pennsylvania Avenue (near Eighth Street) for a department
store he conducted until 1917 when he sold and moved to Rochester and was in business with
his eldest son, Harry in wholesale hosiery.

Morris retired from business in 1935.

MORRIS BARNETT,
Dealer In..... **Ladies' and Gents' Furnishing Goods**
Also a Full Line of Shoes and Carpets.
Pennsylvania Avenue, - - *MONACA, PA.* 1900

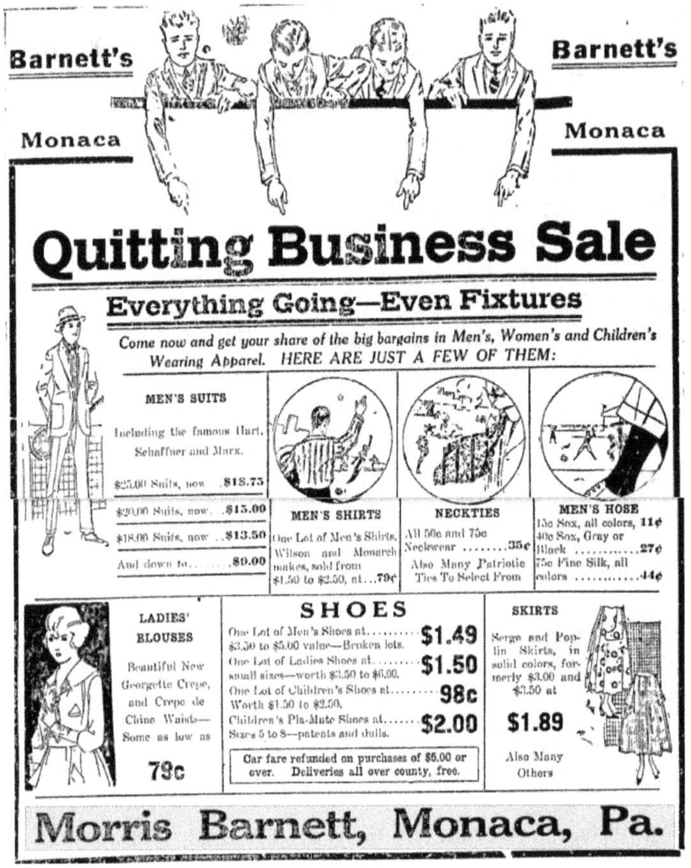

1922

W.(William) L. Dixon – 1135 Pennsylvania Avenue (2 doors from Hotel Hamilton/Pennsylvania and Twelfth Street) 1891 until the late 1920s/early 1930s

- W. L. was listed under "Tailors." He had clothing and cleaning mixed in with his tailoring business. W.L. also ran a nickelodeon in the early 1900s.
- W. L. Dixon and S.D. Hamilton had "a fine picket fence of the latest design erected" "adjoining their residences on Pennsylvania Avenue....." This would indicate that there was only an open lot, if anything, between the two businesses. This also indicates that William Johnston had his business building beside the Hamilton Hotel because Dixon purchased it from Johnston.

W. L. Dixon

—DEALER IN—

Hats, Caps, Gents' Furnishing Goods, Etc.

Pennsylvania Ave., Monaca, Pa.

Feb 1902 ad

W. L. DIXON,

Tailor, Clothier

Gents' Furnisher.

Boys', Men's and Children's Spring Suits. Fine line of Suitings ready-to-wear or made to order.
Trading, Rebate and Keystone Stamps given.

Two doors from Hotel Hamilton, Pennsylvania Avenue,

Monaca, - Penn'a.

1903 ad

Howard S. Scott – merchant of notion store – 1034 Pennsylvania Avenue
1930

       In 1920 Howard and wife Adele were living in Conway; he was machinist on RR.

       By 1940, I do not know if the store was still open since Howard was a salesman for
          Standard Oil Co.

———

Sobel's Quality Clothes – 903 Pennsylvania Avenue (they appear to have only been renting here)
1912 to c1942

       By 1940–Pennsylvania Avenue – Max was owner of a men's shop.   His wife, Fannie, was the
          owner of a ladies' shop. This would have been Minerva Dress Shop at 899 Pennsylvania
          Avenue (their daughter's name was Minerva, so I am sure she was involved with the store to
          some degree considering her mother's age).

       The Sobel's lived in the same building as the business.

       Max H. Sobel, was proprietor from the late 1910s until about 1942.

    Sobel's store is said to have moved in to 899 Pennsylvania after the Carey's closed their store; if so,
          this is either referring to Minerva's Dress Shop (owned by Sobels) or he may have moved all
          his stock to the 899 store, too.   Regardless, by 1949/1950, the 899 building became known
          as Monaca Inn/Monaca Hotel and currently P-Dub's.

       The Monaca Wallpaper Co. moved from 1140 Pennsylvania to 903 Pennsylvania in 1946.

       The next mention of 903 Penna Ave I can find is in 1957 when it was a furniture exchange store.

       In 1972 Samuel Ciccozzi of Beaver Falls applied to open business Chip's Lounge at 903
          Pennsylvania Avenue.

       The Harbison's house was at 901, then the Sobel building at 903 and an insurance company
          would have been at 905.   It appears that one of these three buildings was already razed by
          1974 because it was stated that in 1974 two buildings were torn down for the new
          Dairy Queen to be built …..but…. it also said it would be taking up 3 lots.   Since the Harbison
          building was a frame structure, and the other two were brick structures, a logically deduction
          would be it was the Harbison building was already razed by 1974.

Harbison's Bldg   **Sobel's**   Insurance/Real Estate business

———

Minerva Dress Shop – 899 Pennsylvania Avenue
Jun 1938, 1942, 1941

Nov 1938 ad

There was a Miss Minerva Sobel in 1936 – she would have been in her mid 20s - eldest daughter to Max & Fannie.

The shop may have closed with Minerva's marriage in 1940 because after she married, they were living in Pittsburgh by Apr 1941; or..........perhaps the shop may have been owned by her mother, Fannie; to honor their daughter by naming the shop *Minerva* (which is more plausible), especially since Fannie is listed as being the proprietor of a ladies store in 1940.   The store closed and was sold the same time they closed and sold Sobel's storeroom at 903 Pennsylvania Avenue.

———

Delp's Store – 1099 Bechtel Street (and Welch Avenue)- Monaca Heights (site of current Gallagher's)
1943

Then became……….

Monaca Heights Bargain Center – 1099 Bechtel Street (and Welch Avenue) – Monaca Heights
1960

Owned by Otto Rahe.   Stocked with clothing, jewelry, footwear, hunting equipment, and other general merchandise.   Store burned Feb 20, 1960 – all merchandise was lost – storeroom in middle of building was gutted.

———

Krall's Men's & Boys Wear – 1128-1130 Pennsylvania Avenue (in 1949, 1957)
                    -at least 1963 - at 999 Pennsylvania Avenue
1949, 1967

In 1956 the address from an ad was 1130 Pennsylvania Avenue.
In 1963 located at 999 Pennsylvania Avenue (in the former bank building, across from the
       Municipal Building).
Sold Men's clothing.
His store had some damage from a fire in an apartment at the rear of the store Aug 1963.
Krall's was at 999 Pennsylvania Avenue prior to the public parking lot being put in beside the Municipal Building.
   o   The 2nd floor of this building had Dr. Callaghan's office; the rear of 1st floor was an apartment
        (1963).
By 1979 there was a hair design business moving into 999 Pennsylvania Avenue.

Jul 1949

———

114

Union Clothing Store aka Goldberg, Pearlman & Company –815-817 Pennsylvania Avenue (Dietrich Bldg)
1903, 1904

Opened store the week of Oct 6, 1903.   Closed the store in Feb 1904.

This company from Coraopolis also opened a clothing and gents' furnishing store in Monaca.
Had their grand opening sale the week of Oct 24, 1903.   Gave premium tickets with
every purchase. (opened the business in the Deitrich Building on Pennsylvania Avenue)

Sep 24, 1903 - Had two large signs made by Leary Advertising Co.

An article stated that since "business was very dull", Messrs Goldberg & Pearlman asked Mr.
John Deitrich to release them from the 19 month lease. He refused.   They offered $100
to release them; he still refused.   The owners still began to pack up their goods and
leave, so legal actions might have been needed if an amicable settlement wasn't
reached.

This 811 to 819 Pennsylvania Avenue in 2015

_____

2 Sisters Boutique Resale Clothiers and Accessories – 1206 Rear Pennsylvania Avenue
1996, 1998

Owned by sisters Paulette Wasko and Barbara Horter.

Opened Jul 1996.

Resale shop / consignments.

_____

Spires Apparel and Gift Shoppe - 1140 Pennsylvania Avenue and 1022 Pennsylvania Avenue
1948, 1949, 1953, 1954

Owned by Mildred (Carey) Spires. She married Lloyd Spires.

Mildred was elected to the position of secretary of the Beaver County Chamber of Commerce.
She was the only woman in the county to hold such a position.

She attended classes at Yale University to learn how to be an executive secretary.

Beautiful Blouses
$1.95 to $5.95

Nationally Advertised "Roman Stripe"
and "Fine Feathers"
HOSE

SPIRES
GIFT & APPAREL SHOP
MONACA

Jul 1949

FOR LADIES' WEAR IN MONACA IT'S
MILDRED SPIRES
APPAREL AND GIFT SHOPPE
"MONACA'S ONLY LADIES' APPAREL SHOPPE"

HALF SIZES
ALSO
Junior And Misses

AT SPIRES YOU'LL
FIND

•Lingerie
•Hats
•Blouses
•Scarfs
•Hose
•Purses
•Gloves
•Brassieres
•Sweaters
•Hallmark Cards

MILDRED SPIRES
APPAREL AND GIFT SHOPPE
"Monaca Merchants Appreciate Your Patronage"

1953

_____

Stein's Dept Store –   1128 - 1132 Pennsylvania Avenue (United 5 & 10 moved in this building)
1912, 1922, 1927, 1943
>   Charles Stein – owner - didn't come to America until 1906.
>   In 1920, Charles and his family (wife Lena, 4 children) lived on Pennsylvania Avenue and he
>   was a merchant in dry goods. Charles owned the property.
>   In 1930, they had moved about 5 blocks down on Pennsylvania Avenue. He was known for
>   shoe sales.
>   Built new business building in Sep 1922 (Mitchell Lumber Co. had the contract).
>   Had a clearance sale Sep 1927.
>   Max, their son, was a clerk in the store in 1940.
>   Ad in Oct 1943 stated "Just a few days and Good bye!" which indicates he went out of
>   business at that time, possibly even retired since he was 61.
>   Charles Stein sold this two storey brick building (2 store rooms, 3 apts) in early 1943.

Have A Good Time And Buy All Your Wants in Your Own Home Town...Hurrah for a Big Monaca!

STEIN'S DEPARTMENT STORE
MONACA, PA.

We sincerely greet and wish a welcome, great luck and happiness to Monaca's new born movie insti
tution, erected by Mr. Louis Stoll. Let's all go and be there at the opening and always thereafter
and enjoy a good show at a very moderate price.

ARISTOCRATIC ROBES AT DEMOCRATIC PRICES	LADIES' AND CHILDREN'S CLOAKS AND DRESSES
Just Arrived, New Robes for the Ladies or the Gents	Just received a big variety of Coats and Dresses.
	Look and wonder at the low prices.
$4.00 Robes.....$2.95 Children's Robes	$36.50 Velour & Bolivia Coats..........$27.50
$5.00 Robes.....$3.95 At Very	$30.00 Fine Fur Trimmed Coats..........$22.50
$7.50 Robes.....$5.45 Moderate Prices	$25.00 Broadcloth and Spring Needle.....$19.50
	$10.00 Ladies' Cloth and Jersey Dress.....$ 4.95

COME AND LOOK US OVER—IT'S A VISIT THAT PAYS

1926

COST $30,000—will sell for $22,000 —a bargain—must leave town. two story brick building at 1128-1132 Pennsylvania Avenue. Monaca—2 storerooms 22½x95 feet long each; 3 apartments—4, 5 and 8 rooms and bath each. Income $284 a month. Charles Stein, Monaca, Pa. Phone Rochester 116-R   24-10 Inc

Feb 1943

Batchelor-Starrett Co. –lower Pennsylvania Avenue
1896, 1940   (The company sold furniture, carpets, dry goods, millinery, clothing, shoes.)
>   A. Dickerson Starrett was the president of the company in 1902/03.
>   He married Helen W. __; they resided on Atlantic Avenue.
>   Alonzo S. Batchelor was the secretary and treasurer of the Co. and resided on Pennsylvania
>   Avenue in 1902/03 and Francis M. was the vice president of the company in 1902/03 an
>   resided on Pennsylvania Avenue.
>   Had a large ad in Sep 1903 paper stating they were having a first year anniversary sale.
>   Had a Millinery department.
>   o   Jan 9, 1903 – Miss Minnette Miller was the manager of the millinery department.
>   Had a reorganization sale Jul 1, 1903.
>   o   Mr. A. Dickson Starrett was retiring and Messrs Alonzo Starrett and Frank M.
>   Batchelor were going to manage the big department store.
>   Sold wallpaper among other items.   Ads stated "5 and 10 cent goods," too.

1904 - Built a 2 storey frame building behind their business block and used it as a <u>stable</u> and wareroom.   May 1, 1906 – they announced the installation of a "cash carrier system."

MADE TO ORDER
Suits and Overcoats
$15.00, $18.00, $20.00.

When we say MADE TO ORDER we mean tailor made.

Over five hundred styles to make your selections from, in every new fabric of the season.

Every Suit or Overcoat guaranteed to fit perfectly, or no sale.

ALL SUITS AND OVERCOATS DELIVERED ONE WEEK FROM DATE MEASURE IS TAKEN.

$5.00, $8.00 and $10.00 saved from most tailoring prices.

All clothes are guaranteed and kept pressed for a season free of charge.

COME IN AND LET US TAKE YOUR MEASURE.

Get into the crowd that is making money by saving money.

The most particular dressers in town are wearing

"International" Made=to=Order Clothes

WHY NOT YOU ?

THE
BATCHELOR-STARRETT CO.,
Pennsylvania Avenue.
MONACA,   PENN'A.

Jan 1904 ad

———

Margolis & Stein – Clothing – 1116-20 Pennsylvania Avenue
1910, 1922
　　　Building was built by Henry Margolis.

　　then……………

Margolis Dept Store – 1116-20 Pennsylvania Avenue (corner of Pennsylvania Avenue / Wahl St*)
1925, 1926, 1930
　　　　　*Wahl Street is an alley off Pennsylvania to Pacific Avenue – btw. Eleventh and Twelfth Streets
　　　Margolis was first at 1144 Pennsylvania Avenue in 1922; he lived in Freedom then.
　　　Opened – 1925/26.　　　Closed – Mid Dec 1930.
　　　Henry Margolis owner.
　　　Known as "The People's Shopping Center."　　　They sold clothes, shoes, and dry goods.
　　　He had a two storey brick business and apartment building erected.
　　　　　In addition to a full cellar and first floor storeroom, it was to have 18 rooms on the 2nd
　　　　　floor with two halls and divided into three suites.
　　In May 1925 they started on the foundation of his building.
　　　o　Henry Margolis married Bessie Stein; had 4 children; they lived in Freedom in 1920, and by 1930,
　　　　they had moved to Harrisburg where he had a dry goods business.

DOORS CLOSED

Final Sale Starts THURSDAY Dec. 18 at 9 A. M.   **MARGOLIS DEPT. STORE**   Final Sale Starts THURSDAY Dec. 18 at 9 A. M.

1116-20 PENNSYLVANIA AVENUE.   ——   MONACA.

This Store will be closed all day Wednesday, December 17th to mark down to almost nothing the entire High Grade Stock of Men's, Ladies' and Children's Clothing, Furnishings and Shoes. This Sale will unquestionably be the greatest in History—This is the End—No Sale has ever approached this Sale! Your Last Chance!

QUITTING BUSINESS

We Must Vacate! We Must Sell! Everything Must Be Sold — Prices Smashed!

MEN'S SHIRTS Slightly Soiled Values to $2.00	LADIES' SHOES Values to $3.00	MEN'S SUITS Values to $20.00	KOTEX 50c Value	LADIES' DRESSES Slightly Soiled Values to $10.00
25c	**25c**	**$6.98**	**13c**	**$1.00**
MEN'S PANTS Values to $2.50	MEN'S SHOES Values to $4.00	MEN'S SUITS Slightly Soiled Values to $15.00	CHILDREN'S SHOES Values to $1.50	HOUSE DRESSES Slightly Soiled Values to $3.00
98c	**98c**	**$1.00**	**39c**	**25c**
MEN'S CAPS Values to $1.00	CLARK'S O.N.T. THREAD 10c Values	BOYS' SUITS Slightly Soiled Values to $7.50	LADIES' HATS Values to $2.00	LADIES' COATS Values to $15.00
9c	**2c**	**$1.00**	**10c**	**$1.98**
MEN'S UNDERWEAR Values to 75c	LADIES' CORSETS Values to $2.00	WORK PANTS Values to $2.00	BOYS' SHOES Values to $3.00	CHILDREN'S COATS Values to $5.00
19c	**25c**	**50c**	**98c**	**98c**
MEN'S OVERALLS Values to $1.50		"QUITTING BUSINESS" **Margolis Dept. Store** 1116-20 PENNSYLVANIA AVENUE. —— MONACA. STORE OPEN EVENINGS UNTIL XMAS		CHILDREN'S DRESSES Values to $1.00
50c				**19c**

LOOK FOR THE BIG SALE SIGNS

1920s view of Margolis store - the United 5 & 10 store moved in to this building.

_____

Monaca Men's and Boys' Store – 1114 Pennsylvania Avenue (corner of Pennsylvania Avenue and Wahl Street) 1942, 1965, 1991, 1997

Opened business in 1942.   Owned by John Sabo, Sr.

Originally sold work clothes, but converted to casual and dress clothing (specializing in tall and big sizes).   The business remained owned and operated by family and was still open in 1991.   John Sabo, Jr. was owner in 1982, 1991.

Store was formerly Butler Co. building; was next door to NcNees Jewelry.

John Sabo, Sr. also started the United 5 & 10 store opening it in 1932.

The men's clothing store building was sold in 1998 after the death of John Sabo, Jr.

We Specialize In . . .
BIG & TALL SIZES
MONACA MEN'S & BOYS WEAR
1114 Penna. Ave., Monaca
774-9370

1990 ad

REG. $1.98
Dungarees - - - - **$1.49**
REG. $1.49
Work Shirts - - - - **$1.19**
T-Shirts - - - **2 for $1.00**
Monaca Men's & Boys' Store
"Next to McNees Jewelry"

Jul 1949

Although occupied by a new business, this is a view of the building of the former Monaca Men's and Boys' Store.   The lower front portion of this building was boarded up for many year; then in 2017, there was some work being done to the store front of this building.

_____

J & A Fabrics -750 Marshall Road, Monaca Heights
1972

Harris Cohen – Dry Goods store – unknown
1910
       Harris and Nettie Cohen owners.

———

Cahen & Harris – Pennsylvania Avenue
1903, 1904,
       Dry goods Merchants – founded their business in Coraopolis in 1898.
       Owned by Nathan Cahen and David Harris.   They opened their store in the new Harbison
           building.
       George J. Harbison wouldn't transfer the lease of store to Sol & Morris in 1904.
       They were only in Monaca for a few months and after "opposition" with Sol & Morris, they
           decided to return to Coraopolis with their business.
       David sold his interest in the business to Nathan in 1910 and was run as Cahen's Men's Store.
           Nathan died in 1933 and his son Leonard took over the business.

———

Krieger & Company – Ninth Street within the Citizen's Bank building.   Address just says "Business Block."
1903, 1904
       Dry good merchants - A. I. Krieger and J. Krieger.   Sold shoes, hats, men's furnishings.
       There was an advertising "feud" going on between this company and Sol & Morris in 1903/1904
       (See further on in this section for more on this feud.)
       Krieger & Company became a well known clothier in Pittsburgh.   There was a Krieger Mfg.
           Co.(clothing) on Liberty Avenue in Pittsburgh in 1931. Leon Krieger was part of
           Krieger & Company.

Sol & Morris – Dixon Building on Pennsylvania Avenue (formerly occupied by Wm. Johnston) (2 doors from Hotel Hamilton) – 1100 block of Pennsylvania Avenue

1903, 1904

Opened on Jan 10, 1903.   Owners – Sol Ostrow and Morris Browdy.
This was a well- known business which did business with Pittsburgh merchants frequently. Both men were in their twenties between 1900 and 1910.   Dry Good merchants – gents' furnishing and shoe store.   "Watch Us Grow" was a motto of this company.
An article stated that Sol made an "appearance" of being a Monaca resident, renting residences:
In Aug 1906, he rented a house on the corner of Thirteenth Street and Indiana Avenue.
In Feb 1907, Sol and his wife were reported to have an apartment above the store.
By 1906, Sol Ostrow was the sole proprietor of the company in Monaca and had already closed his store.   He totally liquidated the store and turned all over to the National Salvage Company of Philadelphia to sell off the clothing.   (See giant ad at the end of this section.)

Sol Ostrow Clothing, furnishings and shoe store – Monaca
1906, 1907

Mens, boys, and children clothing, shoes, furnishings; considered a *clothier*.
John Boyd was hired as a salesman in Mar 1907. Harry Harris was a clerk in the store in Apr 1907.
Closed in 1907 – entire stock was put on sale and sold.   Sol's family was living in Pittsburgh, so an educated guess would be that Sol most likely moved back to Pittsburgh.

Even in 1904, "boys" couldn't get along well together all the time!   Monaca found amusement in a "spat" that was going on between a few merchants in town.   I have included a copy of the entire article that was in the newspaper on Jan 12, 1904, where you can read the exact wordings of some of the advertising and fliers that were distributed throughout this "dispute."

When Cahen & Harris's lease expired, the dispute began. Instead of the lease going back to Cahen & Harris, it was said that George Harbison had put the lease "up for sale" with Sol & Morris and Krieger both wanting to buy the lease.   Krieger found that Sol had put some money down to hold it and he went to confront him about this action.   There were punches thrown and all the fisticuffs ended with Sol and Krieger being arraigned before Chief Burgess Irons.   The whole affair stirred up excitement in the community.   And many people found it most amusing!   It all ended with Cahen & Harris moving their business back to Coraopolis, Sol & Morris remained in Monaca, and Kreiger & Co. went to Pittsburgh.   Play nice gentlemen, play nice!

Whole Town Interested in Fight Between Cloth-ing Merchants.

TROUBLES AIRED IN THE POLICE COURT

One Merchant Alleged to Have As-saulted the Other at Railway Sta-tion Because of Trouble Over a Lease From Another Merchant.

That "opposition is the life of trade," has been clearly demonstrated at Monaca during the past few days. Two prominent business men, members of two different well known firms, are the central figures. They are "Sol" Ostro, of the firm of Sol & Morris, and Leon Krieger, of the firm of Krieger & Company. It seems that another firm, Cahan & Harris, who came to Monaca, several months ago, and opened a dry goods store in the new Harbison building, have decided to return to Coraopolis, from whence they came. Their lease not having expired, it was to be offered for sale. It was stated that Sol was the first to make the firm an offer, and that a partial agreement had been effected on Saturday morning, when Krieger, learning that the store room was to be vacated, made an ef-fort to secure the lease.

It was further stated that when Ca-han went to the Pittsburg and Lake Erie station Saturday morning to leave for Coraopolis, Krieger met him at the station. Sol, on learning of Krieger's movements, hurried to the depot, where he found the latter in conversation with Cahan, whom he called aside. This caused more trouble, words were exchanged between Sol and Krieger, and the latter struck Sol a blow. The latter then brought suit against Krie-ger and he was arraigned before Chief Burgess Irons this morning at 10 o'clock, charged with assault and bat-tery and breach of the peace.

Krieger entered a counter charge. Several witnesses were called. Finally Burgess Irons settled both cases by ordering each man to pay the costs of his own case. Krieger paid $10.59 and Sol $5.75. A witness named Samuel Houlette was demonstrating and swore

MONACA AMUSED BY RIVAL MERCHANTS

(Continued from First Page.)

several times. The burgess fined him 62½ cents for each oath, which amoun-ted to about $12 before he was locked up for contempt.

Other complications are likely to set in as a result of the rivalry. Both firms have been conducting a special sale during the past few days. Both firms employed what they thought to be the best medium for advertising said sales. Krieger & Company had large dodgers printed. At the bottom of the dodger were these words:

"Beware of imitators. Of course we are between the Citizens Bank and Hotel Monaca, so don't get lost among stores of our friends, who blow them-selves up, and tell you to watch 'em grow, at your expense. Watch our prices and let your pocketbooks grow."

These were distributed early last week. "Watch Us Grow" has been a motto of Sol & Morris ever since they commenced business in Monaca. When the Monaca Weekly Herald of last week issued forth on Friday, the fol-lowing item appeared most conspicous-ly on the front page, with the firm name of Sol & Morris underneath:

AND HE WAS A GOAT.

A common, ordinary, everyday goat, with a pair of horns and a bunch of chin whiskers. He was a hungry goat. He had wandered around the town looking for an evening meal, but the health commissioners had been pro-perly attending to their duty. Not a tin can or a piece of paper could this poor goat find to devour. The bill poster had been so unkind as to past his bills firmly to the boards.

The more the goat wandered about the hungrier he grew. Finally a piece of paper fluttered in the street, and how that goat did eat.

The next morning the health commis-

sioners found him dead. A piece of paper was sticking in his throat. He had been trying to sup on a hand bill thrown around by a certain unscrupu-lous firm, who are conducting a fake hard luck sale, on a side street of Mo-naca, and offering a suit of clothes free with every hat purchased (?). But he choked on it, for even a goat could-n't swallow that.

Follow the crowds if you wish to save money. The great annual clear-ance sale is still going on at Sol & Morris.

We are growing, and the increase in the number of our patrons proves that we are growing as a result of our fair treatment to all.

There are lots of places to buy gen-tlemen's wear in Monaca but the real place is of   SOL & MORRIS.

The whole affair has created consid-erable excitement, and no end of amusement among the inhabitants of that thriving little town, and further developments will be awaited with in-terest.

***

Liberty Tux – unknown location
1978, 1983

_____

Eugene G. Zigerelli's businesses...............
1946, 1965, 1979, 1985

Zigerelli's Men's Wear – 925 Pennsylvania Avenue (at this address in 1949)
      1945 - Bought the menswear and dry cleaning business from A. C. Birner and
                continued the business.
      Eugene "Gene" Zigerelli – owner.

Ziggy's Cleaners and Tux Rentals - 925 Pennsylvania Avenue
                (across from the Boro Building and Roxy Theatre)
      1955 – Zigerelli changed to a tuxedo rental business with men's wear, cleaning & pressing.
      1970 - moved next door to 927 Pennsylvania Avenue when Eberhardt Insurance moved out.
  *The building at 925 Penna Ave was once many different businesses Guy's Shoe Repair, Birner's, Ziggy's
Tux / dry cleaners, the Wedding Village, and lastly – the Carriage House Antiques (which is now closed);
the building is currently vacant, but most recently was still labeled for the antique store.

Ziggy's Tux and Cleaning – 927 Pennsylvania Avenue
      He continued the dry cleaning business with Bonacci Cleaning – Beaver Falls.
      He also specialized in selling sports uniforms and jackets for a short time.
      Eugene Zigerelli married Julia Primo and bought the business from Birner.
      He was voted Business of the Month in Nov 1979.
      He retired in 1985.
        Sold his business to John B. Yasick of Leetsdale in May 1985 after more than 40 years of
           being in business.   Mr. Yasick was going to continue along the same lines of business.
  *The building at 927 Pennsylvania Avenue had several business over the years, also - Monaca
Hardware in the late 1920s until __; Eberhardt Insurance; Mr. Yasick had the tux shop from
1985; then Deborah's Bridal Traditions was there starting in 1993.

_____

Patty's Bridal and Formal – 1313 Pennsylvania Avenue
1988, 1998
      Opened on Nov 14, 1988, moved in Jul 1998.
      Owned by Patty Hodovanich.

_____

Wedding Village – 925 Pennsylvania Avenue
1981, 1983
      Opened 1981 – grand opening was in mid Jul 1981.   George Cuch – owner.
        Teri Young was a "live mannequin" outside the store.

Photo by Dan E. Stauffer

_____

Deborah's Bridal Traditions – 927 Pennsylvania Avenue
1993, Current
      Moved to 927 Pennsylvania Avenue in 2000 (the former McNees Jewelry Store).

Deborah's
Bridal Traditions
"Service with a Personalized Touch"

Stop In To See Our
New Exciting Lines For
PROM AND
BRIDAL FASHIONS
FOR 2006

927 Pennsylvania Ave.
Monaca, PA 15061
724-774-5055

Bridal and Formal Wear On Sale Now

2005

_____

Arlette's Bridal & Formal – 1515 Indiana Avenue
2003, 2006, current
      Began the custom made formal wear business about 1883/1885.
      Studio / shop on third floor in her home.   She handmade all her dresses.

_____

Marilyn's Bride & Formal – Center Township – intersection 18 & 51 (old Raccoon Golf Course Club house)
2003   (now site of a hotel/motel)
      Taryn Linta Vanderhart – proprietor/manager.

_____

Millinery

Mrs. H. R. McDonald's Store – Pennsylvania Avenue (next door to city building)
1900

> Anna McDonald was owner/operator – closed her store prior to 1910.   In 1900, she moved from her location to former storeroom of Mrs. Schlosser.   Anna was married in 1881 to Rev. Henry McDonald, they lived on Pennsylvania Avenue in 1900; 2 children.

MILLINERY GOODS!

Latest Styles and Best Quality,
— AT —

MRS. H. R. M'DONALD'S STORE

Next Door to City Building,

PENN'A AVENUE,   ·   MONACA.

Summer Opening Friday and Saturday, May 11, 12

———

Mrs. Schlosser's Millinery Store -   Closed in 1900, she moved from the area.

———

Joyce Nary – millinery
1900   She lived on Pennsylvania Avenue

———

Catherine H. Aubrey – milliner
1902, 1903   She lived on Washington Avenue.   She took a position as head trimmer for a large
                        department store in Akron, Ohio in 1903.

———

Mrs. F. H. Brush – 1727 Indiana Avenue
1902, 1903, 1924, 1946   Sold Spencer Individual Design corset and breast supports.

———

Effie M. Rambo – milliner – Tenth Street
1900, 1902, 1903   She lived on Ninth Street.

———

Pearl P. Potter – milliner – Pennsylvania Avenue
1902, 1903   She roomed at J. M. Kirk's.

Miss Potter's Millinery Store – Pennsylvania Avenue
1902, 1903   Owned by Florence E. Potter.   She roomed at J. M. Kirk's.

———

Mrs. Mae Weaver – Ninth Street
1910   Dressmaking and millinery.

———

Wilhelm's Millinery Store – Pennsylvania Avenue (George Zitzman's brick building – close to Ninth Street)
1906, 1907

> Store was closed by Jul 1907.   Miss A. A. Wilhelm, owner.
> Miss Wilhelm & Mrs. Rowland were living above the store, moved to Keystone Bldg Jul 1907.

———

Ladies Style Shop – 303 Ninth Street
1924   Millinery and notions.

———

Nellie Morgan – Milliner
1900, 1902, 1903, 1904
        She lived at Indiana Avenue.   She went into business with her sister, Eva, in 1904.

Morgan Millinery - Ninth Street (rented the Figley building)
1904, 1907, 1908
        Owned by Misses Eva and Nellie Morgan of Monaca.   Opened business on Mar 7, 1904.

———

Anna Ronshausen's Millinery Parlor – Pennsylvania Avenue (close to Ninth Street)– Zitzman's brick bldg
Jul 1907, Dec 1907
        Miss Anna Ronshausen – owner.   She opened an up-to-date millinery parlor in late
            Jul 1907/early Aug 1907, where Miss Wilhelm's store used to be.

———

Mrs. James Moore Millinery Parlors – Washington Avenue
1910, 1911
        Was closed for a period of time prior to Sep 1911, she reopened her millinery parlors and
            advertised of a nice line of pattern hats.   She worked from home.

———

Beulah Hood – apprentice Millinery
1912   She was 17 and living with her parents at 1101 Pennsylvania Avenue.

———

Miss Hazel Williamson – 1000 Pennsylvania Avenue (Mateer Building)
1912   She was from Pittsburgh; opened a dress making establishment.

Seamstress

Hannah Knapper-seamstress - 1860

Rosina Goetz – seamstress - 1860

Rosina Goetz – seamstress – 1860

Mary Guba – seamstress – 1900

Leora Cartlier – seamstress – 1900

Anna Schab – seamstress – 1900

Rosa Schab – seamstress – 1900

Eva Morgan – seamstress – 1900

Harry Neeley – seamstress – 1900

Mary Hunzuker – seamstress – 1900

Lydia Ronshensen – seamstress – 1900

Olive Hinderman – seamstress - 1900

Vera Grant – seamstress in her home – Atlantic Avenue - 1930

Dressmaker

Nancy Donehoo – dress maker - 1860

Clara Landis – dress maker - 1880 (her father was a shoemaker)

Kansas Hemphill – dress maker -1880

Florence Cronin – in 1912 lived at Washington Avenue

Amanda Finn - in 1912 lived at Pennsylvania Avenue

Pauline Fischer – in 1912 lived at Washington Avenue

Matilda Lais – in 1912 lived at Washington Avenue

Cora LeGoullon – in 1912 lived at Virginia Avenue

Mary Preece – in 1912 lived at Washington Avenue

Jennie Urwin – in 1912 lived at Virginia Avenue

Eva Miller – in 1900, she lived at Washington Avenue

Nettie M. Walter – dressmaker in her home – 1902, 1903, 1920 at Washington Avenue

Cynthia J. Hood – dressmaker
1902, 1903   She lived on Ninth Street.   Mary E. Hood also lived on Ninth Street.

Sofia Heckerman – Millinery store – unknown location - 1920 - She lived on Indiana Avenue

Alice Beucke – seamstress in her home – 1920 at Pennsylvania Avenue

Elizabeth Erb – dressmaker in her home – 1920 – at Atlantic Avenue

*** *** *** *** ***
*** *** ***

TAILORS

Francis Zeigler – tailor in 1841

_____

Reyman Gann/Garner/Grant – tailor
1841, 1850, 1860, 1869, 1870   His residence in 1869 was Lacock Street/Sixth Street.

_____

Frank Donehoo – tailor 1860

_____

Conrad Yeison – tailor – 1860

_____

Charles Conti – tailor – Ninth Street
1902, 1903   Charles had a storeroom in Monaca but he lived in Beaver Falls.

_____

Charles Steiss - tailor
1900, 1902, 1903

_____

Joe Zrebic – tailor – 212 Ninth Street
1913   Mr. Zrebic had his business in Monaca and Rochester.
               He married Rosa, they lived in same building as business.

1913 ad

————

Clemens A. Nosky's Tailor Shop –lower 800 or even 700s on Pennsylvania Avenue
1907, 1908
        Clemens came from Allegheny County - he was also a tailor there in 1900.
        1907 – they moved from rooms over Max Barnett's shoe store to new Eckert Building.
        Clemens was from Austria.
        Clemens married Tressa __ and had 3 children; he married #2 in 1905: Katie __.

————

Alexander Cleaning and Tailoring Co. – 1309 Pennsylvania Avenue
1954   Ralph E. Alexander owner/operator.

————

Adolph C. (A.C.) Birner – tailor – 831/833 Pennsylvania Avenue (1927), then 925 Pennsylvania Avenue
1912, 1920, 1924, 1945
        Merchant tailor and gents' furnishings.
        In 1945, sold business to Ziggy's Tux and cleaning.
        Two special lines he carried were Wm. Pitt Hats and Stack Trousers.
        Adolph C. married Anna _; they had 4 children.
          In 1930, they were living at the business building.
          In 1940, they were living at Indiana Avenue.

————

W.(William) L. Dixon – 1135 Pennsylvania Avenue (2 doors from Hotel Hamilton/Pennsylvania and
                                             Twelfth Street)
1891 until the late 1920s/early 1930s, 1953
        In business in Apr 1901 by ad – called *clothier*.   1902/03 lists him as a *tailor*.
        Tailor, clothier, gents' furnisher, boys' – men's – children's suits.   Trading, rebate and Keystone
             stamps were given here.   Conducted business until he retired -- early 1930s.
        The ads state "2 doors from Hamilton Hotel."   In May 1903 in the Monaca news section, it
             stated that W. L. Dixon and S. D. Hamilton had a "fine picket fence of the latest design
             erected yesterday adjoining their residences on Pennsylvania Avenue....."   This would
             indicate that there was some type of an open area between the two businesses.
             If you go by the way Monaca looks today – Dixon's building was either located on one of
             the empty lots, and since has been torn down - beside the location of the former Hamilton
             Hotel (1199 Pennsylvania Avenue); or it was at 1133 Pennsylvania Avenue, which had been
             remodeled and being used in 2016.
        John Dixon worked for Wm. in 1912.
        W. L. was born in 1863; married Sarah __ in 1885; they had 4 children;
             they lived above the storeroom.
        Their daughter married Charles Lindsay who owned the Monaca News Agency.

W. L. listed himself as a tailor in 1900, 1910.   By 1920 and 1930, W.L. was
working in industrial companies. W. L. and Sarah were married 50 years in 1936.

Michael Theil – 1098 Pennsylvania Avenue (near Eleventh Street)
                                                     – then had storeroom built on Ninth Street
1920, 1922, 1924, 1930, 1940, 1943
        Merchant tailor – cleaning and pressing.
        Had ground broken the first of Jul 1922 for his new two storey brick business and apartment
            building; this was a new building erected for his tailor shop on Ninth Street.
            F. A. LeGoullon did the excavation for the cellar; G. H. Lais was awarded the contract for
            the building.
        Michael was married to Mary __; lived at the store building; had 3 children.   He died in 1946.

Bruno Tailor & Tux Shop – 1016 Pennsylvania Avenue
1970s, 1990s   Located beside the Monaca Library in the Keystone Building.

Photo courtesy BCHR&LF
This photo only shows a portion of the Bruno store front (on the right).

1990 ad

Morris Wise – Tailor Shop – Monaca Heights
1910
        His wife Rachel was proprietor of a dry goods store, too.

Alteration Shoppe – 610 Indiana Avenue
1928, 1929

ALTERATION SHOPPE — Fur and
cloth coats and suits relined and remodeled. Will call for and deliver.
610 Indiana avenue, Monaca. Phone
Rochester 1289.   10 15-21inc

————

Peter Equizi – Tailor Shop – unknown location
1930, 1940   He lived on Washington Avenue.

————

Abraham Kleiman – tailor - married Lillie; they lived at Eighth Street in 1912.

————

M. J. Konvolinka – 927 Pennsylvania Avenue
1920   He had ads that stated "Suits made to order." "Drop me a card and I will call with
            samples."

*** *** *** *** ***
*** *** ***

SHOE BUSINESSES and SHOEMAKERS

August F. Blatt – shoemaker – Ohio Street (turned into 387 Atlantic Street Ext)
1860, 1869, 1870, 1876, 1880
        Came to Phillipsburg in about 1853 – lived in frame house at 387 Atlantic Avenue; in 1940
            was still occupied by their only living child – Sophia.
        Was a shoemaker; married Margaret __; had 5 children.

————

Philip H. Goedeker – Pennsylvania Avenue
1900, 1902, 1903
        He lived in Rochester in 1900, 1902/03 but had his shop in Monaca.
        Closed his shoe repair shop May 6, 1903.
                Moved his stock and fixtures to Rochester and continued the shoe business
                    with his brother-in-law, John S. Gremer.

————

J. S. Gremer – lower Pennsylvania Avenue / Stoops building
1901
        Moved his shoe shop business to the Eberhardt building (beside Charles Haller's meat market).

————

Christopher Blume – shoemaker - in 1869

————

James Markey's shoe store – Pennsylvania Avenue
1900, 1901, 1905

James and his wife were given a proposal to make a wonderful deal with the Opalite Tile
Company in late Jan 1900 - it was to sell their property to S. S. Childs of Pgh for the site
of the new works of Opalite Tile Company. The considered offer of the property was
$14,162.50 – in 1900, that was quite a sum of money.

1900 – James received a large consignment of shoes for his new shoe store.

James went to California for the winter of 1907/08 – he visited with W. B. Pugh and family and
Frank Eckles; all went to California in November due to health problems of W. B. Pugh.

James spent the winter of 1907 in Los Angeles and returned home in Apr 1908.

His house was at the corner of Pennsylvania Avenue and Fourteenth Street; George Dockter
bought the house in Oct 1913.

James was born 1844 - died the end of Oct 1919. He had moved to Pittsburgh early in
1919 to live with his daughter. He was a former proprietor of the Central Hotel before it
was destroyed by fire in 1917/18.

He owned quite a bit of property in Monaca including three lots on Atlantic Avenue and three
on Pacific Avenue. They were purchased by the Monaca and Ambridge Street Railway
Company in 1907. In 1906, he sold a lot on Virginia Avenue to William Leffert (James
had a whole plan of lots on Virginia Ave).

In Oct 1903, James took it upon himself to install a fine brick street crossing on Pennsylvania
Avenue in front of the Pennsylvania Avenue Pharmacy at Thirteenth Street for the
convenience of the general public. The comment in the paper at that time said that
there were more crossing needed like this in town; in fact there should be a bridge
constructed over the artificial canal on Pennsylvania Avenue since it was too far
to jump from the curb to the street.

———

John E. Dietrich – 897 Eighth Street, (then George moved plumbing business to Pennsylvania Avenue)
1892, 1893, 1900, 1902, 1903,

John E. married Catherine __ , they lived in same building as the boots & shoes store
Dealer in high grade boots and shoes and did repairing.

A "Carey roof" was put on the Dietrich building by Heidrich & Taylor 1903.

John opened the store sometime in the late 1890s. He rented the rear of the shoe store to son
George Dietrich who started a plumbing and heating business. George converted the
shoe store to his business after his father John died- 1907. Then George moved the
business to Pennsylvania Avenue. George's son, George Dietrich, Jr. and his brother,
John, took over the business; it remained in the family for over 85 years until George,
Jr. sold the business in 1984 about a year after John Dietrich died.

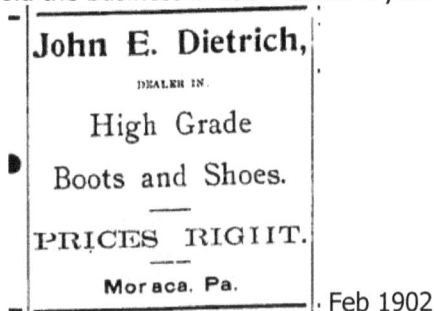

John E. Dietrich,
DEALER IN
High Grade
Boots and Shoes.
———
PRICES RIGIIT.
———
Moraca. Pa.

Feb 1902

———

Julius Schier – shoes – Pennsylvania Avenue
1902, 1903   He married Marie, they lived at same address as shop.

———

Phillip Landis – shoemaker – lived at Pennsylvania Avenue
1902, 1903   He married Rachell A.___.

_____

James M. Aubrey Shoes – Pennsylvania Avenue
1902, 1903   James married Martha J. __; they lived on Washington Avenue.

_____

John Pfeiffer – Shoe Repair Shop – Pennsylvania Avenue
1904
        Closed Apr 1904.   Sold to Angelo Piccano.
        Mr. and Mrs. Pfeifer were going to NY and then to Bavaria.

_____

Angelo Piccano – shoe repair – Pennsylvania Avenue
1904, 1905

_____

John Frank – shoe repair shop - Pennsylvania Avenue (Landis Building)
1904
        Opened Mar 23, 1904 in the Landis Building (formerly occupied by J.A. Schaeffer).

_____

R. C. Jones' Shoe Store – corner of Ninth Street and Pennsylvania Avenue (facing Pennsylvania Avenue)
1907, 1908
        Store was said to be located beside M.W. Carey's place and short distance west of Max Barnett's
                shoe store.
        R. C. went into bankruptcy in Jul 1908; stock was purchased by Stewart Bros. & Co. of Pgh.
        R. C. Jones closed this store by Oct 24, 1908 with Edward Meany opening a gents' furnishing
                store in the store on Nov 1, 1908.

_____

Vincent Iannone – shoe repair – 1309 Pennsylvania Avenue
1928, 1929

_____

Schmuck's Shoe Store – 827 Pennsylvania Avenue moved to 810 Pennsylvania Avenue
                and finally to 915 Pennsylvania Avenue where it is still in business as Red Wing Shoes
1905 to present
        Family owned since it opened.
        Opened 1905 – was across from the First Ward School at 827 Pennsylvania Avenue.
        A custom made shoe and boot shop.
        Frank Schmuck – married Anna – lived at Pacific Avenue.
        1906 – bought larger building – former Ed Winkle's Barber Shop (810 Pennsylvania Avenue).
        Sold that building to "Barber" Wentzel Blasche who had business in 1924 and purchased a larger
                building – Winkle's General Hardware and dwelling at 915 Pennsylvania Avenue.
        Mr. Schmuck used to give shoes to children that didn't have them during the depression.
        Jan 11, 1942 – Frank Schmuck lost his life trying to put out a fire that destroyed
                        the business and home.
        By May 7, 1942, Frank's son, Henry, moved to the corner of Eleventh Street (the M. K. Fronko
                storeroom) and did shoe repairing with equipment that survived the fire.
        Oct 1944 – Henry enlisted in WWII and the repair shop was sold to Guy Battalene and the
                shoe store's stock sold out in his absence.

1947 – Henry was home from the war – Monaca Nat'l Bank gave him a G.I. loan and he
      rebuilt and restocked the new building.
      He discontinued the shoe repair part of the business.
    Mr. Schmuck would let the kids go in and get on the shoe sizing machine he had. It was
      an x-ray type machine that would show the bones in your feet.
Mar 1969 the store became a franchise and became known as Red Wing Shoe Store.
Jan 1978 – Henry's son, Frank's grandson, Eugene took over the business.

Frank Schmuck attends to a customer in his shoe store on Pennsylvania Avenue in the 1920s.
To the right is Schmuck's brother-in-law, Hugo Eder.

1990 ad

Jul 1949

2015

Hugo Eder – shoemaker / shoe shop – unknown location
1930

_____

Karl Fouser – shoe repair
1912   Karl married Marie, lived at 608 Atlantic Avenue.

_____

Andrew Lang – shoe maker - 920 Pennsylvania Avenue in 1912

_____

Thomas S. Mercer – boots and shoes –
1892, 1893

_____

Barnett Shoe Store – 906 Pennsylvania Avenue (and 809 Pennsylvania Avenue)
1882, 1906, 1908, 1909, 1910, 1913, 1914
        Owned by Morris, then Max H. Barnett
            His father Morris Barrett was joined by Max in this business in 1910.
            He worked with his father until 1914, then opened his own shoe store in Rochester.
            Max Barnett rented the lower storeroom of the new Campbell building in Rochester
                in fall 1914 and opened a shoe store there.
    Max's brother, William, assumed charge of the Barnett shoe store in Monaca.
            Morris Barnett had the exterior of his building painted and improved.
            His son Harry had recently opened a shoe store in the building (1906).
            Morris lived at 799 Indiana Avenue and eventually moved to Pittsburgh.
        Max lived at 808 Indiana Avenue until moving to Rochester by 1930.
        At age 21, Max was elected as councilman for Monaca borough – at that time, he was the
            youngest councilman in the state of Pennsylvania.   He was also on the light and street
            committee in 1913 and was instrumental in having the old street gas lights replaced with
            electric lights; as well as seeing that Washington Avenue and Pennsylvania Avenue
            Extension were paved.

BARNETT'S
SHOE SALE
IS NOW ON
BARNETT'S
MONACA, PA.

1909 ad

BARNETT'S
906 PENN AVENUE.   MONACA, PA.
--Monaca's Busiest Corner--

SALE NOW GOING ON—FOLLOW THE CROWDS
THE SHOE EPOCH OF A LIFETIME—   --COME BRING THE FAMILY

1922

BARNETT'S
Established 1882, Over 29 Years Ago,
Are Still Up-to-Date.

IF you want anything beautiful and durable, come and
see our Suits, Hats and Shoes.

BARNETT'S
"Old Reliable"
Monaca.   Aliquippa

Walk · Over Shoes a Specialty
UNION MADE

1911

_____

Daniel A. Steiner – shoemaker – corner Pennsylvania Avenue and Tenth Street
1892, 1893, 1898, 1903
> 1898 directory stated "Boot and shoemaker. Manufacturer of boots and shoes.   Repairing of
> all kinds."

————

John White – shoe dealer
1892, 1893

————

Jacob Bender – shoemaker
1892, 1893

————

John W. Bender – shoemaker – 1121 Virginia Avenue
1900, 1912, 1920
> In his 70s and 80s, he still had his occupation as *shoemaker*.
> John was married to Elizabeth; both b 1845; lived at 1119 Virginia Avenue.

————

Vincenzo Coniglio – shoemaker – 1224 Pennsylvania Avenue
1912, 1930
> Vince was married to Antonia; they lived at Virginia Avenue.

————

John Braccia – Shoe maker – unknown address
1910
> He was in partnership with Joseph Genilli, a barber.   They lived at Beaver Avenue.

————

Guy's Shoe Repair   aka   Battalene Shoe Repair Shop – 923 and/or 925 Pennsylvania Avenue
1948, 1949, 1956
> In business in 1949   (was across from the Roxy Theatre).
> Owned by Guy Battalene.
> He purchased the business from Mr. Schmuck when he left for war service.
> Guy closed his business for a period of time because an ad in May 4, 1948 states "Notice To our
> many friends Guy's Shoe Shop is again open for business at 923 Pennsylvania Avenue
> across from the Roxy Theatre."
> He retired in 1956.   Guy was born in 1893 and died in 1963 (70); married to Silvia __.

————

Andrew Radler – Shoe Repair Shop
1920
     (This was at Nicholas Wurzel's building.)

John Radler – Shoe Repairing/Shoes for sale - 1300 Pennsylvania Avenue
1920, 1924, 1930
     He lived at 1213 Pennsylvania Avenue in 1930.

————

B. Robb's/Rebb's Shoe Store – 906 Pennsylvania Avenue
1924
     B. Robb/Rebb, wife, and children lived over the store.   There was a fire in the building (which
         was owned by Morris Barnett) – caused about $10,000   in damages.
  found it also listed as......
Rebb's Boot Shop –
1924   B. Rebb, prop – sold shoes and hosiery.

————

Joseph Taormina – shoe repair shop – 1206 Pennsylvania Avenue
1923
     He was married to Agatha __; he conducted the shop from their home.

————

Lightning Shoe Repair Shop - 1206 and 1133 Pennsylvania Avenue
1929, 1930, 1938, 1944
     Samuel A Taormina – owner.
     I believe Sam/Samuel was the Americanized version & his proper name was Salvadore.
     In 1930, Sam was in his twenties; living at the same address as store.
     He had his brother-in-law Joseph Cattivera (18) working for him.
     Samuel died in 1971; was married to Helen; they lived at Virginia Avenue.
     He sold his business and went to work for Rheem Manufacturing Co. in Monaca.
     *At some point, the shop moved from 1206 to 1133 Pennsylvania Avenue; it became the
         business of Dom Yacopino.

————

Dom's Shoe Repair –1206 and 1133 Pennsylvania Avenue
1956, 1957, 1986
     Owned by Dom Yacopino.
     Used to do shoe shines.
         Dec 9, 1959 Beaver Valley Times paper said "donations.....to the storeroom formerly
         occupied by Dom's Shoe Repair Shop (which would have been 1206 Pennsylvania).
     Another ad in the Beaver Valley Times – Dec 7, 1959 paper said   "....or to the Oscar Dixon building
         (formerly Dom's Shoe Repair) on Pennsylvania Avenue "
     He used to help different groups in town to earn money by having "shoe shine days."
     Dom retired in 1986 from the repair business and took a job at the Beaver County Area Vo-Tech and
         sold his business to Terry Grimes.

————

Terry Grimes Shoe Repair – 1133 Pennsylvania Avenue
1986, 1988
     Purchased business from Dom Yacopino in 1986.
        o Mr. Grimes was younger when he started his business, and many were
           happy to see a "younger generation" starting a well needed business.
     Terry used to do the shoe shines at Dom's store before opening his own business.

————

Chris's Shoe Repair – 937 (top of hill) Fourteenth Street – Monaca
1965, 1980   Chris Sanfemio – owner.   Business is now closed.

―――――

Salvadore Battaglia – shoe shop – 700 block of Pennsylvania Avenue
1940

―――――

Michael Romisher - Shoe maker / Shoe Shop
1920   He lived at 610 Atlantic Avenue.

―――――

Vincent Cornelius – owned shoe maker shop
1920   He lived at 1220 Pennsylvania Avenue.

―――――

Monaca Hat Cleaning and Shoe Repair –at 1004 Pennsylvania Ave, then at 1016 Pennsylvania Avenue
                                                    (across from Monaca Nat'l Bank)

1938, 1949, 1965   Pete __ - owner

1949 ad   Jul 1949

1956 location of Monaca Shoe Repairing at 1004 Pennsylvania Avenue.

―――――

Taormina Shoe Repair Service
1971

––––––

In 1933 (and during the Depression years), the Monaca Welfare Association established a shoe repair shop in the municipal building where shoes could be repaired at only the cost of the materials.
They also distributed flour to applicants in the first, second, third, fourth, and fifth ward.

––––––

The following were obtained from the census enumerations and or Harris's 1841 Directory:
    The addresses of business were not listed nor found; many of these merchants conducted their businesses from their homes.

George Schnauffer – shoemaker - 1841

Adam Keller – shoemaker - 1841

Tersius Kramer – shoemaker - 1841

Heamline Bimber – shoemaker - 1850

Thaddeus Cramer – shoemaker – 1841, 1850

Andrew Gatse – shoemaker - 1850

Conrad Raese – shoemaker - 1850

John M Sulzle – shoemaker - 1850

George Lais(Lay) – shoemaker – 1841, 1850, 1860,

Charles Schropp – shoemaker – 1850, 1860, 1870

Gottlieb Blum – boot/shoe maker - 1860

John Eitmiller – boot/shoe maker 1860

Charles Rosse – booth/shoe maker - 1860

Conrad Rosse – boot/shoe maker - 1860

William Stewart – shoemaker - 1860

John Davis – shoemaker – 1860, 1869, 1870   His residence was the *bank of river* in 1869.

Felix Lais - boot / shoe maker – 1860, 1870

Phelix Lay – shoemaker – 1870, 1880   His occupation was listed as a *Gentleman* in 1869.

Henry Metchan – shoe maker - 1870

Caspar Pfankucker-boot/shoe maker – 1870

Chas. Schrapp – shoemaker - 1869, 1876 – res Ohio Street (now by Fifth/Sixth Streets.

George Lay –shoemaker– 1869 -res. Third Street/Washington Ave In 1876 he was listed as a *gentleman.*

Casper Pfankuch – shoemaker – 1869, 1876 – res. Ohio Street (now by Fifth/Sixth Streets).

*** *** *** *** ***

CARPET MAKERS and WEAVERS

George Reiff – weaver
1841, 1850

_____

Jacob Duer
1841

_____

C. W. Grimm – carpet weaver – 1608 Virginia Avenue
1912   Charles lived in the same building.

_____

John Baker – carpet weaver
1860, 1870   He was retired in 1880.

_____

John Becker – carpet weaver
1876

*** *** *** *** ***

CLEANERS

W. L. Dixon – 1135 Pennsylvania Avenue
        1912 he had a dry cleaning business mixed in with his clothing and the tailoring businesses.
            See previously under Tailors.

_____

National Cleaners and Laundry – 1103 Pennsylvania Avenue
1928, 1930, 1935, 1936, 1953
        Dry cleaning dresses was their specialty. They also did alterations in 1935.
        In 1936, the address of the business was 1107 Pennsylvania Avenue
        Sep 1953 building was sold and bldg was razed in 1954 for new bank building.

> NATIONAL Cleaners. Monaca—
> Men's suits. $1.00; topcoats. $1 00;
> ladies' plain coats. $1 00. For other
> prices call Rochester 295-R or 1103
> Pennsylvania avenue, Monaca.
>   8 8-14inc

1929

_____

Monaca Cleaners and Dryers – 1307 Pennsylvania Avenue
1929

_____

Alexander's Cleaners – 1309 Pennsylvania Avenue
1956

_____

John's Tailor Shop and Cleaners   aka   John's Tailors & Cleaning –
1965, 1967

_____

Franklin Cleaners – 2089 Pennsylvania Avenue
1957

———

Meryl Ruby – had a cleaner shop – unknown location
1930   He lived at 1103 Pennsylvania Avenue.

———

Chinese Laundry and dwelling – 900 block Pennsylvania Avenue
          Located in the old Ark Building until May 1926.
                    The Ark was razed for the new Penn Theatre to be built (1926).
          1900 – Woht Gee was *laundryman* on Pennsylvania Avenue (located by Morris Barnett and
                    Justus Merkel/blacksmith).
          1902/03 - Sam Wah– laundry – Eighth Street -   He lived at the same location.
          1910 – Sam Young was proprietor – laundry.
          1920 – Ping Fong had business in 2 storey building at 811 Pennsylvania Avenue.

———

Nu-Way Speedy Wash Laundromat – 1103 Pennsylvania Avenue (storeroom)
                              -956-958 Pacific Avenue (plant)
early 1940s, 1952, 1965, 1970, 1974, 1977
          Coin operated in the 1970s.   In 1956 they went by name of Nu-Way Quality Cleaners
                                        "Monaca's only cleaning plant."

> # Grand Reopening
> **A Super Deluxe Cleaning Service**
> **New Modern Equipment**
> ## Nu-Way Quality Cleaners
> Store – 1103 Penna. Ave.
> Plant – 956-958 Pacific Ave.
> **MONACA**
> Phone Rochester 2649

1952

———

Ralph Zigarelli was listed on tax lists as having a dry cleaners at 1004 Pennsylvania Avenue in 1928 - 1943

Peter and Mary Gagianes were also listed as dry cleaners at 1004 Pennsylvania Avenue in 1940 - 1942.

          It is not clear who worked there and/or who were owners during the years the businesses
          overlapped.

———

          The next few listed were/are located where the former Harbison building stood until
                    mid 1932 to 1940s.   A Dairy Queen was built there and the Harbison building was
                    razed along with others. (The shape of the current building originates from Dairy
                    Queen).

Snowy White VIII Laundry – 901 Pennsylvania Avenue

Greenry Laundry -   corner of Pennsylvania and Ninth Street – 901 Pennsylvania Avenue

Laundry Centre – 901 Pennsylvania Avenue - corner of Ninth / Pennsylvania Avenue - Current

*** *** *** *** ***

GENERAL and MISCELLANEOUS BUSINESSES

Tony Olszanski – merchant of general store – 714 Pennsylvania Avenue
1930   He lived in same building.   (See Grocery section, too.)

———

Schnitzler's Store – general store   - in 1901 – corner of Pennsylvania Avenue and Sixth Street
                                    – then 310 Ninth Street - Citizen's Bank Building
1901, 1908
                Owned by Jacob Schnitzler.
                Jacob was selling a dun* driving horse in Jul 1908.
                                    *a dull grayish-brown color

BRING IN THE
BABIES
and Get a Fine
GOLD RING
Free of Charge.

To every baby brought to my store
under one year old I will make them a
present of a fine gold ring.   I also carry
a fine lot of Jewelry at the lowest prices
to be found anywhere and every article
is guaranteed to wear from 5 to 25 years.
See our fine lot of Toys and Holiday
Goods, as well as fine assortment of Men's
and Boys' Dress and Working Shirts.
Full line of Tobacco and Cigars.   Everything up to date at The Racket store,

JACOB SCHNITZLER,
Proprietor.

One Door Below Miller's Bakery.
Cor. Pennsylvania Ave., and 6th St.

MONACA. PA.

Dec 1901 ad

———

Thomas DeSilva – Pennsylvania Avenue
1903
                Thomas DeSilva/DeSilvey proprietor.
                He was formerly of South Sharon, PA, opened a racket store Apr 16, 1903.
                Store was in the new Wurzel building on Pennsylvania Avenue (next to N. Wurzel's real estate).
                Mr. DeSilva and family lived on the second floor as soon as the building was completed.
                The Pennsylvania Avenue racket store closed down and he opened the "Stag" restaurant in
                        Conway in Sept 1903.
                The store was taken over by Joseph McMillan who made it a restaurant.
                        It was 1195, 1317, or 1395 Pennsylvania Avenue (the only information on the exact
                        location I could find stated "close to Twelfth Street").

                *Fun Fact: Most racket stores in the early 1900s were the same as general
                department stores.   They sold many different types of items.*

———

Eddis L. Hood General Store – 1198 Pennsylvania Avenue
1898, 1902, 1903, 1920
          He married Anna L.; they lived at same address as store.

————————

F. L. Wilson & Company – general store - Pennsylvania Avenue
1902, 1904
          He had a five room house for sale in Monaca in 1902.

————————

J. M. Irons – Pennsylvania Avenue
1902, 1903
          Dealer in carpets, wall paper and stationery.
          Dealer in Real Estate and Fire Insurance, too.

————————

A. Dengel's General Store – 1099 Bechtel Street   (now Gallagher's location)
1956   Sold storm windows.   Also had supplies for raising chinchillas.

————————

Monaca Variety / Dry Good Store – 1304 Pennsylvania Avenue
1929, 1930

————————

Leary's Notion Store   aka   Leary's Novelty Store   –1107 Pennsylvania Avenue (in 1911)
1903, 1911, 1913, 1925
          D. F. Leary, proprietor
          Daniel F. Leary lived in Monaca since 1854. He learned the decorating trade and was employed
               at Phoenix Glass Co.   Later he formed the Leary Advertising Company who painted
               many of the valley buildings.   He continued to decorate theatres and hotels.
          See Hardware section for more information.

————————

Henry Finn – Notions Store – 1019 Pennsylvania Avenue
1910, 1912, 1913
          Henry married Lilian ___ and they resided in the same building in 1912. Their daughter, Amanda,
               was a dressmaker.

————————

William Johnston – Notion Merchant - 1200 block of Pennsylvania Avenue (2 doors from Hamilton Hotel)
1892, 1893, 1900, 1910

————————

Gordon's Cut Rate – 906 or 916   Pennsylvania Avenue
1942, 1944
          Sold Easter candies and flowers in 1944.

> Just arrived for your Easter
> Corsage luminous creations:
> orchids, gardenias, roses and
> earrings. Gordon's Cut Rate,
> 916 Penna. Ave., Monaca, Pa.
>   4 3-8 inc

1944

————————

Harry's Dollar Store – 906 Pennsylvania Avenue
1928, 1929, 1931   Harry Burke proprietor; he resided at same address.

————————

Thompson's Cut Rate – unknown address
1954

———

Fisher's Store aka   "The Corner" – 1001 Pennsylvania Avenue (corner of Penna and Washington)
1903, 1912, 1924, 1938, 1953, 1965

> News stand / confectionary store…….. I could have easily listed this store several places because he sold furniture, groceries, cigars, newspapers, greeting cards, confectionery, etc.   It was definitely a *General Store*.
>
> Elmer H. Fisher – owner in 1903.   The family lived behind the building at 315 Tenth Street.   Had a number of improvements made at his confectionary and cigar store in 1903.   Did more improvements to his store room in Mar 1917.   Put a new addition to his store in Jun 1919.   Several news items stated Mr. Fisher only had one arm, but I never found how this occurred.
>
> Fisher's was considered a sub-station for The Daily Times newspaper (also Mullen's News Depot).
>
> Elmer and Clara lived in Monaca from at least 1914 until their deaths.   She was a teacher and helped in the store.   Mr. Fisher was active in the community; he formed a six piece string orchestra in 1903.
>
> o   The home and storeroom were owned by Ms Eleanor Fisher, d/o Elmer & Clara, in 1953 and both the buildings were razed in 1954 for the new bank building to be constructed.
>
> Elmer lived with his parents in Rochester in 1900, Elmer married Clara Dunham; they only had one child.
>
> The family's dedication to Monaca was always evident. There was an Elmer and Clara Fisher Scholarship Fund set up for deserving Monaca high school seniors.

1946 ad

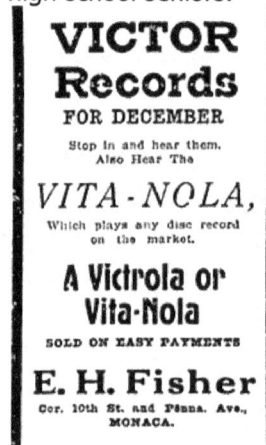

Jan 1918 ad

———

__?__   -   Keystone Block building - Pennsylvania Avenue
1909

> No name, but listed as a "new 5 and ten cent store" that opened.

———

Fred J. Stevens /Monaca Heights Green House
1906   Fred J. Stevens, proprietor.

———

Andy's Store – 100 Fourth Street
1954

———

Simoni's Baseball Cards – Monaca
1990

———

Pop's General Store – 1016 Pennsylvania Avenue
1998

United 5 & 10 - 1116-1120 Pennsylvania Avenue
1931 through 1979
     Originally occupied by a place called Steins, then Margolis.
     Opened 1931.   Founded and owned by John Sabo, then his daughter Violet and her husband
         Jack Hayes took over in 1969.   Closed in 1979.

This building was built by Margolis and he had his clothing store here.

| 1920s | Pennsylvania Avenue | Margolis then 5 & 10 | Wahl Street, then building with awning became Monaca Men's and Boys' Store |

When Jack Hayes decided to close the store after 48 years of being in business, there was a virtual treasure chest of assorted unsold merchandise that had been collecting over the years. Many of the items found in the often ignored basement were from the 1930s. It was a common practice to pack away toys and items after a Christmas season and then the next year new toys and other merchandise would come out, so the old goods just kept accumulating.   With the basement stockroom seldom being used after John's daughter and son-in-law took over, they just didn't explore or clear out the cluttered stock room to see what was actually there until the store was closing.

At the time of the closing, they marked down all the items on the main floor for sale and clearing out shelves, then they had all the items in the basement storeroom appraised and had a special auction and sale of those items.   This sale was not open to the general public, only to interested collectors .

They found "piles" of Depression glass of all sizes, with a large bowl still marked at its original price of 25 cents.   Some of the other items found in the basement storeroom were a whole case of early model projectors- little metal boxes with a bulb in them and a small crank on the side and film loops for them starring Betty Boop, Popeye, Koko, and other comic favorites; many trays, boxes and other items with grand names from Coca-Cola to Big Ben; an expensive doll for her time– a Horsman doll that would have cost $5.95 in her day; a 1930 "Electrocuter" electric mouse trap; toys with the markings "Made in Occupied Japan"; other old glass and ceramic items; clocks made from many eras- some with moving merry go rounds to ones with a gear that represents a moving spinning wheel.   Just shelves and shelves ready for the collectors to purchase.

2016 view of building

The entire first floor of this building was the former United 5 & 10 with access through both front entries.

Jul 1949

Fun fact: Depression glass was originally very cheap, yet very pretty.   It was made with a stamped pattern that resembled cut glass.   Because people could purchase it at such a low cost, people used it for everyday purposes and saved their better quality china for special occasions; therefore a lot of Depression glass was broken during its constant use.   Today's interest in Depression glassware has driven the prices up quite considerably.

Adolphus Bocking – artist – 1860

———

Emil Bott – artist – 1860, 1870

———

Auguste Cimotti – lithographic – 1860

———

Tropic Land – 1306 Pennsylvania Avenue
1955, 1956
    John Sproull proprietor.
    Listed as Pet Supply Center and sold birds, animals and reptiles plus complete line of supplies.

BEAVER VALLEY'S
PET SUPPLY CENTER
Drop in and See
Our Interesting Display
of Tropical Fish

One of the Largest Collections
In Beaver Valley

Canaries—Parakeets—Parrots
or Any Kind of
Bird—Animal or Reptile

Come In and
Tell Us What You Want—
COMPLETE LINE OF SUPPLIES
Open:
12 to 6 P.M. Except Wednesday
Saturdays 11 A.M. to 9 P.M.

1306 PENNSYLVANIA, MONACA, PA.
SPruce 4-5601.

Our Motto: "GREETED WITH A SMILE"
Prop., JOHN SPROULL

2016 view (Now all boarded up.)

———

J. L. Smith Bottling Plant – 307 Ninth Street
1930   (this would have sat on lot at the corner of Ninth and Maple Alley – behind laundry
                    business or building beside Monaca Auto Sales)
    There was a fire at this business Aug 4, 1930.   J. L. was at a desk in the building and saw smoke
        coming from the ceiling area.   The firemen had to cut holes in the roof to control fire. They saved
        the fire from spreading to the American Legion home, a barber shop and other adjoining buildings.
        One storey frame structure, contained large quantities of sugar for manufacturing of soft drinks.
        Building owned by heirs of Paulus E. Koehler the former owner of the building.

———

Nehi Bottling Works – 616 Pennsylvania Avenue
1929

———

A. C. Antoline Advertising and Office Supply Co. – 1526 Washington Avenue
1945, 1988,
       Advertising agency/marketing consultant/office furniture/stationery.   Opened in 1945.

———

Municipal Signs and Sales
1990

———

Tammy's Lil' Treasures – 1108 Pennsylvania Avenue
2003 through 2013   Owned by Tammy DeFelice.

———

Tuma Lawn Service and Landscaping – 1369 Chestnut Street
Opened in 1956, current

———

J. Nicoletta's – 1199 Pennsylvania Avenue
1994

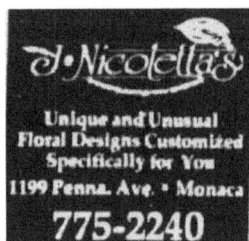
1994

———

Monaca Flower Shoppe – Indiana Avenue
1929
       Miss Esther Steiner was employed in the shoppe.

———

Johnson Flowers – 1034 Pennsylvania Avenue
1958 to 1990
       Opened – 1958.   Mrs. Helen Johnson did flower arranging demonstrations in 1959.
       David Cochran owned the building, selling it the Johnsons in 1975.
       Glenn W. Johnson owner until 1989, they retired and sold business to……
       Gary & Cindy Schwarz owned the building and business in 1990 through 2006.
         Lucenta Schwarz was sole owner in 2006, then sold building to Guy and Tamara Celeste.

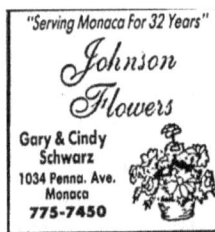
—1990 ad

———

Forget Me Not Flowers – 1206 Pennsylvania Avenue
1995   Kathryn Oravitz – owner.   Sold live and silk and wire flowers.

———

Lily of the Valley Floral and Gift – 215 B Ninth Street
2001, 2002   Theresa Yhelka – owner.

Lily of the Valley
Floral & Gift Shop

HOURS:
Monday thru Friday - 10:00am - 5:00pm
Saturday 10:00am - 3:00pm
215 B 9th Street, Monaca, PA 15061
724-728-7781

*Take advantage of our free delivery
in Beaver County.*

2002 ad

_____

Gift Shop – 318 Ninth Street
1941, 1942
        Ad said "Wanted   Beaver Valley ladies to visit the new Gift Shop at 318 Ninth Street.
        1942 gifts are now on display."

_____

Walsh Flower Shop - 316 Ninth Street
1941

FLOWERS for
TABLE DECORATIONS
at the
COOKING SCHOOL
Come From the
WALSH FLOWER SHOP
316 Ninth Street,   Monaca, Pa.
Floral Table Decorations Given Free as Our Gift to Someone Attending Each Session of the Cook School

_____

9th Street Floral and Gifts – 215 Ninth Street
1995, 1998
        This site was formerly the building of Bittner's Restaurant; currently it is an eatery again.

Fresh and Silk
Arrangements
for
MOTHER'S DAY
9th STREET FLORAL
215 9th Street, Monaca, PA
728-7781
Hours: Mon., Tues., Thurs., Fri. 10 - 5
Wednesday and Saturday 10 - 3

1995

_____

Busy Bee Hive –
1902   Opened Dec 6, 1902. Sold Christmas and Holiday gifts and toys.

_____

Earl Bros. Architects – Pennsylvania Avenue
1903

Owners - John Earl and Charles Earl.
They were hired to prepare plans for a new school building to be built at Allaire.
They prepared the plans for George Bartel's new confectionery store on Pennsylvania Avenue.

Earl Bros.,――――

Plans and Specifications and
Details Furnished.
Architects.

Construction superintended, estimates given, correspondence
solicited. Give us a call before building.

Pennsylvania Avenue,   -   MONACA, PA.

1903 ad

―――――

Harry C. Simpson, Sr. – music store / pianos, etc. – 1298 Pennsylvania Avenue
1901, 1902, 1903, 1920

There is a small building behind 1298, could this have been his store room ?   He married
L. Ada; they resided at same address as store.   He handled sewing machines also.
There was a 2 storey office building adjoining Simpson's building – Dr. Todd was
in the 2nd floor office; building was John Anderson's.

―――――

Louis Love – Music Teacher (private lessons) - 1030 Indiana Avenue

―――――

Blanche Huggens/Higgens– Music Teacher – Atlantic Avenue
1900

―――――

Frank Chamberlain – music teacher in his home – 913 Pennsylvania Avenue
1920

―――――

Eleanor Schachern – music teacher in her home – 1106 Atlantic Avenue
1930

―――――

Helen Schachern – musician in a theatre
1920

She lived at 1106 Atlantic Avenue

―――――

W. F. Frederick Piano Co. – Pennsylvania Avenue
1922

―――――

Guy Alexander – piano rebuilder/piano tuning – 415 Fourteenth Street
1924, 1925

―――――

Frederick Grofs – piano maker
1850

―――――

Frederick Bechtel – Music Dealer – res Atlantic Avenue
1900

———

John E. McMichael – certified piano tuner, repairing – 802 Pennsylvania Avenue
1938

———

Metz's Music Store – Pennsylvania Avenue Extension
1906, 1909
     Owned by Mrs. R. F. Metz.
     She sold records and Edison phonographs and supplies.

1906 Edison

———

Ziegler's Music Store - 1300 block on Pennsylvania Avenue – (a few buildings down from Taormina's)
1978

———

Dr. Doyle's Disco Den – 898 Pennsylvania Avenue - corner of Ninth Street and Pennsylvania Avenue
                                              - then to 1200 Pennsylvania Avenue
1978, 1983
     Tom Doyle of Center Township – owner.   Sold records – new ones came in every Tuesday.   Business was sold, building was razed for the revitalization program for Phoenix's growth; so Dr. Doyle's Disco Den moved to Pennsylvania Avenue (near Twelfth Street) between 1979/80 to 1983.   A picture of the store may be found in Street View section.

Dr. Doyle's
Disc Den
"Lowest Record Prices
in Beaver County"
1200 Pennsylvania Avenue
775-5234
11 - 9 Mon. through Sat.

———

Mars Drums – 1028 Pennsylvania Avenue then 308/310 Ninth Street
2008, 2011
     Owners – Michael Phillis and Craig Zeigler

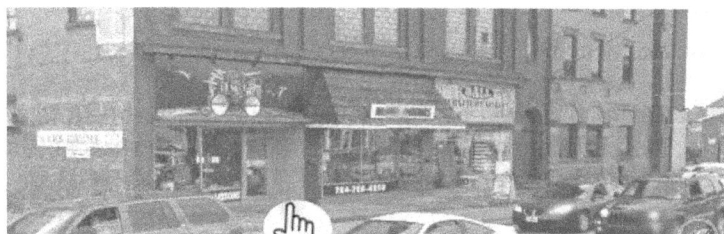

———

Twice As Nice Thrift Store – 1213 Pennsylvania Avenue
1978, 1982   David Chandler and Alberta Chandler of Monaca owners.

———————

John E. Bittner – dancing master –
1898, 1903   John also had a billiard parlor.

JOHN E. BITTNER,
Dancing Master.
All Communications Addressed to
Monaca Will Receive Prompt
Attention.

1902/03

———————

Doris Singer Dance Studio
1956, 2000

DORIS SINGER DANCE STUDIOS

Aliquippa · Ambridge · Baden · Freedom · Monaca
New Brighton · Ohioview · Rochester · Sewickley

Staffed by DMA Teachers

— Dance Masters of America —

Private and class instruction in all
types of dancing.

For Information Ph: CO 6-2113 · 6-0266

Doris Singer

In 2000, Doris was still teaching dance.   Her one studio was in Ambridge then.

Times photos by Sylvester Washington Jr
At age 68, Doris Singer Kokoski is still dancing. In the photo above, she instructs a young student at her dance studio above the Ambridge American Legion on Duss Avenue.

———————

__?__ Monaca Park Dancing Academy-
1919
          Held its first "open to the public dance" given by the local fire department to benefit
               the fund for the "welcome home celebration" for returning soldiers, sailors, and
               marines. This dance was on Saturday, Aug 9, 1919.

———————

Rhythms In Motion - dance classes - 1317 Pennsylvania Avenue
Current

Rhythms in Motion Dance Studio
BALLET • TAP • JAZZ
KINDER DANCE
PRE-SCHOOL • HIP HOP

OPEN HOUSE & REGISTRATION

Our 9th Annual Open House and Registration will be held on the following days:
AUGUST 23, 2007 FROM 4-8 P.M.
AUGUST 24, 2007 FROM 4-8 P.M.
SEPTEMBER 5, 2007 FROM 5-7 P.M.

This is the perfect opportunity to speak with owner, Kim Schlott and the Dance Instructors to plan your child's journey through Dance at Rhythms in Motion Dance Studio!

Call us today at 724-775-4088 for more information.
CLASSES BEGIN SEPTEMBER 8, 2007!
1317 Pennsylvania Avenue, Monaca, PA 15061
www.rhythmsinmotiondancestudio.com

2007

_____

Ceramics by Pauline Icenhour – 1133 Pennsylvania Avenue
1978, 1990
    This location was formerly called "Dixon Building" and Monaca Hardware Supply Co. had business
        in this building; currently the Bluewater Cleaning Service.

"Best Wishes On Your 150th Year"
CLASSES NOW FORMING!
New Students Welcome

CERAMICS
by Pauline Icenhour
1133 Pennsylvania Ave., Monaca
728-5982

1990 ad

_____

Sounds of Success – 699 Pennsylvania Avenue
1995   Car audio store.

_____

Auto Effects – 191 Ninth Street
2006

_____

Steed Audio Inc. – 1133 Pennsylvania Avenue - 1038 Pennsylvania Avenue
1977, 1986, 1992   Sound and lighting contractors.

_____

Evolution Audio – 699 Pennsylvania Avenue
2001, 2004
    Opened in Oct 2001 – rented ½ a barn behind store for workshop and storage.   Had an old barn behind
    the building that burned early Feb 2004. The barn had been the Potter company's and was considered a
    landmark in Monaca.

_____

The Video Hospital – 405 Wahl Street
1990   VCR, camera & audio repair business.

_____

Club Software – 403 Pennsylvania Avenue
1995, 1998   Owners Chris and Judy Dawson opened business in Feb 1995.
            System sales and hardware.

_____

Video Force – 1428 Pennsylvania Avenue
1980s, 1990, 2004

>Opened in early 1980s.   Owners – Paul and Lisa Sylvester took over the store in May, 2004.
They had a personal greeter – Blazer, a black waggy-tailed pug-mix.

1990 ad

_____

Sterling's Photo Parlors – 1034 Pennsylvania Avenue, near Thirteenth Street
1903, 1906, 1908, 1922

>Owned by Harry E. Sterling.   He erected the building in Apr 1903.
>>Daniel F. Leary did the painting and decorating and outside signs.
>Kodaks, Kodak supplies and picture framing.
>In May 1903 they were offering Tin type photos – four for 25 cents; baby pictures were
their specialty.   In 1908 he had the front of his studio painted.

May 1906

_____

Bailey's Photo Finishing and Engraving – old Bank Building – Pennsylvania Avenue
1924

>Don W. Bailey photo-finisher.

_____

Dentzer Studio – Photographer – 1307 Pennsylvania Avenue – 1209 Pennsylvania Avenue (1929)
1912, 1924, 1930

>William Dentzer was the owner.
1209 Pennsylvania Avenue is now an empty lot – no building.

_____

Dellie Martin Studios – 1209 Pennsylvania Avenue
1940, 1990

>Opened late 1940s -Owned by Dellie Alexander & Martin Sebastian – did photography for high
school groups.

_____

Studio One Graphics – 1306 Pennsylvania Avenue, then 1101 Pennsylvania Avenue by 1990
1989, 1990, 1998

      Opened in 1989.   Marsha Wheeler – owner, designer & design consultant;
      Jim Moore was the sign maker.

1306 Penna(now boarded up)

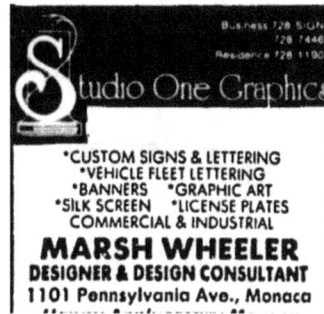

Business 728 SIGN
728 7446
Residence 728 1190

Studio One Graphics

*CUSTOM SIGNS & LETTERING
*VEHICLE FLEET LETTERING
*BANNERS *GRAPHIC ART
*SILK SCREEN *LICENSE PLATES
COMMERCIAL & INDUSTRIAL

MARSH WHEELER
DESIGNER & DESIGN CONSULTANT
1101 Pennsylvania Ave., Monaca

1990

Luci's Studio – 1000 Pennsylvania Avenue
1949

      Photography and supplies.

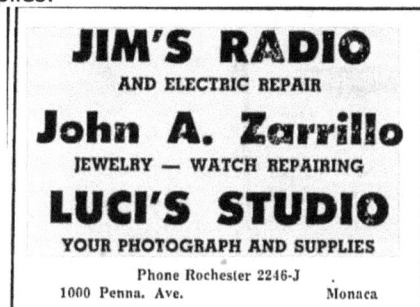

JIM'S RADIO
AND ELECTRIC REPAIR
John A. Zarrillo
JEWELRY — WATCH REPAIRING
LUCI'S STUDIO
YOUR PHOTOGRAPH AND SUPPLIES
Phone Rochester 2246-J
1000 Penna. Ave.   Monaca

Jul 1949

Oak Tree Studios – 1126 Pennsylvania Avenue
2010, 2011
      Production and rehearsal studio.

Imagine That Photography & Design – 309 Ninth Street
2000s

Deem Photographic Illustrations – 1417 Pacific Avenue
1984
      Edward Deem, Jr. owner.

Vaccarelli Studio – 1309 Pennsylvania Avenue
1977   Did portraits, weddings, commercial, group pictures.

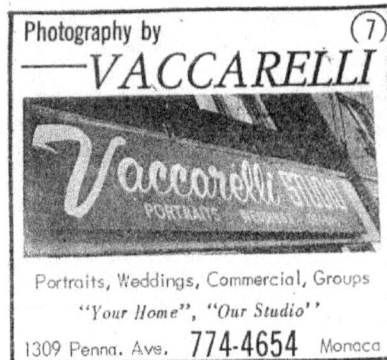

Photography by   (7)
VACCARELLI

Vaccarelli Studio

Portraits, Weddings, Commercial, Groups
"Your Home", "Our Studio"
1309 Penna. Ave.   774-4654   Monaca

Willard Homes (office) – 1136 Pennsylvania Avenue
1940, 1959, 1960   This was former location of fruit business of M. Cortese.

WILLIARD HOMES
OFFICE
1136 Pennsylvania Ave., Monaca   SP 5-6800   1959

Monaca store / Hall of Fame / Souvenir Store – 1098 Pennsylvania Avenue
Current   Opened in 1992.

Beaver County Model Railroad and Historical Society – 416 Sixth Street
Current
        This was the former Sixth Street Pittsburgh and Lake Erie Railroad depot in Monaca.

Western Pennsylvania Operating Engineers Joint Apprenticeship and Training Center – 1136 Penna Ave
1970

Joseph Zigerell – retail cigars and tobacco – 1308 Pennsylvania Avenue
1912   Joseph and Carmine lived at the same building as the business.

Shafer's Racket Store (Schaffer/Schafer) – 715 Pennsylvania Avenue
1903, 1904
        J. A. Shafer – owner.   Sold candy, cigars, and other miscellaneous items.
        They moved into this location; formerly that of Ackerman & Jepson.

William Davis – cigar maker
1870, 1880

———————

John M. Davis – cigar maker
1876

———————

Thomas Smithson – tobacconist
1850

———————

Guy Smithson - tobacconist
1850

———————

Thomas Franklin - tobacconist
1850

———————

Avander Humphreys - tobacconist
1850

———————

V. J. Brucker – Pennsylvania Avenue
1898, 1903   Cigars, tobacco, and confectionery.

———————

Mrs. George Lay – cigars, etc.
1892, 1893   George Lay, Jr. was a clerk in store.

———————

Mrs. James B. McClatchey – cigars, etc.
1892, 1893

———————

James Miller – cigars, etc.

———————

Mrs. Magdalena Varner – confectionery and cigars, etc.
1898, 1903

———————

Nicholas Wurzel – cigars, etc.
1892, 1893

———————

King Beaver Cigars – 1106 Pennsylvania Avenue
Current

———————

The Quilt Basket – 1116 Pennsylvania Avenue
1987, 2002   Linda Bauman & Maxine Holmes, owners.   They had their business since 1987, but I don't
                know if it was always in Monaca.   Sold supplies and offered classes.

———————

Beaver Valley Propeller Service – 1531 Atlantic Avenue
1990   Marine propeller sales & reconditioning business.

_____

Adrian Glass Co. – 1101 Pennsylvania Avenue
1968, 1978

ADRIAN GLASS CO. –
Glasses, stemware, etc.
Beautifully handcut &
decorated. Order for
Christmas. 1101 Penna. Ave.,
Monaca, 774-0200, 9 to 4:00
daily.

_____

The Cornerstone – 1414 Pennsylvania Avenue – 1200 block Pennsylvania Avenue
1978   Owned by Annette Kleist and Ruby Lucci.   Started Sep 28, 1978.   Religious gift store.

_____

Guy's – 1024 Nimick Avenue
1945   Study and reference Bibles, Christian cards and gifts.

_____

Religious Readings by Sister Ann – 1200 (rear) Pennsylvania Avenue
1960

Opening, Fri., July 8th
RELIGIOUS READING
by Sister Ann
Seek the advice of Sister Ann.
She is gifted to read and help
people. Many have come to her
from all walks of life for advice
and guidance.
1200 Pennsylvania Ave.
(In Rear)—Monaca
Open Daily 10 A.M. to 10 P.M.
Sunday 10 A.M. to 3 P M

1960

_____

H & R Block – 1306 Pennsylvania Avenue
1972   Opened the office Jan 1972.

_____

Carriage House Antiques - 925 Pennsylvania Avenue
Opened Dec 1987.
Owners – Tom and Carol Miller of Oakdale.
Remodeled the building (used to be Birner's, then Ziggy's Tux).

_____

Aerial Fire Equipment Co. – 1213 Virginia Avenue
1986

_____

Simon Shafer/Schaffer – proprietor of dance hall – unknown location
1920   He lived on Washington Avenue.

_____

Competitive Nutrition – 615 Pennsylvania Avenue – health food
Closed as of 2015

_____

Fashion Park – 1030 Pennsylvania Avenue
late 1990s/early 2000s, 2012

_____

Kidstuff – 1206 Pennsylvania Avenue
1992, 1993
Business that caters to children and adults – games, videos, movie rentals, candy
Opened Dec 1992.   Diane Henderson and Lauren Henry owners.

_____

Love Me Tender Day Care – 1299 Pennsylvania Avenue
1998

_____

Katy's Place Child Care Center – 819 Washington Avenue
1992

_____

Castle Toys & Games – 1030 Pennsylvania Avenue
2005, 2006
Owners - Jeffrey & Linda Lyden.   Opened business as of Dec 7, 2005.

_____

Family Dollar – 1221 Pacific Avenue
Current

_____

Beaver County Tourist Promotion Agency – 215 B Ninth Street
1992, 2000

Judy Tress and April Koehler – operators.　　The agency produced a calendar of events and a
　　Beaver County brochure that included a map of Beaver County.　All brochures were free.

**JUDY TRESS AND
APRIL KOEHLER**

The Beaver County Promotion Agency
has relocated to 215 B Ninth Street,
Monaca, PA 15061-2028. The agency
promotes Beaver County nationally,
regionally and locally. The agency produced a Calendar of Events and a
Beaver County brochure that includes
a map of Beaver County. All brochures
are free. If you want to promote an
event, know more or need brochures
— call us (412) 728-0212 or (800)
564-5009.

BEAVER COUNTY
TOURIST PROMOTION AGENCY

215 B Ninth Street
Monaca, PA 15061-2028
(412) 728-0212　　　(800) 564-5009

1992

_____

Campbell Transfer and Storage
　　Campbell Moving and Storage – 308 Ninth Street
1945, 1967

　　　　Building was purchased in Sep 1945 by William V. Campbell.
　　　　Building was also used for Coombs Furniture Exchange.
　　　　3 storey brick on the corner of Ninth Street and Washington Avenue.
　　　　Campbell Transfer & Storage Co. was an agent of Mayflower World-Wide Moving Service.
　　　　　(He also purchased the former First National Bank property on Pennsylvania Avenue, near Ninth
　　　　　St....OR....Was this just the Citizen Nat'l Bank building on Ninth Street ????)

Safe MOVING · STORAGE

CAMPBELL

Transfer & Storage
Phone Roch. 30　　　　　　　308 9th St.
M O N A C A

A Mayflower Warehouse

Jul 1949

_____

Former Field Office – 1712 Pennsylvania Avenue

This was former location of Barco Coal business.
(The former bus business building is seen here to the left (it is now razed).

————

King's Pool and Spa   aka   King Construction -2020 Beaver Avenue
Current
Swimming pool dealer – in ground swimming pools, spas, repair parts, pool
accessories, and pool and spas, chemicals.
Founded in 1978 by Glenn E. King.   The parent company is King's Construction which does
general construction and trucking services.

————

Clip and Cuddle – 923 Pennsylvania Avenue
1993, Current
Opened at 911 Pennsylvania Avenue in Feb 199; then moved to 923 Pennsylvania Avenue
(the former business building for Thad's Jewelers).

————

Colonial Supply, Inc. – 1221 Pacific Avenue
Current   Industrial supplies, textile mill supplies.

————

Bluewater Cleaning Service business - 1133 Pennsylvania Avenue
1982 to Current
Opened in Feb 1982.
Apts above – 1131 Pennsylvania Avenue – this bldg was originally called the Dixon Building.
Used to be Monaca Hardware Supply business (1133 Pennsylvania Avenue) and Ceramics by
Pauline.

————

Safety & Security by Veterans – 1307 Pennsylvania Avenue
Current
An independent, veteran owned business.   It provides safety and security gear for a variety of
professional industries, including police, fire, e.m.s, and construction; also have safety and retail
items for the general public.

————

Flesh Mechanics – 1414 Pennsylvania Avenue – tattoos
Current

_____

Magic Ink Tattoo – 1018 Pennsylvania Avenue
Current   Opened in Sep 2001.   Tim Powers - proprietor.

_____

Metro PCS Authorized Dealers – 1120 Pennsylvania Avenue
Current

_____

Dewdrop Gift Shop & Tea Room - 1309 Pennsylvania Avenue
2014, 2015

_____

Salutations Yoga Center – 1230 Pennsylvania Avenue
 2000, 2003
          Opened in 2000.   Formerly started in Bridgewater in 1999. Owners – Rob and Terri Turczany.   The
          center was assisting the CCBC with continuing education classes; also stated to be working side by side
          with *A Sense of Eden Spa and Salon* in 2003.

_____

Jiu-Jitsu Academy – Pride Lands Pgh Brazilian Jiu-Jitsu – 1126 Pennsylvania Avenue
Current

_____

Japanese Karate – One Strike Ichigeki Karate – 1299 Pennsylvania Avenue
2004, Current
          Grant Miller, owner.   Mr. Miller worked in Japan for many years; fluent in Japanese; teaches
          his students about Japanese culture as well as the martial arts; also offers classes in stretching,
          kickboxing, Japanese language, Sumi-e painting.

_____

Troia Eye & Lazer PC – 1100 Pennsylvania Avenue
Current
          Original buildings were razed and replaced with completely remodeled and modernized building
              in 2006; now a one store large, double building.

_____

Kurtz Monuments – 390 Sixth Street (corner of Pennsylvania Avenue and Sixth Street)
Current

_____

Rome Monument Works Artisan Center – 2080 Pennsylvania Avenue
Current
          The company was founded by Michael Dioguardi, a stone craftsman, who immigrated from Italy, settling in
          Rochester in 1930; started his own monument firm four years later. Basic business has been locally and
          family owned since 1934 and employs no commissioned salespeople. Rome Monument is a fourth-
          generation company creating personalized memorials for families in Western Pennsylvania, Eastern Ohio
          and Northern West Virginia.

_____

Daman's Fitt Camp – 390 Sixth Street, rear
2013

_____

Limmelrock Bros. – Moon or Monaca ?
1903   Undertaking establishment.   Also had a large livery.

_____

The LeRoy-Foster Co.
1917
        It appears from this ad, their main store was located in Rochester and they indeed carried quite
        a variety and range of items.   At the bottom of the ad they list their business in Monaca. Where and
        what type of music they were associated with in Monaca is still a mystery; as is the combination of
        the music business and undertaking business. I like that they noted they had a "Lady Assistant."
        I do not have any further information except their ad that was in a 1917 publication.....

THE FARMER'S STORE

where you will find everything needed to furnish the HOME complete.
Dressers, Chiffoniers, Bedroom Suits, Beds in Wood, Iron and Steel and
all colors, Mattresses, Springs, Kitchen Chairs, and Fine Dining Chairs,
Rockers, an endless variety, Pillows, Comforts, Rugs, large and small,
Linoleum, Congoleum Rugs, Couches, Davenports, Kitchen Cabinets, Sewing
Machines, Buffets, Sideboards, China Cabinets, Cupboards, Baby Carriages,
Go-Carts, Cradles, full line of Dishes, Stoves, all kinds, Sheet Music, Musical
Instruments, Edison Phonographs, Victrolas, and full line of records,
Pianos, Player Pianos, Piano Stools and Benches. Goods of Quality at
Lowest Prices.

THE LeROY-FOSTER CO., 82 Madison St., Rochester, Pa.

Near Conway Corners and Bridgewater Bridge

Beaver Co. Phone 5138   Bell Phone 138

THE LeROY-FOSTER CO., Monaca, Pa.
Music and Undertaking
Lady Assistant

_____

Adam and Emil Huff – corner of Pennsylvania Avenue and Fourth Street
1850 to 1906
        Adam used letter head that read "Adam Huff, Manufacturer of and Dealer in Fancy and Common Furniture
            of ALL Kinds – Undertaking a Specialty."
        The entire business was bought out by Batchelor Bros. in Jun 1906.
    Emil W, Adam's son, took a course in embalming and then became his father's partner, both in the
            undertaking business and furniture store; changing the name from just "Huff" to
            Adam Huff and Son.   Emil died in 1905 (44), one year prior to his father's death.
    Their undertaking rooms were in their home.
            See much more Huff's information under Furniture section.

_____

Harper J. Simpson Funeral Home – 1119 Washington Avenue
Current
        Began business in 1972.   This building was the former Dalzell Grocery Store.

_____

Hahn & Reno (Henry Hahn, Joseph I Reno), furniture dealers and undertakers – 422 Fourth Street in
                        Phillipsburg, (Fourth Street became Pennsylvania Avenue)
            Started furniture business in 1874, undertaking business was added in 1876.

Batchelor Bros. – started at 1012, 2nd floor, Pennsylvania Avenue – moved to 998 Atlantic Avenue
1898 to ____
            They also bought out Adam Huff's business.
            See much more of Hahn & Reno /Batchelor's and Huff's information under Furniture section.
        Batchelor Bros. business became.........................

Hall Funeral Homes Inc. – 998 Atlantic Avenue (corner Atlantic Avenue and Tenth Street)

then………

Schleifer Funeral Services, Inc
Funeral Homes & Cremation Services, Inc.
Current

*** *** *** *** ***

Miscellaneous businesses with limited additional information………….

Collectors Dreams – 1307 Pennsylvania Avenue – antiques

Doodlebugs Children's Store – 911 Pennsylvania Avenue – consignment store

Timeless Portraits – 911 Pennsylvania Avenue – Joan Yanchick - photography

Lucci Computers – 615 Pennsylvania Avenue – computer services

Providatek – 615 Pennsylvania Avenue – employment agency

K9 Detection Services, Inc. – 100 Ninth Street – exterminator

Terminix – 100 Ninth Street

S. Shasta Inc. – 300 Ninth Street –

Consultant Life Management – 193 Ninth Street – consultant business

Steel City Aquatics – 1327 Pacific Avenue

Applied Pest Management – 1101 Indiana Avenue

Children's Palace Day Care Center – 1499 Indiana Avenue #A

Children's Institute of Pittsburgh – 1598 Virginia Avenue – day care

Access 995 – 390 Sixth Street (internet providers) - 2010s

Leaf Pest Control – 100 Ninth Street - corner of Atlantic / Ninth Street - Current

Fergy's Vape – at 1030 Pennsylvania Avenue in 2015

Best Vape Shop - 615 Pennsylvania Avenue - Opened in 2016

*** *** *** *** ***

Larger ads Sol Ostrow's Clothing Store

1907

Tremendous Sacrifice Sale!
The Public Benefits!

The public of Monaca, Beaver county, and vicinity, will benefit greatly by the tremendous sacrifice sale of Sol Ostrow's $15,000 stock of clothing and furnishings. This entire stock is now in the hands of the National Salvage Company, of Philadelphia, for quick disposition. The National Salvage Company of Philadelphia, say they propose to sell two-thirds of this entire stock in ten days' time at prices about one-half actual cost of the merchandise. This will be a sacrifice sale of men's, boys' and children's clothing, such as the public of Monaca and surrounding country have never had before, or will ever have again.

The National Salvage Company say they will not move a dollar's worth of the goods away from Monaca, and that at the prices which the entire stock will be sold it should all be sold out inside of ten days' time. It is a sale which the public have an opportunity to attend about once in a life time, and our people of Monaca, Beaver county, and vicinity, will no doubt take advantage of this grand opportunity to secure for themselves clothing and furnishings, at about forty cents on the dollar.

The National Salvage Company informs us that they have engaged forty extra salespeople in order to serve the vast crowds who will attend this gigantic and most terrific sacrifice. We bespeak for this sale a most tremendous business, as The Sol Ostrow stock is practically a new stock of clothing, furnishings, etc., as it has only been established in business in Monaca but a few years, anduring that time he has carried only the most reliable makes and character of good quality clothing. Thousands of people will be attracted to Monaca to attend this sale, as the public well know when they are getting big bargains, and are always ready to save themselves one-half on their purchases, whenever that opportunity presents itself. Merchants from Monaca or surrounding country wishing to buy portions of this stock, or any part of the fixtures, will please call between the hours of eight and nine o'clock a. m., as all other hours will be devoted to the immense crowds of people who will wish to buy this stock out at retail.

Sol. Ostrow's big store at Monaca, which is now closed, will remain closed, in order to get the entire stock invoiced, and every article marked down to the lowest possible limit, in order to sell out the stock rapidly, and the store will not be open for business until the opening day of this great sacrifice Salvage Sale of Sol. Ostrow's stock, which starts Wednesday morning, July 17th, at nine a. m.

Let all who possibly can take advantage of this tremendous sacrifice sale and secure their share of the many grand bargains that will be offered. At the prices we understand this stock of men's, boys' and children's clothing will be sold at, the entire stock should melt away rapidly like a snowfall before a July sun.

The opening day of this big sale, Wednesday morning, July 17th, will be a collossal event. The public will snap up the bargains quickly. In justice to yourself you can't afford to miss this great sale. Drop everything, make your arrangements to be there, remember the opening day, Wednesday morning, July 17th, at nine a. m. If you value money, prepare accordingly. Sol. Ostrow's stock, now in the hands of the National Salvage Company of Philadelphia, and will positively be sold out in ten days at unheard of low prices.

1907

*** *** *** *** ***
*** *** ***

Restaurants and   Bars

Local trade wars between distributors

Wholesale Liquor   and   Brewers

Local "trade wars"

Moonshine

Wholesale Dealers and Distributors

Distributors and dealers of liquor in Monaca

RESTAURANTS and BARS

Monaca never had the lack of a good place to go to get a freshly cooked meal or join in some hometown talks to solve the problems of the world. The "eatery houses," grills, restaurants, parlors, and bars were always a staple in Monaca. A restaurant or lunch room in the mid/late 1800s and early 1900s would not have been quite what is typical nowadays (2016). Seating may not have always been made up of the same type of décor, probably from benches and mismatched tables also with mismatched chairs. Although the aroma of homemade dishes being made and baked goods would have filled the air, along with those would have been the burning embers of the coal or wood being used. What a constant mix of odors people endured in the earlier times.

Speaking of odors, amazing as it may sound, even in the mid/late 1800s and early 1900s, the number of deep fried foods eaten then was extensive. You could have easily found fried fish, fish balls, clams, oysters (very popular), chicken, potatoes, all kind of fritters, and doughnuts in any of the eatery houses. Fried foods were so popular that neighbors of these establishments often times complained of the odors emitted, since there were no high tech air ventilating or filtration systems at that time. It would have been the practice for these eateries to use cottonseed oil or some type of lard for cooking the fried foods; you can bet that very hot cottonseed oil or lard fumes would not have smelled very appetizing.

Coffee was also a popular item served in many of the lunch rooms and eateries, but my guess would have been it was likely outsold most of the time by alcoholic drinks. Up until about the 1890s or very early 1900s, most inexpensive restaurants would have charged 5 cents for a cup of coffee.

Undoubtedly these food establishments would have served foods that were grown or raised fairly close to their locations; most coming from the farm to table without much delay. The owners would have obtained the fresh foods directly from the local farmers, butchers, and hunters. Dairy products were probably the least satisfactory foods for true city dwellers. They could not keep their own cows mainly because of the threat of the cows becoming sick from being penned up and unable to graze. Likewise, the concern with milk being brought in from farther distances since there was a good chance it would not be "fresh." Many urban farmers realized the need for the city folks to have fresh milk; therefore, owning a dairy farm very close to the city was quite a profitable venture. Monaca had several such dairy farms just outside its city limits. Over the years, some of these dairy farms (in Moon / Center Township) were owned by J.A. Patterson, Henry Hartenbach, Frank Schade, Mr. Turnbull, Joseph Dusold, Tom Smoute, Fred Meany, Pete Fenzil, Dusold Family, Ralph Morris, and Jennings Weigel.

Fun Facts:
Family owned Brunton's Dairy in Hopewell Township, Beaver County is still an active
dairy farm after 185+ years in business and also still makes home deliveries (2015).

The Dusold Brothers operated an Echo Point Dairy Store at 1102 Pennsylvania Avenue
in the 1960s and 1970s and had an active dairy farm in Center Township.

Many times, you will notice that the restaurants and eatery houses were operated by women or will notice women made up the work forces that served and worked in them. Many of these women did so since they lacked the experience other than that of housewifery, but wanted or needed to have the funds and income to support either themselves or the household.

Coal and wood were used for the heating and firing of the ovens, stoves, and/or grills; as it became available, gas was next to be used.   By the earlier 1900s many of the businesses had electricity in Monaca.   Even with this luxury, many didn't have fancy lighting fixtures, instead usually but an individual and naked bulb dangling from a wire throughout to illuminate their cafes.   Many restaurants would have large glass front windows to let in natural light.   A well lit restaurant or business was a sign that there was nothing the owner or proprietor had to hide and especially in a gathering place, brightness continued to equate with good times.   Nowadays, a dimly lit room is said to create "atmosphere."

Although these next few pictures are not of Monaca establishments, they will give the reader a look back at what a typical Monaca restaurant or lunch room would have looked like in the very early 1900s.
Make note of the large glass windows that provided extra lighting in both example pictures of business.

Example of small town restaurant/eatery house   (this photo is NOT from Monaca).

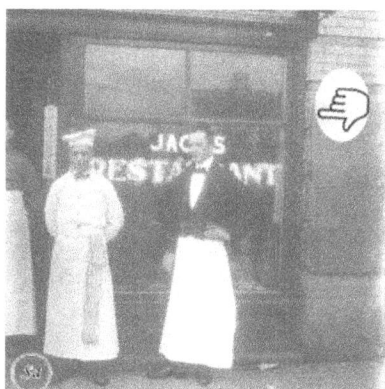

Example of a restaurant from 1903 (this photo is NOT from Monaca).

View of a typical lunch room setting from early 1900s (this is NOT from Monaca).
Nothing fancy for décor.   Note the exposed light bulb hanging from the celing.

It became a common practice for restaurants, cafés, and lunch rooms to also be the local "watering holes" of a town.   Even in today's similar businesses where there is a bar and liquor is sold, you will almost always find food also being served.

During prohibition, and for a few decades after, many of the bars were referred to as "Tap Rooms." This became a common name since the majority of the bar rooms would serve beer from a tap. During prohibition, the phrase "tap room" was most often used in less than flattering means to describe such a business or establishment, often used for places where there was something not totally legal going on.

Prohibition was not a popular time for the bar owners or persons who enjoyed consuming liquors. Monaca had its own share of problems during this era.   In my section on Wholesale Liquor, I have included quite a bit about interesting events and happenings of Monaca during the years of prohibition.   Although Monaca was a far cry from being like New York City or Chicago, it had quite the drama and its own numerous situations.

Typically, since most bars or "tap rooms" were within a café or restaurant, the larger windows for letting in the natural light would have been more common.   Like many other businesses, although the establishment may have been kept clean, there may have been shiny tin ceiling tiles in place, and nicely painted walls, but it would not have been very elaborate otherwise.   Greatly decorated businesses just were not very common in small communities.

The picture below is not from Monaca, but included to give a 1920 view of a bar or "tap room."

Next time you are in an older building, take a look up and see if you can find a tin tiled ceiling. This was a common practice if owners could afford the expense. This would be an example of what a *tin smith* or *tinner* would have done in the earlier eras in case you might have wondered. Today, owners leave the tiles in place but many have found it easier to paint over the tiles rather than try to keep them cleaned and shiny.

The current tin/copper ceiling at 308 Ninth Street. Note how ornate it all is.

———

Within the 1860 census there were two men who had their occupations listed as *eatery house:*

George Duerr and Anthony Simon

There is mention of each of these men having restaurants somewhere in Phillipsburg, but I could not find any additional information on these men, the names of their establishments, or an address of their businesses.

———

Harry Miller – restaurant
1892, 1893

———

Jane Hamilton – restaurant owner / confectionery – unknown address
1898, 1900, 1903
> Jane was widowed and living by herself in 1900; she lived on Pennsylvania Avenue, so the business may have been there also.

———

Lena Sullivan – restaurant owner – unknown address
1890s, 1900
> Lena was widowed in 1900 at age 34 with 4 children.
> Her husband William is listed with a business in the late 1800s, then Lena took over.
> They lived on Pennsylvania Avenue, so the business may have been in the same building.
> > See Confectionery section.

———

Lizzie Baker – restaurant owner – unknown address
1900
        Lizzie was widowed in 1900 at age 45, living with 2 older children on Pennsylvania Avenue.
        The business may have been at the same address.

————

Hood Beanery – Only restaurant in Monaca at that time – 1101 Pennsylvania Avenue
                              -Then corner of Twelfth Street and Pennsylvania Avenue
1900, 1912
        Owned by Hood family – Robert L. and Mary.
        In Mar 1904, he moved from the corner of Eleventh Street and Pennsylvania Avenue to the
            corner of Twelfth Street and Pennsylvania Avenue (formerly occupied by Joseph McClurg).
            They lived in the same building as the business in 1912.

————

Bittner's Restaurant /lunch room and Billiard Parlor – 807 Pennsylvania Avenue (in 1912)
            –1315 Pennsylvania Avenue(1910) - beside Lindsay's which was at 1317 Pennsylvania
                    Avenue - then 215 Ninth Street in 1927, 1928
1900, 1902, 1910, 1916, 1940
        John E. Bittner owner.
            John b 1866 married Ida L. __; they lived at 932 Washington Avenue in 1912.
                John was widowed; still a chef at the restaurant in 1930 at age 64; he was
                living at same address as restaurant - 215 Ninth Street with his son-in-law and
                daughter – Godfrey and Beryl Miller.
                      Also see Wholesale Liquor for more on Godfrey.
        Restaurant was in front of building.
            Pool and billiard room was in the rear.
        Sep 30, 1908 – He was planning to do a number of improvements to restaurant.
        Articles stated hot and cold lunch served at all times – tables in first class condition.
        John was well known for his turtle soup.
        Called "Johnny's" and "Bittner's Beanery."

BITTNER'S

Restaurant
and Billiard
Parlor. ͻ

Hot and Cold Lunch Served at all
Times. Tables in First-Class
Condition.

Pennsylvania Ave., Monaca, Pa.

Feb 1902

        John's daughter and son-in-law took over the business just after 1930 and it became ....

Miller's Restaurant   aka   Miller's Dutch Kitchen – 215 Ninth Street
1930, 1940
        Godfrey and Beryl Miller – operators.   They lived at same address.
            In 1910, 1920 – Godfrey was married to Iva; he was then married to Beryl (Bittner).
            Beryl was a waitress in the restaurant.
                John Bittner was Beryl's father.
            Beryl lost her father and her husband in 1944.
        It was also occasionally referenced as *Dutch Bar.*
        Godfrey Miller was also a dealer in liquors, wines and beers in 1898.

————

Enterprise Restaurant – corner of Pennsylvania Avenue and Eleventh Street

        (probably at 1099 Pennsylvania Avenue since there were other restaurants here)

1902, 1903,

    Frank J. Hoefling proprietor in 1902/03.

        He married Cecilia; they lived at the same address as restaurant.

    Wanted a kitchen and a dining room girl for work in restaurant/lunch room in 1903.

    They were listed for being in the cigar & tobacco retailing, too.

_____

Charles Sweet's pool room and restaurant – basement of the bank building

1907, 1908, 1909, 1910   (there were outside stairs to this business)

    Apr 1907 - ?? Monaca News stated that Charles, of Leechburg, formerly of Monaca, was in town visiting family. I believe while in town visiting, he decided to purchase this business because by Sep 1908 the news stated that he recently took charge of the pool and billiard parlors and lunch room in the basement of the bank building. He was putting in new side walls and would be painting and decorating; with the bowling alleys being repaired and everything put in "first class shape."

    Oct 1908 - he came home to Monaca after a 10 week visit with relatives and friends in Pittsburgh; he must have had someone else who managed the business (?).

    In Mar 1909 he had it newly painted and decorated and added a large sign placed on the exterior of the place. Again, the bowling alleys were also repaired and put in "first class condition." (Either he never did that back in 1908 or they needed it again ??)

    Charles was living in Pittsburgh by 1946, but was still a member of the Monaca Cornet Band.

_____

Mrs. Anna M. Davis's restaurant – 900s Pennsylvania Avenue (btw. Ninth Street and boro building)

1907, 1908

    Mrs. A. Davis moved to Monaca from Darlington and was to conduct a restaurant in N. Wurzel, Jr.'s penny arcade on Pennsylvania Avenue.   Mrs. Davis was a former resident of Monaca. Restaurant opened Aug 3, 1907.

    Anna married Millard Davis, the shoemaker; he died btw. 1910 and 1920; Anna moved to Allegheny County and was living with one of her widowed daughters and grand children.

_____

William R. Preece / "Hank" Preece – restaurant / confectionery – 919 Pennsylvania Avenue

1907, 1929

    William was b 1877 England; s/o Elam and Louisa Preece; moved to Ohio.

_____

Joseph McMillan Restaurant – 1395 Penna Avenue   (might be 1317 Pennsylvania Avenue ??)

1903, 1929

    Opened business on Oct 6, 1903.   Ad stated "fine fresh oysters every day."

    Was formerly Mr. DeSilvey's racket store who had just closed in Aug 1903.

    J. L. McMillan put an addition on his house in Mar 1904 to become a restaurant that he planned to open by Apr 1.   In 1910 Joseph was also a salesman.

_____

Mrs. Jerry Davin – restaurant – unknown location

1910

_____

Nick Wurzel – Restaurant Business
1909, 1910

He did have ownership in the Nickelodeon and family theatre on Pennsylvania Avenue until
Jan 11, 1909; then sold it to his son Cornelius (Corney). Nick continued in the restaurant
business at his old stand.

Nick had ownership of several properties in Monaca, so it is difficult to determine
exact addresses of his business buildings.

_____

Buckley & Curry's ladies' and gents' dining parlor – Pennsylvania Avenue (near Hotel Hamilton)
1907

Opened Sep 1907.
It was located in a storeroom from W. L. Dixon who closed his Nickelodeon by Sept 1907.
Served sea food of all kinds. Meals 25 cents.

> •••••••
> Buckley & Curry's ladies' and
> gents' dining parlor, meals 25 cents.
> Sea food of all kinds. Pennsylvania
> avenue, near Hotel Hamilton.
> ••••••••

1907

_____

Hackett's Restaurant – about 918 Pennsylvania Avenue (former Ark building)
1910, 1912, 1916, 1919

Owner of the business was listed as Mrs. Mary Hackett (building owned by Henry Weirich).
Sold out the business to Mrs. Irene Kuntzelman of KY who had taken charge (Jun 1919). Mrs.
Hackett resided over the restaurant, had moved to the dwelling on Virginia Avenue she
recently purchased.

With the bank purchasing the building, Mary most likely thought she would have had to move
anyway, thus selling her business. As it turns out, the building was left standing until
the spring of 1926. In the mean time, it became a few other businesses including a
Chinese laundry house and dwelling.

All this above occurred after the Ark was recently purchased by the Monaca Nat'l bank as a
site for their new bank building. The same information stated that it was in the Weirich
building/known as the Ark. (The Ark had been built on the lot on Fifth Street in 1884
and moved to the location on Pennsylvania Avenue. The bank never did build on the lot
but instead sold the vacant lot and the Ark property beside it to Louis Stoll who built the
Penn Theatre in 1926. Mr. Stoll razed the Ark building later in May of 1926.)

> Wanted—A good dining room girl.
> References required. Apply at Hack-
> ett's restaurant, Pennsylvania avenue,
> near Ninth street, Monaca, Pa.

1912

Then on tax lists as ......

Hackett's Restaurant – 1129 Pennsylvania Avenue
1930, 1931

Under John Hackett as owner; but both evidently owned it because it was listed as
owned by Mrs. Mary A. Hackett the following year.

_____

J. A. McMellen – restaurant – unknown location
1910

_____

Annie S. Beatty – restaurant – she lived on Pennsylvania Avenue
1910

_____

Karcis Café and restaurant – 1140 Pennsylvania Avenue
1910 (under Paul's name), 1928, 1935, 1937, 1940
        Owned by Paul Karcis. Paul was the son of John and Eva/Mary Karcis who ran a wholesale liquor
                business in Pittsburgh in the 1920s.
        This "beer establishment" seemed to be in the news more times than not.
                1938 newspaper article stated – 3 teenage girls testified Paul Karcis served them, then
                offered to accompany them home, en route, attacked one of the girls.
                Paul went to jail for this.   Supposedly the girls told them they were 22.   The café was
                not charged with any of the accusations/violations but the bartender was charged with
                selling to minors.
        See the Wholesale Liquor and Distributors section for the details on a stabbing
         and trade war incident at this business.

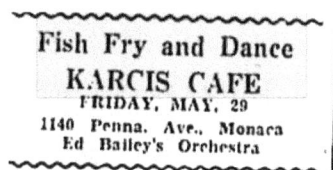

Fish Fry and Dance
KARCIS CAFE
FRIDAY, MAY. 29
1140 Penna. Ave., Monaca
Ed Bailey's Orchestra

_____

Blue Banner Confectionery – 898 Pennsylvania Avenue
1919, 1928, 1931
        Sold home grown Christmas trees in 1930.
        Joseph Runzo – proprietor.
        By mid 1930s this was the location of Spitale's Café.
        (Jos. and family moved here from Beaver the middle of Feb -1928 where
                he owned a fruit and confectionery store on Third Avenue).
        In 1930, they were living at 898 Pennsylvania Avenue.

CONFECTIONERY

Hello, Hello, Fellows, How are you? Hot, isn't it? Come in, Have a Soda. Where? At JOE RUNZO'S. Big Room. Good Service. Fine Sodas, too. Don't forget he handles Blue Banner Chocolate, Also.

Jun 1919

_____

Dew Drop Inn – Ninth Street
1919
        Inn – restaurant and confectionery.

_____

Jack McCarthy restaurant – Pennsylvania Avenue (near Twelfth Street)
1918, 1919
> Closed the business and stored his stock and fixtures in Dec 1919 because they were moving
> temporarily to home in Rochester.

> Jack McCarthy, who conducted a restaurant in Pennsylvania avenue near Twelfth street, is storing his stock and fixtures and will discontinue the business for the present. Mr. McCarthy and family will move to Rochester, where they will make their home temporarily with Mrs. McCarthy's sister, Mrs. John Richardson and family in West Madison street.   . . . Dec 1919

———————

Sabatino Restaurant and Billiards – 1306 Pennsylvania Avenue
1924, 1930, 1937, 1943
> Owner – Ralph P. Sabatino.
> > Ralph P. married Carmella and the family lived at same address as business.
> > R.P.'s daughter Catherine worked in the restaurant. R.P. died 1937.
> The restaurant evidently closed shortly after Ralph's death because Carmella nor any of the
> > children were found working there, or they hired someone to run the business ?

———————

Penn Restaurant – 1018 Pennsylvania Avenue   In 1942 at 1014 Pennsylvania Avenue.
1924, 1929, 1943
> Was owned by Ross Ritchey.   Sold it to Mr. Garner in May 1929.
> In 1929 Mercantile List stated it was at 920 Pennsylvania Avenue.

———————

Marina Schatzinger – lunch room – Colona Heights
1928

———————

Busy Bee Restaurant   aka   Busy Bee Quick Lunch – 1216 Pennsylvania Avenue
1928, 1930, 1931
> Sam Boliono (25 yrs old in 1929), proprietor.
> > Dec 1929, he was visiting a friend in jail and police raided his restaurant. They found a
> > quantity of Moonshine. Sam was taken by surprise when apprehended during a visit he
> > was making at the jail.

———————

__?___ - at 923 Pennsylvania Avenue
1928, 1929
> Demitrios Papademitriou and Demitri Kara - Restaurant owners
> The newspaper said they had to pay bail on Jan 28, 1929 when police found two quarts of
> > moonshine whiskey in the restaurant.
> Wanted a waitress in Sep 1928.

———————

Harvey's Fish Shop – 1206 Pennsylvania Avenue - rear (1923)
                              -308 Ninth Street (1924)
1923, 1924
        Fish store and lunch room.

HARVEY'S
FISH SHOP

1206 Pennsylvania Ave.
MONACA

Halibut Steak Fish,

Ierring and Blue Pike,

Also Fresh Oysters

Cooked Schrimp

Our Restaurant is the
best place in town
to Eat
                                              1923 ad

_____

Monaca Lunch – 1216 Pennsylvania Avenue (1940s)   -1209 Pennsylvania Avenue
1929, 1938, 1940, 1941, 1945
        Gust Ballas was owner.
        In 1940 Gus was owner of restaurant; his wife Anna was cook; daughter Bessie was waitress.
        Ads for help in 1938, 1941, 1945; but then an ad selling complete set of fixtures for restaurant
                in 1945.

WANTED: Waitress over 21, for
Monaca   Lunch. Inquire   1216
Pennsylvania Ave., Monaca.
                                    4|14   1941

_____

Tito Totani – restaurant – 923 Pennsylvania Avenue
1929

_____

Erdeley's Restaurant – Pennsylvania Avenue
1922   Emma Erdeley – proprietor.

_____

Previch Restaurant – 215 Pennsylvania Avenue
1924   Mike Previch – proprietor.

_____

Sam Cohen's Restaurant – Colona
1922

_____

Hays Restaurant – 1310 Pennsylvania Avenue (1922) - 825 Pennsylvania Avenue (1928)
1922, 1930, 1943   Owner - H. F. Hays.

_____

Hick's Restaurant –529 Pennsylvania Avenue – 827/829 Pennsylvania Avenue (1928)
1922, 1930, 1931, 1943
       James Hicks – owner   and   John B. Hicks – owner (1928).
       James had worked in a Un-Gro-Co* grocery store on Pennsylvania Avenue in 1914.
             *Un-Gro-Co. was a trademark – owner C.C. Truax & Co., Toledo Ohio, assignor to United
             Grocer Co., Toledo, Ohio, a corporation of Delaware.   Un-Gro-Co. was used on all their products.
       Several items in the newspaper stated it was always suspected that during prohibition, there was
          a bit of illegal liquor sold here - ? -

_____

Mrs. J. Eiekes – restaurant – 1607 Pennsylvania Avenue
1928, 1943

_____

William F. Ganther – restaurant – 915 Pennsylvania Avenue
1928, 1943

_____

Colonial Bar – 903 Pennsylvania Avenue

_____

Martin Mild – restaurant and billiard room– 912 Pennsylvania Avenue
1928, 1943

_____

Pete Frank's Restaurant – Pennsylvania Avenue
1922   Pete Frank – proprietor.

_____

Sam Affront – restaurant – 1607 Pennsylvania Avenue
1929

_____

Mrs. E. Nichol – restaurant – 1501 Pennsylvania Avenue
1929

_____

Merriman's Confectionery and Grill – 1308 Pennsylvania Avenue
1936, 1941   Edna Merriman – owner.   She resided at the same address.

_____

Eldridge Lunch – 1503 Pennsylvania Avenue
1930, 1931   Mrs. E. Carnahan – proprietor.

_____

Caltury's Lunch–1311 Pennsylvania Avenue - one block up from the Catholic Church
1935, 1940, 1965, 1967
       Opened Aug 9, 1935; was family owned by Frank and Mary Caltury.
       Had sandwich menu, beer and liquor (bar) – restaurant/bar.
       Business was sold in 1967 by Mary who retired the same year.

_____

Ohio Valley Restaurant – 1018 Pennsylvania Avenue
1930, 1931

_____

LeGoullon's Café – 899 Pennsylvania Avenue, then 312 Ninth Street (downstairs)
1936, 1940, 1941, 1942, 1943
> He must have started off using an area in Carey's building, then moved.
> It was also a billiards, bowling alley, and/or arcade business.
> > (The Monaca Athletic Ass'n listed their address as 312 Ninth Street, too.)
> Owned by William C. LeGoullon.

————

Newman's Café – 918 Pennsylvania Avenue
1938   Henry Newman – proprietor.

————

Stathas's Restaurant – 1216 Pennsylvania Avenue
1931   Peter Stathas owner.

————

Dan's Dairy Bar – 916 Pennsylvania Avenue
1942, 1946, 1947
> Firemen fought a fire at the store for 2 hours on Nov 13, 1947 in the kitchen area, which was
> > completely gutted.   Damages total $4,000.

————

Bell's Grill   aka   Bell Restaurant – 920 Pennsylvania Avenue (1930s)   - in 1940 it was
                1014 Pennsylvania Avenue   -in 1943 it was at 1018 Pennsylvania Avenue
1930, 1940, 1941, 1946
> Bell's Grill went in where the old Post Office was located in 1940 (Keystone Block bldg).
> > There used to be an athletic club under this site where area wrestlers trained in the early 1900s.
> Bertha Bell was in a partnership with her son Jesse. In 1943, a news article stated that she
> > went to court and was granted an injunction to dissolve the partnership since Jesse
> > would leave and go to Florida for long periods of time, then return to claim his share of
> > the business profits.
> > Bertha became the sole owner of the grill. She sold bottled beverages, too.
> She bought the building at 920 Pennsylvania Avenue from Anna M. Davis - corner of Ninth Street
> > and Pennsylvania Avenue.
> Bertha became divorced, lived with her daughter Ruth and family in 1940s.
> > She was married to George Bell - lived in Moon Township (became Monaca Heights – Elm Street).
> > They had 4 children.   By 1930, George was living by himself at Pacific Avenue.
> > Bertha died in 1971 at age 80 and was noted for still being a resident of Monaca.
> Bell's Grill provided entertainment during the Great Depression. In Jul 1938, she had
> > Ralph Miller and band to entertain guests.

————

Monaca Grill – 615 Pennsylvania Avenue
1940, 1957

————

Margaret's Restaurant – 827 Pennsylvania Avenue
1940
> In 1940 Roy Brewer and his mother, Margaret Martin, were proprietors of a restaurant
> but I have no address, no name of their restaurant, just the census listing in 1940.
> I believe it was called Margaret's Restaurant.   Evidently it didn't work out because I found
> where *Margaret's Restaurant* was up for sale late in Jun 1940.

————

Park's Restaurant – one block from Monaca Bridge – 215 Ninth Street
1949, 1956

LOOK WHAT'S
COOKING AT
PARK'S

Home style cooking and
delicious home baked
pies . . .

PARK'S RESTAURANT
ONE BLOCK FROM MONACA BRIDGE
MONACA

Jul 1949

Catty's Diner   (also found spelling of Caddy's Bar) –   919 Pennsylvania Avenue
1940, 1957, 1965, 1976
>   Henry Newman was the owner and Ethel was the cook. His obit. stated he ran it for 45 years.
>   Henry was b 1904. Henry, Ethel (Vogt) and 5 children lived at the same address as bar.
>   He had a special project he started in 1957 of collecting monies and donating to the Children's Hospital.
>   Had an ad needing a bartender in Apr 1976.
>   This site became Chips, now (2016) Anthony's Place.

Grater's - dairy bar / snacks and ice cream – 916 Pennsylvania Avenue
1940s and 1950s
>   Mrs. Anna Mae Grater owner and operator - 1940s and 1950s (8 years total).   She lived at 1003
>   Pennsylvania Avenue, then on Indiana Avenue.   In 1956 their address was on Pennsylvania Avenue, to
>   the right of the theatre building.   Sold Meyer and Powers Ice Cream and pizza; also had light lunches and
>   dairy products.   Eugene Biondi, owner in 1956.   This building was adjacent to the Penn Theatre building.

1956

*Fun Fact: Meyer and Powers had their ice cream factory on Hawkins Avenue in North Braddock; were in business in
1922; John C. Meyer was listed as a director in 1952 directory.   They became part of the Tri-Point Ice Cream Co.*

Armstrong's Grill – 1014 Pennsylvania Avenue
1956

_____

Confectionery Store and Lunch Counter – 906 Pennsylvania Avenue
1960
        Was going out of business in Mar 1960.   It was up for sale in Mar 1960.

_____

Neese's Grill – 1018 Pennsylvania Avenue
1965, 1966   _?_ Neese – owner.

_____

Ed Funk's Dairy Store – 916 Pennsylvania Avenue
1940, 1950
        Opened Oct 1940.   Edgar Funk – owner.
        Was a soda bar, sold ice cream, and a luncheonette; also was once a bowling alley
                – completely remodeled with new dairy store equipment and fixtures; soda bar
                made of birch and chrome trimming; red leather stools; contrasting colors of blue
                and yellow were used on the leather seats at the tables.
        Run by a man the kids called "Dirty Dan."
        Had a lunch counter and sold delicatessen foods.
        Edgar S. Funk was also manager and Treasurer of the base dairy company and had the office
                for both the store and the Funk Dairy business in the building.   Edgar was the s/o Mr. & Mrs.
                Lloyd Funk – Lloyd was the founder of the Funk Dairy Company which started in 1919; the
                company was based out of Beaver.

THE HOME OF "CREAMY RICH" DAIRY PRODUCTS
TRY FUNK'S "OWN" SWEET CREAM BUTTER

1956

_____

Elsie's Luncheonette – 916 Pennsylvania Avenue
1964, 1970s
        George and Elsie (Frazzini) Melianos – owners.   Elsie was b 1908; married George Melianos.
        They closed the restaurant and all the restaurant equipment , stock, fixtures and the things in
                accompanying apartment were being sold at an auction because they sold the property
                to the Humble Oil Co. the first of Dec 1971. (A service station was built on that
                corner of Pennsylvania Avenue and Ninth Street and there is now (2016) the Home Mtg.
                Solutions 12 sided building still stands on that corner.)
        She also owned "Elsie's Luncheonette" in Rochester and Conway's Corner Restaurant.
                Margaret Ann Davis Grossi worked at both locations.
        She sponsored a basketball league with the name "Elsie's Luncheonette" on their shirts.
        The building was razed in the early 1980s.

_____

Mona Lunch – 1101 Pennsylvania Avenue
1946, 1956

NOTICE!

MONA LUNCH

We regret the inconvenience to our many patrons of the Mona Lunch, Pennsylvania Ave., Monaca, caused by our closing from July 1st to July 15th. After extensive alterations and complete remodeling of our entire storeroom, we will be open for business on July 15th.

May we have the pleasure of serving you again and renewing old friendships

The Management

1946

_____

Dairy Queen – corner of Ninth Street and Pennsylvania Avenue – 901 to 903 Pennsylvania Avenue
1975, 1977,

Opened spring, 1975.   Dr. Ray Reppert – Monaca dentist owned the building.
Took up 3 lots and 2 buildings were demolished to build it.
It was a larger building, capacity of seating 54.

Dairy Queen
brazier.
MONACA
DAIRY QUEEN BRAZIER
Monaca, Pa.
CHIPPEWA
DAIRY QUEEN BRAZIER
Beaver Falls, Pa.
DAIRY QUEEN BRAZIER
of Zelienople
BEAVER
DAIRY QUEEN BRAZIER
Beaver, Pa.

1975

_____

Rosina's Restaurant – Rosa's Pizza – Italian Restaurant – 1199 Pennsylvania Avenue
1986, 1988

Opened 1986.   Was a new business being built.
Restaurant run by David Halama, Mike Halama, and Greg Burlett
Rosina Cercone was listed as the cook and was grandmother to the men.

_____

John's Family Restaurant – 1102 Pennsylvania Avenue
1976, 1978

_____

Echo Point Dairy Store – 1102 Pennsylvania Avenue
1965, 1970s

Owned and operated by Dusold brothers - John "Jack," Joseph, Donald.
There was the Echo Point Dairy in Moon/Center Township - started in 1925
by Joseph Dusold, father of the Dusold brothers.
Echo Point Dairy received its name since the original dairy farm was situated on a hilltop
and echoes could be heard throughout the valleys.
The dairy supplied milk to Monaca schools in at least 1971.

their 1986 delivery wagon

ECHO POINT MILK
IT'S DELICIOUS

ECHO POINT DAIRY
1102 PENNA. AVENUE, MONACA   774-9814

1965

Photo courtesy Beaver County Historical Research and Landmarks Foundation   1970s

Little Beaver Historical Society   Echo Point dairy truck Monaca - 1956

Original Pita Parlor – 911 Pennsylvania Avenue – grocery / delivery
2009   Became Clip & Cuddle for a period time. Currently it is a hair studio.

————

Lyle Henry's Luncheonette – unknown address
1988   Kathy Hetzler – owner.

————

Chris' Restaurant – 1102 Pennsylvania Avenue
1991 to 1996   Chris Trattoria – owner.

MEET CHRIS TRATTORIA

If you want excellent Italian Cuisine, stop and see Christian LeMatte, owner and chef, of Chris' Trattoria Restaurant in Monaca. Open for lunch and dinner. Chris has a great menu including sandwiches, pizza, pastas, veal and seafood. You will find three daily specials for both lunch and dinner. Soon you will be able to enjoy a nice glass of wine or an alcoholic beverage with your meal as Chris should have his liquor license by May. Stop in, enjoy this lovely Italian atmosphere, great food and excellent service. Hrs. Mon.-Thurs. 11 a.m. to 9 p.m., Fri.-Sat. 11 a.m. to 11 p.m. Take-out available.

Chris Trattoria
ITALIAN CUISINE
1102 Penna. Ave., Monaca
774-8466

1993

ITALIAN RESTAURANT

Chris' Trattoria
OPEN 11-7:30
ON MOTHER'S DAY
CHICKEN PARMIGIANA...... 8.25
HOMEMADE LASAGNA....... 7.95
PRIME RIB.................................. 9.50
MANICOTTI............................... 6.95
SEAFOOD PASTA.................... 8.95
ALL DINNERS INCLUDE SALAD OR SOUP
GARLIC BREAD AND SIDE OF ZITI
1102 PENNSYLVANIA AVE., MONACA
774-8466

May 1991

————

Ricky's Restaurant – 1114 Pennsylvania Avenue (used to be the men's store)
2003   Mexican cuisine was served.

————

Little Echo Restaurant & Lounge - 1534 Pennsylvania Avenue
(open in 1978/1979) 1987, 1990
       Louis Pupi, Paul Pupi – partners; Joseph Dusold and Michael Pupi – partners/managers.
       (Became Slush Puppie Tri-State, Inc. building)

WEEKEND SPECIAL!
FRI. SPECIAL — ALASKAN KING CRAB LEGS | SAT. SPECIAL — ENGLISH CUT PRIME RIB
LITTLE ECHO
Restaurant & Lounge
1534 PENNA. AVE., MONACA — 774-0464
DINNER TUES., WED., THURS. 11 A.M. TILL MIDNIGHT
HOURS: FRI. 11 A.M. TILL 1 A.M.   SAT. 4 P.M. TILL 1 A.M.

      also the business of ....

Slush Puppy – 1534-1536 Pennsylvania Avenue
1999
       Was owned by the Little Echo Restaurant and Lounge people.
          1978 - Louis, Michael, Paul Pupi and Joseph Dusold owners.
       Were advertising for *route drivers* in 1999.

_____

Rossi Pizza & Italian Cuisine – 215 Ninth Street (until 2014)

_____

Big Benny's Sandwiches Nat'l – 215 Ninth Street (2015)

_____

3 Guys - 215 Ninth Street
Current   Opened in 2016.

_____

Tramonte's Pizza – 1140 Penna Avenue - 215 Ninth Street
Current

_____

Bud's Pizza Parlor – Pennsylvania Avenue (1300 block/by Taormina's) –
1973, 1978   next door to Ernest Taormina's Ernie's Superette

_____

Presto's Pizza Shop – 1206 Pennsylvania Avenue
1965, 1972
       Was located on Ninth Street first, then Pennsylvania Avenue.
       Owner/operator – Oresto "Presto" Petrella.

_____

Monaca Pizza –
2000   Eddie Cox, owner.

_____

Unique Pizza Factory Shop – 1038 Pennsylvania Avenue
1999, 2000
 Opened Jun 1999.
 Fran and Kelly Higgins owners of the franchised business.

————————

Yolanda's Restaurant and Pizza – 1601 Pennsylvania Avenue (corner of Sixteenth Street/Pennsylvania)
1989, Current
 Had a fire in Feb 1993 that closed the restaurant for a few weeks/a month.
 Owned by Pete Samovoski, Jr. in 1991.

————————

Rossi's Pizza and Sub House – Pennsylvania Avenue
1968, 1988
 Converted an old house and planned to open late Mar or Apr 1988.
 Had walls painted by James Reynolds of Beaver Falls – did nostalgic movie stars and scenes.
 Guy and Helen Rossi – owners/operators.
  (Guy owned Rossi's Pizza in 1968 and Anzio's Pizza in 1975 also.)

————————

Anzio's Pizza – Monaca
1975 Owner – Guy Rossi (it was named for his father).

————————

Pizza King – Ninth Street – across from the old Monaca Hotel (1976)
1976 In 1977 it was said to be on Pennsylvania Avenue; there were pool tables in there, too.

————————

_?_ - a pizza business – 1031 Bechtel Street (corner of Bechtel and Taylor) – Monaca Heights
 It was at the front of the former #4 Monaca Fire Hall.

————————

Pizza Joes – 815 Pennsylvania Avenue
2014

————————

Jakanna's Pizza – 1032 Pennsylvania Avenue
1978

————————

Anthony Jr's Pizzeria – 815 Pennsylvania Avenue
Current

————————

Pacentro's Italian Restaurant & Pizzeria – 1206 Pennsylvania Avenue, then 1034 Pennsylvania Avenue
2004, 2013
 Moved from 1206 Pennsylvania Avenue – closed all in 2013/2014.
  1206 Pennsylvania Avenue is now an insurance business.
 Opened in Nov, 2004, moved to #1034 by 2006 because #1206 was up for sale that year.
 Guy and Tamara Celeste owners (family run shop).
  They sold the building in 2016.
 Became................

Stumpy's
 Became ....

La Piazza – Italian Cuisine- 1034 Pennsylvania Avenue
Current

This business up for lease as of May 2016.   Formerly housed Johnston Flowers.

(There was no awning or markings on building as of Aug 2016; it appeared empty.)

_____

White House Restaurant – 1032 Pennsylvania Avenue
1988 to Current

Opened in 1988 - owned by Laura Wentz.

WHITEHOUSE
RESTAURANT

1032 Penna Ave., Monaca
774-7003
NOW OPEN FOR DINNER
FRIDAY'S BEST FISH IN TOWN
(Baked or Fried Cod)
Mon. thru Thurs. & Sat. 6:30 a.m. till 3:30 p.m.
Fri. 6:00 a.m. till 7:30 p.m.

————1990 ad

_____

Fountainhead Café – 1038 Pennsylvania Avenue
2009, Current

Opened in 2000s.

_____

Bronze Eagle Restaurant – 1140 Pennsylvania Avenue
2011

Penn Super Market   empty bldg

_____

Graystone Restaurant and Tavern – 1198 Pennsylvania Avenue (formerly the Penn Super Market)
1998, 2000
> Opened Oct 1998.
> Gene Liberatore – owner and chef.
>> Gene was manager at Chauncey's in Pittsburgh prior to opening Graystone and his father owned the LNL Lounge of Monaca.

Then.......

Bronze Eagle Lounge – 1198 Pennsylvania Avenue
2003
> Then.....

Blue Steel then......

Whiskey Rhythm Bar & Grill – 1198 Pennsylvania Avenue
Current

Former Penn Super Market site in 2016

Sakura Japanese Restaurant – 1001 Pennsylvania Avenue
Current
> Opened in 2015.

Downtown Grill – 1400 Pennsylvania Avenue –grill
> In the Get Go/BP station.

Stumm's Tavern – end of Fourth Street on Atlantic Avenue
1840, 1876,
> 1840 - owner was William Stumm.   1876 - merchant C. F. Kaercher lived here until 1932.
> 399 Atlantic Avenue was found in one historic publication to be the address.
> The building is still standing (2016) - turned into an apartment building.

became.........

Shriner's Tavern

> *Fun Fact: Phillipsburg was incorporated on Mar 5, 1840; then about a month later the first election was held the first Monday of Apr 1840 in William Stumm's Tavern.   It has also been recorded that this building was the seminary in 1834 directed by Rev. Ferdinand Winter.*

1840s

Photo courtesy Beaver County Historical Research and Landmarks Foundation

Stumm's Tavern / Shriner's Tavern Building

This building has changed very little since 1840 ....

2015

Rear view

Photo courtesy BCHR&LF

_____

George Lay, Jr. – saloon keeper

1880   From all findings, it appears this "saloon" was in the Lay Building.

_____

Lafayette Graham – tavern keeper

1880

_____

Spitale's café and "taproom" – 898 Ninth Street and Pennsylvania Avenue

1935, 1939, 1940, 1941, 1943

Caroline (Catanese) Spitale/Spitalla and then Antionetta proprietor. It was called a "tap room."

Agnello was also listed as proprietor in 1940.   Alger Hansinger as a bartender at the café in 1940.

There were pool/billiard tables here, too.

There were MANY articles about the mysterious death of her husband (Agnello / Tony).

All articles suspected him to have been "taken for a ride," beaten, shot.

See the section Wholesale Liquor and Distributors for a full story.

_____

Monaca Silver Bar & Restaurant – 1127-1129 Pennsylvania Avenue
1920s, 1940, 1965, 1970s
        Domenico Lucci, proprietor / owner for 50 years; Antonetta was the cook.
          Domenico – b 1898; married Antonetta; lived in same building; had 6 children.

        The business was sold in 2001 and became……..

The Monaca Draft House – 1127-1129 Pennsylvania Avenue
Current
          Victor & Denise Martin - owners

_____

Colonial Inn – 2701 (or 2527) Beaver Street
1938, 1943, 1947, 1969, 1970s
        This establishment had many articles in the newspaper associated with it.   They stated
                there were various charges including for a gambling house and traffic in lotteries.
        John Pevek – proprietor – 1938.
        Keith Ely – proprietor – 1947.
        Mildred Dravich – proprietor – 1969.
        The Colonial Inn had rooms to let out, but was better known as just a bar.
        There is more information on this establishment in the Hotel section.

_____

Monaca Inn   aka   called Monaca Hotel – 899 Pennsylvania Avenue
          (not to be confused with the *Hotel Monaca* which sat on the corner of Washington & Ninth)
1956, 1961, 1968, 1972, 1998
        Restaurant and tavern.   This building was formerly Martin Carey's Grocery store and the site was called
                Carey's Corner.   See Grocery section for more details on Carey's Grocery Store.
        Aug 24, 1942 – building was sold to Ernest C. Springer and Thomas F. Pawka. Until this sale, the
                Carey family had possession of the property.

So.............Carey's former building may have been other businesses, but eventually became the Monaca Inn / Monaca Hotel.

The names of Monaca Inn and Monaca Hotel seemed to go back and forth depending on ownership from 1956.

An ad in 1956 stated they rented rooms by day or week and had the bar open 7 am to 1 pm.

1949 until the 1960s - Les and Martha Jean "Dotty" Fair.

1961 – Called Monaca Hotel in their own ads for fish fries.

1968 – Called Monaca Inn again.

Ad in Beaver County Times for fish dinners says it was "formerly Monaca Hotel."

Owned by Whip & Dorothy Trella.

1972 – called Monaca Inn.

1990 – the Inn was closed down for a while.

Ad to buy the Monaca Inn was in Apr 1990 paper.

45' bar, separate dining room that seats 60, kitchen, and income from hotel rooms.

1991 – called Monaca Inn.

Alan and Natalie Tooch – became owners in 1991, 1998.

Inside of Monaca Inn / Monaca Hotel in 1956

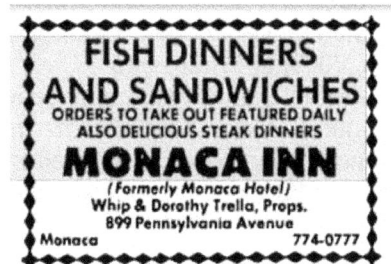

FISH DINNERS AND SANDWICHES
ORDERS TO TAKE OUT FEATURED DAILY
ALSO DELICIOUS STEAK DINNERS
MONACA INN
(Formerly Monaca Hotel)
Whip & Dorothy Trella, Props.
899 Pennsylvania Avenue
Monaca   774-0777

1972

2010 it became...............

P-Dub's and was completely remodeled inside and out
Current

This photo is prior to P Dub's remodeling

———

Namath's Lounge – Monaca Bowling Lanes
1967

———

Ernie's Tavern – unknown address
1963

―――――

Frank's Place – 2000 Beaver Avenue
1931, 1936, 1937, 1940, 1955, 1967, 1969
       Roy Blinn, manager - 1936.
       Frank and Mary Kopecky, proprietor in 1937, 1940.
       Chester (Chet) Waskaski, proprietor in 1955, 1969.
              The newspaper stated that this establishment was connected with charges several times
              (establishing a gambling place, lotteries, and traffic in lotteries) during the 1950s and
              1960s.
       The building is now a nail/hair establishment.

FRANK'S PLACE

DINE and DANCE

Beaver Avenue - Monaca

Phone Roch. 1942

―――――

Chip's II – opened in 1972 at 903 Pennsylvania Avenue
        -then relocated at 919 Pennsylvania Avenue after 1976
1972, 1996, 2005, 2011, 2014/15
       Owned by Samuel Ciccozzi of Beaver Falls.
       Owned by Victor "Chip" Ciccozzi in 1997.
       It most likely moved to 919 Pennsylvania Avenue in the 1970s when Dairy Queen bought up the
           buildings from Ninth Street to 911 Pennsylvania Avenue - no proof of this though.
  now ....

Anthony's Place – 919 Pennsylvania Avenue
Current

Chip's II in 2012

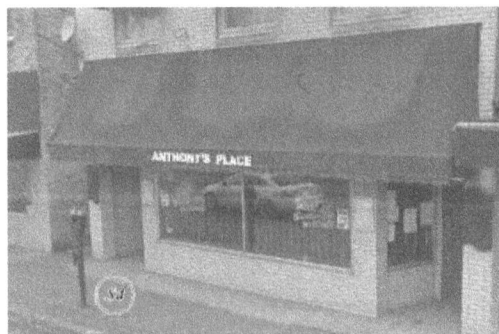

Anthony's Place 2014

―――――

DeCicco's Tavern – 1426 Pennsylvania Avenue
1952, 1963, 1974   Albert DeCicco – owner.

―――――

L N L / "L" Lounge – 827 Pennsylvania Avenue (same side/block as Monaca Inn, a few doors away)
1978, 1990

      Was owned by Gene Liberatore, Robert Nichol and Jack Liberatore.

      Gene Liberatore became the sole owner and his family ran the business.

      Opened St. Patrick's Day 1979.

      Advertised as family owned – food and drink.

      Gene Liberatore, owner in 1990.

————

Dutch Bar   aka   Chick's Dutch Bar – Marshall Road, Monaca Heights
1957, 1969, 1984

      George Eggenberger (Roch) and Adolph "Dutch" Birner (Monaca) – proprietors (1957).

      Pecan Alley was vacated by Linden Street so an addition could be constructed in the rear of
            the bar in Aug 1981.

      Josephine Matko worked at the Dutch Bar for 23 years.

Chick's Dutch Bar
1984, Current

      Thomas "Chick" Nichol (Monaca) – owner in 1984.

————

Two Dog Saloon – 1106 Pennsylvania Avenue
1993 to 1998

      Christian LeMatte – owner of business.   Owner of property Shirley and Leon Faller of Fla.

      The restaurant in the adjacent building to this bar was purchased by Christian LeMatte in 1996;
            but it closed very shortly after the purchase, as did the bar about 2 years later. There were many
            legal problems at this bar – noise complaints, fights, disturbances that would
            spill out into the street; news articles stated it was also cited and fined multiple times by
            the Liquor Control Board for violations.

————

Celeste's Tavern – 1426 Pennsylvania Avenue
1978, 2007,

      Owned by Antonio and Emma Jane Celeste (1989, 1991).

      The newspaper had an article that stated the license suspended in 1991 and then received
      citation for selling beer during the suspension.

      1428 Penna   Celeste's

————

Cellar Door – 1018 Pennsylvania Avenue
1970s, 1980s

COME WATCH OUR
WIDE SCREEN TV

COME ON DOWN

"HOME OF THE ICE PIK"

CELLAR DOOR
1018 Penna. Ave.   728-8631

   and......

Stumpy's Sports Tavern – 1018 Pennsylvania Avenue

   and.......

Jazzy's Lounge – 1018 Pennsylvania Avenue
1991, 1996

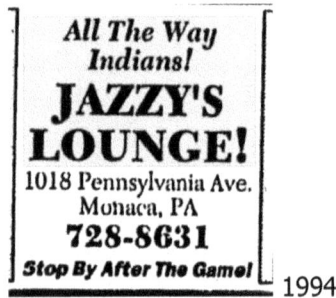

All The Way
Indians!
JAZZY'S
LOUNGE!
1018 Pennsylvania Ave.
Monaca, PA
728-8631
Stop By After The Game!   1994

Sign pointing down stairs

*** *** *** *** ***
*** *** ***

WHOLESALE LIQUOR   DISTRIBUTORS   BREWERS

Monaca is not without its share of drama in the liquor business.   Most reading this book may have heard about prohibition and the government acts to control the selling of liquor without a license.   But prohibition was alive and well in Monaca in 1921.   On Thursday, December 1, 1921, there was a "rum roundup" in Beaver County.   The arrests caused quite the sensation that day in the Beaver Valley since some of the most prominent residents of the district were arrested.   Thirteen of 26 persons were from Beaver Falls, New Brighton, Beaver, Rochester, and Monaca; thirteen from Woodlawn alone.   Liquor valued at many thousands of dollars was confiscated.   Each of the persons who wanted to gain their liberty had to find $2,000 bond; all were scheduled to appear at a hearing on Dec 3, 1921.   Since these names were already publicly published, the names are included further. (none of the Woodlawn names appeared in the paper, but the others came from an issue of The Pittsburgh Press)

Bootleg liquor was quite familiar in and around Monaca for many years.   There was a write up found that piqued my interest because it tied into some stabbings and/or shootings tied to Monaca.   Again, all these names and information were already publicly shared in newspaper articles, so they will be included further.   The Massaro trial with Reynolds was held in Rochester, N.Y.   In finding information below that is more localized to Monaca, I also found out that there was the name of "Spitale" connected in the Rochester, N.Y. area.   In the 1920s there was a bitter feud that had erupted between brothers and a mid-level bootlegger named Sam Spitale who conducted a speakeasy.   While other establishments were being raided, it was noted that Spitale's establishment was left alone. It was concluded by the other bootleggers that Sam Spitale was "informing."   This started a plot for Spitale's demise.   He survived two murder attempts that followed.   The first was when Sam had a sixteen year old wife and in Nov 1928, they were returning to their home when some gunmen took aim and fired several shots.   Spitale made it to the door of the house, but his wife did not; she was cut down by the gunfire and died the following day in the hospital.   Even with this loss, Spitale still continued in his liquor operations.   The second attempt on Spitale's life was in the fall of 1932 when his car exploded as he was about to start it.   He survived again only because six of the seven sticks of dynamite under the car had fallen off and did not explode.   Spitale lived to reach an old age. But my curiosity was peaked with all that I just wrote and ties in with the information futher because of the name "Spitale."   Was this a relative, a connection to events that occurred in Monaca?

*** *** *** *** ***

Local "trade wars"..................

It was reported in early March 1938 that police were blaming racketeers' guns for "silencing" a Monaca beer truck driver who was a defendant in a forthcoming Federal trial involving the operation of an illicit still at Rochester. Anthony Spitale was only about 40 years old and his body was found in shallow water in the Ohio River near Vanport.   He had been shot three times in the back and had been beaten about the head; his clothes were muddy and torn.   The Federal Alcohol Tax Unit at Pittsburgh had indicted Spitale in Nov 1937 in connection with the operation of a still.

Robbery was discounted in the murder, although Spitale's pockets were turned inside out, his watch and chain were not missing.   The beer truck Spitale was driving that day was found abandoned near the RR station in Rochester, the ignition keys in the car.   He had taken his family and a waitress from his wife's café to Rochester on Friday, March 4, 1938.   While the others walked about Rochester, Spitale was said to have entered a tavern of Mike Sashe to make a delivery – this was the last time he was seen alive.   His body was discovered on Monday, March 6th.   Tony Spitale was a former partner of James Tripoli, 43, a beer truck driver who was fatally stabbed in the spring of 1937 during a fight outside Karcis Café at 1140 Pennsylvania Avenue (this would be beside the former location of the Penn Super, and once the Bronze Eagle Restaurant entrance, empty in 2015).
Spitale had been a driver for Tony Ezzo, a Monaca beer distributor.   Caroline, his wife and proprietor of a café / "tap room" at 898 Pennsylvania Avenue, filed for Workmen's Compensation which she received since her husband was killed while on the job.   James Tripoli's wife, Florence, also filed for compensation shortly after his death.

And the plot thickens --- After all was investigated, Virgil Reynolds of New Brighton was sentenced to a life term in the Western penitentiary as being "finger-man" in the "beer racket" murder since he was the one who lured Spitale to the site of the murder and witnessed the killing. Reynolds testified against Louis Tolento stating that he saw Tolento kill Spitale with three shots. Reynolds was brought in from the penitentiary for this testimony because he was already serving a life sentence for the killing of Tony Massaro in December of 1938, a 40 year old Monaca beer baron. The courts were waiting to pile on additional charges for Reynolds pending the outcome of his testimony with Spitale; Reynolds pleaded guilty to a general charge of murder.

And........ Antonio Danna pleaded not guilty and said it was self defense, but was sentenced a 6 to 12 year term in for manslaughter in the killing of James Tripoli in 1937; the fight stemming from an argument outside the Karcis Café. The fight escalated over who had first claim to the license of Danna and Tripoli's former wholesale beer business, the partnership being dissolved previously, and that Tripoli was now taking Karcis's business away from Danna's firm. At the time of James Tripoli's death, Tony Spitale and he were currently partners. Danna pleaded guilty in May, 1937 to the fatal stabbing of his former partner, James Tripoli, but stated it was self defense since he was merely trying to defend himself from a larger, stronger man.

> *Additional Fact: Antonio Danna received over $330 dollars compensation while in the penitentiary on a claim he made for injuries he sustained due to being kicked during the same fight. He declared that he was making $50 a week at that time working for his son, Joseph N. Danna, delivering beer.*

Four known deaths were tied in with Monaca from 1937 to 1938 as a result of the "trade war" between beer distributors. In addition to Tripoli's(1) and Spitale's(2) deaths, Frank Cutrona(3) of Rochester was found in his car, with a 32 revolver gun and a gun shot through his heart. His body was found just 2 hours before the opening trial of Louie Tolento for his connection with Spitale's death. (Louie Tolento was not from Monaca, or in the liquor business, but rather a carpenter in Rochester.)

There were wild conjectures that Frank Cutrona's death was not a suicide, but rather that he had also been slain. Interesting fact – James Tripoli, was somehow connected with Cutrona's business at the time of his death two years prior. Cutrona's death occurred before he had even been questioned or subpoenaed in connection with the trial of Tolento. Tolento pleaded not guilty at his trial. Tony Massaro(4), formerly of Rochester was living in Monaca at the time of his death in December 1938. Virgil Reynolds pleaded guilty to his murder and was sentenced 20 to life sentence. Reynolds stated he was trapped as he sought to pass counterfeit bills he took from Massaro and admitted to his killing. Massaro was described by Federal Secret Service agents as a major figure in a counterfeit ring operating in New York, Pennsylvania, and West Virginia. He was shot to death in a quarry near Pittsburgh on December 10, 1938. (note "New York" – another connection to the opening information)

James Tripoli was not without his own headaches prior to his death. His car was stolen from 920 Atlantic Avenue on Jan 11, 1932 by two men. Peter Canale of Monaca and Mario Bellavia of Arnold stole the car and then were in an accident where they had to be taken to the hospital. Guns were found in their pockets and in the wrecked automobile; they were arrested upon being discharged from the hospital. At the time of James' death early May, 1937, the family was said to be living at 1417 Pacific Avenue; his tombstone in Beaver Cemetery has a picture of him on the stone.

*** *** *** *** ***

Moonshine

Home brewers nowadays should be glad that "raids" are fairly a thing of the past and it is no longer illegal to do some brewing.   There were many incidents in Monaca of moonshine being distilled between 1920 and 1940.   I found a few to be interesting enough to include below.   Even though at the time it was illegal, arrests were made, and names were published in the newspapers, I still felt no need to expose all of those names and exact addresses of the more minor occurrences, but the information was noteworthy.   Talk about having bad luck.........

Nov 1922 - Fourteenth Street – two people were taken into custody Nov 1922.   Police were there to arrest a man on other charges; found a gallon jug of "still warm" moonshine; also found the still in the barn near the house. Both persons were arrested.

Dec 1929 – Busy Bee Restaurant – the owner of a restaurant went to visit a friend at the jail in Beaver.   At the exact same time, police were raiding his restaurant where they found a quantity of moonshine.   Knowing where the owner was at the time, authorities apprehended him during his visit at the jail.

Dec 1930 - Washington Avenue – a man was arrested on a liquor charge when about 10 quarts of moonshine was found hidden in the wall under a bedroom window.

Dec 1931 - Spruce Alley – a man and woman who lived next door to each other were arrested for possession of liquor when a still, some mash and moonshine were found at the man's house and about 100 quarts of beer at the lady's house.

Here is one particularly large "operation" worth noting, as well as several other establishments that also ignored the "moonshine" and illegal liquor laws.   I've included names and places with those below only because they were openly printed in the publications of local newspapers.

Dec 1925 – The Michalic home was raided and two men were involved. Joe Vlasic and Matt Michalic were both arrested and had a trial regarding the operation of a big liquor plant found in the Michalic home in Monaca.   Michalic fled the county, but was later arrested by officers. Michalic entered a plea and was sentenced to pay a fine of $1,000 and to serve one year in the Allegheny County workhouse.
Vlasic also was tried by a jury and although he protested his innocence and declared that Matt Michalic operated the liquor plant, he was still found guilty.   Michalic exonerated Vlasic and a deposition from Michalic was presented to Judge Reader; Michalic took all the blame for the big liquor cache.   Joe Vlasic had a bit of luck in the situation because by Jul 1, 1925 Judge Frank Reader took this deposition into consideration and suspended Vlasic's sentence upon payment of the costs.

With all the raids and arrests, some never learn.......................

Jun 1927 – 1558 Washington Avenue
John Zupcic and Susie Mahalic were arrested during a raid where once again one of the largest caches of liquor was found in the cellar of the Mahalic home.   Two hundred twenty five gallons of moonshine, a 100 gallon still (in operation), 34 barrels of mash, seven cases of beer, one bag of cracked corn, one bag of rye, 300 lbs. of corn sugar were all found and destroyed, along with a large barrel of moonshine that was found under the cement floor of the cellar.   The detectives had been watching the two for some time and when Vlasic was arrested about midnight leaving Susie's home in a roadster. They found a five-gallon can of liquor in the car. This prompted the immediate raid on the home.   Although not home during the raid, Matt Mahalic, Susie's husband was also arrested for alleged illegal traffic in liquor.

During the 1920s, ignoring any positions of importance or offices held, the authorities made a wide sweep and almost simultaneous raids one day. A newspaper article gave a full list of the resulting arrests; the authorities were definitely active that day......

In Monaca -   Julius Roskwitalski – steward at Turners Club
                    They removed a large amount of assorted liquor from the Turners Club.
              H. C. Weirich – baker
                    A large haul of assorted liquor was removed from H.C.'s bakery shop.
              Paul Miller – also charged.
In Beaver -   E. S. Rowse – druggist
                    A large haul of assorted liquor was removed from the cellar of his home.

In Beaver Falls – F. F. Barth – secretary of the chamber of commerce (was a former resident of Pgh)
              W. A. Hoffman, druggist
                  Two truckloads of whisky & wine were taken from cellar of Hoffman's drug store.
              Harry Whitmery, clerk in Hoffman's drug store
              Mrs. Mildred Hays
              Harry May – proprietor of May restaurant in Lincoln Hotel
              Fred Stetler
In New Brighton - Walter Moore – chief of police
             Ralph Molter – street commissioner
             John Weaver
             Frank Fruth (arrested on charge of extortion)
             (took money from a bootlegger)

So many of these were seemingly minor in comparison to many of the major crimes occurring, but at that time, bootlegging and illegal liquor was the topic of the day.

*** *** *** *** ***

Wholesale Dealers and Distributors

Prior to prohibition, the local authorities would hear cases and then would issue licenses to individuals and/or businesses for the brewing and distribution of liquor.   I am sure there were many, but I have only listed as many of these as I could verify.

In the 1850s there were a few brewers in Monaca –
    Oliver Shivas – brewer   Andrew Keller – brewer
    Peter Caldaborn – brewer   James Hazlett - maltster

The Liquor License Court would also review and hear cases for retail and wholesale liquor licenses.   Applicants usually had attorneys with them as well as witnesses to testify the need for such a license at the establishment, area, or business.

1902 – Charles W. Bristol was a wholesale dealer in "fine wines and liquors". He was into wholesaling beer, too; had the Duquesne Brewing Company on the corner of Sixth and Indiana Avenue.   (Charles was married to Jennie ___.)

1902 --Morris Barnet on Eighth Street was also listed as a liquor dealer.

In Mar 1907, the following made applications for retail licenses:

John R. Carmtehael of Moon Township (Monaca Heights in 1907) applied.

Julius C. Coone applied again for a license for the Imperial Hotel at Colona.

Although there were others there to testify for these men, Rev. Hood also testified and stated that a license was not necessary for either.

At the same hearings, the following made applications for wholesale licenses:

Joseph G. Reed – Second Ward

William Carey – Second Ward

Gustave Friebe, Jr. – First Ward

John A. McMillen – Second Ward

Henry E. Vogt – First Ward

In Mar 1912, Beaver County found that the judge was not so generous in granting licenses. He declined almost half of the applications, reducing the number of wholesale stores from 16 to 9. Out of the 42 retail licenses applied for, a total of 31 were granted. In spite of the judge's lack of generosity, in Monaca all the retail licenses were granted and one wholesale license was refused:

Retail Licenses:

Christopher C. Beeler, First Ward - granted

Carl Herbert, First Ward – granted

S. D. Hamilton, Second Ward - granted

Wholesale license:

Bert C. Irons, Second Ward – granted

Gustave Friebe, Jr., Second Ward – refused

There were no brewers or distillers licenses applied for from Monaca, but this doesn't mean Monaca did not have any of them within its boundaries; it just means no one asked for/applied for a license.

***   ***   ***   ***   ***

In January 1934, the first state liquor stores were open in Western Pennsylvania; one each in Midland and Aliquippa. J. Albert Miller, of Monaca, was the manager of the Midland store. There were more storerooms to open soon in Rochester, Beaver Falls, and Ambridge.

Liquor Store – 1130 Pennsylvania Avenue - located across the street from Monaca Hardware

1940s, 1972, 1987

George Darno, Ambridge, was manager in 1982; Joe Mancini was manager in 1986.

***   ***   ***   ***   ***

It was war time and so many men were taken away to serve for our country; but here's an article just to show that women were still repressed.........note the word in the second line......"forced." (Evidently if there had been more men available, then NO women would have been considered or hired.)

73 Women Hired For Liquor Stores

HARRISBURG, May 8— (P) — The manpower shortage today forced the Pennsylvania Liquor Control Board to hire 73 women to clerk in state stores.

Fifty-four of the feminine clerks who will receive the same $1,380 annual salary as men, will work in Philadelphia where the state liquor monopoly has 80 stores.

Others will be located in Aliquippa, Beaver Falls, Charleroi, Homestead, Johnstown, Lansdowne, Monaca, Monessen, Mt. Gretna, Wayne and Yeadon.

— Pgh Post-Gazette – May 1944

***   ***   ***   ***   ***

Distributors and dealers of liquor in Monaca:

Christian Will – wholesale liquor dealer
1898, 1903
> Wholesale dealer in all kinds of liquors, wines, ales, etc.
> Sole agent for the C.L. Centivre Brewery Co., of Fort Wayne, Ind.

_____

Hugh Davis – whole sale liquor dealer - res Atlantic Avenue
1898, 1900, 1903

_____

Henry Levy – liquor dealer
1892, 1893

_____

Godfrey Miller, Jr. – dealer in the best brands of pure wines and liquors – Pennsylvania Avenue
1892, 1893, 1898, 1903   (See Bittner's, too.)

_____

Harrison T. Will – wholesale liquors - corner Sixth Street and Pennsylvania Avenue
1900, 1902, 1903
> Proprietor at Hotel Monaca after Apr 1, 1903.

When You Drop Into a Cafe, Hotel,

Or Bar, ask for "CHESS CLUB," "DUN-MORE" or "MONACA RYE," It will help some. All are A No. 1 brands.

H. T. WILL,

Wholesale Dealer and Sole Distributor.

Feb 1902 ad

_____

Morris Barnett – Eighth Street – wholesale liquor business
1902, 1903
> May, 1903, he moved his stand to Pennsylvania Avenue (near Ninth Street)
> Sold to James Beach in spring of 1903, who continued the business.

_____

James Beach – wholesale liquor business – Pennsylvania Avenue (near Ninth Street)
1903
> This business was purchased in early 1903 from Morris Barnett.
> Officially opening Jun 1, 1903.

_____

Charles W. Bristol – whole sale liquor store - Pennsylvania Avenue
1902, 1903
> Listed as being a wholesale dealer in fine wines and liquors and agent of the Duquesne
> > Brewing Co. on corner of Sixth and Indiana Avenue (based out of Indiana).
> He was selling out his entire stock – no successor was named.
> He had Benj. Anderson working for him.

_____

Anderton Brewing Company – corner of Eighth Street and Pennsylvania Avenue
1903

   Sept 1903 - Had a sign painted by the Leary Decorating Company.   Curiously, it was stated that the main figure was that of a ballet dancer.

_____

John Wuesthoff – Pennsylvania Avenue (moved here from Sixth Street in 1903)
1903

   Offered choice of kind of bottle of free wine with every $1 quart of whiskey.
   He conducted a wholesale liquor store and bottling house.

_____

Bert C. Irons - wholesale liquor dealer - 307 Ninth Street (corner of Ninth Street and Washington Avenue)
1906, 1912,

   Had a "cooler" on Washington Avenue. (I do not know what was meant by "cooler" or what it actually was.)
   He had permission to pave a portion of the street and gutter in front of his "cooler" in the fall of 1906.
   Bert and Margaret lived at 834 Pennsylvania Avenue in 1912.

_____

John Brezgar – wholesale whiskey man –
1905, 1906

   Purchased a handsome team of horses in Aug 1906.   In 1911 he started a coal yard, so he was also a coal dealer (see Hardware section).
   By early 1912, John was listed as a Monaca coal dealer and not the wholesale whiskey man.

   Side story to Mr. John Brezgar ---
   He was under contract to supply coal to the pump station and other borough institutions.
   Unfortunately, it occurred that Mr. Brezgar was handing in bills for more coal than he had been supplying; the contract between him and the Monaca council was therefore null and void.   The council awarded the contract to John P. Potter. It was a bitter council meeting that day.   Brezgar admitted to billing for almost twice as much coal as he was delivering and made strong accusations that the other coal dealers do or did the same thing; but council gave testimony that this was not true.   When all was said and done, Potter had the new contract, Brezgar's contract as annulled; yet council agreed to take 60 to 70 ton of 3-4 inch coal from Brezgar since he had on hand and had purchased it specifically for the borough.

_____

Jacob E. Hicks - Pennsylvania Avenue
1906

   Wholesale liquor business.
   Closed business the end of May 1906 and moved to Homestead.

_____

Duquesne Brewing Co. – corner of Sixth and Indiana Avenue.
1902   Charles W. Bristol was a dealer associated with this company.

_____

Antonio Danna was in the beer distributer business in the 1930s. He was involved in some of the liquor disputes going on in the late 1930s.   He had to serve time in prison for his involvements.
   His son evidently took over the business because on the 1940 census he is listed as the owner.
            See previous under Local Trade Wars section for more details.

_____

Gustave Friebe, Jr. – lower Pennsylvania Avenue
1907, 1909

> Gustave used to be a barber in Monaca, then he sold out of that business and started one in
>> wholesale liquor.   Mar 1907 Friebe leased his barber shop to Carl Stief because
>> Friebe had just been granted a liquor license and was going to open a wholesale liquor
>> store very soon.
> Mar 6, 1909 he was regranted a wholesale liquor license.
> Also the first of Mar 1909, he moved his place of business from lower Pennsylvania Avenue to
>> H. C. Weirick's building known as the Ark on Pennsylvania Avenue (near City Hall).
>> Mr. Weirich planned on remodeling and putting in a new front to the building.
>> 1910 census states he was a *merchant* and he was living on Washington Avenue, so he
>> did not live in the building where he conducted business.
> 1912 – Friebe, Jr. was not issued a license to sell wholesale liquor.
> Friebe, Jr. and family eventually moved to Ohio.

_____

Gelfo Distributing Co., Inc. – 1740 Pennsylvania Avenue
In business in 1949, 1956, 1965

> Owner Samuel J. Gelfo.   Sold his business late 1967/early 1968.
> By 1980s and into the 1990s Gelfo's was located in East Rochester.

1956

1956

The Perfect Companion

For The Hot Sultry Evenings
There Is No Better Snack Than A
Nice Sandwich With A Big Re-
freshing Glass Of Ice Cold Beer.

GELFO
DISTRIBUTING CO.
For Prompt Home
Delivery of Cold Beer

Call Roch. 4127
1740 PENNA. AVE., MONACA

1949

_____

Ezzo Beer Distributor / Monaca Beer Distributor –
1937, 1938, 1939

> Tony Ezzo – owner.   One of his drivers was murdered.   See previous for more information.

_____

Melchiorre Distributing, Inc. – 2420 Beaver Avenue
1990, 1993

_____

Monaca Distributing Company – 900 Pennsylvania Avenue – Rear
1951, 1952, 1958   Bought by Ihja Mijo Marjanovich (owned the Kobuta Hotel).

_____

Joseph Danna – owner / beer distributer
1940   His residency was at Atlantic Avenue.

*** *** *** *** ***
*** *** ***

GROCERY MEAT FISH CONFECTIONERY FLOUR GRAIN

Gardeners

Meat   Butchers   Fish   Poultry

Fruit Markets

Confectionery   Bakery   Ice Cream

Dairy   and   Milk delivery

Grocers

Flour   Grain   Feed

ICE BUSINESS

MISCELLANEOUS INFORMATION RELATED TO GROCERS

GROCERY MEAT FISH CONFECTIONERY FLOUR GRAIN

The businessmen and women in this section provided (literally) the "meat and potatoes" to the town residents and food preparation businesses. People would get their daily food from a variety of sources – butchers, grocers, and produce dealers. These types of businessmen would primarily handle only goods that were impossible to manufacture or process cheaply at home. Some of the most popular items would include flour, sugar, syrups, salt, tea, coffee, tobacco, spices, and dried/fresh fruits. One would find that many of the grocery store owners would exchange their manufactured goods with farmers for their produce. This would be productive for the farmers and the businessmen since the store would then sell the fresh produce in their stores and the farmers then had needed provisions. With many homes not owning any sort of refrigeration besides an icebox, housewives would most likely have shopped almost daily for particular food items. Each storeroom had its own flair and its own strong sources of goods. You will see that some businesses are listed as grocery AND meat or grocery AND fish, while others advertised and were referenced as produce only and others general grocery stores.

Small and more personal stores continue to become fewer and fewer as the number of the larger chain stores grew. Monaca had the Great Atlantic and Pacific Tea Company (A & P) in town. A & P first started by selling teas, coffees, and spices, but in 1912 they introduced economy stores and sold a full line of groceries and at low prices on a cash and carry basis. The smaller stores just could not purchase the larger quantities like the chain stores did, so they also had to sell items at a bit higher price just to keep in business. By the 1930s, large supermarkets were totally challenging the dominance of the small neighborhood stores.

I tried to list all the stores that were in the same type of business together and also to put some that were at the same address together.

*** *** *** *** ***

Gardeners

Nelson H. Trumpeter – gardener – res. on Eleventh St
1880, 1900
> He married Fanny __.
> Whether or not Nelson still did gardening for profit in 1910, he was listed as working
> > for a glass factory.

_____

William Trumpeter – market-gardener – res on Washington Avenue
1900   William married Mable __.

_____

Gilbert Trumpeter – gardener
1880, 1892, 1893

_____

Robert Biddle – gardener – res. on Tenth Street
1880, 1900
> He married to Mary E.__.   Robert was 77 in 1900.

_____

John Trumpeter – gardener – 1299 Indiana Avenue (grocery store)
1892, 1893, 1900, 1928

> He was married to Louisa in 1900; had 4 children; then married to Emma in 1910; had 3 children with her.

2016

_____

Ebert Robinson – gardener
1892, 1893

_____

Wesley Robinson – gardener
1892, 1893

_____

James Irons – gardener
1869

> Res. on Factory Street (now Pennsylvania Avenue Ext, coming into town)

_____

Daniel McClean - gardener
1880

_____

Robert A. Graham – gardener
1902, 1903

> His wife was Mary A.; they lived on Eighth Street.

_____

Joseph Senkovitz – gardener
1930

> He lived on Jefferson Road

*** *** *** *** ***

Meat   Butchers   Fish   Poultry

In 1900, there was one man I could find who laid claim to his occupation being *fisherman* –
Huford Hollerbaugh.   Huford lived on River Street/Road aka Saw Mill that ran from about Ninth Street to
Sixth Street down along the river's shore.   Good location for his home considering his occupation.

_____

Kindleberger & Evans – Pennsylvania Avenue and Fourteenth Street
1916, 1917
Fish market.   Opened ____.   Closed Jul 1, 1917.

_____

John A. Schaefer – fish store – Pennsylvania Avenue
1902, 1903
He married Mary __; they lived on Pacific Avenue.

*** *** *** *** ***

John Schamburgher - butcher
1841

_____

Christian Wack/Mack - butcher
1860

_____

David Brobeck – butcher
1876

_____

Christine Erbeck – butcher
1869, 1870, 1876, 1880   (res. Hanover Street / Fourth Street)

_____

Edmond Reukard /Rutard – butcher
1870

_____

Lewis Halderman – butcher
1850

_____

Adam Hamilton – butcher
1892, 1893

_____

Paul Karcher – Pennsylvania Avenue
1906, 1907
Butcher Shop.
He moved with his family from Pacific Avenue to the rooms over his butcher shop in Apr 1907.

_____

William Eherhardt/Ehrhardt – meat market – 1127-1129 Pennsylvania Avenue
1898, 1902, 1930

Were these the same businesses that just stayed in the family ?

Geo. Eherhardt Meat Market – 1127-1129 Pennsylvania Avenue –(Reader building)
1902, 1910, 1912, 1913, 1920, 1930s
 Opened his butcher shop Sep 1, 1906.
 Mr. Eberhardt was of Pittsburgh.
 Home dressed chickens, home dressed meats & smoked meats, fresh fish & oysters.
 Thomas Cochran had a butcher shop here in 1906 and George then moved in.

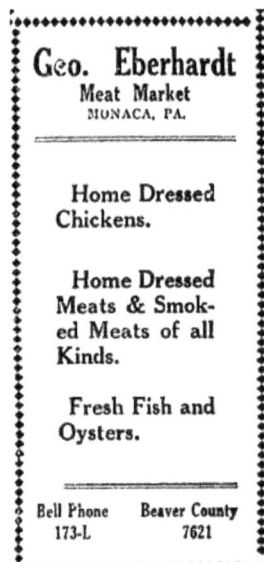

Geo. Eberhardt
Meat Market
MONACA, PA.

Home Dressed
Chickens.

Home Dressed
Meats & Smok-
ed Meats of all
Kinds.

Fresh Fish and
Oysters.

Bell Phone   Beaver County
173-L   7621

Feb 1913

_____

Daniel F. Leffert – Meat Market
1892, 1893

Fred Leffert – Meat Market – corner Pennsylvania Avenue and Eighth Street
1898, 1900, 1901, 1902, 1903
 His wife's name was Lydia; they resided on Atlantic Avenue.
 The 1902/03 Directory only lists him as a butcher and not an owner of a store ?
 1898 Directory stated him as "dealer in all kinds of fresh and smoked meats, poultry and game
   in season at fair prices."
 His shop was bought by Dave Fisher/Fischer the blacksmith.
 He also had a pool room.

 This may have been the same as previous or it was father/son – brother/brother/ etc. ?
 They definitely had separate ads in the 1902/03 directory though ?

John P. Leffert - The Butcher – Pennsylvania Avenue
1898, 1903
 "Purveyor of all kinds of fresh and salt meats, fresh fish, oysters, game, poultry, etc."

_____

Reader's Meat Shop – 1129 Pennsylvania Avenue (became known as Reader Building)
                          (adjoined to the Eberhardt Building which was at 1127 Pennsylvania Avenue)
1800s, 1900, 1904
        Owned by James M. Reader.
                  ○   He married Anna __; they lived at the same address as the shop.
        Offered full line of fresh meats at bed rock prices.   He was also a butcher by trade.
        Opened Jan 1900 in another building; Charles Heller/Haller then also moved in.

————

Joseph Gerlock – butcher – res. Indiana Avenue
1900

————

Chas. N. Haller – 1129 Pennsylvania Avenue
1900, 1902
        Dealer in fresh and smoked meats, dressed poultry.
        Opened business first week of Feb 1900.
        This store was previously rented by J. M. Reader.

Chas. N. Haller,
DEALER IN
Fresh and Smoked Meats.
Dressed Poultry.
Pennsylvania Ave.,
Monaca,   Penn'a.

Feb 1902 ad

————

Thomas Cochran – butcher shop – 1129 Pennsylvania Avenue (Reader Building)
1906
        Had moved out of storeroom by Aug 1906.
        George Eberhardt opened his grocery store and butcher shop there in Sep 1, 1906.

————

Buchholz's Meat Market – corner of Eighth Street and Pennsylvania Avenue
1906
        Owned by Walter Buchholz.
        Was a Clover Farm Store.   Put a new delivery wagon on the road in Nov 1906.

————

Harrison L. Skillman – meat store – Pennsylvania Avenue
1902, 1903   His wife was Addie.

————

Walter McWilliams – butcher
1930, 1940

————

Mateer Bros. Meat Market – 1000 Pennsylvania Avenue (beside Boro building in 1910)
1902, 1909, 1929, 1930, 1943

> Had their storeroom on Pennsylvania Avenue, near Tenth Street in 1902/03, Mar 1907.
>
> > Owned a lot on Pennsylvania Avenue near Eleventh Street, too (1907).
>
> 1912, there is an address for them at 411 Pennsylvania Avenue.   Was this one of their homes ?
>
> John R. and James M. Mateer owners /partners.
>
> > John's step son, Arthur Miller, was a clerk in the store.
> >
> > After John died (between 1930 and 1940); his wife Clara ran the business.
>
> "Cash meat market."   They carried all kinds of seafood, too.
>
> > They rented the store room in one of their buildings where Fred Patton's Jewelry store was to Joe Zigerel (Zigerelli) who had a fruit market on Ninth Street and was using this new store room for his business.   They rented an adjoining room/office to Squire W. W. Morgan in 1903.

Courtesy BCHR&LF

Clara Mateer - grocery store – 1002 Pennsylvania Avenue
1930, 1940

> Clara P. was John Mateer's widow. She must have been married prior to John because she had 3 older children going by the name "Miller" still living with her in 1940 and listed them all as her *sons* and/or *daughters*; but in 1930, when John was still alive, they were listed as step children to John. Her *son*, Arthur Miller, was listed as a clerk in the store in 1930 and then the manager of the grocery store with Clara in 1940.
>
> Clara and older children were living in the same building as the store in 1940.

Frank Gray – corner of Ninth Street & Washington Avenue (Jacob Strawick bldg)
1901

> He had the same business in Rochester and expanded to open one in Monaca.
>
> Poultry and egg dealer.
>
> Opened business Jan 12, 1901, after renovating a room in the building.

The Pittsburgh Premier Poultry Plant – Box No 753, Monaca
1906

BARRED--PLYMOUTH ROCKS--WHITE
WHITE--ORPINGTONS-- BUFF
STANDARD BRED EXHIBITION AND UTILITY STRAINS.

Eggs, $1.00 Per Fifteen; $1.50 Per Thirty; $5.00 Per Hundred. Several Fine Breeds for Sale. Prices a Matter of Correspondence. 'Phone, Write or Visit

The Pittsburgh Premier Poultry Plant,
Box No. 753, MONACA, PA. 237-2 'Phone.

May 1906

Vogt & Glasser – 715 Pennsylvania Avenue (old post office building)
1903, 1904

Opened Dec 1903 - Meat market and groceries.   Owned by Henry E. Vogt and Harry Glasser.
They sold out their business to Lee Musick and William Cornell of New Brighton; it would be known as Musick & Cornell, who took charge of the business on Apr 5, 1904. Mr. Vogt and William Meanor were going to remain in the employment of Musick & Cornell.

Stauffer's M. Musick & Cornell Meat Market – 715 Pennsylvania Avenue (old post office building)
1904

Opened business Apr 5, 1904; purchased business of Vogt and Glasser.
Lee Musick and William Cornell were the owners.
Mr. Vogt and William Meanor remained in employment with them.
The first of Jun 1904 they had the delivery wagon touched up and the name of the firm painted on it.

Stauffer's Meat Market – 1000s Pennsylvania Avenue, then 1101 Pennsylvania Avenue
1911, 1913

Grocery store and butcher shop – home made sausage, home dressed meats, liver pudding, home rendered lard, eggs......
Owner Allen W. Stauffer.   Allen and Ruby lived in the same building as the business.
Dec 1912, the business moved from 1000s Pennsylvania Avenue to the other side of the street at the corner of Eleventh Street and Pennsylvania Avenue – 1101 Pennsylvania Avenue

Stauffer's Market

The Place to Buy

Home dressed meats, butter, eggs, cheese, home-made sausage, liver pudding and home-rendered lard. Also a full line of

Best Groceries

Everything Worth While and

Quality First

B. C. PHONE 7726.
Cor, 11th St. and Penn'a. Ave.,
MONACA, PA.

1913

Central Cash Meat Market – 1012 Pennsylvania Avenue
1931, 1936, 1940

CENTRAL
CASH MEAT MARKET
1012 Pennsylvania Avenue · Monaca, Pa.

EXTENDS CONGRATULATIONS

to members of

MONACA COUNCIL
and other
BOROUGH OFFICIALS

on the occasion of the dedication of the
Municipal Building.

OUR MOTTO—
"HIGH QUALITY AND LOW PRICES"

Central Cash
Meat Market
1012 Pennsylvania Avenue — Monaca, Pa.

Order Xmas Poultry Early!

We're Anticipating Your Christmas Table Needs With a Complete Stock of Full
Home-Dressed Turkeys, Chickens, Ducks and Geese. We Plan to Retail Them to
You at Wholesale Prices, Which Means the Greatest Savings You Can Realize
Anywhere.

FINEST MILK FED VEAL

For Stewing or Stuffing, lb......... 12½c

VEAL ROAST and CHOPS, lb 18c

Extra Special
VEAL STEAK, lb. 25c

SUGAR CURED SKINNED HAM, Half or Whole, lb 17½c

PORK SHOULDERS, Whole or Shank End, lb 14½c

HOME MADE PORK SAUSAGE, 3 lbs...... 50c

HOME MADE COUNTRY STYLE OR LINK SAUSAGE, lb........ 20c

WEINERS, RING BOLOGNA, MINCED HAM, per lb 20c

LIVER PUDDING, Home Made, lb...... 18c

Extra Special
PURE LARD 11c½ LEAF LARD

ROUND | S | 20c
SIRLOIN | T E A |
Tenderloin | K | Lb.

FRESH PIGS FEET, 4 lbs 25c

NECK BONES, PIGS' EARS, 3 lbs........ 25c

FRESH COUNTRY ROLL CREAMERY BUTTER, lb 33c, 2 lbs.......... 65c

FRESH BEEF LIVER, Special, lb........... 15c

PORK KIDNEYS and PORK LIVER, lb..... 10c

SUGAR CURED BACON, Half or Whole Strip, lb.................. 25c

FRESH SPARE RIBS, lb 15c

FINEST SAUER KRAUT, 4 lbs........ 25c

Michael Weber
1930

> I do not believe that Michael had his own shop; instead, he worked for another store.
> He was living at Fourth Street in 1930.

_____

Halford Herchenwrother – butcher – unknown location
1930

> He resided at Wagner Road in Center Township in 1930.
> > It is unknown if his shop was located in the same place or if he worked for
> > another business.

*** *** *** *** ***

Fruit Markets

Joe Scanio – lower 900s Pennsylvania Avenue
1900, 1910

> Italian fruit dealer in 1907.
> Sold fancy California fruit and vegetables.
> In Jul 1907 Joe tired of produce coming up missing, so he got two large dogs by his store who
> > would "react" to intruders.

   then……

Antonio Scanio was the owner – lower 900s Pennsylvania Avenue
1920, 1930, 1940

> In 1920 and 1930, Domenick Taormina had listed *merchant/fruit* on the census.   I suspect he
> > was working for Antonio because he was his brother-in-law since Antonio married Anna
> > Taormina; Domenick was also living with Antonio in 1920.
> In 1933, they moved to Pennsylvania Avenue, located close to Max Barnett's
> > shoe store which was formerly owned by Joe Alessi.   They had their fruit market
> > on street level and lived in an apartment above the store in 1933.
> So, since Antonio and Anna were listed as living at 906 Pennsylvania in 1940, this may
> > have been the address/location of the store.

_____

Joseph Taravella – fruit dealer – Pennsylvania Avenue
1900, 1902, 1903

> Joseph married Antonia; they lived at the same place as the store.

_____

Joe Sigarel – fruit dealer - Ninth Street prior to Apr 1907, then corner Pennsylvania Avenue/Sixth Street
1906, 1907

> He moved from Ninth Street to a store room in the Mateer Bros. building on Pennsylvania
> > Avenue, near Sixth Street.   This store room had been rented previously to Fred Patton
> > Jewelry store who moved to the Keystone building.

_____

Dominick Taormina - merchant / fruit dealer – lower 900s Pennsylvania Avenue
1920, 1940
>It is not clear if Dominick was the owner of his own store. He was listed as a *merchant* which indicates the owner of a business. I found no store with his name alone; but he was the brothe-in-law to Antonio Scanio who did have his own store.
>Dominick lived with Scanio in 1920, then at 1100 Indiana in 1930.
>His wife, Antonie, also listed herself as a *merchant/fruit* in 1930.

_____

Mr. and Mrs. Mike Darrow – grocery and fruit - 1223 Pennsylvania Avenue
1920, 1922, 1924
>In 1920, they bought property.   They planned to open their store room and dwelling there.

_____

Matteo/Matthew Cortese – fruit dealer - 1136 Pennsylvania Avenue
1920, 1930, 1940,
>In 1920 he purchased the business property and the adjoining building which was occupied by Andrew Radler/shoe repair shop (sold from the Nicholas Wurzel estate) but this wasn't near 1136 Pennsylvania .
>In 1940 it was not just a fruit store, but called a grocery store. His wife, Sarah, helped in the store; they lived at same address as store.

_____

Andrew Kurtz - fruit merchant – 1136 Pennsylvania Avenue
1930, 1940
>This business was Cortese's Fruit and Grocery. Andrew either worked for Cortese or had his own section in the storeroom.
>Residency was on Virginia Avenue.

_____

Samuel Taormina – fruit dealer – 1308 Pennsylvania Avenue
1929, 1930

_____

Samuel Kurtz was a fruit merchant – address unknown
1930
>He was living with Samuel Taormina in 1930; he may have just handled the fruit section in Taormina's store rather than have his own business; or he could have been in with Andrew Kurtz (?).

_____

Alessi's Fruit Headquarters   aka   Joseph Alessi – fruit mart and grocery store – 910 Penna Avenue
1922, 1929, 1930, 1931 , 1933
>Building was a one storey frame, owned by Joseph Zigerelli and ____.
>Joseph Alessi operated his fruit market and grocery store in the building.
>>There was an explosion and serious fire at this building at 3:10 a.m. Dec 28, 1929.
>>The entire front of the store was blown out from the explosion, which was suspected to have been from a gas leak.   The building had been erected in 1885.
>>>Mr. and Mrs. Zigerell lived at a brick residence in the rear of the building. When the building was remodeled, it must have been made into two storey OR Alessi moved the business to another building, because........
>He was out of business by Apr 1933 because A. Scanio moved from Indiana Avenue to Alessi's storeroom on Pennsylvania Avenue – using storeroom to sell fruit, living on second floor.
>Mrs. J. Alessi was the owner in 1931.

_____

Samuel Battaglio / Bollaglia - fruit merchant – 1031 Pennsylvania Avenue
1928, 1930, 1931, 1943
> He was living at 1032 Pennsylvania Avenue in 1930, so I suspect he just handled the fruit section
> in Taormina's store or the Monaca Fruit Market rather than having his own business (?)

————————

Mrs. Amelia Petrella – fruit dealer, etc. – 913 Pennsylvania Avenue
1912
> Mrs. Petrella lived at the same address as the business.

————————

Antonio Danna – fruit market – 910 Pennsylvania Avenue
1910, 1912
> Antonio and Rosa resided in the same building as the business.

————————

Joseph Campisi - fruit market – 923 and 1136 Pennsylvania Avenue and 2564 Beaver Avenue - Colona
1912, 1930, 1931, 1943
> In 1930 the Mercantile List states his business at 32 Beaver Street.
> Joseph and Lena lived in the same building as their business in 1912,
> > then living on Beaver Avenue (Colona) beginning 1920.

————————

Monaca Fruit Market   aka Cancilla Fruit and Grocery Market   aka   Cancilla & Company (1925)
> - 1032 Pennsylvania Avenue (1920) then 1200 Pennsylvania Avenue
1920, 1930, 1940, 1960s
> Frank and Virginia Cancilla , owners.   Had business for over 50 years prior to 1977.
> They lived in same building as business in 1920.

MONACA FRUIT
MARKET
1200 PENN'A AVE.,
MONACA
1200 PENN AVE., MONACA, PA.,
WILL OFFER THE BIGGEST
CHRISTMAS SALE OF BEAVER CO.
CHRISTMAS TREES, 40c AND UP.
FRUIT OF ALL KINDS AT LOW
PRICES, WE DELIVER ANY PLACE.
COME ONE, COME ALL. CANCILLA
& COMPANY.   12|21-22-23-24
1925

Come One!
Come All!
To See the Big Specials on
Our
Christmas Trees
AT LOWEST PRICES
50c AND UP
Also All Kinds of Fresh
Fruits and Vegetables.
Phone—We Deliver
Rochester 9114

Monaca Fruit Market
FRANK CANCILLA, Prop.
1200 Pennsylvania Avenue
MONACA
1930

*** *** *** *** ***

Confectionery　Bakery　Ice Cream　Dairy

William Miller – baker – unknown address
1898, 1903
> He had advertisement in 1902/03 for "Wm. Miller Bakery."

_____

Emmett O'Brien – candy store / confectionery – res Pennsylvania Avenue
1898, 1900, 1903
> On 1898 directory, Mrs. E. O'Brien was the proprietor.

_____

Weirich Bakery – 821 Indiana Avenue
1889, 1893, 1900, 1905, 1913, 1921, 1922 (not in business by 1930)
> Owned by Henry C. "Pop" Weirich.
>> 1880 – at the age of 14, Henry was working in a bakery, most likely being "apprenticed" in the trade.
>> 1889, when he married Mary Gray/Nay, Henry was already a baker. The family lived at the same building as the bakery.   They settled and started a family on "Third Ave" which became Indiana Avenue.
> May 1906 - Brick work and stone work was finished on his new building, Indiana Avenue. Known for his coffee cakes.
> Contractor Hemphill finished the brick work and stone work on Henry's new building on Indiana Avenue in 1906.
> Henry had William Stoops and Walter Anderton working as bakers and residing with them in 1900, 1902, 1903.
> Building sat where new social hall is for United Methodist Church (2016).

Weirich home & bakery
Courtesy BCHR&LF

_____

William Stoops – baker
1900
> He was employed by Henry Weirich; he also lived in the Weirich home.

_____

Jimmy Davis Confectionery Store –confectionery and cigar store - 809 Pennsylvania Avenue
1898, 1902, 1907

     James "Jimmy" M. Davis – owner (nephew of Hugh Davis – Moon Township)

     Jimmy started in business with Morris Barnett sometime between 1886 and 1887, but in 1893
          the building was destroyed by fire. Store was located at Pennsylvania Avenue and Eighth Street.
          Then Morris built a large brick two storey brick building on Pennsylvania Ave (near Eighth Street)
          and began his own business.

     Confectionery and ice cream parlor. In 1898 a directory stated "dealer in fine confectionery,
          tobaccos and cigars; fruits in season; manager Western Union Telegraph Co."

     Dec 1900 – enlarged the store, put up new steel ceilings and repainted.

     1902/03 had the store on Pennsylvania Ave; he roomed with G. Heintz.

     Had a "fine new box sign placed in front of his confectionery and ice cream parlors" on
          Apr 4, 1904.

     Added three new show cases in his confectionery and cigar store Oct 29, 1906.

     Mr. Davis died in 1907 and Charles (Charley) K. Lindsay conducted Jimmy's business until the
          estate was settled since Mr. Lindsay had been employed by Mr. Davis since 1901.
          C.K. Lindsay who continued to run a confectionery store for a number of years.   It later
          became the property of James Hicks.

     Building and business was bought by Harry B. Barnett of Monaca.   Mr. Barnett also had a clothing
          and gent's furnishing business in Aliquippa, too – but would conduct both businesses.

     The building James had for his store was among the oldest in Monaca.

     The building was razed in May 1927. The land on which this building stood was owned by the
          Wagner heirs.

     Jimmy's 1902/03 small ad stated again - "Dealer in Fine Confectionery, Tobaccos and Cigars;
     Fruits in Season.   Manager - Western Union Telegraph Co."

It became...........................

Lindsay Parlors – 809 Pennsylvania Avenue
1907, 1912

     Owner, C. K. Lindsay.   Charles K. married Clara ___ and they lived at Virginia Avenue in
          1912. He became the owner of this store in 1907.   Sold ice cream and confections
          and cigars.

When the building at 809 Pennsylvania Avenue was sold, C. K. Lindsay moved and opened ....

Crystal Confectionery   aka   Lindsay's News – 1317 Pennsylvania Avenue
1912, 1921, 1924, 1943

     C. (Charles) K. Lindsay owner.

     He was noted for his confections, ice cream, soda, root beer.

     Had interior of store newly painted and papered.

     Charles also made a specialty in selling sporting goods.

     This business was also referred to as *Lindsay's News* in 1938.

C. K. Lindsay.

Stahl Bakery – Pennsylvania Avenue
1906   Sold to George Schnoedel in 1906.

_____

Mattauch's Confectionery – 699 Pennsylvania Avenue
Early 1900s through c 1940
       Paul owned a confectionery store in addition to his barbershop.   Both businesses were in the
              same building.   I do not know if his daughter, Mrs. William (Emma) Cloughley
              worked in this storeroom; but Paul's wife, Julie, did. It was printed that she sold more
              ice cream than was sold at Junction Park.

       See the Barber section for a large picture of the building at 699 Pennsylvania Avenue.

Photo courtesy BCHR&LF

Julie Mattauch in the confectionery store.

Photo courtesy BCHR&LF

Paul and Julie's daughter, Emma Mattauch Cloughley, in front of her father's
confectionery store.

_____

Jolly's Bakery – 216 Sixth Street
1892, 1893

> The earliest mention of Jolly's Bakery I found was 1870, but I believe he would have been
>> in business prior to that date; most likely from the time Phillipsburg was being established.
> Dickerson A. Jolly no longer had his business in the early 1900s.
> He had Henry Weirich and Harry Miller working for him in the bakery.   Henry Weirich
>> opened his own bakery on Indiana Avenue in c.1899.
> The original bakery building was eventually torn down and a private home was erected on the lot.

––––––––––

Klingseisen Bakery – In 1900s the business was at 919 Pennsylvania Avenue, it then moved
                                                          to 1009 Pennsylvania Avenue
Between 1900 & 1910, 1929, 1940, 1957

> Business was started by Joseph and Francesca Klingseisen (parents of Lothar and Alois)
>> Joseph and family came from Allegheny County between 1900 and 1910 and opened the
>>> bakery on Pennsylvania Avenue (Joseph was only in his early 30s at that time).
>> He came to America in 1889 and was most likely taught the trade of baker in Germany.
> The 2nd location was adjacent to the site of the current (2016) post office and on the property
>> where the Nat'l Bank bldg (the Century Bank) was built- currently a restaurant .   This
>> location was between the Fisher's home, the Fisher newsstand, and a dry cleaning store.
> It was a family business.   Joseph died between 1912 and 1920, Frances, 49, was widowed and
>> listed as the owner of the bakery and had *baker* as her occupation on the 1920 census.
>> Her sons Lothar and Alois (and Lothar's wife, Elinore) were living with her.   Alois was
>> working in the bakery at age 16.   Lothar was a telegraph operator.
> Francesca still owned the bakery in 1930, but it was being run by Lothar and Alois (with Lothar's
>> wife helping I am sure).   Francesca, now 60, was living with Lothar and Elinore at 1009
>> Pennsylvania Avenue; Alois was then married and living on Atlantic Avenue with his
>> family, but still working at the bakery.
> On Aug 27, 1936, Alois Klingseisen, younger brother of Lothar, unfortunately drowned in the
>> Ohio River at age 32 when his motor boat collided with the tow boat *Costanza* by
>> Rochester on the Ohio River.
> Francesca was still living at age 70 in 1940 and her son Lothar was the sole owner of the bakery
>> with Elinore listed as a *clerk* in the bakery. Margaret, Alois's widow, and children were
>> living with Margaret's widowed mother, Alice Potter at 616 Washington Avenue.
> With Lothar and Elinore having no children, it appears that the family business was not
>> continued when Lothar retired and sold their building.

––––––––––

Schier Bakery – bakery and confectionery store - 714 Pennsylvania Avenue
1906, 1912

> Emil Schier opened his new bakery May 23, 1906.   Julius Schier was considered the owner in
>> 1912.   Julius and Marie lived in the same building as the business.
> The store was across from Buchholz' meat market which was on corner Pennsylvania &
>> Eighth Street.

––––––––––

Wm. Figley Ice Cream parlor and confectionery store – Ninth Street
1901, 1903

> Opened in summer of 1901.   This building was used for Morgan's Millinery in 1904.
> Mr. and Mrs. Wm. Figley seemed to have moved out of Monaca between 1904 and 1913(?).
> 1923 there is a Harry Figley of Ninth Street but no business listed.

––––––––––

Edward B. Borr Bakery – Pennsylvania Avenue
1902, 1903
       His wife was Elizabeth __; they lived at the same location as the bakery.

———————

Robert Onstott – Confectionery Store - Pennsylvania Avenue
1903
       Added a one storey addition to his residence and opened a confectionery store.

———————

Martin Konvalinka –baker in his own bakery - Dockter's Heights/Monaca Heights
1910, 1912, 1920

———————

Joseph McMillen – confectionery store – unknown location
1910, 1930
       Joseph lived on Atlantic but I do not know where his business was located or if it was at his home(?).

———————

Walter Auderton – baker
1900
       I found no business of his, so he probably worked for another business; he lived on
          Indiana Avenue.

———————

George Bartel's confectionery store – Pennsylvania Avenue
1903, 1904
       It was called "Bartel building" in 1903.
       In 1904, he took over E. Levy's "Owl Billiard Academy" store room.
       When he opened the new confectionery and ice cream parlor on Mar 23, 1904, he was furnishing
          it with the finest furniture and fixtures and show cases. He formerly conducted the
          "Sugar Bowl" in Rochester prior to it burning.
          He was portioning off the large store room for the rear to be living rooms with the
          confectionery store and ice cream parlor in the front part of the building. The Bartel
          family lived in the rear and he opened the store in the front.
          Anderson Davidson commenced stone work on the George Bartel Building in the Michael
          Wahl plan on Pennsylvania Avenue; frame work started in 1903.

———————

Brack's – candy and ice cream store – Pennsylvania Avenue
Earlier 1900s
       Daniel Bracken (Brack) Winkle - proprietor
       He married 2nd to Josie Guba and they lived in the now razed house which was located just
          outside Monaca. on the right past the railroad trestle. Daniel was also fire chief, vice president
          of the Phillipsburg Building and Loan Association and was a prominent citizen of Monaca; Josie
          was also well known socially.

———————

Mrs. Madeline Varner – confectionery store – 613 Pennsylvania Avenue
1902, 1903   She lived on Washington Avenue.

———————

Markey Confectionery – Pennsylvania Avenue
1914   Ewing Markey – owner.

———————

Helen aka Nellie O'Keefe - 718 Pennsylvania Avenue - 798 Pennsylvania Avenue – 899 Atlantic Avenue
1928, 1930, 1931, 1940, 1941, 1943

> She had 3 different addresses attached to her business and /or residency. What was listed on the tax records may have been errors which would account for the different numbers and/or they listed her home address for a few years instead of the business address (?).
>
> She ran a grocery store, then it was considered a confectionery store, and finally before the whole block was torn down for the revitalization program, it was a confectionery and luncheon counter.
>
> Helen's maiden name was Sullivan and she was married to Christopher O'Keefe in 1917. They had 4 children and then Christopher died in Jan 1925.
>
> 1930 to 1940, listings had them at 798 Pennsylvania Avenue, in 1940 they were listed at 718 Pennsylvania Avenue. Between the 1940s and before she died in 1977, they were at 899 Atlantic Avenue. (As stated, tax lists indicate all three addresses over the years, too.)
>
> *899 was evidently razed – no longer exists; may have been removed for building or "beautifying" of the bridge area (?).

This photo gives a look at Helen O'Keefe's storeroom.   It was located on the right side of Pennsylvania Avenue heading into Monaca, heading toward Ninth Street.   All the buildings along this side of Pennsylvania Avenue within the 700 and 800 blocks of Pennsylvania Avenue were razed for the revitalization project by Phoenix Glass Co. I suspect the building address would have correctly been 718 Pennsylvania Avenue since the adjacent house to the left sat on a corner which was #798.   Possibly Helen and family lived in the house for a period of time which would also explain the different addresses listed on tax records.

Photo courtesy Borough of Monaca

_____

William Eberle's Confectionery Store – 919 Pennsylvania Avenue
1925   There is no indication of who the previous owners were, but William Eberle bought this confectionary store on Jul 1, 1925.
    It then became................

Preece's Confectionery – 919 Pennsylvania Avenue
1928, 1929

> William R. Preece.   Placed an ad looking for 2 or 3 men to work/drive.
> He also ran a restaurant at this address in the 1910s.

_____

Roxy Confectionery – 924 Pennsylvania Avenue
1938

_____

Carl Kortoff – baker -
1930   He most likely worked for another person in their store.

_____

Merriman Confectionery – 1308 Pennsylvania Avenue
1936, 1941   Had a *grill* here, too.   The address of this storeroom might have even been
                at 1301 or 1307 –   the print was difficult to read.

_____

Graters Confectionery Store – corner of Ninth and Atlantic Avenue/ 899 Atlantic Avenue
1920, 1924   Mrs. Elsie Grater – proprietor.   She lived at same address.
                899 Atlantic is no longer there – building was razed for beautifying area of bridge.

_____

John Bell's Confectionery – Monaca Heights
1930s, 1938, 1949
            John Bell also once had a store downtown, by 1938 he was also on the hill.
                His wife Henrietta owned and operated the confectionery store - Bell's Super Market at
                    1014 Pennsylvania Avenue (Mar 1957) – 927 Pennsylvania Avenue (Feb 1957).
            In 1949 Louis Cativera purchased the downtown business from John Bell which was then at
                1014 Pennsylvania Avenue.

_____

Herbert Harrison – Confectionery Store – 914 or 915 Marshall Road - Monaca Heights
1930s   Herbert owned the store; he lived at same location as store in 1930.
                By 1940 he was working elsewhere, but may have still had the store (?).

_____

Renzo Confectionery – 924 Pennsylvania Avenue (next door to the reconstructed Municipal Building)
1937   Made their own ice creams.

We Are Right Next Door To Our
Reconstructed Municipal Center

RENZO CONFECTIONERY
924 Pennsylvania Ave., Monaca

WE MAKE OUR OWN
ICE CREAMS
FRESH DAILY

Come in and watch the process
SPECIAL ALL THIS WEEK!

2 PINTS - - - - - 25c
Any Flavor

Try one of the tasty nickel "High Hats"
Hot Dogs and Hamburgers—
Silix Made Coffee—Soft Drinks—
Tobaccos—Newspapers. ALL THE
LATEST MAGAZINES.

_____

Charles Lacassas was a baker in a bakery, but I have no evidence of his owning his own shoppe
1930   Charles lived at 1096 Pennsylvania Avenue in 1930, the business may have been
                out of his home(?).

_____

Agnes Campisi – confectionery and grocery store -923 and 1136 Pennsylvania Avenue
                                                and 2564 Beaver Avenue - Colona
1940
        Agnes was the daughter of Joe and Lena. She first was a clerk in the store, then
                was the proprietor of the business by 1940.   In 1930 – resided at Beaver Avenue.

_____

John McMichael - owner of a confectionery store – unknown address
1940   They lived on Virginia Avenue in 1940.

_____

Joseph Zigercal/Zigerelli – Confectionery and Grocery Store - 1308 Pennsylvania Avenue (prior to 1956)
1910, 1920
        (Many versions of the name's spelling appeared in the newspaper articles.)
        He came to Monaca in 1901; 1910 Joseph was listed as a merchant in confectioneries;
        1920 Joseph was listed as a merchant in the grocer business.

_____

Stark Candy Co. - 1299 Indiana Avenue, then in 1954 moved to 1140 Pennsylvania Avenue
1951, 1956
        Edward L. Stark - owner

_____

Monaca Home Baking Co. – 1307 Pennsylvania Avenue
1954, 1956

_____

Allen Fredericks was a baker and worked in a bakery.
1940
        I don't know if he had his own store or used his home for a store. He lived at Walnut Street.

_____

Frank Nunzir Bakery – Pacific Avenue
1979   See Grocery section for more information.

_____

Jennie Romisher – confectionery store - 818 Penna Avenue (also residency)
1940
        1940 census states she was a proprietor of a confectionery store and an article stated from about
            1935 to at least 1943 that she partnered in the confectionery business with Susanne (her
            sister-in-law) and Herz Salberg.

_____

Bakery on Fourth Street
1961 to 1975   Amelia "Mama Celeste" Cappella.

_____

Kappel's Confectionery – 1723 Pennsylvania Avenue
1951   They specialized in "charcoal hot dogs."

_____

Mr. Paul's Bakery – 1128 Pennsylvania Avenue
1962, 1967, 1972, 1977

James Braddick was one of the owners of Paul's Bakery, Inc. in 1967, 1969.

He did many cake decorating demonstrations for many various events.

Owned by William Braddick in 1977.

Was closed before 1995.

Fun Note – The first of March 1972, the state lottery program began in Beaver County and – this was the only business in Monaca in 1972 to begin distributing state lottery tickets. On March 16, 1972 , Mrs. Eleanor Ramos of Pennsylvania Avenue won $50,000 from a ticket purchased at the bakery.

WHAT A TREAT!
Home-Baked Quality Goods From
Paul's Bakeries
We Specialize In Wedding Cakes

You'll always remember the exquisite beauty and delicate flavor of your wedding cake, when it's baked by us.

We Guarantee Satisfaction...

BIRTHDAY – SPECIAL OCCASIONS!
PICNIC BAKED GOODS
AND BAR-B-QUE OUTINGS

PAUL'S BAKERIES
WITH FOUR LOCATIONS

511 Merchant Street, Ambridge	CO 6-6052
14th & Merchant Streets, Ambridge	CO 6-8103
Plaza Shopping Center, Aliquippa	ES 8-2706
1128 Pennsylvania Avenue, Monaca	SP 4-1060

Isaly's Dairy Store, Inc. – (beside Johnson Flowers)   1032 Pennsylvania Avenue
1940, 1949, 1971

Building was owned by Glenn Heckman (a hardware store owner).

William Hawkins was manager in 1940.

Isaly's
**BULK PAK
ICE CREAM**
VANILLA OR
CHOCOLATE $1.49
Gal.
1032 Penna. Ave.   Monaca
Phone Rock 9091
1949

KEEP YOUR YOUNGSTERS HAPPY
WITH *Isaly's* SKYSCRAPER
ICE CREAM
CONES
In Choice of
16 Tempting
Flavors
10¢
1953

Vogt & Reed – Pennsylvania Avenue
1907

They had a meat market and also bought out milk route of James Cochran (Moon Township dairyman). Joseph Reed, Jr. member of the business drove the milk wagon.

Main Ice Cream Co. – 1200 Pennsylvania Avenue
1911
They had a matched team of young sorrel ponies for sale in 1911.

_____

Edward M. Johnston – Washington Avenue
1908, 1909
"Manufacturer of fine ice cream and ice cream cones – wholesale and retail."
It was referred to as "the milk depot" business.   He had bay horses for deliveries.

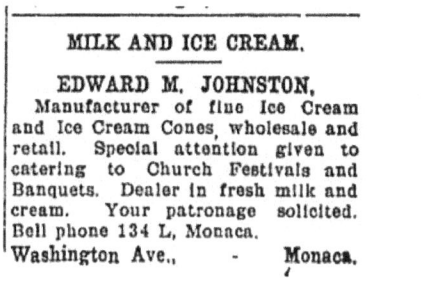

> **MILK AND ICE CREAM.**
>
> **EDWARD M. JOHNSTON,**
> Manufacturer of fine Ice Cream and Ice Cream Cones, wholesale and retail. Special attention given to catering to Church Festivals and Banquets. Dealer in fresh milk and cream.   Your patronage solicited. Bell phone 134 L, Monaca.
> Washington Ave.,   -   Monaca.

1909

and........

E. M. Johnston Dairy – 1200 Pennsylvania Avenue
1909, 1912   Edward M. was known for his homemade ice cream.

_____

George Heintz – address unknown
1902
Sold ice cream – retail and/or wholesale. Advertised special rates on large orders.
George and Bertha had their home on Washington Avenue.   They may have run
their business from their home(?).   George died prior to 1931.

_____

Albert J. Kugel – dairyman
1902, 1903   His wife was Anna A.; they lived on Virginia Avenue.

_____

Charles Kugel – dairyman –
1910   Charles had a dairy farm (in Moon Township which may have been Monaca Heights ?).

_____

August Greener/Grinier – dairyman in retail milk – Monaca Heights
1910, 1911   Charles, his son, was a driver of the milk wagon in 1910.

_____

Lewis M. Chapman – butter dealer and then grocery store – 1099 Pennsylvania Avenue
(corner of Penn and Eleventh Street)
1912, 1920, 1928, 1943
In 1912, Lewis was just a butter dealer.
Lewis and Mayme Chapman lived in the same building as their business.
Was granted a license in 1915 from the Pennsylvania Dept. of Agriculture to sell oleomargarine.
In 1920 he was a merchant of a full grocery business.

_____

Harry L. Ferguson – butter dealer – 1110 Atlantic Avenue
1912   Harry and Fern resided in the same building as their business.

_____

Abraham Levine – 1101 Pennsylvania Avenue
1914, 1915   Abraham was granted a license in 1915 from the Pennsylvania Dept. of Agriculture to sell
                    oleomargarine.

_____

Gus Haller – milk route deliveryman – 1135 Pennsylvania Avenue
1924

_____

Milliron's Milk Depot – 1128 Virginia Avenue
1922, 1924, 1930
          Mrs. Anna Milliron was listed on tax lists as owner of business.   They lived at 1128 Virginia
                    Avenue; the census stated her husband, John, was a *dairyman* for a Dairy Co.
          They may have sold items from their home ?

_____

Monaca Dairy – 1300 Atlantic Avenue
1931

_____

Skeeter Hill Ice Cream Shop - corner of Walnut Street and Taylor Avenue
          Very small wooden building.

_____

Echo Point Dairy –Chapel Road, Center Township
          (This site is currently the Cedar Ridge Estates.)
          1925 Joseph and Genevieve Dusold bought the farm on Chapel Road and started Echo Point Dairy.
                    Tradition says the name was because of the echoes that could be heard from where the house
                    was located up on the hill.
          Until 1950, the 150 to 200 acres were farmed; there were 25 to 50 head of dairy cattle.
          1950 – John (Jack) Dusold bought the farm from his father and along with his two brothers,
                    Joseph and Don, they formed Echo Point Dairy, Inc.
          1963 – they opened the store in Monaca.
                    -Another store was opened in Beaver Falls in 1965, but was sold in 1970.
                    -A delicatessen in Beaver was started in 1968 and as of 1990 was operated by Don and
                              Norma Jean Dusold.
          1978-1987 – the dairy store was sold and Little Echo Restaurant was opened.
          As of 1990, the original farm house was still occupied by Dusolds.
          2016 – the original farm house is still standing.

_____

Hyllmede Dairy Incorporated –
1965   Owned and operated by Beaver County Dairymen.

*** *** *** *** ***

A 1915 report of the Pennsylvania Department of Agriculture contained the following information:

The following were listed in Monaca as having samples taken of their milk, all coming back with no adulteration detected:

H. C. Hartenbach (Lived and had a dairy farm in Moon/Center Township.)
W. M. Engel
Edward E. Winkle   (Lived and had dairy farm in Moon/Center Township.)
Paukray Finzel   (Lived and had dairy farm in Moon/Center Township.)

The following were listed in Monaca and had comments attached:

Edward J. Schachern - Pennsylvania Avenue
Was listed as having "complying" with pure food samples (fish); but was also cited for selling cold storage fish not properly marked in March of 1915.
Martin Mild – was charged in April 1915 of selling milk low in fat and solids, skimmed.
(He lived and had a dairy farm in Moon/Center Township.)
Alexander Eckert – was charged in April 1915 of selling milk low in fat and solids, skimmed.
Frank Kalenoska – was charged in April 1915 of selling milk low in fat and solids, skimmed.
(He lived and had a dairy / general farm in Moon/Center Township.)
Jos. Phibbs – was charged in April 1915 of selling milk low in fat and solids, skimmed.
(He lived and had a dairy farm in Moon/Center Township.)

*** *** *** *** ***

Grocers

Israel Bentel – grocer
1841

Israel was born in Jun 1794 Germany and came from Economy to Phillipsburg.
He died in 1848.   I do not know if Israel had a business and Anthony Knapper (his brother-in-law) was involved in the same business or if they both had their own storerooms.

———

The One Horse Cash Grocery (1898)
aka   McClurg's stand - General Store – corner of Pennsylvania Avenue and Twelfth Street
1898, 1900, 1903, 1904

Dry goods, notions, shoes, tin and granite ware.   Jos. R. McClurg was owner.
By Mar 1904, Joseph was no longer at his business because E. Hood took over the building and the McClurgs moved to a house on Virginia Avenue.
He married Martha __; they had 4 children.
George and Edna had died by 1910. Joseph had his occupation as *laborer, odd jobs* in 1910.   Martha was then living at 1525 Pennsylvania Avenue. Jos. died between 1910 and 1920.   Joseph was also the Street Commissioner of Monaca in 1907.

J. R. McClurg,
DEALER IN
Dry Goods, Groceries, Boots, Shoes, Rubbers.
Cor. Twelfth St. and Pennsylvania Ave., MONACA, PA.
1900

———

Knapper Grocery and Meat Market – from 1837 it was at 111 Fourth Street - then at 424 Pennsylvania Avenue
1837 to 1877 ....

> Opened 1837.   Red brick home was there when still Phillipsburg and the Economites came.
> Owned by Anthony Knapper.   He was one of the earliest postmasters of Water Cure, later
> > Phillipsburg and finally Monaca   (1858 to 1877).
> Anthony married Theodora Wilhelmina Bentel in Mar/Apr 1832. Her brother was Israel Bentel.
> Anthony hired a young George Bechtel as a clerk as his business grew.
> > George Bechtel married Anthony's daughter, Emilie. Both Emilie and their daughter died
> > within a year of the marriage.
> He ran the business from his red brick home on Fourth Street.
> When Anthony died, George Bechtel continued the business.   With no authentic records,
> > Anthony's presumed death date is 1877 since George Bechtel succeeded him as
> > postmaster from 1877 until 1881.
> Then........................

Bechtel Company – 424 Pennsylvania Avenue (opposite the turn leading to the Brodhead Road)
1877 to 1937   (100 continuous years in business!)

> > George remarried many years after Emilie's death to Mary Miksch who helped in
> > conducting the growing business.   George died c. 1886 (I found no authentic record of
> > his death).   The firm of Bechtel Company was formed with John and Henry Miksch
> > being members of the company. John Miksch died in 1908; Henry Miksch was known as
> > a real estate and insurance agent and withdrew from the company.   Mrs. Mary Bechtel
> > ran the store in 1910.   Mrs. Bechtel took her two sons, William and Fred Bechtel into the
> > business & the family carried it on.   Mrs. Bechtel died in 1919; the sons died by 1930s.
> George and Mary's daughter, Emilie Bechtel and her sister-in-law Mrs. Mary Bechtel (Fred's wife)
> > operated the store until they made the decision to retire.
> The location was considered 403 Pennsylvania Avenue when they were running the business.
> The 1902/03 directory listed Mrs. M. Bechtel and H. Miksch as owners; stated it was a grocery
> > and meat market; had all kinds of mill feed, salts, flour and hay, also hosiery and dry
> > goods.
> Fred H. Bechtel, owner in 1912, 1913 and 1927 with help of his sister, Miss Emilie.
> > F. H. lived at 111 Fourth Street.
> This was one of the oldest and largest general stores in Monaca.
> The business closed its doors in Sep 1937 after <u>100 years</u>.

```
::::::::::::::::::::::::::::::

F. H. BECHTEL
_____
Pennsylvania Avenue
Monaca, Pa.
DEALER IN

All Kinds of Mill
Feed and Salts,
Flour and Hay.

Walter's Buckwheat, 5 and 10
   lb. Sacks...20c and 35c Sack
Cornmeal, 10 lb. Sacks, 25c Sack
Conkey's, Pratt's, Dr. Hess' and
   National Poultry Food. Com-
   plete line of Remedies for
   Live Stock.
For Laying Hens Try Our
   Scratch Grains and Mash
   Feed.
_____

Bell Phone 582-R.
::::::::::::::::::::::::::::::
```
1913

Charles Frederick - Retail grocer – unknown location
1870

Dairy and Produce Store - 1102 Pennsylvania Avenue
1897, 1913
        Established in 1897.   Owned by Mr. and Mrs. William Fisher.
        They closed out the business in 1913 to move to Youngstown, Ohio.

        _____

Michael Cachner - grocer – unknown location
1850

        _____

Charles Polen – grocer – unknown location
1892, 1893

        _____

H. A. Orr & Co. – grocer – unknown location
1892, 1893

        _____

Charles O'Brien – grocer – unknown location
1892, 1893

        _____

Vogt Meat Market and grocery – 800 Pennsylvania Avenue
1892, 1893, 1902, 1903, 1912, 1920, 1926
        Daniel F. Vogt was listed as the owner in 1892, 1893.
        Henry E. Vogt was then listed as owner and was a butcher.   He married Elizabeth __; they lived
                at 610 Indiana Avenue.
        Walter Bucholtz purchased and had his business as of Jan 1, 1927.
                See Vogt & Reed   and   Vogt & Glasser

        _____

William Sullivan – grocer and confectionery – Pennsylvania Avenue
1898, 1902, 1903
        William married Lena; they lived at the same place as the store.
                After William died, Lena kept up store and had a restaurant, too.
    Then ....

Sullivan & Hunter – corner of Pennsylvania Avenue and Eighth Street
Very early 1900s
        John Hunter and Peter Sullivan – owners.   William Hunter was John Hunter's father.

    Then firm was purchased by.....................

John Hunter – grocery store - corner of Pennsylvania Avenue and Eighth Street
        Opened   ------ .   Closed Oct 10, 1906.

    John sold the business to Peter Sullivan and it became.........

Sullivan's Produce Market – Pennsylvania Avenue   - Became known as the Sullivan Building.
1906   Had a large glass window pane break in 1906 due to the sinking of the building.

        _____

Carl F. Kaercher – grocery store – unknown location
1869, 1876, 1880,
        The Kaercher family lived on Hanover Street (now Fourth Street), then 399 Atlantic Avenue.

        _____

John Shoemaker – grocer

1869   His resident was on Ohio Street (now Atlantic – where it joins Sixth Street).

_____

William Porter – grocer – unknown location

1880

_____

Peter Julius – grocer – Pennsylvania Avenue

1898, 1903   Sold confectionery, cigars, tobacco, and soft drinks, too.

_____

Martin W. Carey's Grocery store –899 Pennsylvania Avenue

1882, 1893, 1907, 1934, 1942

At the corner of Pennsylvania Ave & Ninth Street; this corner was called Carey's Corner.

Property was purchased by Martin W. Carey from Jacob Bucheit May 14, 1873.

Business was started by Martin W. Carey's father, Martin opened his business on May 12, 1882.

Martin married Mary A.; they lived above the grocery store.

Martin W. Carey (died in 1934) His son helped run business, then took over
when his father died.

Aug 24, 1942 – building was sold to Ernest C. Springer of Monaca and Thomas F. Pawka of Beaver.

Until this sale, the Carey family had possession of the property since 1873.

The property consisted of the corner building (which contained the large storeroom on the first floor and an 8 room and 1 room apartment on the second floor), two adjacent buildings that faced Ninth Street, two that faced Pennsylvania Avenue, and there was a seven car garage.

Daniel Carey was a clerk in the store in 1892/1893.

*This same storeroom/building then became known as ....

Monaca Inn (called Monaca Hotel in 1990s) – 899 Pennsylvania Avenue.

See Restaurant and tavern section for more details on the Monaca Inn.

Post card of street car and the intersection of Ninth Street and Pennsylvania Avenue

Ninth Street and Pennsylvania Avenue
Monaca, Pa.

Carey's on the left   Citizen's Nat'l Bank in back ground (on Ninth)

Courtesy BCHR&LF
Harbison's bldg on corner

_____

LeGoullon Grocery – Pennsylvania Avenue
1880, 1900s,

Lamartine learned to be a merchant from his father by being a clerk in dry goods store in 1870.
By 1880, he owned a grocery store; his son Francis was working with him.
Lamartine was b 1848. He married Clara Bott – children: Francis A., Edward, Cora, Ella,
Blanche, Charles, Emma, Charlotte, Howard, Lamartine
In 1898, Clara was listed as proprietor.   The store was listed as "groceries and provisions."

Then ....

LeGoullon Brothers Grocery – on Pennsylvania Avenue - 1199 Indiana Avenue - 298 Pennsylvania
1902, 1903, 1928, 1931   Avenue (1931)

Francis A. and Edward C. (sons of Lamartine) were owners.
Francis A. was married to Marie and they lived on Pennsylvania Avenue.
Edward C. was married to Lena and they lived on Pennsylvania Avenue also.
Howard W., their brother, was with the store eventually and lived on Fourth Street .

When Bread Was Just 5 Cents A Loaf!

Photo courtesy BCHR&LF

_____

C. Binder – grocer and provisions
1898, 1903

_____

Isaac Onstott – retail grocer - unknown location
1870

_____

J. Lawson – general merchandise (groceries) – Baker's Landing (Moon Township)
1898

_____

John Trumpeter –grocer - corner Thirteenth Street and Indiana Avenue / 1299 Indiana Avenue
1892, 1902, 1903, 1912, 1920, 1931, 1943
      In 1903 he started in the grocery business at 1299 Indiana Avenue and continued in this
            business until his death 1934.
      Had property on the corner of Twelfth & Indiana in 1906.
            Spark's circus held an attraction there in Jul 1906.
      Jun 1910 – he purchased a new horse for his delivery wagon.
      John married Emma; they lived at the same place as the store.
            John, Jr. was a clerk in the store in 1912.

_____

W. A. Dalzell & Son – first at 511 Bechtel Street , then 1011 Bechtel Street, Monaca Heights
      (Bechtel Street must have been renumbered because the store never moved and
      in 1950s to currently, Bechtel Street only goes down to #799.)
1899, 1994 (As of 1994, was in business 95 years.)
      Opened in 1899.   William A. Dalzell was the owner – he was father of C.W. who had
            Dalzell's downtown on Washington Avenue.
      Family home was originally in the back of the store.
      Grocery supplies and orders were delivered to the Monaca station by train from Pgh.
      Dalzells made deliveries; the livery was on the corner of Taylor and Bechtel Street and
            then became garages for the trucks; those were torn down and a home now sits
            on the corner lot.
      The store was once stocked with antiques and other mementos of the past which
            William and C.W. enjoyed collection– it was a mini-museum which depicted
            nearly 100 years of life in Beaver County.
      By 1937, Eugene was in business with his father.
      The store is still in business in 2016 under the ownership of Joseph Nichol.

in 1922

William, Malinda, and Eugene Dalzell standing outside their newly
remodeled Clover Farm Store ..... "the W.A. Dalzell and Son Grocery."

1011
Bechtel St.
Monaca

774-6019
W. A. DAZELL & SON
Food Market

1990

The Dalzell Grocery Store in Monaca Heights was a popular place in 1936. From left are Eugene M. Dalzell, Malinda Dalzell, Simon Palmgust, Katherine Dalzell, Russel Gallagher, Alice J. Graham, William A. Dalzell, Elliott R.L. Palm and Edmund Glass.

This business and building is now (2016).................

Nichol's Market – 1011 Bechtel Street, Monaca Heights
Current

_____

Henry Miksch – grocer – unknown location
1900   He lived on Atlantic Avenue.

_____

Joseph Zigerelli – confectionery and grocery store – 1308 Pennsylvania Avenue
1910, 1922
        He also sold cigars and tobacco at this address in 1912.

_____

McCreary – grocery business – 1119 Washington Avenue
1912, 1920
        Robert and Mary McCreary lived on Washington Avenue in 1912.

_____

Thomas S. Jackson – grocery store - 1229 Pennsylvania Avenue
1909, 1910, 1912   Thomas and Florence resided in the same building as the business.

_____

Michael Dorn's Grocery and Confectionery Store - at Sixth Street and Pennsylvania Avenue (1911)
  – then 1119 Washington Avenue (1923)

1910, 1923, 1928, 1929
    Michael lived on Kay Avenue, Monaca Heights; d 1933 (83 yrs); married Anna __; 3 children.
    1922 Mercantile Tax list stated his business was "Monaca Heights," so he most likely also had a
        store located there or possibly just sold the ice cream from his home ????
    Louis Dorn was a clerk in the store in 1912.
    Sold soft drinks and Rieck's Ice Cream.

MICHAEL DORN,
Sixth Street and Penn'a Avenue,
MONACA, PA.
LIST.
6 Cans Peas, Corn, Beans
    Tomatoes 45c
3 Bars of Soap............. 25c
3 Boxes Noodles........... 25c
7 Boxes Argo............. 25c
7 Boxes Soup Powder...... 25c
All Grades of Coffee...... 24c
3 Cans Molasses........... 25c
3 Cans Baked Beans........ 25c
3 Cans Lemon Cling Peaches 25c
7 Packages Spices..... ... 25c
4 Packages Mother's Hom-
    iny 25c
3 Large Salmon........... 50c
3 Bottles Catsup.......... 25c
All Preserves 10c
6 Packages Tobacco....... 25c
3 Jars Olives............. 25c
6 Packages Corn Starch.... 25c
3 Packages Breakfast Food. 25c
49lb Flour of all Brands in
    Stock $1.45

1911 ad

_____

I tend to stray off the beaten path within this book and delve into interesting facts.   This is one of those times.......

Fun fact: Rieck's Ice Cream
Many establishments were proud to carry the brand Rieck's Ice Cream.   It became very well known by many in Monaca and the surrounding communities and towns.   I found the information on this particular brand of ice cream interesting, so......... I wanted to once again stray off the path a bit and elaborate on some interesting information of a fairly local business.

Rieck's Ice Cream may go back to the early 1900s, but current times tie into it equally as well with the newly consolidated Heinz and Kraft companies.   The H. J. Heinz Co. was a Pittsburgh born company and it makes up 51 percent of the newer formed company with the Kraft Foods Group.   Kraft, which also has deep roots in Pittsburgh, did not always go by the name Kraft but had the name of National Dairy Products Corporation.

*   The National Dairy Products Corp. was formed in 1923 by Goldman Sachs and after it was offered to the public; it made several hard-working men into millionaires.   This corporation was formed by two companies – one was a smaller company called Hydrox, based in Chicago; the other was the larger Rieck-McJunkin Dairy Co. which held 2/3 of the stock when the corporation went public.   One of those men to become involved in the National Dairy Products Corp. was Edward E. Rieck.   He was the chairman of the board and also held a quite large portion of the corporation's new stock.   Edward was the son of German immigrants who were the pioneers of a dairy empire that would soon dominate Western Pennsylvania for more than 50 years and become one of the world's first nationwide dairy companies.   Edward used a $376 inheritance and bought a milk route from his uncle and in 1886 began with driving a milk wagon around the South Side of Pittsburgh.   His father died when Edward was young, but his step father had stepped in to run the business with his mother.   Shortly after 1886, Edward also bought out his step father for $800 and "the Edward E. Rieck Company was born" with 3 milk routes, 4 horses, and 3 wagons which he operated out of the Rieck's rented grocery store location on Jane Street.*

Over the years, Rieck made good use of his ambitious approach to life and made many acquisitions including a local creamery, leasing refrigerated storage space, moving the business to downtown Pittsburgh, hiring 8 men and 5 teams of horses. All this lead to the company delivering 500 gallons of milk and 400 gallons of cream a day throughout the city. He nicknamed himself the "Cream King of Pittsburgh." Between 1899 and 1919, ice cream became a very popular item; especially after the invention of the cone in 1896 and the 1904 St. Louis World's Fair making the waffle cone so popular. Edward did not let this opportunity slip by and he quickly made a name for himself in the ice cream business. His acquisitions continued to grow just as quickly with him buying two dozen dairies between 1890 and 1924. After the founder of the MCJunkin-Straight dairy of Pittsburgh died, Rieck acquired controlling interest. In 1917 Edward merged his own company with this company and it became the Rieck-McJunkin Dairy Company. By 1923 there were 3 plants in Pittsburgh and others in New Castle, Butler, Charleroi, Altoona, and McKeesport. The Rieck name was seen on milk bottles, ice cream cartons, egg cartons, butter boxes, cottage cheese containers, and even had its own radio program "The Rieck Revelers" (a 15 minute gospel music show on KDKA in the 1930s).

Goldman Sachs saw the opportunity to capitalize on the huge appetite for ice cream and sought out the Hydrox and Rieck-McJunkin companies to form a corporation, which he accomplished early in December of 1923. Thomas McInnerney, chairman of Hydrox (who manufactured ice, ginger ale, and other beverages was ½ the size of Rieck's company) and his partners, along with Edward and his 2 sons, Carl and Albert, were all present to close the deal with a unanimous vote to form National Dairy Products Corp. This corporation's first brand, Sealtest, was created in 1935; the red Sealtest label was added to all the products that met the standards of the day, including those of Kraft and Rieck-McJunkin. Sealtest became the name for NDP's entire dairy division. Between 1928 and 1929, NDP acquired many famous brands, such as Breakstone's, Bryers Ice Cream, and Kraft through mergers.

Rieck had more than enough experience to continue to be the chairman of the NDP but he lacked the desire to hold the position, so 2 years after NDP was formed, he left that position to cofounder Thomas McInnerney. In 1925, Edward, now 60, left New York and returned to Pittsburgh where he purchased the dairy farm of his dreams, a 1100 acre tract of rolling hills and white wooden barns owned by John Bell of Moon Township. He stocked his Rieck's Bell Farm with the finest champion pedigreed Holsteins and ran a spotless dairy farm to produce the highest standard of certified, unpasteurized milk and products. By 1941, wartime had the government buying acreage for air bases. Rieck's farm was in the location of what is now the site of the Greater Pittsburgh International Airport and the Army wanted to purchase the land. He was 76 at this time; since he had not served in an of the armed forces, he felt that if he gave up his farm to the Army, it would be his way of serving his country. The sale was done in 1942 and less than a year after selling his Bell Farm, Edward died of pneumonia. At his death, he was still a Director of National Dairy and Chairman of the Board of the Rieck-McJunkin subsidiary. Rieck's Ice Cream and other dairy products were known as the best tasting of the day because of Edward's insistence on using certified, high quality, unprocessed milk.

1920s/1930s tray

The storerooms at 1119 Washington Avenue seem to overlap some within the information found on each….

Trumpeter grocer – 1119 Washington Avenue
1890s, 1901, 1902, 1903, 1904
    William Trumpeter was the owner.
        He was engaged in this business for some time; he later became employed by the Standard Sanitary Manufacturing Co. and also by Jones and Laughlin Steel Corporation at Aliquippa; then became first custodian of the new High School building. Perhaps through this all, he may have had someone else manage the store.
        William married Rosa Mabel Carey, they lived on Washington Avenue; Wm. died between 1920 and 1930.

This storeroom at 1119 Washington Avenue became Dalzell's....................

Dalzell's Food Market – 1119 Washington Avenue
1929 to 1971
> Opened business Jul 23, 1929.   He closed his business in 1971(42 years total).
> Charles W.'s family moved to Monaca Heights in 1904.   His father opened a grocery store on
> > Bechtel Street.   C.W. opened a Clover Farm Store.   He featured fresh produce and
> > poultry grown on his farm in Potter Township .
> He was inducted into the Monaca Community Hall of Fame in 2002. C. W. died in 1985.
> > **My mother worked in this grocery store prior to marrying my father.

_____

Mary Fronko's Store – She had a store behind where Yolanda's is now located.
1910, 1922, 1928, 1929, 1931, 1949, 1951
> Owner – Mrs. Fronko.   In 1912, they lived right by the business at 1552 Virginia Avenue.
> Opened store on Eleventh Street in 1923 (across from the Junior High building).   Michael, Jr. was
> > a clerk in the store in 1912.
> Owners became -   Michael K., Jr. and Susanna Fronko; in 1940, they lived at 300s Eleventh Street.
> Advertised "fresh salt and smoked meats."
> Retired from business in 1951.

I do not know the connection, if any, to.............................

Fronko's Meat & Grocery Market - 1598 Virginia Avenue (in 1912)– 1101 Pennsylvania Avenue in 1923
> and also 363 Eleventh Street (which would be rear of 1101 Penna Ave).

_____

Mrs. Olive Coene – 1910 Mercantile Tax list had her listed as being located in Colona.
1914
> Bought the grocery business from Mrs. Lilly Mets (see further) and was going to continue the
> > business there.   Mrs. Coene was widow of Julius Coene who formerly was proprietor
> > for Colonial/Imperial Hotel in Colona.

_____

Jackson's Grocery – Pennsylvania Avenue (Near Thirteenth Street)
1907, 1910   Added a frame awning in front of his grocery store in Mar 1907.

_____

Robert M. Winkle – Grocer - Pennsylvania Avenue
1900, 1903, 1906
> He was reported to be papering and "otherwise improving interior of his grocery store" in 1906.

_____

Lyman C. Householder – grocer – Pennsylvania Avenue
1902, 1909   His wife was Cinnie B.; they lived at the same address as the storeroom in 1902/03.

_____

Metz Grocery Store – 1306 Pennsylvania Avenue - also corner Pennsylvania & Eleventh Street (1910)
1907, 1910, 1912, 1914
> Richard Metz – owner; his wife, Mrs. Lillie Metz, also listed as owner.
> Large plate glass window of Mrs. Lilly(wife of R. F.) Metz's grocery store was broken in 1912.
> Opened business in 1907 – sold it in Oct 1914 to Mrs. Olive Coene.
> In 1912, Lillie was living in the same building as the business.
>> (?) Jan of 1911 through Jan 1912, Richard and Lillie appear to have owned two store rooms
>> because both are listed as being grocers – Richard at Eleventh Street & Pennsylvania
>> Avenue; Lillie at 1306 Pennsylvania Avenue (?)

1306 Pennsylvania Avenue

———

J. B. and Lena Kramer – grocery store – 718 Pennsylvania Avenue
1910, 1912, 1920, 1928
> John B. and Lena lived in the same building as the business.
> Only Mrs. Lena Kramer is listed on mercantile tax in 1922, but only J.B. is in 1928.

———

Anthony Damo – produce and grocery store – Pennsylvania Avenue
1910

———

Peirce's Grocery – Pennsylvania Avenue
1902   Edward and Anna M. Peirce – owners.   They lived in same building.
            By 1920, they were living in Pittsburgh; he was a manager in a bakery.

———

Levine & Bellan Grocery and Meat Market – 1140 Pennsylvania Avenue
            -then at 1101 Pennsylvania Avenue (corner of Pennsylvania & Eleventh Street)
1912, 1917, 1920
> Abraham Levine and L. Bellan were the owners of this business.
> In 1920, Abraham was residing at the same location as business.

———

Roy H. Kauntz – Grocery store – unknown location
1910   Roy lived on Ohio Avenue in 1910.

———

Alexander Sproul – Grocery Store – unknown location
1910   He lived on Jackson Avenue in 1910.

———

Julia Carnahan (Mrs. E.)– merchant in grocery – 300s Jackson Avenue - Colona Heights
1910, 1922
> They lived on Jackson Avenue in 1910.

———

Giovanni DiMarchi – grocer – 815 Pennsylvania Avenue
1912, 1910s   Giovanni and Mary lived in the same building as the business.

_____

Charles Fagerstrom – Sixteenth Street and Pennsylvania Avenue
1910, 1911
   He had a couple newspaper ads in Jul 1911 that said he was selling "good grocery store with a well established boarding house connected with it" – reason for selling, poor health. He also stated he was selling "cheap to quick buyer."   One of the ads stated the sale included entire stock and fixtures.

_____

The Atlantic and Pacific Company   aka   A & P Store   -   There were several locations
        and   multiple stores open at the same time ---1014 Pennsylvania, 1133 Pennsylvania,
                        927 Pennsylvania, 1022 Pennsylvania
1917, 1930, 1931, 1943
   The store at 1014 Penna Ave - Mar 25, 1930 - sustained damage due to a fire (Keystone Bldg).

Women On the Job

The wheat surplus mess is a home problem

1930

Hughes' Grocery – 1416 Pennsylvania Avenue
1901, 1903, 1912, 1913
    Andrew Hughes – owner /operator.
        His wife was Ida; they lived at the same address as the storeroom in 1902/03 and 1912.
    Opened in 1901.
    Groceries and Provisions, flour and feed.
    In 1906, they added on to stockroom and living rooms above and bought the adjoining lot to
        his store.

1913

Lorenzo Mariano - rented the storeroom owned by Joseph DiMarchi (Grocer) – 815 Pennsylvania Avenue
1916, 1920
    (I found DiMarchi and family in 1910 not 1920; did not find Mariano in 1910 or 1920 census.)

Miller Bros. aka William Miller Bakery and Confectionery – 615 Pennsylvania Avenue
1900, 1901, 1908, 1920, 1928
> Harry W. and William (married Mary __) owners.
> Harry was 24 and William only 16, both living with parents on Atlantic Avenue in 1910.
>> They were the sons of James and Mary Miller.
> The business and home was located one door from Jacob Schnitzler's General Store in 1901
>> (corner of Pennsylvania & Sixth Street).
> There was an ad in the Jul 1911 newspaper that said the Miller Bros Monaca had the produce
>> business up for sale – must sell at once.   But yet I found information in 1920 and
>> in 1928 on the business, so they may have never sold it or whoever bought it kept the
>> name since it was already established -?-

———

Miller's Super Market –   498 Pennsylvania Avenue
1907, 1908, 1929, 1940, 1956
> Grocery market was owned by Harry Miller in Feb 1902/03, 1907.
>> o Married Flora__, they lived at same place as the market.
> Handled home dressed poultry, turkeys, chickens, ducks, and geese.
> H. E. Miller opened a store in the Keystone Block Building the first of Dec 1908.
>> o Advertised a fine line of fish, oysters, butter, eggs, and cheese. Sold flowers, too.
> 1943 – was in chain of Triangle Food Stores.
> 1932 – was in the Clover Farm chain of stores.
> The building he used was used as a lodge in 1880s – in 1994 it was apartments.
> Catherine Miller –was the owner operator of the Miller's Super Market; retiring in 1949.
>> She married Leland Weyand.

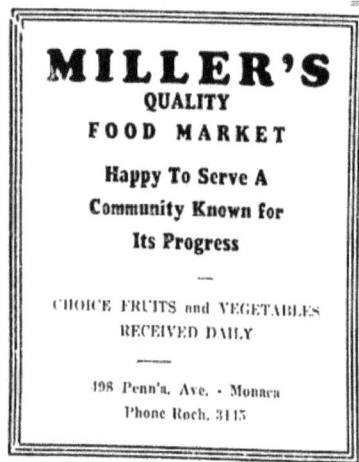

MILLER'S
QUALITY
FOOD MARKET

Happy To Serve A
Community Known for
Its Progress

———

CHOICE FRUITS and VEGETABLES
RECEIVED DAILY

498 Penn'a. Ave. - Monaca
Phone Roch. 3115

———

Bednasz Groceries – 1723 Pennsylvania Avenue
1922, 1940   Albert Bednasz – owner.

———

Charles Cianfarno – grocery store – 1610 Pennsylvania Avenue
1928, 1929, 1931, 1943
> This building has been razed and is an open lot/parking area as of 2015.

———

Robert Hood – grocery store
1910

———

Eddis Hood – grocery business - 1198 Pennsylvania Avenue
1902, 1912, 1920

>Succeeded his brother __?__ in the business.   1902 listing stated him as proprietor of a
>"general store."
>Eddis and Anna lived in the same building as the business.
>Then was a storekeeper for Colonial Steel Company.
>By 1920 Eddis was widowed; he still had the store, but sold it within that same year.
>>He worked in a steel mill, too.   By 1938 he was living on Atlantic Avenue.

Then became.........

Monaca Cash Market – 1198 Pennsylvania Avenue / corner Twelfth Street and Pennsylvania Avenue
1920, 1928, 1929, 1942

>Run by Samuel Balter and H. B. Bazell of Freedom.
>They bought the building from Eddis Hood – 2 storey frame bldg & 2nd floor was residence of
>the Hood family.
>>1928 – James Pecorri was listed as the former proprietor. He purchased a grocery and meat
>>market in McKees Rocks with the family moving there about mid Jun 1928.

MONACA CASH MARKET

J. FALLER, Proprietor

1198 PENNSYLVANIA AVENUE   -   -   PHONE ROCHESTER 845

Will open SATURDAY, SEPTEMBER 15th to offer you the finest, freshest MEATS, GROC-
ERIES and PRODUCE the market can possibly afford, at the most reasonable prices you
would ever think of, realizing the quality of the merchandise that we are offering you.
Visit our market and enjoy the CLEANLINESS, COURTESY and SERVICE that await. You
FREE TREAT FOR THE KIDDIES

OPENING DAY FEATURES

Butter	Finest Creamery Roll or Print	2	lbs.	**57c**
Flour	Pittsburgh Leader	24½	lb. sack	**95c**
	Pillsbury - - - - -		$1.13	
Brooms	Regular Value 40c			**29c**
Smoked Hams	Whole or Shank half		lb.	**20c**
	Center Slices, lb. - - - - - 32c			
Ground Meat	Freshly Ground		lb	**10c**
Potatoes	U. S. No. 2		peck	**15c**

PORK CHOPS—Lean. Meaty · 2 lbs 35c

COFFEE, lb. - - - - - - 19c	PORK and BEANS, can - - - 5c
Our Own Freshly Ground	Large CATSUP, 2 bottles - - 23c
COFFEE, lb - - - - - - 29c	21 Ounce size
Chase & Sanborn	SUGAR, 5 lbs. - - - - - 27c
Kellogg	Chocolate Cream Filled
CORN FLAKES, 2 boxes - - 13c	CAKES, lb. - - - - - - 15c
Standard Brands	JUMBO or RING BOLOGNA
CIGARETTES, 2 packs - - 25c	WEINERS, lb. - - - - - 15c
Singles, 2 packages 19c	CHUCK ROAST, lb. - - - 12c
Popular Brands	Meaty Cuts CENTER CUTS, lb. 16c
MILK, 4 cans - - - - - 25c	ORANGES, each - - - - - 1c
P. & G. SOAP, 2 cakes - - 15c	LEMONS, each - - - - - 1c
ONE OXYDOL FREE	ONIONS, 10 lb. bag - - - 29c
Soda or Graham	CABBAGE, 5 lbs. - - - - 10c
CRACKERS, 2 boxes - - - 19c	PEPPERS, each - - - - - 1c
O - JELL, It Jells Quickly, pkg. - 5c	SWEET POTATOES, 6 lbs. - 25c
IVORY FLAKES, large - - - 23c	
ONE SMALL PACKAGE FREE	

mid Sep 1934

The bottom of this ad stated they had "free delivery," too.

Monaca Cash Market was evidently right beside Penn Super. I found no closing date for the cash
market, but it was at least by the time Penn Super made their addition to their store in 1964/65
because the property became part of Penn Super Market.

————

Penn Super Grocery Store – 1198 Pennsylvania Avenue (corner of Pennsylvania Avenue and Twelfth Street)
1928 to   1994
Opened in 1928.   Closed Jan/Feb 1994.
Was owned and run by Jacob and Yetta Faller; Jacob died in 1946 and Yetta retired in 1956.
Their sons Harry and Bernard took over and expanded the store in 1964/65.
Now the building is a bar/tavern.

The original store front of the Penn Super Market.

This is a picture from a newspaper the first week of Nov 1964.   The quality of this picture is not very good at all, but it is showing the remodeling being done on the former Penn Super Market. This was a new addition being added to the left of the old building.   The addition gave the building a store space of 64,000 square feet; it was expected to be completed by Jan 1965.

William Kaye was manager of a grocery store – was it his own.... ?
1930
> They resided at 1110 Atlantic Avenue in 1930; his son Robert was also a manager of grocery store in 1930.

Thomas Liston was manager of a grocery store – was it his own... ?
1930   He lived at 935 Indiana Avenue in 1930.

Charles Shedlosky was manager of a grocery store – was it his own?
1930   He lived at 1125 Virginia Avenue.

Joseph Setting – grocery store – 1219 Pennsylvania Avenue
1928, 1930, 1931, 1943
> Joseph was also residing at 1219 Pennsylvania Avenue.   (The building is designed to have been a business.)   Apartment was rented out at this address, too.

Trumpeter's Grocery – 1219 Pennsylvania Avenue
1938   Mrs. E. Trumpeter – proprietor.

Power's Grocery Store – 1416 Pennsylvania Avenue
1930, 1931   E. M. Power – owner.

Frank Fabi – grocery store – 1107 Pennsylvania Avenue
1928, 1930, 1931
> Frank Fabi was the owner.
> He resided at the same location.

————

Frank Nunzir General Grocery Store – both on Pacific Avenue
1950s to 1979
> Frank's real name was Nunziato, but he said his first grade teacher had trouble pronouncing it and changed it to Nunzir.
> He first had a general store at the front part of his house, then started a small bakery at the rear of the home with his specialty being bread.   He not only delivered to neighbors, but also as far away as Midland and Ambridge.
> His house, along with all the others on the 800/900 blocks of Pacific, was torn down to comply with the redevelopment project and the reconstruction/ expansion of Phoenix Glass Company plant in 1979/1980.

————

9th Street Food Market – (address unknown, but presumably on "Ninth Street")
1938

————

National Cut Rate Foods – 1006 Pennsylvania Avenue
1938

————

Buchholz Bros.   - 800 Pennsylvania Avenue   aka
   Walter Bucholtz – merchant of grocery store - corner of Pennsylvania Avenue and Eighth Street
1927, 1930
> Walter had home at 917 Washington Avenue.
> His store was across from / opposite 714 Pennsylvania Avenue in 1906.

————

Alois J. Chambers – grocery merchant – 699 Bechtel Street – Monaca Heights
1928, 1930, 1931, 1943
> They resided at 699 Bechtel Street in 1930.

————

Mrs. Peitsch – groceries and provisions -   corner Ninth and Pennsylvania Avenue
1924

————

P. H. Butler Co. - grocers – corner of Wahl Street and Pennsylvania Avenue – 1114 Pennsylvania Avenue
- other addresses found were: 308 Ninth Street   and 1313 Pennsylvania Avenue
1922, 1928, 1929, 1931, 1943
     Mercantile Tax List (1928, 1929, 1931) has this company at all three locations.
     They had a nice striped awning installed in the 1920s with their name on it.
     1114 Pennsylvania (This address became Monaca Men's and Boys' Store.)
     (Margolis Clothing/Department Store was on the opposite corner on Wahl Alley; it
        became the United 5 & 10 store.)

1920s   Margolis   Wahl St.   P.H. Butler

———

Fred S. Karcis - grocery store – 1140 Pennsylvania Avenue
1920s and 1930s   Fred lived at the same address.   Also see Karcis café.

———

Karcis Meats and Groceries   aka   Karcis Cash Market – 434 Pennsylvania Avenue (until 1930)
                                                -1140 Pennsylvania Avenue (1931)
1922, 1930, 1931
     Paul S. and Mary Karcis – owners.
     Martin Misicko was the meat cutter for this business and John Gaydos was a butcher for him.
     In 1930 Paul was living at 1140 Pennsylvania Avenue, but with Penn Super adjacent to this
        building, I am not sure this would have been the location of his store.

———

Bell's Economy Super Market   – 1018 Pennsylvania Avenue (Mar 1957) (in Keystone Bldg)
                                       and 927 Pennsylvania Avenue
1930s, 1957
     Henrietta (Thomas) Bell was the owner/operator.   Was a Clover Farm Store.
        Henrietta also owned and operated the Dorca's Style Shop.
        She was married to John H. Bell who had a confectionery store on Monaca Heights.

———

Eagle Grocery Co. – 1142 Pennsylvania Avenue
1928

———

Francis Taormina – 1034 Pennsylvania Avenue
1949   Was a Triangle Food Store.

———

Angelo Farri - grocery merchant - 1198 Pennsylvania Avenue.
1930, 1931

_____

Eighth Street Market – 800 Pennsylvania Avenue
1931

_____

Steve's Clover Farm Store –1299 and then 1301 Pennsylvania Avenue
1938, 1940, 1949, 1952
          Stephen Ogrizek – owner (When at 1299 Pennsylvania, its ads stated *Butcher Shop.*)

_____

Dale Leifer's (or Leiper's) A.G. Stores – quality meats and groceries – 1301 Pennsylvania Avenue
1955   Dale Leifer/Leiper – proprietor.

_____

Cecula Fruit and Grocery Store – 1101 Walnut Street (Taylor & Walnut Street)
1931, 1940, 1943
          Anna Cecula is listed as owner in 1940 (her husband John died in Jan 1940).
          In 1931 they were living in Rochester.

_____

Tony Parona – grocery merchant – Monaca Heights
1929

_____

David Patton – grocery store – 1317 Pennsylvania Avenue
1928

_____

Hartman & Stifler – grocery store – 1301 Pennsylvania Avenue
1928, 1929

     Then.................

Anthony Hartman – grocery store – 1301 Pennsylvania Avenue
1929, 1931

_____

Olszanski's Store – groceries – 714 Pennsylvania Avenue
1928, 1930   Tony Olszanski – owner.   (See General Store section, too.)

_____

City Cash Market – 1106 Pennsylvania Avenue
1928, 1930

th
ce   LOST—Lady's white gold cameo
nt finger ring, between City Cash Market
·J. and Eighth street. Monaca. Reward.
   Frances Eckley, care City Cash Mar-
nc ket, Monaca, Pa.   1.10-16inc
          1928

_____

Martha Pietsch – merchant in grocery – 898 Pennsylvania Avenue
1920, 1922   She lived at 898 Pennsylvania Avenue in 1920.

_____

Hughes' Grocery – 1003 Pennsylvania Avenue
1938, 1940　　　　　　　James H. Hughes – owner.　　(this was most likely Andrew and Ida's relative)

_____

Frank Taormina was the grocer in a grocery and produce store.
1930, 1940　　　　　　　Frank lived on Eleventh Street.

_____

Anthony Taormina was the owner of a wholesale produce store 1940.

_____

Taormina Groceries – Mary Taormina at 310 Ninth Street
1940
　　　　　There was a Mary Taormina from Bridgewater – could this have been her store ?

_____

Evans Thrifty Market – 1598 Virginia Avenue
1938, 1943, 1949, 1965, 1971
　　　　　In 1943 they were under Triangle Food Store chain.　　Clyde Evans – owner.
　　　　　In 1991, Dr. Mike Dragonjac had an office there (ad for dental asst).
　　　　　In Sep 1938 there was a sleeping room for rent at 1598 Virginia Avenue.
　　　　　　　(Fronko's was listed as having a grocery store at this same address.)
　　　　　By 2005, it was Project Star – the Children's Institute/Child Welfare Agency (ad for clerk).

_____

Marie Lollhart was the grocer in her own grocery store, but I have no address for this.
1940　　　　　It may have been by 1171 Walnut Street.

_____

Anna Cecla was the grocer in her own grocery store – 1101 Walnut Street
1940　　　　　She lived at the same address.

_____

Mac's Superette – unknown location (found mention of business in an article).
1871

_____

Donald McDonald – grocery store – location unknown
1930　　　　　They lived at 130 Colonial Avenue in 1930.

_____

Louis Bernstein – grocery store – 1601 Beaver Avenue
1928, 1930, 1931
　　　　　They were living in the *Colona* area.　　His wife Nettie worked in the store, too.

_____

Herk's Super Market – 937/941 Fourteenth Street (top of Fourteenth Street Hill)
1930, 1957, 1971　　　　　　　　　　　　　　　　　　also listed as 509 Bechtel Street
　　　　　Halford Ray Herchenroether, owner.　　The building became a carwash at the top of the hill.

_____

Amelia Rambo was a grocer in her own store.
1940　　　　　I have no address for her store; it may have been at 1207 Marshall Road.

_____

Benjamin Eisner Grocery Store – 2598 Beaver Avenue
1913, 1930, 1940, 1943
Opened store in about 1913.
He used a building owned by Morris Barnett for his store and residence in 1913.
They were living in *Colona* in 1930.
Benjamin Eisner was the owner of business (died in 1957), put his business up for
sale Nov 13, 1943.

_____

Leon Bovish's/Bobish's grocery store – 615 Pennsylvania Avenue
1930, 31   Leon's home was at same address.

_____

Martynke's – 701 Walnut Street
1949   J. Martynke – proprietor.

_____

Zindren's Superette – 1098 Marshall Road
1940, 1954, 1957
Pete Zindren – proprietor.   Was a Triangle Food Store.

_____

Dewey's Deli – 801 Allaire Avenue
1983, 1990
Opened Nov 1983.
Was built on a triangular lot at the intersection of Colonial Avenue and Allaire Avenue.
Charles Dewhirst was the owner.
Charles had a Paneling and Carpentry business at this same location in 1970.

_____

E. Mangiarelli & Sons – Wholesale Groceries and Confectionery -   1543 Pennsylvania Avenue
1910, 1912, 1924, 1930, 1943
Emidi Mangiarelli – owner – he married Joanna and they lived by the business
at 1541 Pennsylvania Avenue.

_____

George Mangiarelli – grocer – Colonial Avenue
1930, 1931

_____

Franz R. Birner – grocery store – 1605 Washington Avenue
1922, 1931
Mrs. F. Birner is listed as owner in 1931.

_____

Tew's Clover Farm Store – Ridge Road
1956

_____

Martin Yanik Grocery store – res 1699 Virginia Avenue
1920, 1922
By 1930, the family was living in Trumbull, Ohio and Susanna (wife) was retailer in grocery;
either they had the store in Ohio all the time or started a new one there - ? –

_____

Beaver Falls Cash Market – 1101 Pennsylvania Avenue
1922

_____

Kroger Grocery & Baking Co.   aka   Krogers – 1142 Pennsylvania Avenue
1929, 1949   -also found a listing at 1022 Pennsylvania Avenue in Jul 1940

Kroger's

1142 Penn'a. Av., Monaca; 684 3rd Av., Freedom; 452 Adams St., Roch.

SPECIALS IN OUR MEAT DEPT.

MEATS SOLD IN MONACA STORE ONLY — 1142 PENNSYLVANIA AVENUE

LIKE YOU PROTECT YOUR HEALTH DO LIKEWISE WITH YOUR CHRISTMAS DINNER — BUY THE BEST TURKEY AND AT THE LOWEST PRICE IN BEAVER COUNTY — KROGER'S AVE., MONACA, PA. — ALSO MEAT DEPT., 1142 PENN'A. FULL LINE OF CHICKENS, DUCKS AND GEESE.

CUT FROM PRIME STEER BEEF		
CHUCK ROAST, per lb	13½c	
RIB ROAST, per lb	18c	
ROUND, SIRLOIN AND TENDERLOIN STEAKS, per lb	18c	
GROUND MEAT, Fresh Ground, lb	15c	
RUMP ROAST, Boneless, per lb	20c	
SHOULDER ROAST, per lb	17c	
BEEF LIVER, Sliced, per lb	18c	
PORK SAUSAGE, Bulk	2 LB.	35c

CUT FROM CORN FED PORKERS		
PORK LOIN, Rib End, per lb	16½c	
Pork Chops 20c lb		
PORK SHOULDERS, per lb WHOLE OR CALA HALF	13½c	
FRESH HAMS, per lb	20c	
PIGS FEET	3 LB.	25c
NECK BONES	3 LB.	25c
SPARE RIBS, per lb	15c	
HOG LIVER, per lb	14c	

SUGAR CURED SKINNED HAMS, lb ... 18c
SUGAR CURED CALAS, lb ... 13½c
SUGAR CURED BACON, lb ... 25c
Link or Country, Pure Pork 2 LB. 43c

CUT FROM MILK FED CALVES
VEAL BREAST, Per lb ... 13c
VEAL CHOPS 2 LB. 35c
SHOULDER ROAST, Per lb ... 15c
VEAL STEAK, Per lb ... 24c
LAMB STEW 2 LB. 25c
LAMB LEGS Per lb ... 22c
LAMB SHOULDERS, Per lb ... 15c
LOIN OR RIB LAMB, Per lb ... 22c
COTTAGE CHEESE FULL CREAM 2 LB. 25c
WEINERS OR RING BOLOGNA, lb ... 20c
LIVER PUDDING, RING, lb ... 15c
JUMBO BOLOGNA, SLICED, lb ... 25c

Specials in Grocery & Provision Department

CANNED PUMPKIN 1 CAN MAKES 2 PIES - - 3 LARGE CANS 25c
ALL BRANDS CIGARETTES AT THIS LOW PRICE - Carton $1.15
BARBARA ANN TOMATO SOUP - - - - 4 CANS FOR 25c
MIXED NUTS, lb ... 25c
CALIFORNIA WALNUTS, LB 33c
FRUIT CAKE ... 2 lb 85c
3 LB. FANCY TIN $1.35
ORANGE AND LEMON PEEL, 1-4 lb Pkg ... 13c
CITRON PEEL, PKG 19c
COUNTRY CLUB RAISINS ... 3 Pkgs. 25c
CURRANTS, Pkg. ... 12c
BULK DATES, lb ... 12c
MINCE MEAT NONE SUCH, Pkg. ... 15c
BULK MINCEMEAT, lb ... 19c

TOMATO OVAL SARDINES, Can ... 10c
ASSORTED Cream & Jellies ... 2 lb 29c
ASSORTED CHOCOLATES, lb ... 21c
HENKEL'S FLOUR, 5 lb Sack ... 29c
COUNTRY CLUB OLIVES, Stuffed, Pt ... 39c
1-2 PT 23c—PLAIN, PT. 21c
COUNTRY CLUB PEACHES, No. 2½ Cans 22c
PALMOLIVE SOAP ... 3 Bars 19c
STORAGE EGGS ... 2 Dozen 45c

Fresh Fruits and Vegetables

250 SIZE FLORIDAS ORANGES ... 2 Dozen 39c
ICEBERG LETTUCE 2 Lge. Hds. 21c
80 SIZE GRAPEFRUIT ... 5 for 25c
54 SIZE 1 FOR 25c CAULIFLOWER, Each 19c
MUSHROOMS, lb ... 45c

CABBAGE ... 10 lbs 25c
SWEET POTATOES ... 4 lbs 25c
JONATHAN APPLES ... 4 lbs 25c
DELICIOUS, 3 LBS 25c
NEW SPINACH ... 3 lbs 19c
YELLOW ONIONS ... 10 lbs 20c

1930

_____

Willo Foods   aka   Willo Grocery Store – 1416 Pennsylvania Avenue
1936, 1944, 1949   Will Oyster – owner.

_____

Colonial Market – 2598 Beaver Avenue
1949

_____

Taormina's Market– 1301-1302 Pennsylvania Avenue
1931 to 2016
  Opened market in Monaca in 1931 by Sam and Josephine Taormina.   Closed 2016.
   o They had their first store in Freedom in 1926 and then moved into Monaca.
  The store in Monaca first opened at #1302 which was in front of their house.
  1930 and 1940 – Joseph their son worked in the store, too.
  1943 – was a Triangle Food Store chain and located at 1034 Pennsylvania Avenue.
  1949 – Two separate businesses were listed - Sam Taormina was listed at 1302 Pennsylvania
   and Steve O'Grizek was at 1301 Pennsylvania ?
  1961 – the store was moved next door to 1036 Pennsylvania Avenue.
  The business was passed down through the family and in 1990 Ernie Taormina, Sam & Josephine's son,
  was owner until he retired; Ernest and Mary Taormina became the new
   proprietors.
  1964 – Ernie and Mary purchased the building at 1301 Pennsylvania Ave and relocated the
   grocery store where it is still located, although currently closed (2016).
  After the move in 1964, the store expanded from groceries and a fruit stand to a full service
   store with cold beverages, meats, cards, newsstand, snacks, ice cream, and PA lottery.

_____

Ridge Market – 2100 Ridge Road, Monaca Heights (this may be the same as Tew's).
1920, 1940, 1963, 1971
  Building erected in 1920 – dark red brick – two story.
  Anthony Wasilowski – 1946;   Norbert Wasilowski – 1946.
  Owner/operated in 1963 – Norbert J. Wasilowski (they lived in the building, too).

_____

Ed's Place – 711 Pennsylvania Avenue (formerly Keck's Furniture Exchange)
1993, 2000s   Edward G. Knox of Monaca - owner of BP station – convenience store.

_____

Mamula's Market – 200 Ninth Street
1990s

_____

Swan's Quality Meat & Deli – unknown location
1990

_____

Shank's Superette – 711 Pennsylvania Avenue (in Citgo station)
Recent business.

_____

Betty Dengel was the grocer at 1099 Bechtel Street
1940,

    Became ....

Gallagher's General Store

    Then it became known as ....

Gallagher's Market – 1099 Bechtel Street
1961 to current
        Started business – 1961 (as of 2016, in business 55 years).
        Groceries, dairy products, drugs.

1994

_____

Slush Puppie Tri Point Inc. – 1534 Pennsylvania Avenue
1972, 1990
        1972 – Slush Puppie Tri Point Inc. was started /operated by Jos. Dusold, Jr. & son Gerald
            in 1990.

_____

Just 'N Case - dried and dehydrated surplus food store – Pennsylvania Avenue
1975   John and Ellen Smego, owners – opened first of Mar 1975 – closed_?_.

_____

L & M Market – 823 Pennsylvania Avenue
1947, 1956, 1958, 1960s

      Closed in the early 1960s.   **L**eitshaft **&** **M**auber owners.

      Fire did damage to the business on March 3, 1958, but they stayed open.

      This building was shared by Paul's Garage (in rear of building) and there was an
           apartment area within the building also.

1958

IF YOU WANT THE BEST IN
MEATS
AND
GROCERIES
SHOP AT THE
L & M Market
823 PENNA. AVE.
MONACA

1954

Parona Grocery – 2000 Marshall Road – Monaca Heights
1930, 1940, 1956   Tony Parona owner.

    Became ....

Troy's Market – 2000 Marshall Road
1984   Owned by Charles Cumberledge.
      Built a small multi apt building with a convenience store underneath in 1985.

    Became ....

J & W Market – 2000 Marshall Road
1999

    Became ....

Pappy J's – 2000 Marshall Road
Current   Bought by John and Linda Hall in Aug 2004.

(2015)

***   ***   ***   ***   ***

In Oct 1962 there was a Food Distribution Program.

One of the surplus food headquarters was at 1534 Pennsylvania Avenue in Monaca.

_____

Tax records stated the following stores were in Monaca in 1910; no additional information found on them:
G. H. Dodds – grocery store – He lived on Indiana Avenue.
James Moore – grocery store – He lived on Pennsylvania Avenue.
Frank Fife – produce store – He lived on Pennsylvania Avenue.
Joseph Demarchi – grocery store – He lived on Pennsylvania Avenue.

*** *** *** *** ***

Flour - Grain - Feed

Forner & Figley Flouring Mill – unknown address
1892, 1893   John B. Forner and William Figley owners.

_____

Frank M. Todd – flour and feed store
1892, 1893

_____

A. Davidson & Co. – flour mill near the Sixth Street railroad station
1902
        Allen Davidson and H.J. Eckert ran the business.   See further - Monaca Roller Mills

_____

Poultry Supply and Feed Store   aka   Davidson Feed Store   aka
                Davidson Flour, Feed, Hay, Grain and Seed Store – 422 Pennsylvania Avenue
1911
        Opened 1904/05.   Allen Davidson owner.
        He also had ½ interest in the Sheffield Flour mill which ran from 1890 to 1897.
        In 1898 he moved from Hopewell to Monaca and bought the Monaca Roller Mills.
        See further - Monaca Roller Mills

Allen Davidson

_____

Monaca Produce Co. –713 Pennsylvania Avenue (1929); then 1034 Pennsylvania Avenue and by 1957 at
                1534 Pennsylvania Avenue
1929, 1941, 1955, 1957
        Wholesale business.

_____

Monaca Roller Mills – 698 Pacific Avenue (along the railroad tracks, by the former depot)
1897/98, 1911, 1922, 1944

       Opened in 1897/98 - owned by Mr. Henry Hild – flour miller;
then..........

       In 1900 owned by Allen Davidson (of my Davidson family).

       Was called A. Davidson & Co.; H. J. Eckert was in business with Davidson.

       By 1912, Henry Eckert was owner – he lived at Fourteenth Street Ext. then

            Allen was married to Sarah and lived on Fourth Street in 1902/03 and

               Henry J. Eckert was living in Colonial Heights.

       Also had a grain and feed store at 422 Pennsylvania Avenue.

       Newspaper article said Eckert ran the Monaca Roller Mills until 1904 – did it close then or was
            this just a date of reference ?

       In 1920 and 1930 Mr. Hild was considered the miller and owner again.

        (It may have been a partnership or he just worked in some capacity at the mill ?)

           Mr. Hild resided at Indiana Avenue.

Allen Davidson was living in Columbiana, Ohio by the end of Apr 1919 since he came back into town
    and was visiting friends.   His brother Anderson, was still living in Monaca at that time.

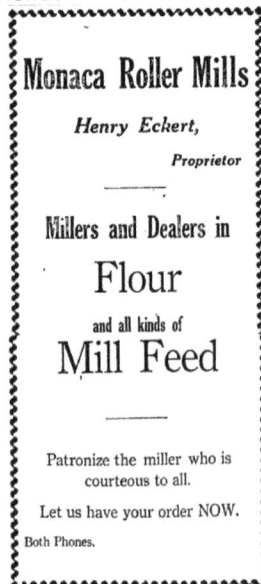

1911

Wm. Penn Supply Co. – wholesale dealer – 1543 Pennsylvania Avenue
1929

*** *** *** *** ***

MISCELLANEOUS GROCERY AND FOOD STORE INFORMATION

Many of the grocery stores were run under The Clover Farm Stores chain.   This Dec 1930 ad
was more or less a blanket ad for the stores that participated with them. The Clover Farm company carried their
own brand of many, many items; equivalent to the "store brands" you find in grocery stores nowadays.   They
had their brand of coffee, canned fruits, canned vegetables, spices, dairy products, cookies, paper products, etc.

Stores that would choose to be a participating Clover Farm Store would be given a large marquee to hang above
their storeroom doors to indicate they were one of the Clover Farm Stores.

I do not know if the Clover Farm Stores company would pay for these ads, but there would not be individual ads for
each proprietor's store, just one blanket ad.   All participating Clover Farm Stores would then honor the prices as
advertised.

1920s ad

This is a copy of a postcard showing an unidentified meat and poultry market in Monaca. Although I could not find the name of this storeroom, it was too interesting to ignore and not include in the book.

This is another unidentified grocery store in Monaca; again, such an endearing photo. It reflects the simplicity, structures, and life styles of some of the businesses.

The Pennsylvania Department of Agriculture used to grant licenses for the manufacture and sale of oleomargarine and renovated butter. Several of the restaurants and lunch rooms who served milk were also listed in a few other publications. The government was keeping an eye out for the consumers at least by 1910. Their 1912 monthly publication of the Dairy and Food Division listed every food establishment in Pennsylvania, by county, and whether they passed or failed or were granted licenses. Just a few of the Monaca business people who were granted licenses for just Jan 1, 1911 to Jan 15, 1912 were Andrew Hughes (grocery dealer) – 1416 Pennsylvania Ave.; Richard F Metz (grocer) – corner Eleventh Street and Pennsylvania Ave.; Mrs. Lillie Metz (grocer) – 1306 Pennsylvania Ave.

Checking on what the consumer was purchasing and ingesting, as well as how the grocers were handling the foods in their stores was monitored in the grocery stores also and not limited to just restaurants and diners.   The government was very interested in the marketing and selling of grocery items.   I enclosed a few samples from a 1912 report below.   It discusses adding artificial colorings, selling rancid eggs, low butter fats, limit of benzoate of soda (used in packaged foods as preservative), to the proper refrigeration of foods.

The law of Pennsylvania permits the use of a limited quantity of benzoate of soda in the preparation of certain food products. But it is unlawful to use more than one-tenth of one per cent. Sometimes the manufacturer becomes careless and indifferent and the result is too much benzoate of soda in the articles sold by him.

During the year 1910, a considerable number of cases were prosecuted and terminated against manufacturers or venders of non-alcoholic drinks. The dealers had forgotten the requirement of the law, hence the trouble which came to them, overtaking them suddenly like a thief in the night. Some of the agents of the bureau collected samples of milk containing added water and some from which a portion of the butter-fat had been removed. Some cream was likewise found to be below the legal standard, 15 per cent. butter-fat. Also a large number of ice cream cases were terminated in which the frozen dainty failed to comply with the provisions of the ice cream act.

We are pleased to report that the line of canned goods put up in this country, consisting of potted meats, soups and vegetables, have all been found to comply with the requirements of the Pennsylvania pure food law. This is complimentary to the manufacturers and an assurance of safety to the consuming public.

During the year 1910, Special Agent Cassidy found his troubles in Philadelphia, some of which were due to the persistency of dealers in rotten eggs or eggs which were really unfit for human food. This nauseating evil was remedied, in part at least, by the arrest and prosecution of some offenders. This business of selling putrid eggs is one of the most revolting in which any human being can engage.

package marked 'artificially colored,' the householder, in buying the noodles, will be cheated, for she will get noodles without any nutriment in them at all.

"Here is some mustard made from wheat flour, colored with coal-tar dye and flavored with a little real mustard.

"The entire point of the thing is this—while the law permits such artificial coloration when the label is so marked, I do not think it should be allowed by law, because people who buy foodstuffs are careless, the majority of them do not read the labels and often when they do, the mark 'artificially colored,' does not deter them from buying.

"This is the question the buyer should ask himself, 'Is this artificial coloring necessary? Have they not left out something from the composition of this article they want to conceal by the presence of this dye? Have they left the eggs out of the noodles, or the cake? If they have, I do not want that article."

I enjoyed the miscellaneous notes found throughout the same 1912 publication; the wording of some of these were quite interesting. Here are a few of them:

MISCELLANEOUS NOTES.

The householder will do well to scan with attention products suspected of cold storage experiences.

Labels do not always tell the truth; nevertheless it is good policy to examine them carefully. Under the National Food and Drugs Act it is always possible for a lying label to get the producer into trouble.

Whenever the nation or the state confronts the deliberate adulterator of food with the prospect of a prison sentence there will be fewer violations of law. The prison has terrors that no fine can produce.

With millions upon millions of pounds of butter swiftly gathered up and stored away is it any wonder that the butter supply is not ample enough to provide all the people with a generous share at a reasonable price?

Recent events seem to confirm the view of those who have been putting a large share of the responsibility for the high prices of food products on the shoulders of the cold storage managers. They likewise increase the urgency of the popular demand for government supervision of this business. It has its good features as well as its vicious ones. The former should be preserved and strengthened; the latter should be eliminated.

Vinegar seems to be a favorite vehicle of the adulterators. In spite of what has been done by the federal government and some of the states a very considerable percentage of the country's "cider" vinegar never saw any cider.

Ordinary prudence should teach the housekeeper that the only safe food products are those free from doubtful foreign products.

A little poison will kill nobody, unless it be extremely powerful; but account should be taken of the cumulative effect of swallowing it in your food from day to day.

Another practice of the oleomargarine people which is deprecated by the dairymen and farmers is that of labeling their product with a name wholly suggestive of genuine butter.

The cold storage folks are furnishing some convincing evidence against themselves. When they unload upon the market and prices go rapidly down they seem to prove all their critics have been saying.

To educate the coming generation in a knowledge of the properties of food products and to familiarize it with the effects of various preservatives will be to add to the length of human life.

ICE BUSINESS

Ice would be cut out of the Ohio River, some streams, and/or ponds, then hauled to the ice houses. The ice would be packed in sawdust, this process would keep the ice for sometimes up to two years.   Especially dealers in dairy and/or meat products needed the ice to keep their products cold.

There was a former ice house by the site that became the Elvidge's Service Station on Pennsylvania Avenue.   Since Elvidge's was at the corner of Pennsylvania Avenue and Fifteenth Street, this ice house would most likely have been the Barco and Huffmyer's ice house.

Barco and Huffmyer - ice men – 1498 Pennsylvania Avenue
1927
   They dealt in coal and were also local ice men.

————————

Ice Dealer – 300 block of Atlantic Avenue (once called Ohio Street)
 In 1912, William Volhardt was listed as the ice dealer.   William lived at 715 Washington Avenue.

Photos courtesy Beaver County Historical Research and Landmarks Foundation

  This barn was used as an ice house and was located by the corner of Fourth Street and Atlantic Avenue;
  in the 300 block of Atlantic Avenue.

  Both the barn and the house beside it were razed.   If you look closely on the right side of the
   picture on the right – you will see a workman in the process of dismantling the house.   (Both the
   barn and house would have faced toward the river.)

This barn / ice house would have probably been William Volhardt's with the location of Henry Volhardt's
home being just a short distance further on Atlantic Avenue extension and Henry's shoemaking shop being along
this stretch of Atlantic, too.   (William was Henry's son.)

*** *** *** *** ***
*** *** ***

Teamsters and Livery

Tanner

Saddlers

Wagon and Buggy Makers

Horseshoers

Blacksmiths

TEAMSTERS   LIVERY   BLACKSMITHS   WAGON MAKERS   TANNERS and SADDLERS

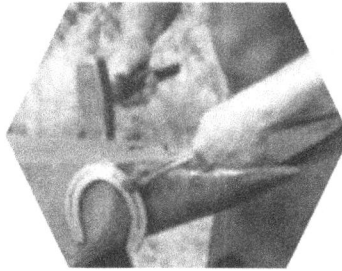

Teamsters   and   Livery

The livery and blacksmiths, wagon makers, livery owners, along with tanners, and saddlers were quite necessary prior to the popularity and accessibility of automobiles.   Livery owners were once common since most of the people did not have the funds, or facilities to own and board their own horses and rigs.   Those who did have horses or mules to use along with their line of occupation would have their own horses, but not always a place to keep them.   In this book, I have only included information beginning at 1850.   I am sure there were more individuals in all these occupations much earlier than 1850, but with no available documentation of occupations of residents then, I could not list them in this book.

Connected with the subject of this section, there was one special interest connected with Monaca that occurred in 1976. A group of people celebrated the bicentennial by making trips across the country by wagon train. There was also a water unit to this pilgrimage; this involved a bicentennial barge, the "Victory."   This wagon-bearing barge left Paduka, Kansas on April 5, 1976 empty except for the crew and a photographer, it traveled up river to Omaha, Nebraska and the Oregon Trail wagons were loaded. It proceeded to Independence, Missouri, where the Santa Fe Trail wagons were loaded on May 8th.   With a total of 19 covered wagons, mules, horses, and humans now onboard the *Victory* barge, it was on its way to begin meeting up with others traveling on land.   When the *Victory* barge docked at the shores of the Ohio along Monaca's Water Works, it marked the first stop of the water unit in Pennsylvania and the first time the land and water contingents had united in many months of traveling.   With many towns and areas having celebrations and parades, these wagon trains were invited to participate as often as possible. There was one of the wagon trains that made its way from Beaver Falls to Monaca one Saturday afternoon in June.   Bud Brown of Arizona made a six month Bicentennial Wagon Train Pilgrimage from his home state to Philadelphia, Pennsylvania, with his team of mules and wagon train all traveling through Beaver County.

The *Victory* barge docked at Monaca Water Works.

Parade of wagons traveling
on Pennsylvania Avenue.

This is teamster Bud Brown driving his
wagon toward Monaca in 1976.

While researching, I did find several men who had *teamster* listed as their occupation, primarily in the 1850s and 1860s. I was ignoring these individuals thinking in today's terms as their belonging to some type of union. Then I ran across some articles and information that brought a new meaning to the word. It seems that in the 1800s, a teamster was a person who drove a team of horses or a wagon drawn by a horse. Teamsters were used by those in the construction, building, hauling, and delivery businesses.

With all that being said, listed below are the names of *teamsters* that I found who were living in Monaca, followed by livery/liverymen, tanners, horseshoers, saddlers, wagon makers, blacksmiths. I may have some of the men listed individually, when in reality, they may have been working with the owner of a shop or storeroom and did not specifically owned their own building. The job of teamster was hard work and I felt it was important to give them credit where credit was due whether they owned their own shop or not, so I've listed all of the individuals.

Teamsters

1850	**1860**	**1870**	**1880**	**1900**	**1912**
Francis Bomat	Francis Bimat	- - -	Richard Jolly	Mary Boak	John Dunfee
Isaac Baker	Adam Meaner		Stameda Jolly	Roy Boak (her son)	John Manor
	Gilbert Trompeter			William Rowan	John Potter
	Benj. Stright			Austin Laird	Harvey Taylor
				James Hicks	Joseph Erb
	1892/1893		**1876**		Charles
	Robert Fleming		George McCauley		Huffmyer
					Edward Jackson
					Isaac Stephenson

Also, listed as "drivers" in 1900 were:
        Henry Vogt on Indiana Avenue   and   Albert Mateer on Ninth Street

Ever hear of a drayman ?

Historically, a drayman was the driver of a dray which was a low, flat bed wagon without sides that was pulled by horses or mules.   A dray would be used to transport all types of goods. More modernly, the term is used for brewery delivery men, even though the routine horse-drawn deliveries are extinct.

Monaca's Drayman in 1912 was Charles R. Cain who lived at 1108 Virginia Avenue.
Charles delivered coal. He eventually had a coal delivery business with trucks he kept in a garage at the rear of their home in 1934.
He was listed as *general hauling* in 1929 at 1200 Virginia Avenue.

LIVERY

Liverymen covered many duties.   We can compare them to or describe them as an early day taxi at times. Visitors to a town or area could leave their horses at a livery stable during their stay. You could say that a livery was more of a hotel for horses. Liverymen would feed, water, and provide a stall for the animals.   At the livery stables people who did not own a horse could often rent one; buggies, wagons and sleighs could also be rented. It was not unusual to find men gathered at a livery stable to talk; it was a place where they exchanged stories, exchanged information and ideas, and just relaxed.   People could hire a liveryman to transport one person, a family, or groups of people to different events throughout the year.   There were some livery businesses available that provided carriages for funerals and transporting the casket; yet other livery businesses relied on the income from boarding and caring for the horses of other people who did not have facilities to keep their horses.

Bert Allen – liveryman
1902, 1903   His wife's name was Martha E.; they resided on Indiana Avenue.

_____

J. B. Shumaker Livery Stable   - Moon Township

_____

Simmelrock Bros. Livery – unknown address
This business was out of Pittsburgh – on the South Side.   Many Monaca businessmen made trips to Pittsburgh on a fairly regular schedule.   This livery/stable was mentioned in an Aug 1888 article of the Pittsburgh Daily Post, as well as in the local newspapers for Monaca.

_____

Burgess Paulus E. Koehler's stable – Peach Alley
1906
(Peach Alley runs parallel with Pennsylvania Avenue - between Eighth and Ninth Streets)
I do not know if Paulus was actually a liveryman, but he did have stables.
Horses from the Monaca Vol. Fire Dept were moved from Potter's Livery in 1906 to Paulus's stable until the new stable for the horses was built.
He served 2 years as a member of the borough council, two terms as burgess and as Justice of the Peace. He also was tax collector of the borough for 22 years, until his death.
Paulus built the old Monaca Hotel which he conducted two years before selling it, then he entered upon his various borough activities and did much toward making Monaca a thriving municipality.   With his own stables, it would have been beneficial so he could provide boarding services for the Hotel Monaca patrons' horses.

_____

Sidney Huffmyer – Pennsylvania Avenue and Ninth Street
1914

Liveryman.   Sidney and his brothers and sisters were step-children of Edward Stoops in 1900
(their father, Wm., had died and his mother remarried to Edward).

By 1910, Sidney had moved to Center Township; married to Anna and had 2 children; his
occupation was *farmer*.   Sidney was married 3 times: 1) Lenore Mateer; 3 children;
2) Anna Myers; 1 child;   3) Gula Baker; no children.

Photo courtesy BCHR&LF

Charles Huffmyer – 1498 Pennsylvania Avenue, near Fifteenth Street
1907, 1909, 1910

His livery was next door to Heidrick & Taylor's hardware store.

Charles was associated with Edward Stoops through the years (see previous).

He hired Abner Hindman in 1909.

Charles was the son of Wm. and Laura Huffmyer (who married E. Stoops after Wm. died).
Charles married May __; 1 child ....then married Lena Cain; 3 ....then married
Mollie; they had 4 children.   In 1910, Charles and Lena were living at the same location
as the shop.

They used to reside in the Monaca Chess Club building on lower Pennsylvania Avenue, but in
Apr 1907, they moved in to the new building on upper Pennsylvania Avenue.

Potter's Livery – 612 Washington Avenue (near Sixth Street)
1886, 1902, 1929, 1937, 1944, 1953

John P. Potter was the owner & started his business in 1886 when Monaca was still called
Phillipsburg.

John and Alice lived at 612 Washington Avenue, right by the livery barn.
It was a very large two storey barn behind 699 Pennsylvania Avenue.

The barn burned in early Feb 2004.

There was also a home at 699 Pennsylvania Avenue in 1940s.

It was noted he purchased a fine carriage team of dapple greys in Jul 1906.

He was also listed as a local contractor.

Horses from the Monaca Vol. Fire Dept were moved from here to Koehler's stable on
Peach Alley until the new stable for the horses was built.
George Erb was one of the employees at this business.

One of the famous Potter wagons.   Photos courtesy of BCHR&LF

James Harper owned the property at 699 Pennsylvania Avenue and the barn in 2001.

Potters were known for being the leader in hauling machinery weighing many tons.
Had 10 head of horses, 4 drivers, and 25 to 30 laborers in 1911.
He was considered a "Teaming Contractor."
Along with providing the livery services, John P. began to use his teams for hauling construction
materials and thus the beginning of not only a livery business, but John would be called
for moving heavy equipment, building blocks.   Eventually the business expanded into
installing block windows and building foundations for buildings.   John P.'s sons joined
their father and eventually took over his business and the name of the business morphed
into ....

Potter Brothers Construction Co.

They had their main business being done at the Potter Barn – behind 699 Pennsylvania Avenue;
they also had a very small business building at the other end of town that was still standing in
2015 – between Johnstone's and Slush Puppie offices, across from Yolanda's.

See Hardware Section for a bit more information on the hauling business.

John P. was a lifelong resident of Monaca, b 1869; married to Alice Figley; they had 9 children.
The Potter family:
    John Presley Potter b 1867; married Alice Figley; 9 children:
        Zacharias b 1892; married Ann __ ; he was a contractor.
        John B. b 1894 in Monaca; married Alice _; 2 children .... married Grace _; 2 children.
        Robert G.- b 1895 in Monaca; married Edna Weigel; he was a contractor.
        William- b 1897; married Margaret __, had at least 1 child.
        Raymond - b 1900.
        Charles - b 1902; married Grace Reynolds.
        Margaret -b 1905.
        Lillian - b 1908 (was not on the 1920 census).
        Alice - b 1913.

> For Sale—Good fast driving horse.
> Thoroughly city broke. Inquire at
> Potter's Livery, Monaca, Pa.

1913

With his sons continuing in John P.'s business, it was considered one of the oldest continually operated businesses in Monaca as of 1974.

1910 - Zach and John B. were teenagers and listed as livery drivers for their father.

1912 - John B. and Zachariah were drivers for the business.   I do not know if they drove horse drawn vehicles or if the Potters had purchased trucks by this time.   Both sons still lived at home at this time.

1920 – Robert, Wm., Raymond, and Charles were all *teamsters* for their father; John B. was a *mason in contracting*.

1930 - the horses and teams were probably being phased out because they owned a truck by then and Charles was the driver for the company.

This was the Potter's livery barn that listed at 699 Pennsylvania Avenue.   If my memory serves me correctly, the barn was actually located just behind the current building at 699 Pennsylvania Avenue (which would be Jim Harper's Barber Shop) and sat on the corner of Maple Alley and the unnamed alley that runs between the gas station and barber shop.   It was definitely one of the landmarks in Monaca
since it was built in 1892.   It remained in the Potter family until 1999 – a total of 107 years.

Potter's Livery/ Barn

Current view of site

On Feb 8, 2004, the barn burned down......what a shame to lose such a well known building.

All that was left of the livery/barn after the fire.

The former livery / barn was being used as a "rent a space" warehouse and workshop in 2004.   Todd Gnarra and Jay Funkhauser were co-owners of Evolution Audio and the barn, purchasing it mid 2002.

_____

Moses Casper – teamster / livery
1920   He lived at 600 Pennsylvania Avenue in 1920.

_____

Michael Schuster – teamster / livery
1920
        He lived at 417 Pennsylvania Avenue in 1920.

_____

Edward S. Stoops – 616 Pennsylvania Avenue
1901, 1902, 1903, 1904, 1906, 1912, 1920, 1922, 1930
        He built the livery and sale stables in Apr 1901.   They were built by Cochran Bros.
        Edward's wife was Laura – they lived by the livery at 698 Pennsylvania Avenue in 1912.
            In 1920, they were living at 616 Pennsylvania Avenue.
            He had George D. Hott and Wesley Arnold working for him; they also lived/boarded with Edward and Laura.   George Mateer also worked for him in 1902/03 and lived with them.
            Edward and Charles Huffmyer were close associates, working together and possibly shared a barn at times because there were several articles stating both their names.
            Ex - E. S. Stoops and Charles Huffmyer bought a team of cab horses in 1906; in their absence to attend this sale, they left Harvey J. Taylor in charge of the barn.
        Edward had Charles McCullough working with him in 1912.
        1920-21 - Wm. S. Stoops was listed as proprietor.

> ********
> Liveryman Stoops purchased a fine match team of bay horses on Saturday, which are quite a valuable acquisition to his livery outfit.
> ********

1904

          *** *** *** *** ***

Tanners

Peter Markey – Tanner
1850 through 1880
        Peter was born 1809 - d 1881; married Nancy Stewart; 4 children.
        They had lived in Monaca since 1838; residence was on Pennsylvania Avenue.
            Nancy lived to be 95 years old; died in 1903.
        James Markey worked in the tannery in 1870 (he became proprietor of Central Hotel).

_____

Lewis Calb – Tanner
1850   Was 19 years old in 1850 and apprenticed/worked and lived with Peter Markey.

_____

Charles Hemphill - Tanner
1850   Was 28 in 1850 and working for Peter Markey.

_____

George Lay – Tanner
1900

_____

George W Weinman – Merchant in leather
1920   He lived at 810 Indiana Avenue.

          *** *** *** *** ***

Horseshoers

James Bryan – 399 Eighth Street
1912   His trade was *blacksmith*.

_____

H. W. Shaffer – 211 Sixth Street
1912

*** *** *** *** ***

Saddlers

Millard F. Wolf
1902, 1903
     He was a manufacturer and dealer in handmade harnesses and full stock of horse furnishings.
     He was married to Ida M. __; they lived on Atlantic Avenue.

_____

James Finn/Lynn – saddler
1860

_____

Sylvester Johnston – harness maker
1892, 1893

_____

Edward Johnston – harness maker
1900

> **E. M. JOHNSTON,**
>
> Manufacturer of HARNESS and dealer in Collars, Whips, Robes and Horse Furnishing Goods. Repairing a Specialty.   MONACA, PA.

_____

R. E. Goettman –
1909   Sold harnesses and horse supplies.

> **HARNESS AND HORSE SUPPLIES.**
>
> R. E. Goettman,   Monaca, Pa.
>
> A fine line of harness and horse supplies. All repairing promptly attended to.

1909

_____

Christian Erbeck
     Had his own shop where he practiced the trade of saddler and upholstery. He retired from this business and did farming and butchering in Moon Township, turning to farming only.
     Christian married Philippine Wagner, d/o of Jacob and Christine Wagner.

*** *** *** *** ***

Wagon and Buggy Makers

The horse drawn vehicles, carriages and buggies were intertwined with the livery business in that often times a wagon maker might additionally have a livery business, too.   This dual business would be for income between sales and then storing/servicing of a wagon.

The wagon makers from Monaca would have had smaller shops, yet adequate to serve the limited region. The size of a shop would not diminish the craftsmanship that was applied to their craft.   These men were also like an early version of AAA because they were called upon when a wheel would come off a wagon or break or any type of maintenance was needed.   They were true craftsmen and always took pride in their products.

Types of horse drawn wagons and buggies a liveryman might have used and/or the wagon makers would have produced were varied.   Monaca, Moon/Center, and Potter residents could have owned or would have seen any one of these on a regular basis in the earlier years.

Buckboard

Spring wagon

Piano box runabout

Doctors Buggy

Hearse

Augustus Greiner – wagon maker
1900, 1902, 1903
> August was b 1871 in Germany; married 1893 to Amelia; 1910 lived at Washington Avenue;
> they had 7 children.
> By 1910, August was out of the wagon making business and they moved to Monaca Heights;
> he was then a dairyman/retail milk.

Peter Folland – wagon maker – Hanover Street (now Fourth Street)
1850 through 1880
> His shop was beside their home – at about 135 Fourth Street (2015).
> Peter was b 1823 and d before 1900; married Mary __; 7 children.

Oliver Weigle – wagon maker – Monaca Heights
1902, 1903
       His wife's name was Enzeennetta; they lived in Dockters Heights.

————————

Henry Frederick – wagon and buggy maker
1860
       Henry was b 1830; married Dortha; 2 children.

————————

Joseph Shafer – wagon maker
1860
       Joseph was b in 1827; married Clementine; 5 children.

————————

Philip Wagner – carriage maker (age 19)
1860
       At such a young age, I would imagine he was working for one of the other wagon
           makers in town.
       His father had passed away several years prior to 1860 and his step father had also died by then.

————————

J. Bergmann – general blacksmith and wagon maker
1898, 1903
       By 1929, a J. Bermann is listed as a barber on Ninth Street.   This could either be
           the same person, or possibly a son.

*** *** *** *** ***

Blacksmiths

Any one of the men who worked in a blacksmith shop was considered to be an individual of great skill. These men had studied and were taught metal crafting. They could take a piece of iron and shape it into many items, including tools, horseshoes, and wagon-wheel rims. It was a familiar sound to hear the blacksmiths' clanking as his hammer would pound out the metal on his anvil. Just as familiar was the sound of the horses' shod hoofs hitting the paved (brick lined) streets as they passed through town. The need for the livery stables and the blacksmith shops began to wane by the mid 1900s with the introduction of the automobiles to the towns, communities, and areas. Many of the younger blacksmiths found jobs in mills and industry with their skills of working metal was continued, although slightly altered.

The following five men were blacksmiths in Monaca and all were referenced at the same address throughout the span of 1841 to 1926. This blacksmith shop was quite popular by all the articles and information I found on it. There appears to have been one or two adjacent buildings. The men seemed to cross over during the years as working and or owning the business. I have listed the years I found information on their being a blacksmith, but it was too difficult to determine exactly who actually was considered the owner during any given years.

"Pat" McKee – Eighth Street and Pennsylvania Avenue
1840, 1892, 1893, 1901
>   Had David Fisher as an apprentice and taught David well because he continued the trade
>   through out his lifetime.
   and.....

Merkel Blacksmith shop – corner of Pennsylvania Avenue and Eighth Street (beside Wagner House).
1840s, 1869, 1900, 1901,
>   Owned by Justus T. Merkel.   Started in the business in the 1840s.
>   Immigrated to America in 1847 – landing in Philadelphia and came to Phillipsburg in 1850.
>   Learned the blacksmith trade in Germany.   Lived at 705 Pennsylvania Avenue.
>   Young boys and girls used to pass time at his shop.
>   He was considered to be frugal and industrious and had a natural business sense. Justus
>   amassed a considerable fortune, allowing him to acquire a large amount of real estate.
>   i.e. 1526 Pennsylvania Avenue (still standing in 2015)
>   Justice Merkel purchased a frame house from Geo. Zitzman and moved it a short distance
>   west on Pennsylvania Avenue. The newspaper article stated Mr. Zitzman intended to
>   move his store building from Ninth Street to the lot where the house had stood; was to
>   add an additional storey to the building.
>   The old blacksmith shop was torn down.
>   o Justus b 1824 Germany-d 1907 Monaca, s/o Henry and Marie; married Margaret Mateer and
>   they had no children; he then married Marie Eistner and they had 4 children.

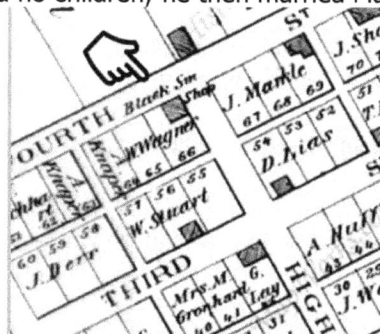

(Fourth Street became Pennsylvania Avenue and High Street became Eighth Street.)

And.......

James P. Bryan – Eighth Street and Pennsylvania Avenue
1901, 1908, 1916, 1926

James was said to have acquired the business about 1901 from Justus Merkel when he retired.

Was the village smithy. He had one of the oldest landmarks in Monaca, but it was razed in the mid 1930s.   He became owner of the shop in 1901.

- James learned his trade at the Patterson-Blackmore blacksmith shop and first worked at Clinton, Bavington, and Midway.
- Originally established by Justus Merkel about 1841.

John B. Potter, general building contractor and liveryman, was Mr. Bryan's first customer in 1901.

Operated the blacksmith shop until 1915 (at which time he became Sheriff of Beaver County).

At the end of his term as sheriff, he and his family returned to make their home in Monaca and he again entered his profession which he carried on until 1926.

In 1927, the Bryans moved to Beaver; he served as postmaster in Beaver.

James P. Bryan

And......

"Dave" Fisher's Blacksmith Shop (also had a hardware – appliances – furniture section in shop...1898)
1898, 1903, 1915

His shop was a "hang out" of many of the old timers who met there daily to swap stories as "Dave" would be pounding out horse shoes.   Dave was doing well in his business in the early 1900s because he purchased the building that Fred Leffert had his meat market in and was having repair work done to the building.

He also ran a hardware business (see Hardware Appliances Furniture section).

Jonathan D. Wagner (married Mollie__, lived on Fourth Street) was working in the shop in 1912.

And......

William Wagner
1876, 1912, 1919, 1926

William ran the business with his brother in law David (Dave) Fisher (who had apprenticed under "Pat" McKee).

Re-opened his business after serving term as Sheriff of Beaver County.

He continued the business until 1926 then they moved to Beaver.

The building was considered the "supreme court" of Monaca – James H. Markey was "chief justice."   Many stated missing the establishment and said even though the "court" has long since passed, memories linger on.

James Markey moved from Pennsylvania Avenue to Pittsburgh in Apr 1919.

William, like Dave Fisher, was also in the hardware business.

The building was razed prior to 1940.

See complete Wagner family history in Prominent People section.

_____

Simon Wagner was listed as a blacksmith in 1841. It would be logical that he worked in the family shop, but proof of this was not found.

_____

Samuel Boak – blacksmith
1892, 1893

_____

Harland L. Gamble - blacksmith
1892, 1893

————————

Emphraim Powell - blacksmith
1892, 1893

————————

Sidney Powell - blacksmith
1892, 1893

————————

Claude C. Leister – blacksmith – Pennsylvania Avenue
1902, 1903
    His wife's name was Anna L.; they resided on Washington Avenue.

————————

Reed & McKnight – blacksmiths – Sixth Street
1902, 1903
    Michael W. Reed (married Catherine M.) and Frank B. McKnight (married May A., resided on Sixth
    Street). Michael W. Reed had Nellie McKnight living with him in 1902/03.

————————

These men were working as blacksmiths, but it is very probable that none of them had their own shops, but then I
found nothing to say that they did not have individual shops, so……..

1841	Bernard Zeigler	Jacob Veiginger
	George Zeigler	

1850	Robert Adkinson – blacksmith	Orias Bouton - blacksmith
	William Calhoun – blacksmith	Philip Metshan – blacksmith
	Henry Rivar – blacksmith	Andrew Rivar – Blacksmith
	George Smith – blacksmith	Samuel Tregellas - blacksmith

1860	Frederick Frank – apprentice blacksmith	Terenline Lee - blacksmith
	William Wagner – blacksmith	

1870	James Irons – blacksmith	Justice Michael – blacksmith
	James Patterson – blacksmith	

1880	Edward Blatt – blacksmith	Robert Merriman – apprentice blacksmith

1900 and 1902, 1903
    Michael Reed – blacksmith   John Wagner – blacksmith
    Charles Doherr (Mary) – blacksmith
    George M. Dunn (Nancy) – blacksmith
    Philip Meyers(Kate) – blacksmith
    William Wright – blacksmith - He roomed with A. Temple.
    Edward S. Flick [Anna C.], blacksmith
    George M. Flick [Carrie E.], blacksmith

1912   L. Bert Emerick, married Lizzie, lived at Ninth Street.
        Anthony Hagerty, married Margaret, lived at Ninth Street.

*** *** *** *** ***
*** *** ***

TONSORIAL ARTISTS   BARBERS

SALONS   BEAUTY SHOPS

TONSORIAL ARTISTS / BARBERS   SALONS   BEAUTY SHOPS

As with the blacksmith tradesmen, some of the persons listed within these occupations may not have had their own shops or businesses, but rather worked for others.   I have listed as much information on each as could be found.

Alexander Gempill – barber
1841

————————

Joseph Kreg – barber
1841

————————

Conrad Gann – barber
1841

————————

George Hartzel – barber.
1890s   Had his own shop in the 1890s.   George left Monaca in 1897 and went to Marion
                           Township, but returned in Apr 1904 and secured a position at Jacob Burry's shop.

————————

Henry Krausse - barber
1892, 1893

————————

Paul Mattauch – started at Pennsylvania & Fourth Street, then built shop at 699 Pennsylvania & Sixth
          Street; purchased the storeroom and dwelling owned by the late William Johnston on
          Pennsylvania Avenue (may have been at #616).
1893 to 1977
          Opened his shop in 1893.
          Paul retired the week of Jan 9, 1942 after 56 years in business.
          Mr. Mattauch's son Henry Paul Mattauch ran the business for 50+ years and retired in 1977.
          He learned his trade in Czechoslovakia in 1885 where he also did his apprenticeship.
          In 1890 he arrived in America, landing in New York; he then went to Pittsburgh and worked
                 there for 3 years.
          In Nov 1893, he came to Monaca.   He started his first shop in a small building on Pennsylvania
                 Avenue and Fourth Street; after it was established, his mother also came to America to
                 live with her son.
          His business outgrew this first building and Mr. Mattauch built a one storey building at the corner
                 of Pennsylvania Avenue and Sixth Street.   He remained at this location until 1900.
          1900 - he purchased the large dwelling and storeroom owned by the late William Johnston; this
                 building became the home of the Mattauchs and the location of his barber shop at 699
                 Pennsylvania Avenue. Paul had his barber shop newly painted and beautified in Jun
                 1907.   Even before inside plumbing, the barber shop provided hot and cold baths.
          Mr. Mattauch was not only a barber, but a mentor and taught the trade to at least nine other
                 men; several opened their own shops.
                 Some of these men were Paul Schlosser of Beaver and Carl Stief of New Brighton, his
                 nephews Richard Keilner and Carl Mattauch, John Bergman, Earl Arbogast, Gustave
                 Friebe, and Wenzel Blasche, all of Monaca, and Emil Berger of Pgh.   William Peitsch,
                 formerly from Monaca, then of Rochester, also was an apprentice but he did not follow
                 the trade.
          Emil Berger was boarding at the barber shop in 1902/03.
          Earl A. Arbogast was working here in 1902/03; he lived on Atlantic Avenue.
          Carl Mattauch and Wenzel Blasche were employed by Mr. Mattauch for some time.
          Frank Lockhart worked for Paul in 1912.   Frank lived at 1125 Virginia Avenue.

Paul was president of the Monaca Federal Savings and Loan Assoc, of Monaca from 1934 to
beyond 1942.

He married a Miss Julia Linke of New York in 1899 and they lived their married lives in Monaca.
They had three daughters and a son.

After 56 years as a barber, Paul turned the keys over to his son Henry when he retired the first of
Jan 1942.   Henry had an assistant, William Irons, who was a grandson of Paul.
Henry Paul died in 1985.

The original building was torn down in the mid to late 1960s and replaced with a one storey
building.   James Harper bought the business in 1977/78.

See Grocery section – the Mattauch's had a confectionary store next door to the barbershop.

Photo courtesy of the Great Arrow Historical Association collection
This is Mattauch's Confectionery and Barber shop building.
Paul Mattauch and "Pickle" Douds (on right) are pictured.

Paul Mattauch
Photo courtesy of the BCHR&LF

—————

Carl Mattauch – barber – 1303 Pennsylvania Avenue
1912
Carl (Paul's nephew) branched out into his own business; his shop opened at the other
end of town by 1912.   He still lived at 699 Pennsylvania Avenue and was considered *a boarder*.

—————

Harper's Barber Shop / Harper's Styling– 699 Pennsylvania Avenue
1978, 1990, Current   Owned by Jim Harper.

—————

Jacob Burry – barber - 806 Pennsylvania Avenue (near Eighth St)
1892, 1893, 1900, 1902, 1903, 1911, 1918

Started Aug 2, 1881 (when it was known as Phillipsburg).

In Sep 1911, Jacob was the oldest living business man in Monaca.

Jacob married Caroline Kugel in 1876. They had four daughters. Jacob died in 1918; Caroline continued to live in the house until she died 1942. They are both buried in the German Lutheran Cemetery. Their home had been at 810 Pennsylvania Avenue.

With Caroline being in her mid 70s at the time of her death, one would believe that she possibly went to live with one of her 4 daughters prior to her death since the home at 810 Pennsylvania Avenue (near Eighth Street - owned by Jacob Burry) was razed mid Apr 1941. The conclusion of her living with one of the daughters is made because the building had been purchased in 1940/1941 by Harry E. Keck and resold to Bryan Mamula of Aliquippa and then the building was razed -- there was no mention of her moving during all this.

It was one of the oldest buildings in Monaca in 1941 when it was razed.

Jacob had W. F. Patterson working for him in May of 1903 (W.F. left for Pittsburgh to work as a bartender for his father who had opened up a saloon there).

Jacob hired George Hartzel in Apr 1904 when he returned to town after being gone for about 7 years. (George had his own barber shop in 1890s before leaving town.)

In 1902/03 Jacob had William F Patterson working with him and William lived at the same location as the shop.

Jacob Burry

Vetter & Nique – corner of Pennsylvania and Ninth Street – 898 Pennsylvania Avenue
1902, 1908, 1910, 1911, 1912

In 1902 and 1903 A. C. Vetter was the sole proprietor and it was referenced as the "Sanitary Barber Shop;" then listed as owned by Alvin C. Vetter and Alvie/Elvie Nique.

Alvin took in Lee Cain to teach him the barber trade, but Lee resigned in Sep 1908 for health reasons.

Alvin was boarding with G. Friebe (barber) in 1902/03.

They added an electric massage machine to their tonsorial parlor.

Alvin married Yetta in 1909 and they started their family, living on Pennsylvania Avenue. He was working in a steel mill in 1920; living at 810 Washington Avenue.

Elvie (Elva/Alvie) Nique came from Ohio and went back to Ohio to live after the barber shop closed; he was married and living there in 1920.

A. C. Vetter

Edward B. Winkle's Barber Shop –   business at 810 Pennsylvania Avenue (near Eighth Street -known as
1902, 1903, 1906, 1909, 1913   the Burry building)

> The building at 810 Pennsylvania Avenue was eventually sold to Schmuck's Shoes in 1906.
> > Mr. Winkle's shop was in the basement area of the new Keystone building by Nov 1903; by
> > > 1905 he was located at 911 Pennsylvania Avenue.
> > > o   He also put a new barber pole in front of this place of business at the Keystone Bldg in Dec 1903.
> > Edward lived on Pennsylvania Avenue; then Edward B. and Edna lived at 1103 Virginia Avenue.
> > Prior to opening his own shop in Monaca, he was working at Harry Faust's shop in Freedom.
> > Apr/May 1906 - he made changes to the front of his barber shop on 911 Pennsylvania Avenue –
> > > moving the door to one end of the building from the center of it to give more room on
> > > the inside.   He remodeled and beautified the interior of his shop in Jun 1907.
> > The paper referred to him as "the tonsorial artist."
> > Carl Stief worked at E. B. Winkle's shop in spring of 1907.
> > In 1909 he sold his shop at 911 Pennsylvania Avenue to Wenzel Blasche, Sr.
> > The end of Mar 1909 he said he would soon be opening his shop in the new Zigerelli Bldg on
> > > Pennsylvania Avenue (#1414); but no further evidence was found if he actually did.
> > > He accepted a position with the P & LE RR in Feb 1913; so if he did open this shop, he
> > > may have had it open during hours he was not working at the railroad or just
> > > owned the shop and business and had another barber(s) working for him.

This picture is at Winkle's barber shop at 911 Pennsylvania Avenue in 1905.   Ed Winkle (at the 2nd chair), sold
this shop to Wenzel Blasche, Sr.   The man at the first chair is a customer, Harry Kuhn.

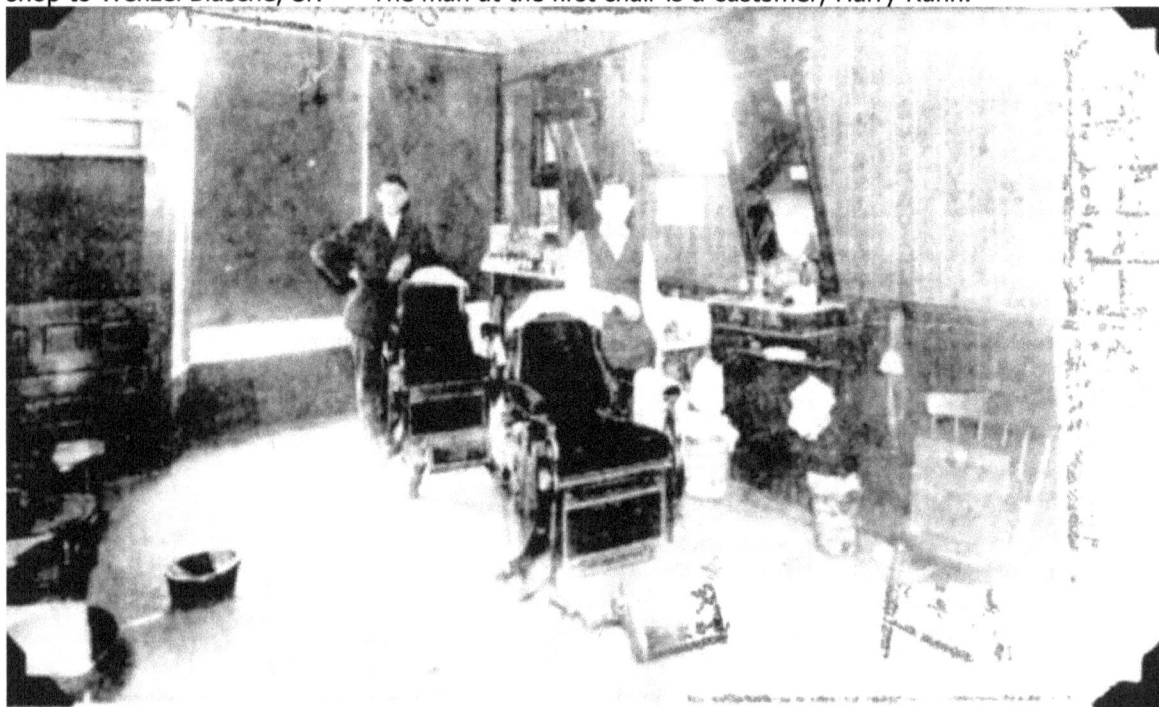

Photo courtesy Fritz Blasche in 1991 to Karen Heibling of the Beaver County Times

————————

Jerry O'Brien – barber
1900
> He lived on Pennsylvania Avenue

————————

Gustiav A. Friebe, Jr. – *tonsorial artist* – Pennsylvania Avenue
1898, 1900, 1902, 1904, 1907
        Gustav Friebe, Sr. b 1843 was a decorator in a glass plant.
        His son – Gustav Friebe, Jr. b 1877 was the barber.   He lived on Washington Avenue.
           He vacated his building the end of May/first of Jun 1902 (F.L. Wilson & Co. Real Estate
                agents moved in bldg); but an article from Apr 1904 – said he beautified and painted the
                interior of his barber shop....................
                    So............it appears he must have moved the shop or started it back up by 1904 ?
        The Friebe family lived on Washington Avenue in 1900 and 1910.
        1907 - Carl Stief was employed in Gustav's shop and leased the shop from Mr. Friebe.
        Gustav was granted a license and was to shortly open a wholesale liquor store.
        As of Nov 1919, Gustave was living in Toronto, OH.
                  See Wholesale Liquor section for more on Gustave Friebe.

————

Blasche Barber Shop – 911 Pennsylvania Avenue (used to be Ed Winkle's shop)
1909, 1975
        Opened his own shop in 1909 and bought Ed Winkle's shop in 1913.
        Wenzel R. Blasche owner.
        Learned his trade in Austria.
        Had this business for 72 years, retiring in 1975 at 90 years old.
        The red and white barber pole was still standing outside the building in 1976.
        Wenzel had his home on Atlantic Avenue from 1920.
            He married Marie ___ ; they had 8 or 9 children.
        Wenzel, Sr. was born 1886 and died at age 96.   Their home was at 820 Pennsylvania
            Avenue in 1912.
        Fritz and Rudy Blasche took over and operated the shop; they had helped with the shop
            prior to 1975.   Fritz died in 1995 at age 84.
        The shop was still open for business in Aug 1977 when it had some windows shot with pellets.

————

Earl Arbogast, the barber – Pennsylvania Avenue (next door to Nat'l Bank)
1906, 1907
        In business Jul 1906, Aug 1907.
        Bought a driving horse from Mr. Huffmyer in Jul 1906.
        In early Aug 1906, he bought a "handsome new buggy and set of harness for the driving mare."
        He lost the use of his right arm in Jun 1907. He was working and all of a sudden his arm from
            the elbow down became paralyzed; he is said to have recovered and was back at work
            before the end of Jun 1907, yet he had a help wanted ad for a full time barber in
             Aug 1907.
        He married Jennie Huffmyer of Monaca in 1907 and they lived on Ninth Street.

————

Joseph Genilli – Barber Shop – address unknown
1910   Joseph was partners with John Braccia who was a shoe maker.
          They both lived together on Beaver Avenue.

————

Joseph Karban – Barber – (no location of shop)
1902, 1903   He lived on Pacific Avenue. Joseph died Apr 1904.

————

Thomas A. Bailey – barber - (no location of shop)
1902, 1903   His wife's name was Ada M.; they lived at Atlantic Avenue.

————

Louis Brown – paper listed him as "the colored barber" – (no location of shop)
1903   Committed suicide near Colona; he was buried in the old Monaca cemetery.

_____

There were many different barbers that run their businesses in a space/shop that was located
in the basement of the Hotel Hamilton.   It seemed that each barber occupied this space for no more than a few
years at a time.   It is unclear if they rented the space for their businesses or if they were employees of the Hotel
Hamilton.......................

Harry Faust Barber Shop – basement of Hotel Hamilton
1902, 1903, 1904
        Opened his barber shop Nov 17, 1903; had the furniture and fixtures installed Nov 16, 1903.
        Harry lived on Washington Avenue in 1902/03.
        On Apr 6, 1904, Harry and his two sisters left on the steamer "Queen City" for Kentucky
                to visit relatives; then they were heading to California where they planned to locate
                permanently.
        These plans were carried out because his obit stated he left Monaca, settled out west;
                he changed professions and became a painting contractor.
        Harry had married Louise Koehler.   He died Jan 1945 at age 67.
                His father was also "Harry" and was a glass blower at Phoenix Glass before working for
                William Reagel, a local painter; following the painting business until he died in 1903.
    and......
Charles Ash – basement of Hotel Hamilton
1906, 1907
        The newspaper stated "a well known colored barber, of Rochester,...."
        He took charge of the barber shop/ business in Apr 1906.
        Mrs. Charles Ash and family moved from Pennsylvania Avenue to her old home in Bridgewater on
                Jan 8, 1907. (Why is Charles not mentioned in this move ? -- and by Apr 1907, there
                was a new barber using the space Charles had in the hotel ?)
    and.....
John Riar – basement of the Hotel Hamilton
1907   Opened his barber shop in Apr 1907.   John was from Rochester.

    and......
E. Forrest Barber Shop – basement of the Hotel Hamilton
1908
        Was out of the business, moved from Monaca by Sep 1908 , living in Cincinnati, Ohio.
    and......
McLaughlin Barber Shop – basement of the Hotel Hamilton
1910
        Was called "tonsorial artist." Had the shop newly papered, painted and fixed up in "fine style" – Nov 1910.
    and.....
E. C. Ertel / Estel – barber – basement of the Hamilton Hotel
1912, 1920   Elmer C. and Elsie lived at 419 Ninth Street (1912); at 1200 Pennsylvania Avenue (1920).

_____

Alexander Abnarth – barber - (no location of shop)
1902, 1903   His home was on Atlantic Avenue.

_____

Paul Schlosser – barber – Monaca Heights
1910   He apprenticed under Paul Mattauch.

_____

William Cleu – barber
1920
It is likely he just worked at a shop and didn't own his own.
He lived on Virginia Avenue in 1920.

_____

John Zigerelli – 1414 Pennsylvania Avenue
1920, 1930, 1940, 1954
Barber Shop.   He owned the building and had his shop here, lived there with his family.
By 1955, it was listed as John Zigerelli's Hardware and Confectionery Store.

_____

Frank Lockhart – Barber - Pennsylvania Avenue
1924
Frank filled in for Paul Mattauch in Aug of 1912 when Paul had a wrenched knee. Frank
formerly worked at the Blasche shop a few months earlier.
In the 1924 Monaca Yearbook, Frank was listed as *barber* on Pennsylvania Avenue, but I have
nothing else on this; he may have been with Paul Mattauch or also may have had his
own shop at that time.
Frank had his barber shop in Freedom in 1903 prior to opening the shop in Monaca.

_____

Nicholas Boris – barber
1930, 1940   He lived in the 1200 block of Pennsylvania Avenue.

_____

John Bergman – Barber shop – Ninth Street
1929, 1930
There was a blacksmith business in 1898 – no address; this was either the same man, or
possibly his father who started this business.   John was lodging on Indiana Avenue in 1930.

_____

Whippo Barber shop – Ninth Street (beside Ed Meany's Tailor Shop)
1929, 1930
Miller Whippo, owner.
He lived at 318 Ninth Street; this was most likely the same location as his shop.

_____

Frank Zogoria – Barber - unknown location
1930   He lived at 45 Beaver Avenue in 1930.

_____

Joseph Tomacella /Tomasello / Tomasella – Barber shop – Pennsylvania Avenue
1929, 1930, 1940
Joseph lived on Indiana Avenue in 1930.
He was the son-in-law to Frank Taormina who was retired in 1930.

_____

William Radakovich – Barber Shop – unknown location
1940
He lived on Wagner Street in 1940.

_____

Hemer's Barber Shop – 946 Fourteenth Street
1951, 1957   George Hemer – owner.

_____

Lou and Warner's Barber Shop – 1012 Pennsylvania Avenue (Keystone bldg)
1949, 1965, 1990
        Opened in 1949.
        Louis Cattivera purchased the business from John Bell.
                Louis was a barber in 1940 (no location as to where).
        Werner Agner was hired in 1950.
        Originally located where Bruno's Tailor Shop was in 1990 (which was 1016 Pennsylvania Avenue).
        After Louis passed away in 1981, Werner became sole owner and it was named.........

Warner Hair Styling
        After Werner retired, it became..............

Irons' Hair-Nails-Tanning
        About 1996/97, they moved to 2000 Beaver Avenue (former "Frank's" place).
        This business changed its name yet once again and is now ....

Designs by Dana – 2000 Beaver Avenue – beauty salon
2013, 2014/2015

_____

Christy's Barber Shop – Marshall Road
1977   Owner and operator – Christy D. Antoline.
        Formerly lived on Brodhead Road, Center Township, operated a barbershop there since 1946
                while he was employed at J & L Steel in Aliquippa.   He retired from J & L in Feb 1977
                and opened a barber shop in his new home on Marshall Road where he was a full
                time barber.   Mr. Antoline was born in 1919 in Monaca and died in 2003, Monaca.

_____

Anthony Ippolito's Barber Shop – 800 block Pennsylvania Avenue
1974

_____

Elmo's Barber Shop – 1206 Pennsylvania Avenue
1978

_____

Jeff Michaels Hair Salon – unknown address
1991

_____

Ramon Ramos Barber Shop – Pennsylvania Avenue
1993   Resident of Monaca since early 1960s.
        Operated a barber shop for several years.

Elmer's Barber Shop – (near Twelfth Street) – Pennsylvania Avenue
1983

*** *** *** *** ***

Susanna Ramsey – beauty specialist / beauty parlor – unknown location
1930   She lived in Colona.

—————

Bertha's Beauty Shop – 1107 Pennsylvania Avenue
            Bertha Reynolds Williams – Owner.

—————

Grater Beauty Studio aka   Anna M. Grater Beauty Shop (1929) aka Miss Anna M. Grater, Beauty Specialist
1928, 1929, 1940, 1943
        Anna Grater, proprietor.   She moved her parlor/shop around quite often.................
            - 1003 Pennsylvania Avenue on tax list in 1929
            - 1026 Pennsylvania Avenue beside the Batchelor Furniture Store -2nd floor (1930)
            – 316 Ninth Street (at least here in Aug 1940)
            - opened her shop in the Roxy Theatre building (Oct 1940) - 920 Pennsylvania Avenue
            - and finally to 1206 Pennsylvania Avenue
    When in the Penn/Roxy Theatre building, Anna decorated it with new furnishings - in the colors
        of black, cream, and red.   She also was ahead of her time and offered treatment to
        reduce "those bulges while you relax".

Formal Opening Wednesday
GRATER BEAUTY STUDIO

New Location

ROXY THEATRE BLDG., MONACA
(Former location—316 Ninth St., Monaca.)

Completely Remodeled, Redecorated
and Refurnished

DOOR PRIZE — OPENING DAY
$5 PERMANENT WAVE
ALSO DOOR FAVORS

We feature Parker-Herbex scalp treatment and Program
Cosmetics, oils for the skin.

Hours 10 A. M. to 8 P. M.
Phone Rochester 2159.

Oct 1940

RELAX--and REDUCE the
SLENDA VOGUE WAY

A streamlined, vital body, that looks and feels like a million.
Visit our Slenderizing Salon soon. It's our latest asset to
accommodate the request of our patrons. We can reduce
those bulges while you relax. One 40-minute treatment is
worth hours of strenuous exercise.

GRATER BEAUTY STUDIO
920 PENNA. AVE.   PHONE ROCH. 2459   MONACA

May 1941

—————

Susanna Kelly – Her own Beauty Shop – address unknown
1940   She lived at 1110 Pennsylvania Avenue in 1940.

—————

Marguerite Taormina – her own beauty shop – address unknown
1940   She lived at 1100 Indiana Avenue in 1940.

—————

Elizabeth Frick – was a beauty operator / beauty shop – address unknown
1940   She may have had a shop in her home or worked for someone else.
                She lived at 1050 Walnut Street.

—————

Kelsey Beauty Salon – 1107 Pennsylvania Avenue
late 1930s, 1940s

MISS HELEN LEONARD
BRODHEAD ROAD, MONACA
a graduate of the Wilfred Academy of Beauty Culture, is now affiliated with the

KELSEY BEAUTY SALON,
1107 Penna. Ave., Monaca.

Miss Leonard, as well as Miss Kelsey Vogt, holds both a teacher's license and operator's license. The Salon features a special price of $1.00 for a shampoo, wave set, and manicure, and 75c for a finger wave and facial, every Monday, Tuesday and Wednesday. For a limited time only a Hollywood Oil Croquignole Permanent will be priced at $2.00. Telephone Rochester 2423 for appointments.

───────

Barbara's Beauty Shop – 812 Pennsylvania Avenue
1941, 1956, 1969, 1979
    Barbara Salinshick was a border at 818 Pennsylvania Avenue in 1940 and worked as a cleaner for a glass company; then she opened her own beauty shop. She was born in 1913 in Yugoslavia. Her father, Paul Salinshick who owned Paul's Garage-823 Pennsylvania Ave, came to America in 1913, remarried, and saved his money to bring Barbara to America in 1926. She lived with Dan and Susan Romisher for many years, then lived in the Monacatootha Apartments for several decades. Barbara lived to be 99, dying in 2012.

Barbara's shop was in the first bldg on the left (a larger picture is located in Street Views section).
This building was erected in the 1880s and originally housed Adam Kemmer's Tin Shop.

───────

Dominic Saltarelli – Beauty Shop – unknown location
1940   His wife Lena was a beautician in the shop.

───────

__?__ Beauty Shop
1942   Proprietor – Winifred Catherine Gonet (became Mrs. Ketterer).

───────

Maxia's - beauty shop – 1422 Pennsylvania Avenue
1956

───────

Bea Rambo's Beauty Shop – 1005 Elm Street
1957

───────

Velma's Beauty Shop – 1107 Pennsylvania Avenue
1952, 1956

_____

Nichol Beauty Shoppe – 1054 Walnut Street
1951, 1952, 1956   Mamie Nichol, owner.

_____

Ann Salamay – Beauty Shop - 1065 Linden Street – Monaca Heights
1956, 1957

_____

Velma B. Makowiecki – unknown location of shop
Prior to 2004   Operated a beauty shop in her home prior to 2004.

_____

Leslie's Beauty Salon & Spa – 215 Ninth Street
2005

_____

Bessie's Beauty Shop – unknown address of shop
Prior to 1978   Owner/operator for over 50 years – Elizabeth (Bessie) Deveney.
                           She lived at 1229 Indiana Avenue.

_____

__?__ beauty shop – Monaca Heights
Prior to 1997   Operator – Mrs. Jane (Porter) Hicks.

_____

European Flair – 309 Ninth Street
2002, 2003   Opened March 2002.   Constantina Hahn – owner.   Now located on Third Street, Beaver.

_____

Virginia Silvestri's Beauty Shop – unknown location
Prior to 2001   Owner/operator – Virginia Silvestri (prior to 2001).

_____

Lela's Beauty Shop – Ninth Street
1965   Owner – Lela Donahey.

_____

Millie's Beauty Shop – 203 Ninth Street
1965, 1978   Owner – Mildred (Millie) Bennett (died 1988).

_____

Something Different in Hair Design – 999 Pennsylvania Avenue
1979   Richard Smith of New Brighton owner.

_____

Silhouette Beauty Shop – 1206 Pennsylvania Avenue**
1961   Co-owners – Carolyn Davis Paliotte Hoover and Randall Davis.

Carolyn Paliotte Beauty Shoppe – 1206 Pennsylvania Avenue**
btw 1961 – 1974   Owner – Carolyn Paliotte Hoover.

LaCoupe Hair Styles – 1206 Pennsylvania Avenue
1978   Co-owners – Carolyn Paliotte Hoover and Randall Davis.   This went into business in Nov 1974.

**1206 Pennsylvania Avenue had many hair stylist businesses; then it became a Pizza restaurant in
    2004 and was up for sale by 2006...............other prior businesses -- fish market, trucking firms.

MONACA   INCOME $100,000
1206 Pennsylvania Avenue
Excellent Investment Opportunity!! Over 2800 square
feet of Prime Commercial Space currently occupied by
two secure commercial tenants! The second floor
offers an apartment. This building is well maintained
and offers the investor a solid return! Ample off street
parking is adjacent and owned by the Borough!
MLS # 602982
Lorraine Ross at 724-624-4528

This ad was in paper Jul 17, 2006   There is currently an insurance agency business in the building.
The Ace Transport had a business in the rear of the building in 2005.

_____

Mr. Anthony's – 1302 Pennsylvania Avenue
1963, 1966   Was located across from Taormina's Market.

PERMANENT WAVE CLEARANCE
PROTEIN WAVE NOW $3.99 Reg. $6.95
HAIRCUTS EVERY MON TUES WED 99c
NO APPOINTMENT NECESSARY! NO WAITING!
SHOP HOURS: 8 A.M. - 9 P.M. DAILY
All Work Guaranteed By Experienced Operators
MR. ANTHONY'S Budget Permanent Wave Center
162 BRIGHTON AVENUE, ROCHESTER
2nd FLOOR OFFICES 2 AND 3—775-6480
1302 PENNA. AVE., MONACA—775-4161
911 7th AVE. BEAVER FALLS—846-6021
RAYS WIRETON SHOPPING CENTER—457-7540

_____

Flora's Beauty Shop
1972, 1973   Employed Miss Ridenour in 1973.

_____

___?__ beauty shop - (prior to 1980)
1979, 1981   Mrs. Madeline Petrella, owner.

_____

Zupsic's Beauty Shop – 1107 Pennsylvania Avenue
1978, 1990

_____

The Beauty Shop – 1201 Pennsylvania Avenue (corner of Twelfth Street and Pennsylvania Avenue)
1978

_____

The Fresh Look – 1103 Pennsylvania Avenue
1988, 1990   John and Cynthia Biskup, owners.

_____

Yolanda H. Mandish – owner/operator of hair salon in her home prior to 1995
1994, 1995

_____

Precision Hair Styling – 1130 Pennsylvania Avenue
1980, 2000's, closed by 2015   Owner was Linda Bell.

_____

Massey's 2 – beauty salon– 1120 Pennsylvania Avenue
2000s   This was the former United 5 & 10 store; Massey's was in the left of building.

_____

Fresh Look Hair Salon – 355 Eleventh Street
2010s

_____

Jackie Lee's Hair Hut – 1529 Pennsylvania Avenue
2015

_____

Leonard's Hair Design – 1608 Pennsylvania Avenue
current   Opened in 1992.

_____

Main Street Barbers – 1130 Pennsylvania Avenue
2013, current

_____

Sunspot Tanning – 699 Pennsylvania Avenue #2
2015, current

_____

Hair Styles by Kathy Schad / Guthrie / Rosemary Hair Design – 1213 Pennsylvania Avenue
Current

_____

Hairazors – 355 Eleventh Street – barber shop
Current

_____

Starr Styles – 1107 Pennsylvania Avenue
Current

_____

Style Nails – 1230 Pennsylvania Avenue
Current

_____

Hartley's Hair Studio – 911 Pennsylvania Avenue
Current   Established in 2014 -- small two storey sandstone building on the left of Red Wing Shoes.

_____

Fun Fact: 911 Pennsylvania Avenue was Blasche's Barber Shop, a place of business in 1909 that dealt with cutting hair and 107 years later, in 2016, after other businesses being in the building, it is back to being a hair salon business.

*** *** *** *** ***
*** *** ***

APPLIANCES

FURNITURE

APPLIANCES

Johnston Bros. – 1004 Pennsylvania Avenue
1926   Sold radios – Atwater Kent Radios exclusively.   They had weekly payment plans, too.

SPECIAL XMAS WEEK ONLY!
Any Radio Purchased This Week
We Will
INSTALL FREE OF CHARGE
EXTEND VERY EASY TERMS
NO INTEREST TO BE ADDED
This Offer Positively Expires Dec. 26, 1925, 11 P. M.
We Can Deliver and Install Before Christmas
THE FOLLOWING RADIO SETS:

ATWATER KENT—The Largest Selling Radio in the World.
FRESHMANN—Masterpiece at the Price.
CROSLEY—The Lowst Priced Radio Made.
PENNSYLVANIA—Using U. S. Navy Patents.
HOWARD—A Piece of Art.
A-C DAYTON—A Wonderfully Constructed Set.
KENNEDY—The Royalty of Radio.
ERLA—A Reflex Circuit.
GILFILLAN—Neutrodyne.
THOMPSON—Neutrodyne.
GREBE—Synchrophase.
AKRODYNE—A Real Buy
RADIOLA—Needs No Comment.
FEDERAL—Ortho-Sonic.
PHILCO—"A" and "B" Power.
BALKITE—"B" Eliminators and Chargers.
TUNGAR—Battery Chargers.

Rochester **Johnston Bros.** Monaca
Largest Radio Dealers in Beaver County. . Both Stores Open Evening.

Dec 1925

_____

Monaca Electric Appliance Co. – 1004 Pennsylvania Avenue
1922, 1924

_____

Radio and Electric Shop – 924 Pennsylvania Avenue & 1300 Pennsylvania Avenue (1930)
1928, 1931, 1943   Arthur A. Reith was owner.

*Expert Radio &
Electric Service*
On All Makes of Radios and
Electrical Equipment
Authorized Dealer
MAJESTIC — SPARTON
PHILCO — MAJESTIC
ELECTRIC REFRIGERATOR
Radio Electric Shop
924 & 1300 Penn'a. Ave., Monaca
Phones Roch. 3060 & 2018

1930

We Service Any Make of
ELECTRIC
REFRIGERATORS
WASHING MACHINES
AND RADIOS
Authorized Dealer for
PHILCO, MAJESTIC and
SPARTAN RADIOS
& MAYTAG WASHERS
RADIO ELECTRIC SHOP
1308 Pennsylvania Avenue
Phone Roch. 3060—MONACA

1932

Balamut Electric Shop –at the Penn Theatre building in 1934, then 1213 Pennsylvania Avenue
1925, 1931, 1949, 1958, 1967, 1970s, 1980

Opened in 1925.

Louis Balamut – owner.

He was located in the Roxy Theatre building in 1940 which was at 920/922 Pennsylvania Avenue
in Aug 1940.

Purchased the "Sarah Radler Building" on Pennsylvania Avenue (near Twelfth St.) in Aug 1940.
A two storey buff brick structure at 1213 Pennsylvania Avenue; his business was on first
floor; the 2nd floor was rented out.

Had General Electric and Maytag products; had Philco and Zenith Radios.

Balamut's closed in the early 1980s.

RADIOS and ELECTRICAL
APPLIANCES REPAIRED
L. BALAMUT
Penn Theatre Bldg —Monaca
Phone Roch. 2330—Res Roch. 1073-R

1931

GE TELEVISION
NOT LAST YEAR'S OUTMODED SETS ... BUT BRAND NEW 1958 MODELS!

TRAILERLOAD SALE

WE DARE NOT SHOW PRICES! FAR TOO LOW TO ADVERTISE

OPEN EVERY NIGHT

UNHEARD-OF SAVINGS!!
ON NEW
PORTABLE TV's
DURING THIS SALE
OPEN EVERY NIGHT 'TIL 9

DRIVE IN YOUR CAR OR STATION WAGON AND TAKE YOUR NEW G-E TV

IF YOU DON'T HAVE ALL 3
YOU'RE BEING CHEATED ON ALL THE WONDERFUL ENTERTAINMENT COMING YOUR WAY!

ALL MODELS CARRY A FULL YEAR'S WARRANTY ON ALL PARTS, TUBES, INCLUDING PICTURE TUBE!

AUTOMATIC TUNING

SLIM SILHOUETTE

MODULATED FIDELITY

BALAMUT ELECTRIC SHOP
"EVERYTHING ELECTRICAL"
1213 Penna. Ave., Monaca   SPruce 4-2077
"24 YEARS OF PERSONAL SERVICE"

1958

HERE'S THE NEW
WASHER FOR YOU!

was 149.95, now
$109.95
ONLY
$1.75
PER WEEK
after small down payment

YOU GET— • G-E QUICK-CLEAN WASHING—with Activator®
Washing Action. Each piece washed individu-
ally and thoroughly.
With Pump As Shown $119.95
• FULL 8-POUND CAPACITY • ONE-YEAR WARRANTY
• FINGERTIP CONTROLS • EASY TO MOVE, LOCKS IN PLACE
• ADJUSTABLE WRINGER

COME IN FOR A NO-OBLIGATION DEMONSTRATION TODAY!

BALAMUT
ELECTRIC SHOP
1213 Penna. Ave., Monaca   Phone Roch. 2330

1953

1213 Pennsylvania Avenue in 2015

Standard Refrigeration – appliance store - 1003 Pennsylvania Avenue (1946, 1949) - 1034 Pennsylvania Avenue (1953)
1946, 1953, 1956, 1957

Earl Keener – owner and manager.

This was also listed as the location of National Cleaners – they may have shared the store room (?).

COOL OFF with CARRIER
Room and Office Air Conditioners

For these scorching days and there will be many more,
climatize your room or office to comfort at a reasonable price.
Free estimates—no obligation. See our all-new "Carrier"
Freezer.

Standard Refrigeration
EARL KEENER, OWNER
1003 Penna. Ave.   Phone Roch. 2337-J   Monaca

1949

BUY IN MONACA --- HELP HER GROW

Shop in your own home community . . . Monaca is growing
and you, the people of the Monaca vicinity are to be con-
gratulated . . . but there is still a lot of business going out
of town that could help Monaca . . . The next time you buy
. . . Buy in Monaca!

SEE OUR 1954

Crosley Automatic Electric Range

Two complete ovens—each with bake and broil
units handle large meals easily. Bake in one
oven while you broil in the other!

Revolutionary new Crosley Bake-Unit design
distributes even heat more evenly than any other
range tested! And self-sealing oven doors keep
the heat inside so breads and pastries come out
uniformly golden brown every time.

Push-button Controls for seven-heat speeds.
No more guesswork about proper heat for surface cooking. Push a button and get exactly
the degree of heat you want.

"Mastermind" Clock Control lets you cook whole
oven meals automatically . . . and times appliance outlet, too. Dozens more wonderful
Crosley features, including popular divided-top
design. Get it now . . . and be a wonderful
cook automatically.

STANDARD REFRIGERATION
EARL KEENER, Owner
Ph. Roch 2337-J   Monaca

1953

OF COURSE IT'S ELECTRIC
CROSLEY ELECTRIC STOVE

STANDARD	DELUXE
$194.95	$279.95

Standard Refrigeration
EARL KEENER, OWNER
1003 Penna. Ave.   Phone Roch. 2337-J   Monaca

J. Radler – radio dealer – 1213 Pennsylvania Avenue
1928, 1943

_____

Reliable Refrigeration – storage storeroom – 1031 Bechtel Street (corner of Bechtel Street and
                                                    Taylor Avenue) Monaca Heights
      This building was the former Fire Hall #4; it had a pizza place in the front of it, then used by
      Reliable Refrigeration for storage.

_____

Guzik's Reliable Refrigeration Service – 715 Washington Avenue
1956

_____

Monaca TV Sales & Service – 1140 Pennsylvania Avenue
1952, 1956

_____

Weber's – 1018 Pennsylvania Avenue, 924 Pennsylvania Avenue, 1098 Pennsylvania Avenue
1957, 1965
      Sold and tested television tubes; had toys and hobby supplies.   May have either / or but most
      likely not both #1018 and #1098 (one or the other might have been a misprint).

_____

Al Jaros – TV/Radio Repair – 1220 Pennsylvania Avenue
1957

_____

Charles Dwyer – Repairs to pressing machine boilers - 403 Pennsylvania Avenue
1944

_____

Monaca Radio Service – was at Ninth Street and Washington Avenue
                                        – moved to 1000 Pennsylvania Avenue Oct 10, 1945
pre 1945, 1949
      Radio service and sold records, phonographs, radios, refrigerators, electrical appliances.
      They did pickups and deliveries.
      The business became "Jim's Radio and Electric Repair" by 1949 and it shared the storeroom with
            John A. Zarrillo – Jewelry Watch Repairing – 1000 Pennsylvania Avenue   and
            Luci's Studio – photograph and supplies – 1000 Pennsylvania Avenue.

1946 ads

_____

Jim's Radio and Electric Repair – 1000 Pennsylvania Avenue (1949 to 1953), then 355 Eleventh
1949, 1957, 1978   Street (1954, 1957)
        Sales and service business.

JIM'S RADIO
AND ELECTRIC REPAIR
John A. Zarrillo
JEWELRY — WATCH REPAIRING
LUCI'S STUDIO
YOUR PHOTOGRAPH AND SUPPLIES
Phone Rochester 2246-J
1000 Penna. Ave.   Monaca

Jul 1949

_____

Gnu Tubs – 999 Pennsylvania Avenue (used to be old bank building)
1990, current
        Started business in 1979, but came to Monaca at a later date.
        Family owned business

_____

AM Parts Company – 1038 Pennsylvania Avenue and then 1548 Pennsylvania Avenue
1978, 1983, 1984, 1985, 1998, 2002
        A/C , refrigerators, washers, dryers, ranges, furnace business.
        Started in Rochester in 1972 by Ralph Stockhousen, Sr.
            o   Ralph and Cheryl Stockhousen were still owners in 2001.
        Opened at 1038 Pennsylvania Avenue, then moved to 1548 Pennsylvania Avenue
            between 1984 and 1990 (which is now Johnstone Supply).
        There was Hardware and Supply Company previously at 1038 Pennsylvania Avenue and
            Unique Pizza moved into 1038 Pennsylvania Avenue Jun 2000.

Your Search is Over ...
Gas Grill
Replacement Parts
FOR MOST MAKES & MODELS

• BURNERS/VENTURIS
• VALVES
• REGULATORS
• GRIDS
• GRATES
• WARMING RACKS
• ROTISSERIES
• ADJUSTABLE ROAST RACK
• FISH/CHICKEN BASKET
• POTATO/RIB RACK
• CHAR-BRIC • BRIQUETTES
• LAVA ROCK
• UNIVERSAL POST
• HANDLES
• COVERS
• KNOBS

with this ad
Save $1.00
on Briquettes

WE ARE A CHARM GLOW DISTRIBUTOR
AM PARTS
COMPANY
Distributors of Major Appliance Replacement Parts
1038 Pennsylvania Ave., Monaca........ 775-8041
3337 Babcock Blvd., North Hills 363-8040
Bon Aire Shopping Center, Butler .. 283-9100

1984

AM PARTS
COMPANY
1548 Pennsylvania Ave., Monaca
775-8041
BEAVER COUNTY'S MOST
COMPLETE APPLIANCE
PARTS DISTRIBUTOR

1990 ad

_____

Appliance Outlet – 1020 Pennsylvania Avenue
Current
        Business in the Batchelor Building, beside the former Batchelor Furniture business building.

*** *** *** *** ***

FURNITURE

As you go through all the businesses listed here, you may notice that they were not only in the trade of cabinetmaker and/or furniture making, but that the same business was listed along with *Undertaking*. Through many of the earlier years furniture business and undertaking went hand in hand since the cabinet makers who made furniture were called upon to also provide caskets. With their skill and knowledge of handling wood, they found it profitable, and craft wise, and easy to also make the coffins. Many of the cabinetmakers and furniture making men did not personally perform the actual process of embalming. A partner or apprentice in cabinet making who was working for them most likely had training to embalm. It was found that although their services were eventually needed, the frequency of selling the furniture they made was more profitable than waiting for someone to die. In later years, the two businesses divided and became complete and separate entities.

Huff Furniture and Undertaking – then became........
 Adam Huff & Son Furniture and Undertaking   - corner of Pennsylvania Avenue and Fourth Street
                  Before the street names were changed, it was "corner of Factory Street and Hanover Street."
1849, 1880, 1906

 Adam Huff - owner; then his son, E. W. Huff joined him the business.
 Adam was a cabinet maker; came to Phillipsburg in 1848 from Germany. He built the house
     pictured further. The house sat beside (to the right) of the former location of the
     Soldiers' Orphans Home. The sturdy home was torn down in 1963 to make room for the
     water treatment plant.
 As with most cabinet makers, he also began to make coffins.
     Huff family tradition states that he used to ask his wife to lie down in a new coffin
      to see how it looked.
 In addition to being a carpenter, cabinet maker, and undertaker, he opened a storeroom
      to sell the furniture he was making. He built a storeroom on to the front of the house,
      it was later converted into the porch (see picture).
 Adam used letter head that read "Adam Huff, Manufacturer of and Dealer in Fancy and
      Common Furniture of ALL Kinds – Undertaking a Specialty."
 Elizabeth, his wife, raised chickens and sold eggs in the neighborhood and she eventually
      purchased cows and sold milk, too.
 Their son, Emil W., took a course in embalming and then became his father's partner, he
      joined his father in the undertaking business and furniture store; changing the name
      from just "Huff" to *Adam Huff and Son*.
 In mid Jun 1906, Batchelor Bros., the Monaca undertakers, bought out Adam Huff.
      Mr. Huff was 85 years of age at that time (the oldest resident of Monaca in 1906) and
      due to his advanced age, was retiring from his 60 year old business.
 Adam b 1823 d 1906; married in 1849 at St. Peter's Church to Elizabeth Appel b 1827 d 1897;
      their children were George, Adam, Charles, Emil, Edward.
      Emil W. b 1861 d 1905; married Maggie Cochran.

Photo courtesy of Mrs. Lillian Huff Jansen in 1984
The roadway to the left of this picture was formerly called Factory Street (now Pennsylvania Avenue Ext; the street in front and off to the right of this picture was formerly called Hanover Street (now Fourth Street).

Hahn & Reno (Henry Hahn, Joseph I. Reno), furniture dealers and undertakers – 422 Fourth Street in
Phillipsburg, (Fourth Street became Pennsylvania Avenue).
1874, 1876, 1892, 1893.....   .
In business in 1874 with just furniture, and by 1876 the undertaking business was added.
Henry Hahn and Jos. I. Reno were owners.   Joseph Reno founded the business
in 1874 and became a great uncle of Elvin Batchelor.

They eventually became known as............

Batchelor Bros. Furniture and Undertakers– 422 Pennsylvania Avenue, then beginning in 1902 at
1020 Pennsylvania Avenue
1896, 1930, 1940, Apr 1970
Alonzo S. Batchelor started to work for his uncle Jos. Reno as the manager of the store
after Henry Hahn had died.
A. S. Batchelor took over the business in 1896.   With his brother, Frank and Clinton C. Aughenbaugh,
they moved the business in 1902 to a new building on upper Pennsylvania Avenue.
Later the funeral home moved from the 2nd floor of the Batchelor Building on Pennsylvania
Avenue to a new location on Atlantic Avenue where it remained with Elvin W.
Batchelor as the supervisor.
A.S. and Frank M. Batchelor were the remaining members of the firm by 1928.
C.C. Aughenbaugh was a member of the firm prior to 1928, as was his son Joseph
Batchelor Aughenbaugh until his death in WWII.
Elvin W. Batchelor was an undertaker and embalmer beginning in 1930 and was the owner and
operator of both Batchelor Bros. Inc. Funeral Homes in Monaca and Rochester.
By 1957, Frank M. Batchelor was president of the firm, joined by two second generation family
members, Elvin W. Batchelor (s/o Alonzo S.) and Frank H. Batchelor (s/o Frank M.).
1916 they placed an ad looking for a man to work in the furniture store.
Closed Monaca store in 1970; opened new store in Beaver Valley Mall.
The first storeroom was located on 422 Fourth Street in 1896.   It was a frame,
partial one store building with parts that had two stories.   There was either a two storey business
building or private residency beside it at that time.
They then erected a "modern building" in 1902. This building was located at 1020-1024
Pennsylvania Avenue.   It was a three storey brick building, erected and owned by the Batchelor
Brothers – A. S. Batchelor, Frank M. Batchelor - and C. C. Aughenbaugh.

In 1930, the Batchelor Brothers had another new two storey building erected beside their
current building; it was nearing completion the end of Jul 1930.   This newest building was
constructed with a stone façade and large glass display windows. It had a storeroom on the ground
floor and office spaces on the second floor.
Nov 15, 1945, there was a legal fictitious name application made for Batchelor Brothers Co.
of 1020 Pennsylvania Avenue. It was made by Frank M. Batchelor of 999 Atlantic Avenue and Elvin
W. Batchelor 464 Mecklem Avenue, Rochester........evidently there were other names involved in the
business and they were legally changing the names.
Early in 1952, Batchelors completely remodeled their entire building at 1020 Pennsylvania
Avenue.   They made all 3 stories into areas of showrooms and also the basement area – making 4
floors of new display areas for the items they sold – rugs, appliances, all types of furniture,
televisions, and miscellaneous accessories for decorating. They held a grand 're-' opening the first
week of June, 1952.
It was a family business and by 2003, it had been in the area for 106 years.   A son and nephew
of the originators (Frank, Alonzo, and Joe) were running the business. Frank was the owner of
the sole store located in the Beaver Valley Mall, with the Monaca, Rochester, and Northern Lights
stores having been closed prior to 2003.   Monaca's store closing in 1970.
Batchelor Bros. also had an ambulance vehicle as early as 1903.

1896 ——— 1940

This is a view of the smaller storeroom on lower Pennsylvania Avenue in 1896.   This photo is not of the best quality, but shows A.S. Batchelor, C.C. Aughenbaugh, and Frank M. Batchelor in the picture.

Since our business started in this small storeroom, on lower Pennsylvania avenue, 'way back in 1896, we have strived to give Monaca a store whose merchandise and prices would appeal to everybody! To date you have welcomed us with co-operation at every turn . . . substantiating our claims with your loyal patronage. A store and the community it serves are one . . . with interests mutual. During the growth this business has enjoyed, it has tried, for its part, to repay you with values that only honesty can achieve. To those who have shared in its benefits we offer our sincere thanks!

A. S. BATCHELOR   C. C. AUGHENBAUGH   FRANK M. BATCHELOR

Photo originally shared by Elvin W. Batchelor

The Hahn-Reno Furniture and Undertaking Co.   Reno is the second person from the right, Henry Hahn is fourth from the right; beside him is Alonzo Batchelor.

1022-1026 Pennsylvania Avenue   Batchelor Furniture   Keystone Block Bldg   2015

The Batchelor Bros. erected this building in 1902.   It was remodeled in 1952 and again underwent remodeling it in 1957.   The front has changed, but the building still stands (2016).

1952

1970

Fun fact (or eerie fact, depending on your view) – the Batchelor Bros. were not only into the furniture business, they were also in the business of undertaking. Before purchasing and building their funeral home at the corner of Atlantic and Tenth Street, the brothers conducted their undertaking business from the 2nd floor of their three storey furniture building on Pennsylvania Avenue. A person could easily be shopping for some item to decorate or furnish their home while right above them there was embalming being done.

_____

Floyd B. Coene - casket maker
1920   Floyd was living at 913 Washington Avenue.   He may have worked for another
               business or had his own business (location unknown).

_____

Chott's Furniture Exchange –previous address (?) prior to 1946, then at 308 Ninth Street
1924, 1946
        Started in business at 308 Ninth Street in Jan 1946.

1946

_____

L. H. Stitt – 1018 Washington Avenue
1937
        Furniture repaired and upholstered.
        Antiques refinished.
        L. H. Stitt owner/operator.

_____

Monaca Furniture Co.   - 903 Pennsylvania Avenue (1963) and   308-312 Ninth Street
1963, 1967, 1969
        Owned by Harold O'Hara of Brighton Township.   Run by Wm. Glenn Thomas & Ray O'Hara.

_____

Economy Furniture Exchange – 903 Pennsylvania Avenue
1956, 1957
        They were associated with Economy Home Furniture in Rochester in Mar 1956.

1957

_____

Keck's Furniture Exchange –711 Pennsylvania Avenue
1938, 1948, 1956, 1963, 1972

Sold new and used furniture and had rental tools and Glidden paints.

In business in Sep 1938 (ad), Jun 1944 (ad), Feb 1946 (ad), 1956 (ad), 1963 (ad).

Business investment ad in 1941 says "two storey brick building with frame house in
rear – 711-713 Pennsylvania Ave."

Harry Keck owner; they lived in Rochester in 1930 and he was into general hauling
which may have led him to gathering used furniture and items to sell.

Harry and family moved to Monaca between 1930 and 1940, lived at 802 Pennsylvania
Avenue.   Their house was on the corner of Pennsylvania and Eighth St, across the
street, but closer to the store.   He married Clara A.; they had 3 children.

In 1941, Harry purchased the old Burry barber shop building on Pennsylvania Avenue, near
Eighth Street, and resold it to Bryan Mamula of Aliquippa who razed the building
right after the purchase.

The business/store closed in 1972.

WANTED: To buy bed room
suites, dining room suites,
breakfast sets, chairs, cup-
board, twin beds, table top gas
ranges, Frigidaires and small
radios. Keck's Furniture Exchange, 711-713 Penna., Ave.,
Monaca.   Fri.-Tues.*
                                    1946

May the most preci-
ous gift be bestowed
upon all this Christ-
mas — "Peace on
Earth".

NOEL....
KECK'S FURNITURE
EXCHANGE
711 Penna. Ave   Monaca Pa.   Ph. Roch. 4585-J

early 1972

Cochran Exchange Mart – 1034R Pennsylvania Avenue
1960

Owned by Walter and Katherine Cochran.

Buy and sold furniture, appliances, used tools, etc.

Johnston Flowers was in the front of the building with Cochran's using the rear of the building.
David Cochran owned the building as of 1975 and sold it to Glenn and Helen Johnson.

Coombs Furniture Exchange – 308 Ninth Street (Mayflower building) – basement
1943, 1945

Ad stated many, many household furniture and items for sale.
Coombs sold the business and it became Chott's.

FOR SALE: Gas and electric hot plates, ice refrigerators, porch swing, gliders, radio, gas ranges, victrola, dining room suite, living room suites, beds, dressers, vanities, twin beds, bunk beds, etc. Visit our basement show room. Coombs Furniture Exchange, 308 Ninth St., Monaca. 4 12-14 Inc.

1944

FOR SALE: Walnut bedroom suite, electric victrola, roll top desk, chestarobe, electric hot plates, kitchen cabinet, Army bunk beds, ice boxes, side oven gas ranges, glider, living room suites, beds, dressers, breakfast set, like new, and many other items of good used furniture. Coombs Furniture Exchange, 308 9th St., Monaca. 5 9-15 Inc.

1945

Ball Furniture Outlet   aka   Ball Furniture Outlet and Interior Contracting, LLC – 308 Ninth Street
2011, current

Randy Ball, Owner.
Started with just one of the three storerooms in the former Business Block/ Citizen's Bank/ Campbell's Storage Building; currently uses the entire building (all floors) for hid business and storage.

In just right side section.

In the entire building.

*** *** *** *** ***
*** *** ***

Hardware / Home Improvements / Builders / Contractors / / Trades

Coal

Miscellaneous related businesses and Tradesmen from censuses and directories

HARDWARE   HOME IMPROVEMENT

BUILDERS / CONTRACTORS   and   TRADES

David Fischer was well known blacksmith and hardware merchant – Eighth Street
1860, 1880, 1900, 1903, 1907

> David first apprenticed as a blacksmith, then had his own business.
>
> David erected a new blacksmith shop in the rear of Bittner's restaurant – 807 Pennsylvania
> Avenue.
>
> The old shop on the corner of Pennsylvania Avenue and Eighth Street, formerly Fred Leffert's
> meat market, was bought by David and to undergo a lot of remodeling. It was used
> by Mr. Fisher as a store room and warehouse.   David resided with his sister and family
> Wm. and Wilhelmina Wagner in 1900, 1902/03, 1910.
>
> He was b. in 1857 and doesn't appear to have married; d Jul 1913 in Monaca; s/o Christian and
> Anna Fisher who lived on Washington Avenue.

_____

William Wagner – blacksmith and hardware store
1880, 1892, 1893, 1900

> William apprenticed as a blacksmith with David Fischer/Fisher and then, along with being a
> blacksmith, followed in the hardware business, too.
>
> By 1900, William was only listed as *merchant* ; in 1910 he had *none* as his occupation (age 60).

_____

W. B. Pugh Hardware Store – 1030 Pennsylvania Avenue   (beside Eckert Bldg & one door from Leary
1905, 1907   Bros.'s store in 1907)

> Opened business in 1905.
>
> Mr. Pugh was born in 1862.
>
> He sold business to S.F. Fair of Beaver.
>
> > Mr. Pugh went to California for health reasons and engaged in the grocery business with
> > Frank Eckles who previously was a clerk for him while in Monaca.
> >
> > J. P. Dickerson worked in the store and would travel to Pittsburgh for business.

_____

Winkle's General Hardware Store – 915 Pennsylvania Avenue
1900s

> The building was bought by Schmuck's Shoes.

_____

Fair Hardware   aka   Fair Bros. Hardware – 1030 Pennsylvania Avenue
1907, 1908, 1910

> Samuel J. Fair (from Beaver), owner.
>
> He purchased the business from W. B. Pugh the first of Sept 1907.
>
> He sold gas and coal heating stoves and coal ranges.
>
> Fair Hardware was purchased by Heckman Bros. Hardware in Jan 1910.

_____

John P. Ackerman   aka   Ackerman & Jepson – Hardware dealers
                          located - 2nd floor/ 715 Pennsylvania Avenue & 1100 block of Pennsylvania Avenue
1902, 1903, 1904

> Started business in 1902 – was in _?__ (cramped quarters).
>
> Ads stated their business was "Above post office" in 1904.
>
> Leaders in hardware – sold gas range, would furnish kitchen, sold paint, and guns.

They moved into their new storeroom in the Eckert Block on Sep 10th, 1903.

The Eckert Block was in the 1100 block on Pennsylvania Avenue.

John P. and Alida W. lived on Virginia Avenue.

Business was also listed as owned by John P. Ackerman and C.H. Jepson.

J. A. Shafer/Schaeffer moved his candy and cigar store into the room vacated by Ackerman & Jepson.

(This could have been at 715 Pennsylvania Ave. or the 1100 block of Pennsylvania Ave. ?)

Heidrick & Taylor – hardware and tinners - 1428 Pennsylvania Avenue
1902, 1903, 1905, 1913, 1922

Owned by H. Harry Taylor and James M. Heidrick. James lived at the same place as store.

Evidently also did some type of painting & roofing and/or hardware type business from the various ads and articles......one stated Taylor was painting a roof, another said a gas stove was donated by Heidrick & Taylor.

Also had ads in paper for a good strong boy to learn the tinners' trade – one ad stated "not under 16 yrs of age;" the other stated "age 18 to 20 years."

Their ad in 1902 stated "corner Penna. Ave. and 15th St., Opp. Catholic Church..."

There was a Harvey Taylor, a carpenter in the late 1800s/early 1900s; married Mary K.__; lived on "Fourth" (which have become either Fourth Street or Pennsylvania Avenue).

H.H. Taylor was from Pittsburgh, where his parents still lived in 1903. H.H. married Frances Ella. He was in Monaca in Nov 1902, but she did not join him until the end of Apr 1903. The Taylors eventually bought a home at 1121 Atlantic Avenue. Harry died prior to Dec 1952; Frances Ella died Dec 1952. Harry H. Tayor lived at corner of Pennsylvania Avenue and Fifteenth Street in 1902/03 (info from Monaca Directory). Prior to 1940, had a hardware business. Sold it in the 1930s and retired.

James M. Heidrick was also married – his wife was from Brookville, PA. 1902/03, James lived at corner of Pennsylvania Avenue and Fifteenth Street, too.

Taylor and Heidrick dissolved the partnership Apr 1, 1913 by mutual consent. The business of the dissolved firm was continued by H. Harry Taylor under his own name.

Fun fact: Due to store being broken into several times, they installed a new instantaneous burglar alarm system in the store room in May, 1904. The alarm would shock an "unwelcomed visitor of the night." The burglar alarm was in the shape of a large and vicious thorough bred bull dog. Shortly after obtaining this "burglar alarm," Mr. Heidrick could not enter the store one evening because the "burglar alarm" denied him admission. Mr. Taylor was called and the dog was coaxed off to allow Mr. Heidrick entrance.

Heckman Brothers   aka   Heckman's Hardware – 1030 Pennsylvania Avenue
1910, 1924, 1965, 1971, 1973

William C. and Miles A. Heckman started their business in 1910.
They purchased the business from Samuel Fair.
In 1929 it was referenced Heckman Bros. Hardware.

General hardware and home furnishings.
William and Anna Heckman lived at 1105 Washington Avenue as of 1912.
Miles and Laura Heckman lived at 934 Indiana Avenue as of 1912.
The business remained in the family with Glenn Heckman being the last owner.
Glenn closed the store in 1973.
He died in 1989, married to Mabel Buckenheimer; 2 children.

Bell Phone 218-W   Beaver Co. 7477

Heckman Brothers
General Hardware, Cutlery, Stoves, Paints,
Glass, House Furnishigs, Etc.
Reznor and Coal Heaters, Novelty Pumps,
Guns and Ammunition.

No Matter What You Want in the Hardware Line
WE HAVE IT.
A Trial Order will Make You Our Customer.

HECKMAN BROTHERS

1911   PENNA. AVENUE   MONACA, PA.

Heckman Bros. Hardware   Photo courtesy of BCHR&LF

c 1928

Miles Heckman is pictured above standing in front of the storeroom.

Anderson's Hardware – 323 Eighth Street
prior to 1912
    This business became the Monaca Hardware Company.

Monaca Hardware Co.   aka   Monaca Hardware and Supply Store
1912, 1924, 1927, 1946, 1958, 1964, 1971
    Was formerly Anderson's Hardware which was at 323 Eighth Street.
    Various addresses for the business:
        first at 323 Eighth Street (1912)
        -308 Ninth Street (1919)   -2098 Pennsylvania Avenue (1922)
        –927 Pennsylvania Avenue (1928)   - 1428 Pennsylvania Avenue (1940)
        –1133 Pennsylvania Avenue (across from Liquor Store in 1945)
        and lastly at 1038 Pennsylvania Avenue (1954)

Boss Ovens
AND
Hot Plates
Best On The Market.
Stop in and See Them.
Monaca Hardware Co.
308 Ninth Street.   MONACA.
1919

DOLLAR DAYS SPECIALS!
WOOD
STORM **$12.00** Regular
DOORS $19.95
SHOP OUR STORE! OPEN UNDER NEW MANAGEMENT!
Car 'N Home Wastebasket - - Reg. $1.49 $1.00
Pint-Vacuum Bottle - - - - - Reg. $1.49 $1.00
Figure Skates - - - - - - - Reg. $14.75 $10.00
Nationally Advertised FISH LURES – Values To $2
NOW . . . . . 3 for $1.00
MONACA HARDWARE
1038 PENNA. AVE.
FREE KITCHEN TOOL WITH $1.00 PURCHASE!
1960

In 1922 a glass front was in place and the new business building was nearly completed.
A 1939 ad stated this business was "formerly Anderson's Hardware."

Wilfred L."Posey" Flowers conducted the business in 1912, 1927.   Mr. Flowers lived at 318 Eighth
        Street.   Emil Troy was the owner in 1951.
1954 - Constructed a new two storey building – 25 x 85 feet/roman brick construction.
        This seems to be when they began to use The Monaca Hardware and Supply Company
                name.
        He built this new building at the rear the current building - at 1038 Pennsylvania Avenue.
        Was to be finished and open for business by Christmas 1954/Jan 1955; two apartments
                were planned on the 2nd floor.
The Monaca Hardware and Supply Company was affiliated with American Hardware Supply Co.
Had ads in paper for bicycle tires, tea kettles, and other items.
        (2015 – Bluewater Cleaning Service business was at 1133 Pennsylvania Avenue
        and Fountainhead Café is at 1038 Pennsylvania Avenue.)

Just arrived large and small roasters; roaster pans and Dutch ovens, all heavy aluminum, limited stock; wheelbarrows; 43 piece pastel dish sets: copper coils; dishpans; heavy metal waste baskets all colors. We carry a full line of fertilizers, grass seed, and house cleaning supplies. Monaca Hardware and Supply. 1133 Penna. Ave. Monaca. Call Rochester 3252.   4 3-9 Inc.

1946

1038 Pennsylvania Avenue in 1958   Monaca Hardware bldg

Kemmer Hardware store – 812/814 Pennsylvania Avenue
>   (sat in the area adjacent to the rear of current CVS drug store lot – torn down in about 2002)

1890, 1912, 1922
>   In 1892 Directory listed as "Kemmer, Adam - Hardware, stoves, tinware, etc. on
>   Fourth Street" (Fourth Street then was renamed Pennsylvania Avenue).

Owned and operated by Adam Kemmer.

Adam was a tinner by trade; owned a tin shop in town at 812 Pennsylvania Avenue.

1887 – He built a very large, long, two storey building beside the original frame tin shop and
>   opened his hardware store.

He owned the first hardware store room in Monaca and the family lived in the same building.

From all the accumulated information….Adam didn't move to Monaca until 1883.
>   In 1880, Adam and family were living beside Christian Kemmer in Allegheny County –
>   Christian had a tin store and Adam was a tinner there.

After Adam died, his wife & daughter continued the hardware store for a number of years.

1898 Directory had Mrs. Adam Kemmer (Elizabeth) as proprietor of hardware store.

Between 1910 and 1940, I cannot find what the store room was used for, but the resident
>   portion of the building and ownership of the building changed hands several times.

The Kemmer store building was used in early 1900s for a school room (as was the city hall
>   building and the Lay Building.). In 1912 they added more seating in the TWO school
>   buildings and did not use it.   Mrs. Kemmer, then 52 in 1900 and 62 in 1910, had her
>   married daughter and family (Christopher & Christina Lindsay/Lindsey) with her.
>   Christopher Lindsay was a carpenter in 1902/03; married Christina; lived on
>   Pennsylvania Ave.

The Robert Lindsay family moved to the Kemmer property in May 1912.

The Lepper family lived at 814 Pennsylvania Ave in 1920 census. Mrs. Kemmer and her
>   daughter and family (Chris Lindsay) moved and were living at 1101 Indiana Ave.

James Flishaker and family were living at 814 Pennsylvania Avenue in 1920.

Henry Thompson and family moved from the "Burry cottage" (810 Pennsylvania) to the
>   Kemmer Building in Jul 1922.

In 1930 and 1940 – Robert Werner owned and was living at 814 Pennsylvania.

Adam had built a miniature tin house that his daughter donated in 1940 to the Connelley
>   Vocational High School in Pittsburgh to use as an inspiration in the school's shop class.

Kemmer family:
>   Christian Kemmer – b 1836 in Germany; married Christine ___; Christian had a tin store.
>   Adam Kemmer – b 1850 in Germany; married Elisabeth ___ b 1848 PA , they
>   had a daughter Christine b 1876; Adam was also a tinner.

(an extended view of the area is under Street Views)

Mecklem Bros. Lumber Company – 1548 Pennsylvania Avenue
1920, 1924, 1942
> Organized in Monaca in Apr 20, 1921.
> > o   Began in 1912 when brothers Joseph and William Mecklem purchased the
> > Copenhaver Shane Lumber Yard in North Rochester and changed the name to Mecklem Bros.
> Company in Monaca had a 250 feet frontage; was one block deep (to the P & LE railroad tracks).
> Until 1918 they used hitched team of horses to pull their deliveries.
> > o   In 1918 they bought a Model T Ford with an Olsen chain driven truck rear end.
> The business was burned out in a fire in 1924.
> > o   Hazel (Mecklem) Hutchison was trapped in office, but rescued.
> There was a William J. Mecklem listed as a carpenter in late 1800s/early 1900s; married
> > Ida M. __; lived on Indiana Avenue.
> 1942 – the owners dissolved the business and only Roy H. Mecklem had Monaca company.
> > Lester Mecklem retained the North Rochester location and the name Mecklem Brothers.

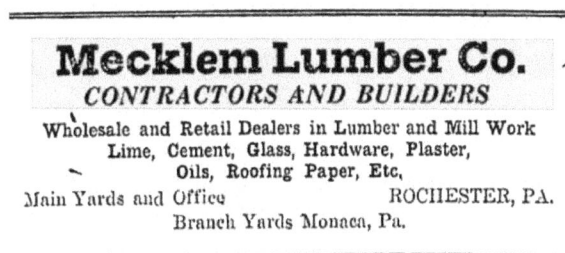

Mecklem Lumber Co.
CONTRACTORS AND BUILDERS
Wholesale and Retail Dealers in Lumber and Mill Work
Lime, Cement, Glass, Hardware, Plaster,
Oils, Roofing Paper, Etc,

Main Yards and Office   ROCHESTER, PA.
Branch Yards Monaca, Pa.

1923

When Roy H. Mecklem became the owner of the business in Monaca he changed the name ....

Roy H. Mecklem Lumber and Builders Supplies
1942 to 1983
> 1954 added a new hardware department – completed a 2 storey brick and block addition to the
> > current building – addition was finished by Oct 1954.
> > > Clifford Schnuth, Jr. – store manager – designed the addition.
> 1960 another fire caused heavy damage to the business.
> Then the building was destroyed by a tornado in Sep 1970.
> 1972 – Roy H. Mecklem formed a family corporation & gave his ownership to Clifford Schnuth, Jr.
> > who was still president of the corporation in 1983.
> 1977 - a ready mix concrete facility was added and they delivered wet mixed concrete into a
> > trailer for consumers to take to project sites.
> 1982 – in house computer was installed to control and update operations.
> > Also in 1982 there was a heated borough meeting where the borough had a boycott
> > against Mecklem's stating that they were being overcharged for items.   Clifford Schnuth
> > disputed the charges and the boycott was lifted.   All of the dispute was for over paying
> > $42 for two shovels. The borough had done their business through Mecklem's in the
> > past but with finances being tight and overspending an issue, the borough said they
> > would now seek to find the best competitive price for future purchases.
> Still in business in 1983.
> Roy Mecklem was born in 1900; married Edna H.; 3 children; they lived at Atlantic Avenue.
> > He was the s/o William J. (carpenter/contractor) and Mary Mecklem.

Fun fact – Roy Mecklem celebrated his 95th birthday the first of Feb 1995.
He was officially retired then and living in Florida.   He owned and operated
Mecklem Lumber Co. in Monaca for 65 years.

FLAT ENAMEL PAINT
GOES ON LIKE MAGIC
"REAL OIL BASE"
Qt. $1.25 Gal. $3.85
ROY MECKLEM
LUMBER & BUILDING SUPPLIES
Phone Rock. 2310
Penna. Ave.   Monaca

1949

LUMBER AND BUILDING SUPPLIES
For Better . . . Building
Use the better building supplies. It pays in the long run!
Order seasoned lumber, insulation and other supplies from
us for dependable quality and a fair price!
Roy H. Mecklem
LUMBER AND BUILDERS' SUPPLIES

1949

Mecklem's new store – Pennsylvania Avenue   1954

After Roy H. Mecklem closed, then came………………..

Johnstone – 1548 Pennsylvania Avenue
current
> Business building was the former Roy H. Mecklem business building.
> Wholesale HVAC/R Distributor

_____

John Zigerelli Hardware and Confectionery Store – 1414 Pennsylvania Avenue
1955
> He had the building erected; previously had his own barber shop in the building.

_____

Nichols Wire, Sheet & Hardware Co. – Pennsylvania Avenue
1931

_____

Charles Cain – general hauling – 1200 Indiana Avenue
1929

      Also see Livery section, Charles was considered a *drayman*.

—————

Fleming Hardware Co. – 1428 Pennsylvania Avenue
1928, 1931

1428 Pennsylvania Avenue (now boarded up).

—————

Westport Home Improvement Center – Seventeenth and Washington Streets
1977

Oct 1977

—————

Michael Bickerstaff – lumber dealer in the late 1870s and the 1880s
1870s, 1880s

—————

Baldwin & Baldwin – Sixth Street and corner Virginia Avenue and Fifteenth Street
1902, 1904

> Dealers in coal, stone, lime, cement, brick, contracting & hauling.
> Owned by Frank D. Baldwin of Washington Avenue and Irwin Baldwin of Indiana Avenue.
> Had their office on Sixth Street. Their stables were on the corner of Virginia Avenue and Fifteenth Street.
> They also had a saw mill near the pump house/station.

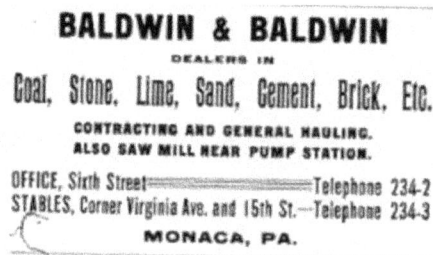

BALDWIN & BALDWIN
DEALERS IN
Coal, Stone, Lime, Sand, Cement, Brick, Etc.
CONTRACTING AND GENERAL HAULING.
ALSO SAW MILL NEAR PUMP STATION.
OFFICE, Sixth Street———————Telephone 234-2
STABLES, Corner Virginia Ave. and 15th St.—Telephone 234-3
MONACA, PA.

Potter Brothers – 612 Pennsylvania Avenue
1800s, 1910

> Their business included general contractors - building supplies - heavy hauling – house moving – grading contractor   and   coal and coke dealers.
> They also had a small business building in front/to the side of Johnstone's - at 1538 Pennsylvania Avenue).   It was still standing as of 2015.

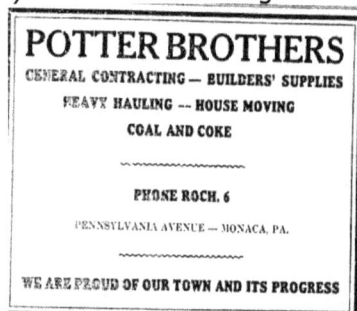

POTTER BROTHERS
GENERAL CONTRACTING — BUILDERS' SUPPLIES
HEAVY HAULING --- HOUSE MOVING
COAL AND COKE

PHONE ROCH. 6

PENNSYLVANIA AVENUE — MONACA, PA.

WE ARE PROUD OF OUR TOWN AND ITS PROGRESS

> J. P. Potter was well known for the business of heavy hauling and the transferring of machinery weighing many tons.   He had a stable on Washington Avenue, near Sixth Street, maintaining a team of excellent horses beginning in about 1886.   In 1911 he had 10 head of horses, employed five drivers, and used 25 to 30 laborers.   The Potters were also involved in the coal business because of their ability to make large deliveries.

> (See more information on the Potter Brothers under Livery   Blacksmith section.)

Potter Bros. – 1538 Pennsylvania Avenue
1871, 1931, 1956

(Very small building located between current Johnstone and Slush Puppie.)

Dewhirst Paneling and Carpentry – 801 Allaire Avenue / triangular corner of Colonial Ave. & Allaire Ave.
1977, 1983
> Established in 1977 - owned and operated by Charles Dewhirst (see Dewey's Deli).   Opened his
> > Deli at this location in Nov 1983.
> In 2004 Humbert Heating and Air Conditioning moved their business to this site.

_____

Robert W. Boggs – filing / sharpening business - 829 Pennsylvania Avenue
1928

_____

W. R. Keefer – architect – Pennsylvania Avenue office
1902, 1903   W. R. resided in Beaver Falls in 1902/03.

_____

Roth Marz Partnership – architects - 2020 Beaver Avenue
2001
> Carl G. Baker, architect in Beaver, was in charge of this office.
> They specialized in designing in the educational, recreational, medical, and commercial fields.

_____

Orr Baker – surveyor
1892, 1893

_____

Thomas Cochran – contractor – Pennsylvania Avenue
1902, 1910
> Boarded at J. Burry's in 1902/03.   Staying at Hamilton Hotel in 1910.
> > (There was also a Thomas Cochran that had a butcher shop in Monaca in the early 1900s.)

_____

George Henry Lais – 714 Washington Avenue
1870, 1882, 1910, 1922
> G. Henry – b 1844; was a carpenter by age 16 and active in business as contractor by age of 25.
> Awarded many contracts in Monaca – a few being…. 1922-Ninth Street for M. Theil, Tailor Shop;
> > Monaca First Ward School building in 1882; the Presbyterian Church in New Brighton.
> (See more information on the Lais family in Prominent People.)

_____

F.A. LeGoullon & Son   and/or LeGoullon Coal and Builders Supplies– 298 Pennsylvania Avenue Ext
1926, 1922, 1926, 1958
> Owned by Frank LeGoullon for 50 years, then his son L.L.
> Was considered a "wholesale business."   Advertised for many things – mostly coal – coke – ice.
> Erected a coal tipple - Pennsylvania Avenue in 1922, along tracks lower Pennsylvania
> > Avenue (along RR tracks over roadway, leaving town).
> Did the cement work and provided the building materials for new Penn Theatre in 1926.
> Still in business in 1956, 1958.
> Lamartine L. LeGoullon, Sr. died in 1972.   He had been in business, first with his father, and
> > then on his own for 35 years. The business was dissolved several years prior to 1972.
> F. A. LeGoullon was awarded many contracts for excavation of cellars and/or moving and
> > hauling: 1922—Theil's Tailor Shop – Ninth Street.
> Frank had a frame building between Tenth and Eleventh Streets on Walnut Alley that he used as
> > a truck shed.   There was a large barn and wagon shed adjoining the building in 1922.
> Francis A. LeGoullon died at age 92 in spring of 1965.

_____

C.B. Frye & Sons Contractors – 499 Fifteenth Street
1965

_____

Glenn H. Brobeck – General contractor - 1335 Washington Avenue
1956, 1959

_____

John Dickey – engineer
1892, 1893

_____

John McCullough – engineer
1892, 1893

_____

E. E. Skroul – engineer
1892, 1893

_____

R.S. Bowser - engineer
1892, 1893

_____

Melchiorre Brothers Construction – 2420 Beaver Avenue – contractors
        (Express Transmission has the same address.)

_____

Pringle-Nero Land Surveying – 2020 Beaver Avenue

_____

Beaver Valley Construction – 403 Pennsylvania Avenue
1978, 1980   Owners – Jim Sundry/Rochester and John Menoher/Monaca.

_____

Rosso Construction Co. – 1134 Washington Avenue
1986

_____

A. F. Jolley – contractor
1892, 1893

_____

Hiram Hicks - contractor
1892, 1893

_____

Oliver Reed – contractor
1892, 1893

_____

Harry C. Rogers – contractor
1902, 1903   He most likely worked from home; found no office for him.   His wife's name was Dora;
                they lived on Virginia Avenue.

_____

N. Wurzel – contractor
1902, 1903

      N. Wurzel is associated with everything from billiards to groceries to hardware to nickelodeons to contracting.   Either there were quite a few "N. Wurzel/Nicholas Wurzel" people in Monaca, or he was one venturous and ambitious business man.

————

Nelson Hamilton – was a painter and had a storeroom - Pennsylvania Avenue
1902, 1903

      He lived in the same building as his storeroom.

————

Faiance Decorating Company – corner of Sixth Street and Pennsylvania Avenue
1903

      Opened Dec 12, 1903.
      Sold wall paper, paints, rugs, etc.

————

The Beaver Valley Decorating Co. – Monaca
1926

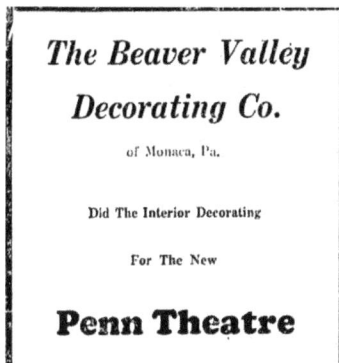

The Beaver Valley
Decorating Co.
of Monaca, Pa.

Did The Interior Decorating

For The New

Penn Theatre

1926

————

Monaca Wall Paper Company -at 1012 Pennsylvania Avenue - Keystone building in 1928, 1930
                    -at 1014 Pennsylvania Avenue in 1931   - at 1114 Pennsylvania Avenue in 1941
                  - at 1140 Pennsylvania Avenue (across from Eagle Building) 1944, 1945
                  – at 903 Pennsylvania Avenue in May/Apr 1946, 1949
1924, 1946, 1949

      1923 to 1941 - Charles Konvolinka was proprietor of Monaca Wall Paper store.
      In 1930 when in the Keystone Building, the storeroom sustained damages from
         a fire; the store was located on the ground/street floor.
      Konvolinka rented the storeroom on Pennsylvania Avenue formerly occupied by the
         Monaca Flower Shoppe since his was destroyed by the fire; opened at this location the
         end of Mar 1930.
      As of Dec 1941 this company was at 1114 Pennsylvania Avenue.
      1944 ad stated "Under New Management" - 1140 Pennsylvania Avenue– across from the
         Eagle Building, then moved and located at the corner of Pennsylvania and Ninth
         Street – 903 Pennsylvania Avenue.
      An ad on Apr 1946 says "We are now open for business....." so they just moved to this
         location (903 was Sobel's clothier former location).
      Charles Konvolinka died Oct 1941; his home was at 101 Kaye Avenue in 1930.

Leary's aka   Leary Decorating Company – first located in lower Pennsylvania Avenue (near Fifth Street)
– 1107 Pennsylvania Avenue in 1911, then 1032 Pennsylvania Avenue
- In 1925, at 1100 Pennsylvania Avenue

1903, 1911, 1913, 1917, 1925
> Daniel F. Leary, proprietor.
>> Daniel lived in Monaca since 1854 – learned the decorating trade and was employed at Phoenix Glass Co.   He was listed among some of the oldest residents of Monaca in 1911.
> John Pettit worked for the Leary Advertising Company in 1903; he took employment in Canonsburg and Mr. and Mrs. Pettit moved there in Jun 1904.
> Daniel and Mary lived in the same building as the business in 1912.
> His business consisted of selling wallpaper, moldings, paints, and novelties and he did painting and decoration and making signs.
> He decorated the Novelty Family Theatre.
> The store had "dressed dolls" the week of Christmas in 1912 – pictorial Advertisements.
> A 1912 directory listed his business as selling china and dinnerware, too.

> Later he formed the........

Leary Advertising Company which painted many of the valley buildings; he was still decorating theatres and hotels.
> Leary's store sustained smoke and water damage in Jul 1917 when the store beside his, rented by Hyman Finn as a Dry goods store, burned.   Daniel Leary had a two storey frame building – first floor was a novelty and wall paper store and his residency was on the 2nd floor.
> In 1925, an article stated "one of the best known of Monaca's business places...."
>> The building he occupied in 1925 was formerly at Fifth Street and Pennsylvania Avenue and was moved to the present location.
> By 1920, Daniel was basically out of the notion business and had expanded the painting portion of the business, specializing in auto painting. He purchased a spraying system and other equipment and his son Frank had become associated with his father in the painting business.   They also did specialty design signs.
> Daniel was b 1859; married __; 2 children. In 1900, Daniel was widowed, living with his children on Washington Avenue.   By 1910, he had married 2nd to Mary E. ___. Daniel died in 1925. A few months after his death, his widow, Mary, went for an extended visit with her family in Mass.
> To attest to Daniel's ability at painting and decorating, the following was printed in 1908 in an article about the remodeling of the Masonic Temple in Rochester.......

Leary's Notion Store,
Penn'a. Avenue.

D. F. Leary, the proprietor, is one of the old residents of Monaca, moving to the town in 1854. He learned the decorating trade and was employed at the Phoenix Glass Co. Later he formed the Leary Advertising company, which company painted many of the prominent buildings in the valley The Leary store has an excellent patronage. Mr. Leary still does decorating of theatres and hotels. He wishes in this way to thank the people for their patronage of the past and solicits their future patronage.

1911

A Full Line of

St. Patrick's Day and Easter Novelties

—AT—

LEARY'S
Pennsylvania Avenue
MONACA

1913

John Dinsmore - was a painter and had a storeroom – Pennsylvania Avenue
1902, 1903
> John married Lizzie; they lived at same address as storeroom.

Broman Paint Store   aka   Brothers Paint   – at 1003 Pennsylvania Avenue
> - then to 1000 Pennsylvania Avenue
> - and finally across the street to 999 Pennsylvania Avenue

late 1940s, 1951, 1976, 1987
> 1953 and 1956 ads stated 1000 Pennsylvania Avenue.   In 1961, the borough decided to purchase the Gormley and Batchelor properties which were between the Keystone building and the borough building and put in a public parking lot. These properties were housing the storerooms of Broman's, Monaca Shoe Repair, and others.
>
> Earnest Herman and Ellert Harold Broman first started the business about 1947.
>
> In 1987, Ellert Harold and Irene Broman owned and operated the business and it was stated that the Bromans had the business for 50 years.
>
> 1000 Pennsylvania Avenue was the original store room, then in the mid-1950s, the business was moved to the old National Bank Building at 999 Pennsylvania Avenue (now occupied by Gnu-Tub).
>
> In 1963 the Krall clothing store was at 999 Pennsylvania Avenue but the E. Harold Broman's family was living in the apartment at the rear of the building on the first floor.   (There was a small kitchen fire in the apartment in Aug 1963.)
>
> The move to 999 Pennsylvania Avenue was most likely needed because the borough was putting in a new parking lot.
>
> Erik and Ruth (Dahlstrom) Broman were both born in Sweden in 1907 and 1913 respectively; Erik worked in the wire mill in 1920; they had 5 children.
>> By 1930, Erik was widowed and living on Marshall Road, Center Township with his children. By 1940, he was remarried to Astrid and they added 1 more child to the family.
>>> One of the children, E. Harold was one of the owners and operators of Broman's, with his wife Irene helping run the business.

1953

Business at 1000 Pennsylvania Avenue – 1956.   (Note the borough building to the right of picture.)

John Glass – Tin Shop – Monaca Heights
1910, 1920,
     He worked for Heidrick and Taylor at one time.

Humbert Heating and Air Conditioning – 801 Allaire Avenue
Current
     Owners – Ray and Jane Humbert.
     Located in the 801 Allaire Avenue location in 2004.

Foehringer Sheet Metal & Heating – 834 Pennsylvania Avenue
1940, 1956
     George Foehringer owner.
        George and Dorthea lived in the same building as business.

————

Beaver Valley Sheet Metal Co. – 1213 rear Pennsylvania Avenue and 1215 Pennsylvania Avenue
1956, Current
     Incorporated in 1956 – Chris Mangin was president in 1990, 2000.
     Installed and serviced heating and air-conditional equipment; also source-removal duct cleaning
        and sanitizing.   A showroom and offices opened in the spring of 1998, next door to the
        sheet metal shop which is at the rear of 1213 (next door).

beaver Valley sheet metal co.

HEATING – AIR CONDITIONING
1213 Penna. Ave., Monaca
775-7300

bryant
HEATING COOLING
Best Wishes on Your 150th Celebration!

1990

————

Harper & Alexander   aka   J. Edward Harper   aka   Harper's Tin Shop
               In 1912 at 316 Tenth Street then moved to 1126 Pennsylvania Avenue.
1909, 1924, 1928, 1942, 1955
     Furnace work, tin, slate and composition roofing.
     John C. Harper & __ Alexander started the business.
        J. Edward Harper took over business from his father.
     Known as "Sheet metal man" or "Reliable Tinsmith of Monaca."
     Spouting, tinning, heating, and all sheet metal work.   Exclusive agency for furnaces.
     John C. Harper (Hartup) – b 1847 married Mary Miller; they lived on Pennsylvania Avenue.
        Edward J. Harper was born in 1884; married Theo Hicks; 2 children; they lived at Virginia
          Avenue, then Pennsylvania Avenue.   His son was an apprentice to him in 1930
          at age 19.
     The #1126 Pennsylvania location was beside the Magnolis store / United 5 & 10.

TIN AND SLATE ROOFING.

Harper & Alexander,   Monaca, Pa.
Tin and slate roofing, spouting
and general repair work. Estimates
promptly furnished.

1909

Tinning & Roofing

For The Beautiful New

PENN THEATRE
OF MONACA, PA.

by

J. E. HARPER
MONACA, PA.

1926

————

J. C. McMillan – Washington Avenue, then 1395 Pennsylvania Avenue
1909, 1929
> Tin and slate roofing, repair work, full line of furnaces.
> John McMillan married Nellie.   His brother Harry lived with them on Washington Avenue in 1910.
>> John was a tinner and Harry was a apprentice tinner.
> By 1929 it was run by Joseph McMillan and was at 1395 Pennsylvania Avenue.

TIN AND SLATE ROOFING.
___

J. C. McMillan,   Monaca, Pa.
  Tin and slate roofing; repair work.
A full line of furnaces.
J. C. McMillian,   Washington St.,
          Bell phone, 105-J.
___

1909

George J. Zitzman – Heating & Roofing Co. – had his own storeroom
> first located at corner of Ninth and Washington Avenue, then on Pennsylvania Avenue
1898, 1900, 1901, 1908, 1910s
> George was considered *a tinner*.
> 1898 directory stated "Dealer in stoves, ranges and house furnishing goods. Tin, slate, and
>> iron roofing, general repairing of roofs and spouting."
> A frame house of Geo J. Zitzman was bought by Justice Merkle.
>> It was moved a short distance further west on Pennsylvania Avenue.   George Zitzman
>> intended to move his store building from Ninth Street to the lot from which the
>> house was removed and add an additional storey to it.
> In Nov 1945, the Borough wanted to extend Pacific Avenue west through land
>> owned by Ellsworth J. Zitzman and the Phoenix Glass Co. ------ E. J. and Phoenix
>> agreed to convey this land to the borough if they gave other land to E. J.
>> The Borough owned land adjoining the property they wanted, so they were
>> going to give that to him.   (This was all around Pacific Avenue and Spruce Alley.)
>> (The borough did a couple deals with residents – one was extend Pacific Avenue from
>> Twelfth Street to a plan of lots on Spruce Alley again.)
> He had Patrick E. Shaughnessy working for him; Patrick also was boarding with George.
> They were living in Beaver Falls by 1920.   George was b. 1879; married Sadie __;
>> 3 children.
> George had moved to Beaver Falls prior to 1920; he sold the business to W.C. McDowell.

GEORGE J. ZITZMAN

Stoves, Ranges, Housefurnishing Goods.

Tin and Slate Roofing. Furnace Work.
Bridge Street,   *MONACA, PA.*

1900

Note "Bridge Street" on this ad – this was often used for "Ninth Street."

Hiram Hicks – stone and brick contractor - 609 Pennsylvania Avenue
1912   He most likely worked from home; found no office for him.

W. C. McDowell – Heating & Roofing Co. - Washington Avenue
1908

      He took over Geo. Zitzman's business when Geo. moved to Beaver Falls.
      He most likely then moved from Washington to Pennsylvania Avenue and into Geo.'s storeroom.

```
:••••••••••••••••••••••:
: How About :
: a Furnace? :
:——————————————:
: In Furnaces We Have :
: CANTON PERFECT BLAST, :
: BOOMER, STANTON, FOX, :
: PECK-WILLIAMSON, :
: MONARCH and MONCREIF. :
:——————————:
: W. C. McDowell :
:     Phone 157-1t     :
: Wash. Ave.,   Monaca, Pa. :
: If your roof leaks just phone us :
: and we will fix it in a hurry :
:••••••••••••••••••••••:
```
    1908

_____

Monaca Building Block and Construction Company – 2012 Pennsylvania Avenue
1922, 1937

      Organized Mar 22, 1922; began operations Apr 25, 1922.
      Handled building materials and concrete building blocks.
      Orazio Zaccardi and Teodoro Rossetti – owners.
         Orazio was called "The Hustle Man" because he tended to do things fast.

_____

Edward M. Kaye, of Monaca, although this was not his line of work............
      was granted a patent by the government for some type of building block or brick.
         This patent was granted in 1909 for the method of manufacturing the building blocks
         or bricks and glass facings.
      This information came from a magazine devoted to the uses of cement, so I have no
         additional information as to if any company in Monaca applied his method or if buildings
         in the area were built with products using this method.
      He was listed in 1908 in "Clay Record," a brick trade publication, and in 1909 "The Cement
         Age," a magazine devoted to the uses of Cement.

_____

George J. Harbison – was a carpenter and had a storeroom- 901 Pennsylvania Avenue
1902, 1903   He married Ida B. __; they lived at same location as the storeroom.

_____

Cochran Bros. Lumber Company – between Fourteenth Street and P & LE railroad
1898 to 1906

      George Cochran and J.M. Cochran of Woodlawn/Aliquippa, owners.
      In business in 1898 to the end of Jun 1906 when they sold their stock of lumber
         for their Monaca company (keeping Woodlawn's) to J. S. Mitchell & Sons*, Beaver Falls.
      The P & LE railroad bought that property from Cochran Bros. to erect a new passenger depot on
         the site in Jun 1906, thus the reason they sold their stock since they were closing.
      Changed name to Beaver County Building Company at Monaca (also had another business,
         same name, in Woodlawn/Aliquippa in 1906).
    *J. S. Mitchell lived in Monaca in 1920 and 1930, his son James S. started Mitchell Bus Company by 1930.
    See further for the J.S. Mitchell company/business.

_____

The next company at the same location as the former Cochran Bros. Lumber Company that I could find was.......................

Beaver Building Block Company – corner of Fourteenth Street and P & LE RR
1920, 1922

Had a machine in their plant that could make 800 blocks every 10 hours.

> **NEW MACHINE INSTALLED**
>
> A new Besser automatic machine just installed in the plant of the Beaver Building Block company, corner of Fourteenth street and Pittsburg & Lake Erie railroad, was put in operation today. The machine has a capacity of 800 blocks every ten hours. A switch to facilitate shipments is being constructed at the plant.
>
> ———
>
> Aug 1922

then.........

Keystone Cement Products Company   – Fourteenth and Colonial Streets
                     – along Beaver Avenue heading toward Aliquippa

1926, 1929

Owned by John Ogrizok.
John was president; W. J. Mecklem-vice president; H. S. Malone-treasurer;
Jas Bonidy- secretary.   General Manager in 1927 was Everet C. Smith.
They were at this time rated as the largest business in cement block in Beaver County.
Each block they made was impressed with a "Keystone" – their trade mark.
This business, used for making concrete building blocks,
It was sold at a sheriff sale in Aug 1929.
It was located in the area of Colonial Avenue, by the American Glass Specialty Glass Co.,
Fourteenth Street, and the railroad tracks.   There were several buildings – all
concrete.   Had slag and composition blocks in stock.

> **Keystone Cement Products Company**
>
> MONACA, PENNA.
> Phone Rochester 1559
>
> We wish to announce to our regular customers and to those contemplating fall building, that we have added another class of building blocks to our products, known as the "CINSLAG" construction unit on which we are pleased to quote:
>
> Plain .... .14
> Rock, Panel or Plain Faced....... .17
> Rock, Panel or Plain Corners..... .20
>
> Above Prices f. o.b. Monaca, Penna.
> For waterproofed block add 2c per block extra to above prices.
>
> 1926

Then........

Marcello Block Co. – 933 Washington Avenue - 1425 Beaver & Fourteenth Street
1929, 1996,
John Marcello, owner.
In 1929, 1931 Tony Marcello was doing business at 933 Washington Avenue.
Prior to 1940, the address of the company was once Fourteenth Street and Colonial Avenue
then Colonial Avenue became known as Beaver Avenue.

Concrete specialties and builders supplies.
Sep 5, 1970 – was totally destroyed by a tornado.
As of 2015 – A large warehouse/storage building is still being used for various enterprising activities.

(See Weather Events section for more on the tornado.)

Marcello
BLOCK MFG.
High Quality

● High Test Concrete Blocks   ● Sand
● Gravel   ● Cement   ● Lime   ● Sewer Pipe
● Septic Tank   ● Wall Coping   ● Drain Tile
● Fuel Lining   ● Steel Windows
●Chimney Blocks   ● Coal

CALL ROCH. 3479

At 11th St. R.R. Crossing

1425 Beaver Ave.   Monaca

Jul 1949   1956

In 1938

Robert G. Onstott   - was a carpenter and had a store room on Pennsylvania Avenue.
1880, 1902, 1903
        He lived at the same location as the storeroom.

Adam Huff – cabinet maker – lived at corner of Fourth Street and Pennsylvania Avenue
1850, 1860, 1869, 1870, 1876, 1880, 1900
        Still called himself a cabinet maker at age 76.
                (See all information on Adam in the Furniture section.)

Augustus H. Lindsay – carpenter work
1904
        He received the contract for the Monaca Young Men's Christian Association Hall in Mar 1904.
        He married Elizabeth _; they lived on Virginia Avenue.

Ellis Figley – carpenter/contractor –1099 Pennsylvania Ave.(1929) - 1003 Pennsylvania Avenue(1931)
1929, 1931

_____

Monaca Lumber Company –2098 Pennsylvania Avenue (across the street from Pgh Tube)
1929, 1956, 1965, 1971
      Organized in Mar 1929.
      Used the former buildings of the Opalite Tile Company with improvements and additional
            buildings added.
      Was across the street from Pgh Tube Co. who in 1965 owned the property.
      Owned and operated lastly by John R. Skinner – 3rd generation family member.
            In 1920 Alexander was owner of a garage; he started the business.
            Alexander's son, John Martin Skinner was then owner/operator (census 1930) –
            The next owner was John M.'s son John R. Skinner.

BUILDING & REPAIR — Material for your every need. Free estimates on building and remodeling material for new building or remodeling. Monaca Lumber Co. 2098 Pennsylvania Ave., Monaca, SPruce 5-0440.

1958

Get It Done In '51

Always See
MONACA
LUMBER CO.
FIRST
- Lumber
- Rock Wool and Zonolite
- Paints
- Hardware

PHONE
Rochester
5297 or
5298

OFFICE AND YARD
2098 Penna. Ave., Monaca, Pa.

1951

MAKE PLANS NOW
FOR YOUR DREAM
HOME IN 1952

Come In And Let Us Help You In Selecting The
Right Materials And Plans Now . . .

MONACA LUMBER CO.
PHONE ROCH. 5297 OR 5298
2098 PENNA. AVE.   MONACA, PA. 1952

_____

D. J. Mitchell Lumber Yards –1224 Pennsylvania Avenue
1919, 1924, 1940
      David J Mitchell – s/o J.S. Mitchell became owner/operator of his own business.
      David was living at 1101 Pennsylvania Avenue in 1940.

_____

Robert Kerr Cabinet Work – 928 Grant Street Monaca Heights
1956

_____

J. S. Mitchell & Sons   aka   Mitchell Lumber Co. – 1224-1226 Pennsylvania Avenue
1902, 1907, 1917, 1919
      J.S., F.S., and David J. owners. (D.J. became owner – see further)
      Contractors and builders.   (in 1902, had their main office in Beaver Falls)
            They had a planing mill and lumber yard and manufactured cement blocks.
      Dealers in lumber and builder's supplies.
            David J. 's wife was Mary L. __; they lived on Washington Avenue and then in
            1912 at 914 Atlantic Avenue.   I did not find the other Mitchell's living in Monaca.

Called J. S. Mitchell & Sons in 1907.   (J.S. and F.S. did not live in Monaca)
Had a new floor put in their office building in 1907.
Sold lumber, lime, cement.
In early 1907, it was reported that the employees of the J. S. Mitchell & Sons company
        cleaned and swept the second floor of the planing mill and started to use it
        as a skating rink.
In Oct 1919 – a strip of property on the Mitchell Lumber Co. yard was condemned so the
Borough could purchase it and make an official roadway since people were using it as a shortcut
from Twelfth Street to the RR station.
        It was a 40 x 100 foot section – the opening to Pacific Avenue from Spruce Alley and
        then from Twelfth Street (this would be the section of Twelfth Street that runs along the
        side of the Band Room building (2016) and former Penn Super Market.

J. S. Mitchell & Sons had lumber businesses in both Beaver Falls and Monaca in 1906
        and they purchased the stock of the Beaver County Building Company in
        Monaca/ aka Cochran Bros.
Mitchell Lumber was purchased by Mecklem brothers in late 1919 and moved to
        1548 Pennsylvania Avenue.

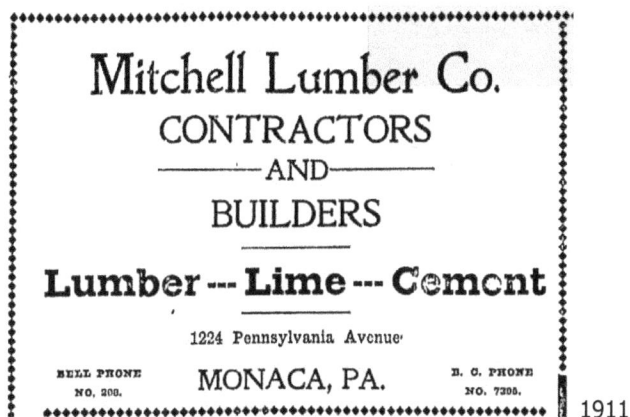

Mitchell Lumber Co.
CONTRACTORS
—AND—
BUILDERS

Lumber --- Lime --- Cement

1224 Pennsylvania Avenue

BELL PHONE
NO. 208.   MONACA, PA.   B. C. PHONE
NO. 7208.

1911

───────

Beaver Concrete & Supply Inc.   aka   Rock Concrete Supply – 10 Industrial Park Road
1998
        Business included - contractors who specialize in patios, ready-mix cement, sand, gravel foundation
        contractors – concrete & cement.   Locally/family owned.

───────

Lawson Lumber Co. / Lawson Equipment Inc. – 10 Industrial Park Road
1972
        Ready mix concrete.   Rock Concrete Supply Co.
        Established in 1972.   Richard Lawson – owner.

───────

Sids Flooring – 403 Pennsylvania Avenue (first ward)
2006   Wanted to put up a business sign in 2006.

───────

Flooring Options by Erika – 403 Pennsylvania Avenue
Current

───────

Eagle Carpet – 924 Pennsylvania Avenue
1977

EAGLE CARPET
Linoleum - Tile
Carpeting Sales
& Installation
FREE ESTIMATES
924 Pennsylvania Ave.
774-7758

_____

Harry Blatt – Carpet Store – upholster and carpet layer
1920   He lived at 387 Atlantic Avenue.

_____

Heritage Place Gallery of Floors – 609 Pennsylvania Avenue
1993, 1999, 2000
        Opened in Jun 29, 1992.   Was closed at 609 Pennsylvania Avenue by 1999.
        Owners in 2000 – David and Elaine DeLuco.
        Flooring materials and accessories.

HERITAGE PLACE
Gallery of Floors, Inc.
Complete line of Carpet, Ceramic,
Vinyl and Wood Floors
609 PENNSYLVANIA AVENUE
MUNACA, PA 15061
(412) 728-8227   1994

        Now.....

Abbey Carpet and Flooring - 105 Pleasant Drive, Center Township
current

_____

Thomas Jobe – had his own upholstery business – Pennsylvania Avenue
1922, 1930

_____

Al's Rental Service – 714 Pennsylvania Avenue
1956   Al Guantonio, owner.   Had tools of all kind for rent.

_____

Jeffers & Leek Electric – 1302 Pennsylvania Avenue
        (not here in 2015)

_____

Monaca Elect. Supply & Motor Repair Co. – Pennsylvania Avenue
1922

_____

Miller Elect. Supply & Motor Repair Co. – Pennsylvania Avenue
1922

_____

Haley Electrical Store – unknown location
1930
      Olin Haley proprietor.

_____

George Reeb – plumber - Pennsylvania Avenue
1898, 1903
      Practical plumbing, gas fitting, and sewering.

_____

Elmer E. Sproull – plumber - 1237 Washington Avenue
1903, 1912
      Elmer and Margaret lived in the same building as he listed his business.

_____

McKay Bros. – Plumbers - Pennsylvania Avenue (near Fourteenth Street) , Monaca Heights, too.
1907, 1908, 1910
      Thadys McKay – owner.
      Were installing a water system to benefit the residents on the hill.
      Ad stated "for plumbing and gas fittings come to us….."
      Broke ground Jun 10, 1908 for new three storey brick building, store room, and dwelling
            on Pennsylvania Avenue (near Fourteenth Street).
      Jun 19, 1908 –council granted them a permit to erect a TWO storey brick building on
        Pennsylvania near Fourteenth Street, so I am guessing the 3 storey building was not built -?-

1908

_____

George Roth – Plumbing Shop – unknown location
1920
      He resided at 1229 Pennsylvania Avenue in 1920.

_____

Biskup Plumbing & Heating – 2028 Beaver Avenue
1965, 1990
      In 1990, Carl Lee Biskup was the master plumber/owner.

_____

Ray Hall - plumbing and heating
1956, 2000
      Owner in 2000 – Brad Hall, Sr. – formerly owned and founded by his father in 1944.
      New construction, repair work, gas and water line replacement, water heaters.

_____

Deitrich's Plumbing & Heating – 815 - 817 Pennsylvania Avenue
1902, 1903, 1912, 1985
> Opened in the early 1900s.
>> Family business started by George Dietrich, Sr. in the rear of a shoe store operated by his father, John, on Eighth Street.
> George E., Sr. converted the store to a plumbing and heating store; lived in the same building.
> The 1902/03 Directory has him as doing practical plumbing, gas fitting and sewering, gas stoves, and being on Pennsylvania Avenue at that time.
> Owned by George, Jr. and John Dietrich (brothers) in 1957 when George, Sr. died. They lived above the store.
> When John died, George, Jr. sold the business to Ron Henry of Monaca.
> Ad said "practical plumbing" – sold stoves and electric fixtures, too.
> Business was bought out by Henry's Plumbing, Heating, and Supply in 1985.

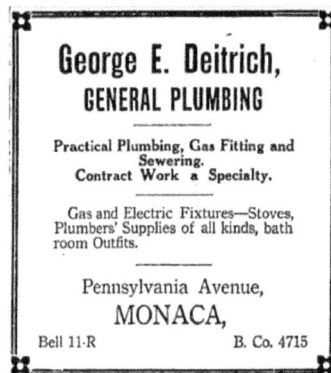

George E. Deitrich,
GENERAL PLUMBING

Practical Plumbing, Gas Fitting and Sewering.
Contract Work a Specialty.

Gas and Electric Fixtures—Stoves, Plumbers' Supplies of all kinds, bath room Outfits.

Pennsylvania Avenue,
MONACA,

Bell 11-R   B. Co. 4715

Deitrich's Plumbing & Heating   Photo courtesy of BCHR&LF

This is an enlarged portion of the 1972 ad – see next image.

THEN AND NOW

DIETRICH'S
PLUMBING & HEATING
Free Estimates
775-0302

WE
SPECIALIZE
IN SERVICE,
INSTALLATION,
AND SELLING...

From laundry to bathroom,
check us for new laundry
trays, water softeners,
hot water heaters, vanities
and bath fixtures.
Gas Repairs —Electric
Sewer Cleaning.

Serving
Beaver
Valley
For
Over
70
Years

DIETRICH'S
PLUMBING
& HEATING
817 Penna. Ave., Monaca
775-0302

1972 ad

_____

Placidi Construction / Placidi Plumbing – 1136 Pennsylvania Avenue
        J. Placidi – proprietor.   This address was also the residency of the Placidi family in 1979.

_____

Brook Fleming's Plumbing Service – 1520 Indiana Avenue - current
 ? to current

_____

Advanced Heating & Air Conditioning – 1311 Pennsylvania Avenue
1991, 1995   John Hodovanich, owner.

Advanced Plumbing and Mechanical – 1317 Pennsylvania Avenue
1998, 2001   Patricia Hodovanich-president and controller; John C. Hodovanich-vice president and
                  project superintendent.
                  In 2001 they were planning on moving to Aliquippa.

————————

The Frederick Webster Company – (in Citizens National Bank Building) – 308-312 Ninth Street
1901, 1903, 1904
        Frederick Webster – pres. and treas.   He married Maud S. __; they resided in New Brighton.
        R. M. Wilcox, Manager (1904).   Ads said "modern plumbers."   1902/03 Directory states
        "plumbing and gas" (had stores in Leetsdale and New Brighton, also).   Given contract
        for the plumbing and gas fitting at the Monaca YMCA Hall – Mar 1904.

"UP TO YOU!"
GET OUR REDUCTION
PRICES ON STOVES.__ .
"SEE US FIRST."
The Frederick Webster Co.,
MODERN PLUMBERS.
MONACA, LEETSDALE, NEW BRIGHTON.
                                    Jan 1904 ads

"SHAM"DELIERS,
COMMONLY
Called Chandeliers, Are
Found in Other Places.
                    WE SELL
THE REAL THING
"See us first" for our stock is the largest and
most complete outside of Pittsburg.
THE FREDERICK WEBSTER COMPANY,
MODERN PLUMBERS,
LEETSDALE,   NEW BRIGHTON,   MONACA.

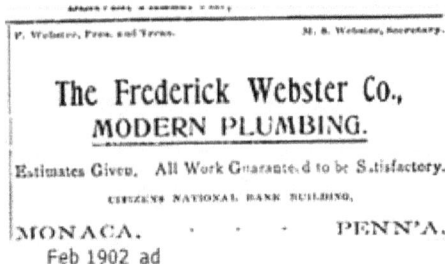

P. Webster, Pres. and Treas.   M. S. Webster, Secretary.
The Frederick Webster Co.,
MODERN PLUMBING.
Estimates Given. All Work Guaranteed to be Satisfactory.
CITIZENS NATIONAL BANK BUILDING,
MONACA.   ·   ·   ·   PENN'A.
        Feb 1902 ad

MOST
REFRESHING
IS A
SHOWER BATH.
Let Us Tell You About
Them.
We Sell Them As
Cheap As $15.00
THE
FREDERICK WEBSTER CO. MODERN PLUMBERS
LEETSDALE, PA. NEW BRIGHTON, PA. MONACA, PA.
        1904 ad   (note this shower)

————————

Henry's Plumbing, Heating & Supply – 817 Pennsylvania Avenue
1985, 1991
        Ron and Roberta Henry, owners.   Opened in 1985 (Had been Dietrich's Plumbing & Heating).
        Services were expanded to include complete renovation of commercial and industrial bathrooms,
        such as ceramic tile floors and walls; plans also include expansion to office and interior
        renovations.   Specializes in complete custom design bathroom and kitchen remodeling.

1990 ad

_____

C & P Kitchen Supply – 600 Pacific Avenue
1977

_____

Robert Kramer – machinist
1870

_____

John Smith – machinist
1880

_____

Sharp Merriman – machinist apprentice
1880

_____

John Bergman – machinist – Tenth Street
1900

_____

Koehler Bros. Machine Shop – 822 Washington Avenue
1914, 1956, 1990, 1995
 Owned by Howard Richard Koehler – s/o Paulus and Maria Schilling Koehler.
  Howard was b 1887 d 1973; retired in 1959.
 Established in 1914 - opened in 1916 (as of 1995, in business 81 years).
 1990, 1995 owned by Jimmy G. Koehler.
 Metalizing – welding and general machine work – experimental work.

1990

_____

S. P. Kohlman – machinist – 823 Pennsylvania Avenue
1928, 1929, 1931

_____

Kovac Machine Shop – 1209 Indiana Avenue (REAR)
1956

_____

Monaca Welding – 1250 Beaver Road
1936, 1956, 1987
> Opened in 1936.
> Used electric and acetylene methods of welding.
>> This would have been located somewhere close to Marcello's, on the other side of the tracks from where the passenger station sat – there are only a few home sitting on this section of Beaver Avenue (2015).

_____

Master Sweeper Sales & Service – 615 Pennsylvania Avenue
1991, 1992   Opened in 1991.   Owner – Robert Buffington.

_____

J. Anderson Davidson – stone mason
1941
> Resided in Monaca for many years and then moved to Center Township; married Rachel; lived on Pennsylvania Avenue.   His brother Allen Davidson owned the flour store.

_____

Halama Brothers Electric, Inc. – 1598 Virginia Avenue
1977, 1990, 2002
> Founded in 1977 by Michael and David Halama.   Opened new building in 2001.
> Michael and David helped run the Rosina's restaurant/pizza in 1980s.

_____

Electric Garage Door Sales (Lift Master) – at ? , then due to a fire, they relocated to 609 Pennsylvania
Avenue (1991)   -1993 at 1128 Pennsylvania Avenue
1964, 1978, 1990, 1991, 1993, Current
> Garage door opener business.   Had experience in business since 1964, but was all this in Monaca ?
> Ray and Nancy Heberling became owners in 1978; bought business from E.P. Barker of New
> > Castle.   They also employed Chris Heberling-Mngr., Robert Eichenlaub, Keith Reed, and
> > Wylie Reehern in 1991.

_____

Allied Piping Engineering & Fabricators Inc. – 20 Sycamore Street – Monaca Heights
1956

_____

Joseph McCorry – local electrician of Monaca
1908

_____

A C TV – 1201 Allaire Avenue – Monaca Heights
1977, 1978   Al Cianfarano – owner.   Electronic repairs service.

_____

Mesta Painting Co. – 300 Ninth Street – painters
Mesta Industrial Contracting, Inc. – 300 Ninth Street
1977, Current
> Business is in the original Hotel Monaca building.

_____

KG Electric – 1199 Indiana Avenue – electricians

_____

Suica's Home Maintenance – 417 Pennsylvania Avenue (?)

_____

Interstate Amiesite Corp. – Twenty-first Street and 1901 Beaver Avenue
1939, 1954, 1965, 1976, 2013
> Blacktopping business.   (See Mills section for more information.)

*** *** *** *** ***

See upcoming pages for additional listings of the men with occupations related to hardware, tinners, carpenters, painters, etc. from the 1850s through 1900.   With no found references for their locations or other miscellaneous information, there is just a list of names with the years in business and their occupations.

TRADESMEN

Although not listed as having a specified storeroom or business, the following men were listed with their occupations on the censuses and or in directories.   Most of these occupations would have been a business that did not require a storeroom, therefore the majority of these men may have worked for someone else or may have worked from their homes.   Since they would have contributed greatly to the constant growth and expansion of Phillipsburg and Monaca, I thought they should be included and recognized in this section.

With the wonderful find of the 1841 Directory of Phillipsburg residents and their occupations, I wanted to share the following names.   I found no other information to give indications of specific businesses and/or where storerooms may have been located though.

1841 Directory

Carpenters	Bricklayers
John Bell	Rheinhold Frank
Henry Sunk	August Schmidt
John Trompeter	Christian Authenriet
Casper Koehler	
George Voght (Vogt)	Tinner
David Lais (Lay)	Christian Smith
Henry Young	

Coopers	Surveyor
Jacob Sanders	Charles Kramer
M. Faut	
Andrew Faut	

***   ***   ***   ***   ***

The following men were from the 1850s, 1860s, 1870s, and 1880s:
(Indented names are sons or relatives of the name above them.)

Adam Keller – potter – 1850

Nicholas Wenzel – tinner 1880
David Brubeck – tinner 1880

Anthony Faut – cooper 1880
George Kaem – copper 1880
Henry Brobeck - moulder 1880

Emil Bott – painter/artist 1850
Frederick Blatner – painter 1880

Wesley Carey – carpenter 1880
John Duerr – carpenter 1860
David Durr – carpenter 1860
Charles Huff – carpenter 1880
George Kroeber – cabinet maker 1860 1870 1880
David Lais – carpenter / house carpenter 1850 1860 1870 1880
David Lais, Sr. – house carpenter 1880
Charles Lais – carpenter 1870 1880
William Miller – carpenter 1860-

Jacob Schafer – carpenter 1850
Milo Stewart – house carpenter 1870
Jacob Stroheker – apprentice pattern maker 1860
John Trompeter – carpenter   1850
Gilbert Trompeter – carpenter 1850
George Vogt – carpenter   1850 farmer & carpenter 1860
     George Vogt – cabinet maker 1860
     Louis Vogt – pattern maker 1860
     Henry Vogt – wood turner 1860
Henry Young – carpenter   1850
Samuel Bickerstaff – carpenter – 1869
_?_ Grossmyer – carpenter – 1869
Henry Lias – carpenter – 1869, 1876
David Lias – carpenter – 1869, 1876
Charles Lias – carpenter – 1876
David Lias, Jr. – carpenter – 1876
John Meany – carpenter – 1869
William Schnobel – carpenter – 1876

Rudolph Cramer/Cranner – machinist – 1869
John Smith – machinist - 1869
William Cavanaugh – stone mason 1880
Mikle Walter – stone mason   1860
Edward Frank – stone cutter 1870
George Groth-stone mason 1870
James Hamelton– stone mason 1870 1880
Andrew Jolly – stone contractor 1869, 1876, 1880
Oliver Reed – stone contractor 1880
Robert Routh– stone mason 1870
Mikle Walter – stone mason 1860
Farquhar Smith – quarryman 1860
James Hamilton – stone mason – 1876
Robert Routh – mason – 1869
Joseph Walters – stone mason – 1869, 1876
Oliver Reed – stone dealer - 1876

Robert McClain – brick layer 1860 1870

Fred Hagan – cobblestone merchant – 1869

*** *** *** *** ***

On the <u>1892/1893 Directory</u>, the following persons were listed:

John R. Haney – cooper
E. B. Stelfle – cooper
Chas. Sweet – cooper
E. P. Sweet – cooper

M. V. Chambers – stonemason
James Baker – stonesmason
Thomas Short – stonemason
Joseph Walker – stonemason
Morris Hemphill – stonemason
E. R. Frank – stonemason
John Irons – stonemason

Samuel Hamilton – painter
Nelson Hamilton – painter
Chas. Heidiger – painter
Harry C. Glasser – painter
John Glasser – painter

A. Wentworth – carpenter
James Taylor – carpenter
James Moore – carpenter
Adolphus Muller – carpenter
Chas. Lias - carpenter
David Lias – carpenter
A. H. Lindsay – carpenter
Wm. Merriman – carpenter
Chas. Huff – carpenter
Henry Hartman – carpenter
Geo. Harbison – carpenter
W. J. Chambers – carpenter
John C. Figley – carpenter

***   ***   ***   ***   ***

I did not find any additional information on specific addresses of storerooms or business but their residencies were listed in the director so I included them. They were listed in miscellaneous Monaca directories and/or census enumeration. I did include their occupations.

"res" indicates their place of residency;   "bds" indicates with whom they were boarding;   "rms" indicates where they roomed; wives' names are in brackets

<u>1902/03 Directory and/or on the 1900 census</u>

Bricklayers
Charles Dower, [Mary], bricklayer, res Indiana Avenue
Richard Wincott, bricklayer, bds Point Breeze Hotel
Thomas Martin [Hattie], bricklayer, res Virginia Avenue
Reuben Reed, bricklayer, bds Central Hotel
John Sebold [Emma M.], bricklayer, res Indiana Avenue
Joseph Swartswelter , bricklayer, bds J Dinsmore
James Welch, bricklayer, bds Point Breeze Hotel
Homer Weigle [Mary], bricklayer, res near Bath Tub Works
Joseph Walter, bricklayer, res Washington Avenue (also a stone mason & cuter in 1870 & 1880)
Harry Zollinger [Ella], bricklayer, res Indiana Avenue

Cooper
George A. Beringer [Mary A.], cooper, res Indiana Avenue
William Beringer [Callie L.], cooper, res Atlantic Avenue
John Haney [Margaret], cooper, res Ninth Street
Gust Rose, cooper, bds W. H. Beringer

Carpentry

James C. Brown [Susie H.], carpenter, res Atlantic Avenue
Clark Cadwell, carpenter, bds Point Breeze Hotel
William S. Carner [Maria], carpenter, res Virginia Avenue
William B. Davis [Emma M], carpenter, res Pennsylvania Avenue
Otto Elias – Cabinet maker – res Pennsylvania Avenue
George C. Haller [Sadie B.], carpenter, res Washington Avenue
Norman D. Hall [Lilly M.], carpenter, res Indiana Avenue
Harry W. Gross, carpenter, res Virginia Avenue
John C. Figley [Ida L.], carpenter, res Indiana Avenue
Henry A. Hartman [Elizabeth M.], carpenter, res Washington Avenue
William Irvin, carpenter, rms Mrs. A. Hood
John McCullough [Mary A. E.], carpenter, res Virginia Avenue
Joseph S. Henderson [Elizabeth], carpenter, res Washington Avenue
William F. Hershey [May], carpenter, res Indiana Avenue
Nathan H. Jones [Mary E.], carpenter, res Washington Avenue
Harry Lias [Alice], carpenter, res Pacific Avenue
Harry A. Kronk[Nellie G.], carpenter, res Indiana Avenue
James A. Kronk [Amanda], carpenter, res Virginia Avenue
Charles Lyle, carpenter, bds J Dinsmore
James Moore [Ida M.], carpenter, res Washington Avenue
David Morris, carpenter, res s s Pennsylvania Avenue
Cornelius Mowry [Martha], carpenter, res Sixth Street
Jonas A. Sayers[Lucy], carpenter, res east end of city
Fred R. Schwartz [Amanda M.], carpenter, res Washington Avenue
Henry Schwartz, carpenter, bds Central Hotel
Elmer E. Winch [Mary K.], carpenter, res Washington Avenue

Paperhanger

Adolphus Blatt, paperhanger, res Atlantic Avenue
Allard Stewart [Mildred I.], paperhanger, res Atlantic Avenue

Plumber

Rooney Beganski, plumber, bds Hotel Monaca
William Keane [Frances T.], plumber, res Twelfth Street
John Madden [Stella T.], plumber, res Indiana Avenue
Charles Chapman, plumber, rms Mrs. M A Jenkins
John Haase, plumber, rms C Doherr
Charles Westbrook, plumber, bds Hotel Monaca

Electrician

John Edwards, electrician, bds J Dinsmore
Harry H. Hughes [Augusta M.], electrician, res Atlantic Avenue

Painter

William Donovan[Frances A.], painter , res Washington Avenue
Henry Faust [Fanny], painter, res Washington Avenue
Jacob M. Glasser, painter, res Washington Avenue
William M. Reagle, painter, bds Point Breeze Hotel
Alexander Temple [Margaret E.], painter, res Eighth Street

Plaster

Frank M. Hayes [Mary L.], plasterer, res Ninth Street
Henry C. Martin [Mollie M.], plasterer, res Eighth Street
Joseph Tate [Fanny], plasterer, res Atlantic Avenue

Gas fitter

Clarence W. Weigle, gasfitter, res Dockters Hts.

Stonemason

Lemont L. Campbell [Maggie], stonemason, res Atlantic Avenue

Edward Rinehart Frank[Jennie], stonecutter, res Indiana Avenue (stone mason and farmer in 1850, 1860)

Ernest Gallop, stonemason, bds J. Dinsmore

Martin Heffinger [Anna], stonemason, res Dockters Hts.

Morrison Hemphill [Elizabeth], stonemason, res Pacific Avenue

Hugh L. Shellito [Clara], stonemason, res Virginia Avenue

Angus Smith, stonemason, res Pacific Avenue

William Smith, stonemason, res Pacific Avenue

Paver

Charles Meads, paver, res Atlantic Avenue

Slater

Fred Harris, slater, bds F. Purtle

*** *** *** *** ***

COAL

coal tipple ....   A **tipple** is a structure used to load coal either from railroad cars or at a mine to load the extracted product for transport.

This is an image of a coal tipple that would have been similar in appearance to LeGoullon's which was along the railroad tracks where they cross over the jointure of Brodhead Road and Pennsylvania Avenue coming into Monaca.

Prior to gas and electric, the main source for heating homes and for cooking in the homes was wood and then either wood and/or coal with furnaces primarily coal burning. Many of the older homes in towns and communities may still have a "coal chute door."   These were used to access the coal storage area in their basement.   The coal provider would deliver the coal to individual homes and use the coal chute on the outside of the home to shovel or shuttle the coal in for the homeowner.   If you take time to walk by or drive slowly past homes in an older town, you will most likely spot many of these chute doors; although no longer used for coal delivery, they are still in place.

_____

R. H. Hamilton – dealer in Coal
1898, 1903

_____

Joseph Benth – coal oil refiner – unknown location
1860

_____

Hall W. Hogan – coal merchant – unknown location
1860, 1869   His residence was on Fourth Street (became Pennsylvania Avenue).

_____

Frederick Hogan – coal merchant – unknown location
1850

_____

John Brezgar – coal business – Pennsylvania Avenue Extension
btw 1900-1910, 1912
> In early 1912, John was listed as a Monaca coal dealer.
> John and Margaretta lived at 802 Pennsylvania Avenue. He was also a wholesale whiskeyman.
> He was under contract to supply coal to the pump station and other borough institutions.
> Unfortunately, it was said that Mr. Brezgar was handing in bills for more coal than he had been
>> supplying; his contract with Monaca Borough was therefore null and void*.
> The Monaca council then awarded the contract to John P. Potter.
>> *It was a bitter council meeting that day.   Brezgar admitted to billing for almost twice as
>> much coal as he was delivering and made strong accusations that the other coal dealers
>> do or did the same thing; but council gave testimony that this was not true. When all
>> was said and done, Potter had the new contract; Brezgar's contract as annulled; yet
>> council agreed to take 60 to 70 ton of 3-4 inch coal from Brezgar since he it had on hand
>> and had purchased it specifically for the borough.

_____

LeGoullon Coal and Builders Supplies– 298 Pennsylvania Avenue
1900s, 1922, 1926, 1958
> Owned by Frank LeGoullon for 50 years, then his son L.L.
> Erected a coal tipple - Pennsylvania Avenue in 1922, along tracks lower Pennsylvania
>> Avenue, along the RR tracks that pass over the roadway as you are leaving town.

_____

William Stoops – coal dealer and had coal tipple
1920 , 1922
> His livery was at 616 Pennsylvania Avenue.
> He was living at 6?4 Pennsylvania Avenue.

_____

Barco and Huffmyer, – Coal and Ice - 1498 Pennsylvania Avenue
1927
> Mr. Barco and Clevan Huffmyer were partners.   They dealt in coal and were also among the local
>> ice men.   Delivered at least 6,000 bushels of coal each month.

_____

Clarence Huffmyer – coal dealer – 1199 Virginia Avenue
1920s

> **COAL!**
> Buy Good Coal—Save Money
> CLARENCE HUFFMYER
> 1199 Virginia Ave.,   Monaca, Pa.
> Phone 2162

1928 ad

_____

Daniel Sabella – coal dealer – unknown location of business
1940   He resided at 203 Ninth Street.

_____

Henry Hild – owner of a feed and coal business – unknown location
1940   He resided at 1124 Indiana Avenue.

_____

Barco Coal & Supply   aka   Barco Coal Co. – 1712 Pennsylvania Avenue
1940s, 1965
> Frank and Ann Barco, owners. Ann ran the company after her husband died; Ann died in 1998.
>> Ann married second John Michaluk of Center Township.   The Michaluk family had been
>> previous owners of the Triangle Tavern/Store in Center Township.

_____

Monaca Feed and Coal Company – unknown location
1951

_____

Monaca Coal Company – 698 Pacific Avenue
1956
        Mike Wilczek owner

_____

Herzog Coal Distributors – 1111 Pennsylvania Avenue
1956   Kenneth W. Herzog owner.

_____

Champion Coal and Disco – 1712 Pennsylvania Avenue
1965
        Sold blocks, cement, mortar, sand, sewer pipe, steel sashes.

_____

Rochester Coal Co. – Eighteenth Street & Beaver Street
1940, 1954
        Improvements and addition done in 1953/54.

_____

Rochester Coal, Trucking and Contracting Co. –
1954
        Had locations in Monaca and Rochester.

1954

*** *** *** *** ***
*** *** ***

GARAGES / SERVICE STATIONS

CAR DEALERS

TRUCKING

GASOLINE / OIL

GARAGES/SERVICE STATIONS
CAR DEALERS
TRUCKING
GASOLINE/OIL

Fun Fact: In 1960 there were 19 service stations in Monaca; by 1997 there were but 3 stations.   Most stations didn't survive and were closed due to the gasoline crisis of the 1970s, or the mill closings, or the 1982 closing of the Rochester-Monaca bridge.

Gasoline stations and garages began to spring up as the popularity and availability of automobiles spread.   The pumps at the early gasoline stations did not afford such luxuries as the ones of 2016.   They did provide the convenience of pumping gasoline into a car, but it was the attendant's job to monitor the amount sold. There were no automatic sensors or shut off devices. A motorist would have to monitor how many miles they had driven, what the average mileage per gallon their vehicle would get, and then ask for sufficient gasoline – making sure to get a bit less gas than the car's tank could hold so there would be no running over.   In 1925, the spread of a new "correct measure" system was added to the gasoline industry. There were two brands of these pumps being used locally; "Correct Measure" and "Fry Visible" pumps were being installed in all local service stations and garages. Although this "correct measure" was not being manufactured in Monaca (factories were actually in Rochester and Fallston), it was definitely sought after and found to be an added convenience by the operators of the stations in Monaca, as well as the owners of the cars.

The principle of the Correct Measure Pumps was to give true and visible measurement of gasoline. The motorists could see he was actually receiving the number of gallons he asked for.   There was a device on the operating handle for the attendant to set the number of gallons desired, and the gasoline would be pulled up and come to the level at the top of the measuring tube/glass container. This also made it easier on motorists to know how many gallons of gasoline they should ask for; and again there would be no mistaking the actual amount of gasoline delivered.   The "correct measure" system would allow a motorist to ask for maybe 4 gallon of gasoline; provided there was no run over, then maybe say "add another gallon" and would find the exact amount of gallons he would need in his tank with no chances of it running over.   The Correct Measure Pumps were electric, speeding filling and draining and accuracy.

1926

Correct Measure

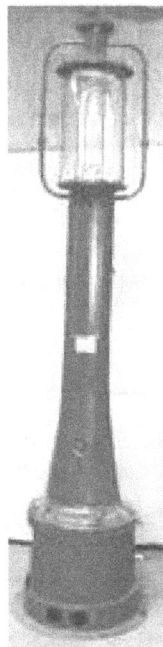

Fry Visible

Wayne Texaco Pump

Another convenience taken for granted nowadays is a radio coming automatically in an automobile or truck. In 1925, there was a branch service business on Pennsylvania Avenue in Monaca for installing radio sets into motor vehicles. The base business was owned by brothers R. Chas. and Harry C. Johnston; the Johnston Bros. of Rochester. They opened the branch business in Monaca in 1925 to continue to accommodate the fast growing demand for installation of the radio sets in Beaver County.

Many of the Monaca garages and service stations tried to handle nationally advertised goods. They found that quality did pay and rather than carry cheap uncertain quality merchandise, the residents preferred quality over quantity. Some familiar names for products in the 1920s were: Mazda lamps, Goodrich tires, Atwater Kent and Grebe radios, Boycite gas, Western Electric products, Eveready flash lights and batteries, Dragon batteries, Englert Cord tires, Hyvis Pennsylvania oils, Mobiloil line products. These same Monaca stations seemed to prefer to purchase the gasoline and oil products through Sutton Oil Company of Monaca and other credited and local distributors such as Chippewa Oil Works.

When was the last time you saw a free road map available in a service station? Free maps were a fixture beginning in 1914. A Pittsburgh advertiser, William Akin, gave his idea for the maps to an oil company. Slowly, over the years from about 1972 on, there was a cost to obtain a map; starting at 5 cents to a dollar and now it costs much more per map. With the expenses involved to print and mostly in the distribution of the maps in modern days, mixed in with the technological improvements and in car navigation devices, the multi folded-paper-"free road map" is gone. There was an estimated amount of over 240 million free maps handed out by oil companies and state highway departments in 1972.

Leaded premium gasoline was also becoming a thing of the past by 1978; it was replaced by super unleaded gas which also had a higher octane quality. The sale of such gasoline was only in the east and Midwest in 1978, but was soon to spread everywhere.

The "Fuel Crisis" was a very serious concern in 1973. There were fears of a gasoline shortage in the late spring and summer of that year. The supply belt was being tightened more and more every day and motorists were being told to "fill 'er up now" and then conserve. Residents were warned about the dangers of trying to "stock pile" gasoline in containers in homes, carrying it in containers in a car, and/or residential garages; explaining the dangers of this practice and telling of how gasoline has a "low flash point." Service stations were closing early or only open on certain days. There was also a great fear of the voluntary Sunday ban turning into a mandatory closing of stations on Sundays because of the shortage. Many station operators were just providing garage services and keeping what gasoline remained in their tanks for their own uses.

There are still garages and service stations out there that ran tried and true to helping and doing things for the motorist and customers, but they are becoming far and few between compared to even 40 years ago in the mid 1970s. Even with the conveniences of modern day computerized equipment and power tools, until you do business with or even have made a visit to a garage or service station that personally pumps your gasoline, checks your oil, cleans your windows, and can personally help with a flat tire or other more minor automotive problems, you will not appreciate how hard working, and most likely personable, the individuals of such garages and service stations actually were and still are.

With all the listings of Monaca's service stations (and all businesses in this book for that matter), many of the addresses and years of being in business may seem to "cross over" with each other. But bear in mind that any intersection of where a street and avenue crossed each other, there are usually four (4) corner lots. For example, when the address may be "Ninth Street and Indiana Avenue", there were actually four (4) corners to chose from that could be listed as "Ninth Street and Indiana Avenue," thus the reason some seem to be during the same years/time periods.

GARAGES and SERVICE STATIONS

W. B. Smith's Service Station – Sixth Street and Pennsylvania Avenue
1924, 1931, 1943
>   Wilbert Smith – owner.
>   Vulcanizing and tire repairs.

_____

The Silk Service Station –corner Ninth Street and Atlantic Avenue
1923, 1932, 1943
>   Opened Dec 1923.
>   Sold Motopower gasoline in 1924.   Sold Canzol Motor Fuel in 1927, 1928.
>   Sold Firestone tires in 1932.
>   A. Lloyd Daugherty worked or owned the store in 1929; then he had his own business on
>   a corner at Washington Avenue and Ninth Street.

_____

Morris Service Station - 390 Sixth Street - Corner of Sixth Street and Pennsylvania Avenue
1935, 1939, 1956
>   Don Morris completely renovated his service station; was to open Jun 10, 1939.
>   First offered Freedom brand gas and oil; then sold Mobil products and sold Firestone tires, too.

TIRES

6x6:16 **$9.95** plus tax

2 Gallon Oil $1.69

Morris Service Station

DON MORRIS, PROP.

6th and Penna. Ave.   Monaca

Jul 1949

1939

This station became Speer's Mobil Service Station by 1960.

Spear's Mobile Service Station – 390 Sixth Street
1959, 1964, 1970, 1976, 1978
        Floyd Speer operator.

_____

Grater & Daughterty Service Station – Ninth Street & Washington Avenue
1936
        By 1940, it was just Daugherty Service Station.

_____

Jack Cameron's Boron Station – 800 block Pennsylvania Avenue

_____

Baker's Service Station – Ninth Street
1937 to 1970s
        Sold Mobilgas and Mobiloil – Goodyear tires – U.S.L. batteries – did repair work.
        Co-owners for 37 years –– David and Florinda Baker.

_____

Grater's Service Station – Ninth Street and Atlantic Avenue
1936, 1940
        Guy Grater, operator.   Sold Atlantic gas & oil, Exide batteries, and Lee tires in 1940.

GRATER'S
SERVICE STATION

Extends Good Wishes To Members of
Council and Other Officials of Monaca on the Occasion of the Dedication
of the New Municipal Building.

GUY GRATER

Atlantic Gas and Oil

Willard Batteries — Goodyear Tires

Ninth Street - Monaca | 1937

GRATER'S
SERVICE STATION
Ninth St., Monaca
Good Service
in a
Good
Town

ATLANTIC
GAS & OIL
•
EXIDE
BATTERIES
•
LEE TIRES   1940

_____

Monaca Service Station – corner Washington Avenue and Ninth Street
Nov 1931
        H. Parsons – manager.

Announcement

We wish to announce to the public of Beaver County the
opening of Monaca Service Station, corner Ninth street and
Washington avenue, Monaca.   You are invited to come
and get acquainted with our service and prices.   Repair
work on all makes of cars.   Batteries recharged.

W. M. KRIGER, Mechanic.
H. PARSONS, Manager.

        Then ....

Pat's Amoco Service Station – corner of Ninth Street and Washington Avenue
1960 to 1997 (in business 37 years)

> Pat opened it in 1960.
> Closed Mar 29, 1997.
> Business was owned by Pat McDonald from 1960; he leased the property.
> - Prior to starting his own business, Pat worked at the old Esso station, then at the Atlantic station (which became Smith's Auto Sales).
> - Pat began his work at the station owned by Avery Smith at 191 Ninth Street (in 2016 Auto Effects); before that he worked at an old Atlantic Station.
> - Pat's met his wife Harriet when he was working at the Atlantic station.
> In 1960, there was but one other employee at this station, William "Butch" Petke of Georgetown.

Photo by Pete Sabella

————

Kohlman Garage – corner Washington Avenue & Ninth Street
1924

> S.P. Kohlman, owner.
> Had a machine shop and car repair garage at 823 Pennsylvania Avenue, too.

————

McCullough Service Station – Indiana Avenue and Ninth Street
1943

> W. B. McCullough operator.

————

Daugherty Service Station aka Daugherty & Son Service Station – corner Washington Avenue and
1940, 1956   Ninth Street

> Lloyd E. Daugherty, owner.

————

Denny's Sunoco Service Station – Pennsylvania Avenue
1976, 1977

————

Roy's Mobil Gas Station – Ninth Street
1954 to 1972

> Owner – Roy Kindelberger of Rochester.

————

Beaver Valley Quick Lube – 198 Ninth Street (corner Indiana and Ninth St)
1996, 2000
       Opened Feb 1996.
       Owned, managed by Jim and Teresa Witkosky in 2000.
       Preventative maintenance services, inspections, emissions, winterizing, tire rotation,
           brake and exhaust replacement, and other minor and major repairs.
       (2016 – Carl's Auto Service.)

FAMILY OWNED AND OPERATED
BEAVER VALLEY QUICK LUBE
198 Ninth Street, Monaca   728-9227
"We don't give you the time to miss your car"
"15 Minute Oil Change"
• RADIATOR FLUSHES
• STATE INSPECTIONS
• Brakes • Tire Rotation • Wipers
• Batteries • Bulls • Hoses
WE ACCEPT
PENNZOIL
WORKS LIKE LIQUID BALL BEARINGS™

1997

————

Ostridge's Station – corner Washington Avenue and Ninth Street
1940
       George Ostridge – owner.

————

Dauler Benzol Co. Station – Ninth Street and Atlantic Avenue
1930, 1931
       Opened Apr 1, 1930.
       On opening day, they gave away one free gallon with a five gallon purchase.

————

F. Edward Garvin was the proprietor of a gas station – location unknown
1930   He lived at 832 Atlantic Avenue in 1930.

————

Derringer's Esso Station – Ninth Street and Indiana Avenue
1936, 1940
       A. W. Derringer – owner.
       His son Park worked with his father at the station.
       Offered complete lubrication service.

————

Probst & Johnston Mobilgas – Sixteenth Street and Pennsylvania Avenue
1952

————

Tony's Sunoco Station – Fourteenth Street and Pennsylvania Avenue
1955

————

Al's Esso Service Station – unknown
1954, 1955

————

McKeel's Service Station – Monaca/Aliq. Blvd (1954), corner Fourteenth Street and Walnut Street
1954, 1956

_____

Lou's Atlantic Service Station –
1987

_____

Hill's Atlantic Service Station – 191 Ninth Street and Atlantic Avenue
1944

_____

Smith's Auto Sales – 191 Ninth Street and Atlantic Avenue (adjacent to the gas station in 1970)
1951, 1968, 1969, 1970, 1977
        Owner/operator – Wilbert Smith in 1951.
        Avery Smith – manager in 1970.
        Emerson Smith also worked at this station.

_____

The Standard Oil Company purchased the corner lot at Ninth Street and Indiana Avenue for erection of a
        service station – the lot was bought from Mrs. Leah M. Mateer – Jun 1930.
Standard Oil Company of Pennsylvania – Ninth Street
1930, 1932
        Erected a large signboard at the station – the placement of this sign prompted the
                Boro to present zoning ordinance that stated such boards would have to be placed
                only in the manufacturing district and at least 100 feet from the sidewalk.   Attny.
                McCreary was to handle having the sign moved from its location near the sidewalk
                to the rear of the property.
        James McElwee was an attendant in 1931, 1932.

_____

Good Gulf Refining Co. Station - one of the corners of Ninth Street and Indiana Avenue
1930, 1936

_____

Shively Service Station – 2030 Beaver Avenue
1940

_____

BP Oil gas station – 711 Pennsylvania Avenue (formerly Keck's Furniture Exchange)
1993, 2000
        Owner – Ed Knox.

_____

Esso Service Station –Ninth Street and Indiana Avenue
1954, 1956
        Owned by Stephen G. Soltes.
        Also mentioned in paper at Pennsylvania Avenue. (This could have been an error.)

_____

Smith's Atlantic Service – Ninth Street and Atlantic Avenue (was adjacent to a used car lot)
1951, 1970
        Wilbert Smith – owner/operator in 1951;   Avery Smith – manager in 1970;
        Emerson Smith, too.

_____

Humble Oil Co. constructed a new service station – corner of Pennsylvania Avenue and Ninth Street
1971, 1972,
>   They did own property at corner of Indiana Avenue and Ninth Street, but it was sold to Fast N
>   Friendly Food Store in 1972.
>   Humble Oil Co. chose to construct their new service station at the intersection of Pennsylvania
>   Avenue and Ninth Street instead.

Exxon Gas Station (formerly known as Humble Oil Co) – corner of Ninth Street and Pennsylvania Avenue
>   Closed prior to Apr 9, 1978.

Colony Federal Savings and Loan Assoc. planned on opening a new office at this location.
They intended to remodel the gas station and install drive up windows.   They planned to close
    their office at 1299 Pennsylvania Avenue once this location was opened for business.
(2016 – this is the site of the Mortgage Solutions twelve sided building).

_____

Sabo's Esso Service – Ninth Street and Indiana Avenue
1964, 1969

_____

Paul & Ted's Super Service – 404 Pennsylvania Avenue (corner of Fourth Street & Pennsylvania Avenue)
1948, 1987
>   This was located as soon as you came through the RR tunnel and made the bend onto
>   Pennsylvania Avenue.
>   Sold Sterling Gasoline & Quaker State Oil.
>   Did tires, batteries, car washing, greasing.
>   US Tires and Batteries.

_____

C. C. McCreary's Service Station – Pennsylvania Avenue
1942, 1943

_____

Julius Carper Station– Pennsylvania Avenue (near Twelfth Street)
1919
>   Opened in Sep 1919.
>   Was the site of a nickelodeon building owned by Abel Finn.

_____

Albert Campbell –/ auto repair –
1920
>   He may have worked for another business or had his own shop.
>   Mr. Campbell lived in Monaca Heights.

_____

Earl Schweinsberg Service Station – Fourteenth and Pennsylvania Avenue
1975   Earl was operator in 1975.
            He gave up the service station to become an officer on the Monaca Police force.

_____

Yolanda's Gas Station – 1501 Pennsylvania Avenue
1994

_____

Beaver Valley Auto Detail – 1501 Pennsylvania Avenue
1997

_____

Boren's Gulf Service – Ninth Street and Indiana Avenue
1929 to 1978
            Began in 1929; Ross Boren was the operator of the station at that time, but didn't
                        own it until 1953.
            Closed Oct 1978.
            Known as "Ross Boren Gulf Service Station" in 1975.
            Just shy of 50 years of service.

Paul's Auto Body Shop – 1227 block Pennsylvania Avenue
1978
            This site is currently Pin Point Custom painting (2016).

_____

Kehna and McCartney Day and Night Towing – 1230 Pennsylvania Avenue
1951, 1955

_____

William's Service – 1742 Pennsylvania Avenue
1965, 1968
            Quaker State products.

_____

Liberatore Service – 1501 Pennsylvania Avenue
1965
    Auto repairs, state inspection.

_____

Swink's Mobil Service Station – Ninth Street and Atlantic Avenue
1948
    Would flush out radiator and block.

WE CARE
SWINK'S AUTO PARTS
AND SERVICE INC.
*Towing Service Available
*Auto Body *Collision
*All Major Insurance Companies
Accepted
775-0791
1800 Penna. Ave., Monaca

1990

STOP
Is your car overheating?
See us for a reverse flush in your
radiator and block . . . Quick Service . . .
SWINK'S Mobile Service
Phone Roch. 9010
9th and Atlantic Ave.   Monaca

Jul 1949

_____

Ray's Sunoco Service – Fourteenth Street and Pennsylvania Avenue
1954, 1956

Famous Kelly Springfield
TIRES
AT THESE LOW PRICES
ALL PRICES ARE PLUS TAX AND OLD TIRES

SIZE	One Tire	Four Tires
600 x 16	8.95	35.80
650 x 16	15.95	62.95
670 x 15	13.95	54.95
710 x 15	14.95	58.95
760 x 15	16.95	66.95

All Kelly Tires
Sold by Sunoco
Carry Our
Liberal 2 Way
Guarantee
Without Limit
Of Time or
Mileage

LIBERAL TERMS   COME IN SOON
ONE WEEK SALE AT
Ray's Sunoco Service
14th & Penna. Ave., Monaca, Pa.
Phone Rochester 9123

1954

_____

Cogis Service Station – 1501 Pennsylvania Avenue (Pennsylvania Avenue and Fifteenth Street)
1987, 1989
    Owned by Steven Cogis of Center Township.   Closed after Aug 1989.
    A company was hired by Pennzoil to remove the gasoline tanks from the station and one of the
        tanks exploded and caught fire putting one worker in very critical condition and the other
        in serious condition.

_____

Red Top Oil Co. Service Station – started at Twenty-first Street & Pennsylvania Avenue; then Sixteenth
1957, 1964, 1968, 1977   Street and Pennsylvania Avenue

_____

Wilson's Garage – Twenty-first Street and Pennsylvania Avenue
    In business Oct 25, 1982.

_____

Paul's Garage – 823 Pennsylvania Avenue
1930, 1937, 1959, 1977
        Paul Salinshick – owner.
                Paul came to America on the vessel Majestic, via Ellis Island, in Feb 1913 from
                        Austria/Hungary and was naturalized in Nov 1921.
                Paul came to Monaca between 1920 and 1930; on the 1940 census and WWII information.
                Registration of 1942, he states occupation as being the owner of an auto garage and
                residence at 823 Pennsylvania Avenue.   Paul was b 1892, d in his 90s.
        Located on what used to be the site of the Monaca Skating Rink – 823 Pennsylvania Avenue.
        Did body and fender work & PA state inspections.
        Ford sales and service.
        The Salinschick family lived at 818 Pennsylvania Avenue in 1930; then when he married Mildred,
                they were in the apartment within the building at 823 Pennsylvania Avenue.

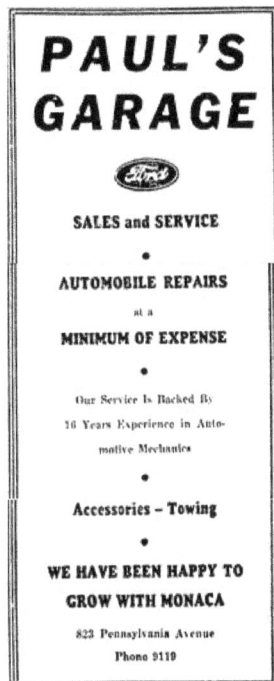

PAUL'S GARAGE

SALES and SERVICE

AUTOMOBILE REPAIRS
at a
MINIMUM OF EXPENSE

Our Service Is Backed By
16 Years Experience in Automotive Mechanics

Accessories – Towing

WE HAVE BEEN HAPPY TO
GROW WITH MONACA

823 Pennsylvania Avenue
Phone 9119

Cain Service Station – just above Twenty-first Street (Beaver or Pennsylvania - on the Monaca-Aliquippa road)
1936, 1937
        In business Feb 24, 1936 (Pgh Post-Gazette).
        Complete service – gas, oils, greasing.
        A trailer truck overturned Aug 6, 1937 and crashed into the station moving it 6 inches off
                its foundation.

Marie Gas Company Service Station – Twenty-first Street and Pennsylvania Avenue
1940s
        In business Jun 28, 1940.
        I believe this was closing soon because there were a few ads starting on Oct 3, 1945,
                that there was an 8 ft long store counter, two ice pop coolers, one ice refrigerator for
                sale at this station.
        Herbert Reynolds (17) was an attendant in 1940.

Falcon Gas Station – Beaver Avenue
1973, 1977
        Charles Fila – manager in 1973.

––––––––––

Zupsic's Pennzoil Station – 1501 Pennsylvania Avenue (corner of Fifteenth Street and Pennsylvania Avenue)
1973, 1978, 1980
        Frank Zupsic, Jr., owner.

ZUPCIC'S PENNZOIL
"11 years in Business..."
1501 Pennsylvania Avenue
⊙ on Map
774-9593
Complete Auto Repairs
Towing and Road Service
FRANK ZUPCIC, Jr., Owner

––––––––––

Verrico Sterling Service Station – 402 Pennsylvania Avenue (Brodhead Road and Pennsylvania Avenue)
1944
        Sold used cars, too.

FOR SALE: Model A Ford coach, model A Ford coupe, both in good condition. Verrico's Sterling Service Station, Brodhead Road and Penna. Avenue, Monaca. Phone Roch. 3457.   3 31   1944

––––––––––

Crescent Oil and Gas Company of Pittsburgh – 1100s Pennsylvania Avenue
                              (between Eleventh and Twelfth Streets)
1904, 1906, 1909, 1912, 1920, 1922
        The company first came to the borough for a permit to lay gas mains in the borough and to furnish the heat and light for the borough.
        Oct 1915 - Had a new brick building erected to be used as the local headquarters of the company.

––––––––––

Johnson Service Station – 1001 Marshall Road
1956

––––––––––

Doc Henry's Service Station – Beaver Avenue
1942

––––––––––

The Public Motomart – 823 Pennsylvania Avenue
1924, 1925
Opened Apr 1924.   W. H. Nash, manager in 1924.
In Jun 1924, the manager reported sales were up since opening.

ANNOUNCING—

A NEW INSTITUTION DEDICATED TO PUBLIC SERVICE

TOMORROW an unique business will be opened at 823 Pennsylvania Avenue, Monaca.

It is a public institution operating without profit.

It is called THE PUBLIC MOTOMART and is one of a national chain dedicated to serving the buyer and seller of used cars operated under the supervision of Percy Chamberlain Associates, Inc., Detroit, Michigan.

Here the car owner who desires to dispose of his automobile can do so with the least inconvenience and obtain the top market price.

Here those who seek full value in a used car can buy in absolute confidence.

The principles and ideals of this institution protect both the buyer and seller of "unused transportation"—its policy is based upon giving maximum service to the public.

And because it is operated without profit it can render this service better than any private organization.

When a car is brought here for estimation, trained men make certain what is needed to bring it to a standard which will assure the buyer a definite value for his money.

The necessary work is done by the dealer who handles the car in this city. His work must be guaranteed.

The owner then is issued a Consignment Receipt which can be used in purchasing a new car or as collateral for a bank loan.

When the car is brought to Motomart Standard, it is placed on the display floor.

All cars carry price tags plainly marked —the prices representing their actual value.

Those who are looking for good used cars can select from a complete stock with every opportunity to make comparisons. They can bring their family or friends here because they will find a clean, orderly place of business that can be visited without embarrassment.

And they can buy in confidence because every car not only looks good but actually is good.

If you are planning on buying or selling a used car, it will pay you to investigate this different institution.

Its manager, Mr. W. H. Nash, is bonded to the public, and it is his duty to see that both buyer and seller get full value.

Come in and see the attractive values at the Motomart.

You will be surprised how little it costs to get a car that looks like new and runs as good as it looks.

COME IN AND SEE THESE ATTRACTIVE BARGAINS

FORDS	GRAY	JEWETT
BUICKS	NASH	OVERLAND
DODGES	STUDEBAKER	CHEVROLET
HUDSONS	ESSEX	AND OTHERS

The PUBLIC MOTOMART

823 PENNSYLVANIA AVENUE   MONACA, PA.

Apr 1924 ad

Jun 1924 ad

Elvidge Service Station –1501-1505 (corner of) Pennsylvania Avenue and Fifteenth Street
1925, 1929, 1940, 1956, 1964
    1927 - it was operated by Wm. Leigh and Geo. McCormack.   Carried Pennzoil gas and oils.
    William R. was the owner-operator; retired in 1964 after 35 years. But I found ad in 1925 ?
        The ad from 1925 stated that the station was "open all night."
    W. R. lived on Atlantic Avenue; he died in 1975.

1940

Boron Oil Co. – 711 Pennsylvania Avenue between Apple Alley and Eighth Street
1971, 1989
      Aug 15, 1972 - the borough granted the Boron Oil Co. a permit to construct a service
            station on Pennsylvania Avenue between Apple Alley and Eighth Street.
            (Keck's Furniture was located on this site.)
      Henry Hughes, manager in 1976.

This would be where (2016) the Citgo station now sits.

_____

Homick's Service Station then Hardy's Service Station

_____

Crescent Fuel & Supply – Pennsylvania Avenue Ext
1931

_____

Fezell's Super Service Station – Pennsylvania Avenue and Brodhead Road
1938, 1940,
      H. J. Fezell – owner.
      Opened this station mid Dec 1938.
      H. J.'s son, William, was the operator of the station.
         (William also ran the Fezell's Linmar Service Station in Aliquippa.)
       "Slim" Hartling and Mike Weber worked with William at the station.
      Sold Quaker State oil .

Fezell's Super Service Station – Pennsylvania Avenue and Brodhead Road

_____

Zig's Service Station – Pennsylvania & Brodhead Road
1942, 1943

_____

Automotive Performance Specialties   aka   APS   - 310 Ninth Street
1977, 1982, 1993, 1996
      Opened 1977 – was at the rear of the building.
      Specialty car parts store, owned by Mark Campbell.

_____

Fath's Body Shop – Fourteenth Street and Pennsylvania Avenue
1940
> Auto painting, fender and body repairs.

_____

AAMCO Transmissions – 1730 Pennsylvania Avenue
1969

_____

Capitol Collision Center – 2100 Pennsylvania Avenue
1990
> Complete collision repair.

_____

Ed. Stoop's Garage – 616 Pennsylvania Avenue
1910, 1924
> Building was razed for the Phoenix revitalization project.

_____

S & S Garage & Body Shop – 616 Pennsylvania Avenue
1956, 1987
> General auto motor repairing – body work & painting – wheel balancing.
> This building was originally Edward Stoops's Livery from 1890s to 1920s.
> Car and tires for sale in 1942 – so it was some type of automotive business.

_____

Monaca Auto Body Shop – 609 Pennsylvania Avenue (corner of Pennsylvania Avenue and Sixth Street)
1941, 1965
> Owned by Graeser Bros. – Bob, Philip, and Red.   Bob started the Graeser Auto Body Shop in 1941.
> The house of Jacob Schaefer was built here in 1830s – it was one of the first Economite
>> homes in town and was torn down in 1961; was located on the same corner.

> Became known as ......

Graeser's Auto Body Shop
1968, 1969, 1983
> Bob and Red Graeser retired from the business in 1983 and the shop was then owned by
>> Tom and Jean Schier, former employees.
> A few other business were in this building after Graeser's closed.
> The building is now home to the Monaca Public Library (2016).

_____

Rowe Roberts Garage – 2400 Beaver Avenue
1969
> Tune-up, Electrical & state inspections.

_____

Gibson's Auto Body Shop – 2456 Beaver Avenue
1956

_____

Monaca Auto Parts and Supplies – 1220 Pennsylvania Avenue and then 1133 Pennsylvania Avenue
1961, 1965
>Opened at 1220 Pennsylvania Avenue in Sep 1961, then........
>>Dec 1962 – the application was made to "officially" start the business.
>Owners – John A. Tufano/Monaca and Willard Morris/ Aliquippa.

**MONACA
AUTO PARTS
NOW OPEN**
9 A.M. TO 6 P.M.
DAILY INCLUDING
SATURDAY
"Where You Buy For Less"
1220 PENNSYLVANIA AVE.
MONACA   1961

———————

Kohlman Garage – 823 Pennsylvania Avenue
1927, 1931
>Owner – S. P. Kohlman.
>>He is listed a few times in this book since he had a machine shop at 823 Pennsylvania
>>Avenue and a station at Washington Avenue and Ninth Street.
>Sold Chevrolet / General Motor products.   He was a machinist.
>1927 - had a 1927 Oldsmobile coach, fully equipped for sale - $1,050.

———————

McKinney's Garage – 1028 Beach Street (just off Eckert Road), Monaca Heights
1946
>R. F. McKinney – owner.

———————

Bumper Mart – 2585 Beaver Avenue
1960s, 2002
>Opened in 1960s.
>Robert Gibson, owner of the business and building had added on to the building
>>over the 20 years it was there.
>Closed that building in 2002.
>2002 building was owned by Robert Gibson.
>A huge fire destroyed the building Jan 1, 2002. The building was empty and up for sale
>>2000/2001, business moved to former Colonial Inn site, a little farther south and on
>>opposite side of road.
>Between 2013 and 2015, what remained of the original and burned buildings was torn down.

———————

Swink's Auto Parts – 1800 Pennsylvania Avenue
1930, Current
>Opened in 1930 – Calvin Swink founded business.
>May 5, 1933 Swink's Auto Parts and Service Inc. was incorporated.
>1977 – business was purchased by Vince Carothers and was again approved to be
>>incorporated on May 26, 1981.
>Additional remodeling and expansion in 1988/89 – manager was Janet McCartney.
>The business sells new and rebuilt auto parts and used cars.

———————

Edgar Folland – private shop – auto repair
1920   He lived at 124 Fourth Street.

_____

A. Howard Brown
1924   Automobile repairing, etc.

_____

Hustler's Service Station - 299 Ninth Street
1928

_____

Beighey's garage –
1939
        Grant Beighey owner.

_____

Elmer W. McCartney Garage – 1230 Pennsylvania Avenue
1956, 1965

_____

Good Ol' Boys Collision & Auto Repair – 1227 Pennsylvania Avenue

_____

International Auto Repair – 417 Fifteenth Street
1977   Willy Muller – owner.

_____

Keystone Service Station – 1742 Pennsylvania Avenue
1928, 1931
        Jack P. White was the mgr./operated this station.
        Ken Kugel (l.) and Edwin Dinsmore (r.) are pictured (1928).

Picture was originally presented by Edwin Dinsmore, Jr. & on file at historical societies.

_____

Jack Moorehead's   aka   Jack Moorehead's Garage –   616 Atlantic Avenue
1956, 1965, 1987

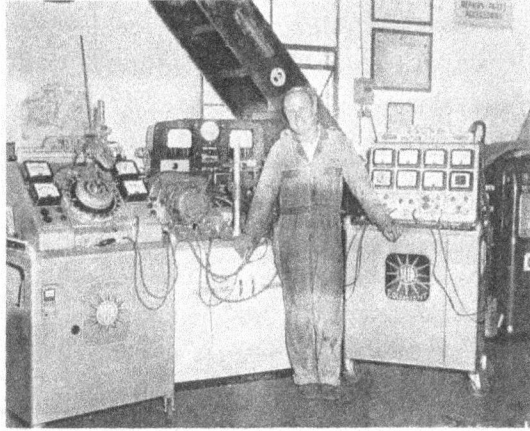

_____

Sherman Motors – automobile merchant business – 1227 Pennsylvania Avenue
1929, 1930, 1931, 1943
        Harry Sherman – automobile merchant.
        He lived at 1228 Pennsylvania Avenue.

_____

Pin Point Customs – 1227 Pennsylvania Avenue – classic car restoration
Current

_____

Monaca Heights Service Station – 1001 Marshall Road
1940, 1943
    then….
Johnson Service Station – 1001 Marshall Road
1956
     then…
Federated Car Care – 1001 corner of Marshall Road and Elm Street
1980s

(2016)

_____

Frick's Service Station – 403 Wagner Avenue / top of Fourteenth Street Hill - Monaca Heights
1940, 1943

_____

Shick's Auto Service – top of Fourteenth Street Hill / 1000 Walnut Street
1951

_____

European Auto – 1230 Pennsylvania Avenue
1984, 1985, 1990, 1992
>   Specialized in foreign car services.   Company owned by Willy Muller and George Stormfels.
>   Started the business in 1970.
>   There was a fire in the building Mar 1984 – destroyed the roof and front of the building
>   and most of the materials inside were burned or water damaged.
>   Willy Muller immigrated to the U.S. from Germany in 1962.

*** *** *** *** ***

AUTO SALES

Stutz Motor Cars – unknown address
1924
>   R. W. Baggs, Prop.

_____

Chas. Wagner, Jr. Auto Sales – 1543 Pennsylvania Avenue
1941

Better see us now, while you can still buy a car on our small down payment plan. Fifty re-conditioned, guaranteed autos to choose from. Chas. Wagner, Jr., Auto Sales. Rochester end. Monaca bridge, and 1543 Penna. Ave., Monaca. Not open for business on Sundays, but drop in and look around.

1941

_____

Bruce Gayle Enterprises – new car broker – Pennsylvania Avenue
1978

_____

Mateer and Wagner Car Sales   then   Mateer Auto Sales – corner of Brodhead Road and Marshall Road
Current   Started business in 1953.

_____

Arienzo Auto Sales – 303 Ninth Street
1986

_____

Monaca Auto Sales – 303 Ninth Street
Current

_____

Mitchell Motor Company - 3228 Pennsylvania Avenue
1919, 1924, 1929, 1930
        David J. Mitchell owner.
        Columbia six star cars, international trucks.   Sold Ajax tires and Star sedans.

Briscoe B, No. 34
Leader of Lightweight Cars
TOURING — ROADSTER   SEDAN — COUPE

The Pilot 6-45
THE CAR AHEAD

Bessemer Heavy Duty Truck
1 Ton 1½ Ton 2½ Ton 4 Ton

Ajax Tires- Cord and Fabric

Mitchell Motor Co.
MONACA, PA.

_____

Cleveland Motor Cars – 823 Pennsylvania Avenue
1924, 1926
        Robert W. Baggs, Prop.   He sold Chandler-Cleveland Motors Corporation cars – "Chandler."
        Most likely part of "The Public Motomart" business that was here.

What is a Chandler car you ask................................

Sold for about $995 in 1926 – 4 wheel brakes, thermostatic water control,
self adjusting spring shackles, air cleaner, oil purifier.

_____

E. E. Groth Motor Sales – 1226-1230 Pennsylvania Avenue
1930, 1940, 1942,
     Their grand opening was held the middle of Jul 1930.
        This was then considered a *super station.*
           (They had show room in Rochester from 1923 to 1930.)
     Sold new and used Plymouth and Chryslers.
     Were approved to put up an electric sign in Jan 1934.
        Did extensive alterations in the building in 1936.
     They had two gasoline pumps which also allowed them to serve as a *pull in* service station, too.
        Also had facilities to wash cars and do oil changes, inspections, service
        department (in rear of the building).
     E. E. Groth was the manager.

E. E. Groth Motor Sales Co. – 1230 Pennsylvania Ave   1940

GUARANTEED BARGAINS
E. E. GROTH MOTOR SALES CO.
1226 Pennsylvania Avenue, Monaca
Phone Rochester 48.

Willys Knight — Willys
Chrysler — Plymouth

1930 Ford coupe	.$350.00
1929 Chevrolet Six coach	350.00
1927 Hupmobile 8 roadster	225.00
1928 Whippet coach	175.00
1926 Oldsmobile coach	125.00
1928 Willys Knight sedan	485.00
1926 Whippet coach	100.00

SPECIALS:
  1926 Chevrolet coach
  Columbia sedan   **$35**
  1926 Chevrolet sedan
Your Choice   1931

Became...................................

Kehna and McCartney GMC Truck Co., Inc. – 1230 Pennsylvania Avenue
1948, 1954, 1956
Opened in 1940s.
Large trucking firm.

Kehna and McCartney GMC Truck Co., Inc. - 1956

*** *** *** *** ***
*** *** ***

TRUCKING

Schachern Trucking Co. – Monaca
1923
> Trucking and transferring – local and long distance moving.

_____

Charles Anderson – 1242 Washington Avenue
1920
> Teamster – general.

_____

Emmett Korenty – teamster – general hauling – 1129 Washington Avenue
1920

_____

W. B. Stoops – R. D. #1 Monaca
1930
> General hauling.

_____

Hugh C. Johnston – 912 Washington Avenue
1923, 1924
> Local and long distance hauling and moving, dump trucks for hire.
> Known for being a local dealer, too.

_____

James Rubino – unknown location
1940
> Trucking company.
> He lived at 1096 Pennsylvania Avenue.

_____

Hunter Atkinson Hauling - 1500 Pennsylvania Avenue
1968

_____

Charles J. Lowery Hauling – 1060 Linden Street, Monaca Heights
1948, 1956
> He advertised excavating cellars was his specialty; all kind of grading and clearing, too.

_____

Truck Technology Training – 1307 Pennsylvania Avenue (Oct 1999), moved to rear 1206 Pennsylvania
1999, 2003, 2007   Avenue
> Founded in Jul 1999.   William Manner, instructor.
> 2003 owners – Steve Krizan/Kruzan and Bill Black.   Also had sites in Leetsdale and at the CCBC.

_____

Ace Transport, Inc. – 1206 Rear Pennsylvania Avenue
(2005, 2006) current
> Opened 2010.   Steve Kritzan/Kruzan of Monaca – owner.
> Transportation services.

_____

Journey Cartage LLC – 1425 Beaver Avenue
2013

_____

Truck Tech Transportation – 1146 Hickory Street
2008

_____

Wm. Herzog Tractor & Trailer Repair – 407 Pennsylvania Avenue then – (in 2015) 4152 Brodhead Road
1974, 1990, 2000, current
      Began business in 1974.
      Diesel repair.

24-HOUR TRUCK REPAIR **HEAVY DUTY WRECKER SERVICE**
WM. HERZOG
TRACTOR & TRAILER REPAIR
407 Pennsylvania Ave., Monaca   728-3596
WE WISH THE COMMUNITY A HAPPY 150th!

      1990 ad

_____

    The following 4 businesses were all housed in one building/structure at 1999 Beaver
    Avenue/Road and all were owned by Sam Piccinini of Rochester.

Rochester Coal and Trucking Company   aka   Rochester Coal, Trucking and Contracting Co.
1953, 1965
      In 1954 did updating/additions to building at 1999 Beaver Avenue; had large plate glass
          windows.
      Owner Sam L. Piccinini.

Rochester Motor Sales – 1999 Beaver Avenue
1954
      Was a Studebaker and Packard Agency.
      Owner Sam L. Piccinini.
      Added Studebaker show rooms and enlarged and improved garage facilities for servicing.

Monaca Mack Sales – 1999 Beaver Avenue
1954
      Had additions to the building in 1954.
      Heavy truck agency.
      Owner Sam L. Piccinini.

The Industrial Piping and Plumbing Company – 1999 Beaver Avenue
1960
      Owner Sam L. Piccinini.
      Did all types of industrial piping, fabricating and maintenance work.

***   ***   ***   ***   ***

MISCELLANEOUS AUTOMOTIVE RELATED BUSINESSES

North Star Transfer Company – located off Rte 51/Constitutional Boulevard
1951, 1961, 1975, 1981, 1983

> They had a "molasses" terminal at this location.
> Was a division of North Star Coal Co., Monaca (barge hauling and railroad hauling company).
> In 1973, there was a serious fire on a barge docked at North Star Coal Co.
> They had a large 15 million gallon storage tank that sat along Constitution Boulevard /
> Rte. 51, between Aliquippa and Monaca. It was used to store molasses which came from
> barges on the river.   There were also two additional tanks that are situated on the very
> edge of the banks of the Ohio River, or actually <u>in</u> the Ohio close to the shore line that were
> owned by the Transfer Company.

> *Fun fact A: The tanks that sat along the boulevard and Elkhorn Road
> were used as water tanks for the P & L E railroad for many years.   In the
> later 1940s or early 1950s, the tanks were then used for storing molasses.
> The molasses was brought in by barges and steam pumps would drain it
> into the tanks.   The molasses was then taken from the tanks and hauled
> out by tank trucks being taken to cattle feed mills in the area to be mixed
> with feed for livestock.*

> *Fun fact B: The name "Elkhorn" was said to have come from the Indians
> of the area because the creek that ties in with Elkhorn Road had so many
> branches to it that it resembled an elk's horn...............thus Elkhorn Run
> Creek and Elkhorn Run Road.*

A & D Transfer Company – Seventh Street and Pennsylvania Avenue
1950

> Owned by Raymond Donaldson of Beaver.   One storey frame structure.
> Totally destroyed by fire in Sep 1950.
> The fire did some damage to six private garages located close to the Transfer Co.

Car Wash – 937-941 Fourteenth Street – top of the hill
> In 1971 it was still Herk's Market.
> Closed c. 2011/2012 – fire department purchased the property.

Leonard Bauers – Junk Dealer – Beaver Avenue
1910

> He resided on Beaver Avenue.

George Otey – Junk Dealer – unknown location
1920   He lived at 110 Atlantic Avenue.

_____

Charles Springer – contractor / oil driller - Colona Heights
1928

_____

Frank Purtle – oil driller
1902, 1903   His wife's name was Adessa; they lived on Ninth Street.

_____

The Dayton Taxicab Company, Inc. – Pennsylvania Avenue - near Seventeenth Street
1923
        Leased the Deidrick Glass Co. plant in late Nov 1923 – one year lease with option to purchase
            property.   They built taxicabs and had a plant in East Pittsburgh also.

_____

Dr. Glass of Beaver County – Fifteenth Street
1987, 1989
        Established in 1979 in Beaver Falls by Raymond Killen.
        Jeffrey Shawger bought the business in Jan 1987 and moved business to Monaca.

*** *** *** *** ***

Recent or Current businesses and/or those with minimal information:

Auto Effects – 191 Ninth Street - Opened in 2000 – Closed 2017.   Owned by Ryan Eichhorn

Ryan's Auto Detailing – 191 Ninth Street

Monaca Auto Sales – 303 Ninth Street   -   Current

Carl's Auto Service – 198 Ninth Street   -   Current

Citgo – 711 Pennsylvania Avenue   -   Current

Anthony's Automotive Inc. – 1230 Pennsylvania Avenue – auto shop, dealer, sales   - Current

COGOs – 1400 Pennsylvania Avenue – gas station   -   Current

D & R Glass of Beaver County Inc. – 1500 Pennsylvania Avenue (417 Fifteenth St.)–auto service-Current

Mike's Pit Stop 1501 Pennsylvania Avenue – garage   -   Current

Geared Up – Motorcycle gear shop - 1416 Pennsylvania Avenue   -   Current

Roger's Kustom Shop – 1500 Pennsylvania Avenue   -   1977, 1980, 2002

Penske Truck Rental – 1501 Pennsylvania Avenue

EJP Machine Inc. – 822 Washington Avenue – auto machine shop

Trans and Auto Rep Express – 2420 Beaver Avenue (auto repair shop)

Trasport Nardick Auto Sales - 2002

Simply Honda – 421 Fifteenth Street - current

*** *** *** *** ***

WHOLESALE   and   GAS COMPANIES

Freedom Oil Works company –
1900, 1907, 1915

> Property of James A. Harvey (of Freedom) was offered $12,500 in late Jan 1900 for his property in Monaca for the Freedom Oil Works company.
>
> In Sept 1928, arrangements were made for a Monaca sports team to use the Freedom Oil Works property in Monaca so they could have a place for home games.
>
> In Aug 1915, there were 3 large businesses that were interested in purchasing a 12 acre plot of the old Freedom Oil Works – what did they mean by "old" ?   Did the Oil Works have just offices in the area by 1915 or had they moved their plant someplace else ?
>
> They celebrated their 50[th](golden) anniversary in Aug 1928 which means they started in 1878 – but where ?

Sutton Gasoline Co.   aka   Sutton Sales Co., Inc. – Twenty-first Street and Pennsylvania Avenue (2000 block), then in 1931 at Pennsylvania Avenue Ext.

1924, 1930, 1940, 1946

> Dorsey P. Burtner of Beaver was the manager in 1942.   Wholesale Oil sales branch.

THE NEW Hi-Test TYDOL Green
Anti-Knock Super-Power Gasoline
AT NO EXTRA COST

DISTRIBUTED IN BEAVER VALLEY BY

THE SUTTON GASOLINE CO.
OF MONACA

With Retail Service Stations at

'hird and Buffalo Sts.,   Third Avenue,
Beaver, Pa.   New Brighton, Pa.
Pennsylvania Avenue,   Riverside Drive
Monaca, Pa.   West Bridgewater, Pa.
Sutton Gasoline Co., Associated Dealers

KRESS SERVICE STATION   J. S. KRZEMENSKI
Beaver Falls and New Castle Highway   Bennetts Run, Beaver Falls, Pa.
Koppel, Pa.   PARAMOUNT TIRE REPAIR CO.
WAGNER & KRIBBS   Beaver Falls, Pa.
Beaver Falls, Pa.   ABRAHAM YOUNG'S SERVICE STATION
REYNOLDS AUTO LAUNDRY   Sunflower Road
New Brighton, Pa.   RICHARD WILSON,
R. C. CALHOON SALES & SERVICE Co   West Bridgewater, Pa.
Beaver, Pa.   MITCHEL MOTOR CO.
JOHNSTON BROS,   Monaca, Pa.
Rochester, Pa.   A. A. WEHR
SNYDER GARAGE   Baden, Pa.
Conway, Pa.   PETER DEFELICE
WAGNER & KRIBBS   Aliquippa, Pa.
Ambridge, Pa.

WATCH FOR THE G R E E N PENNANTS
Save 3 to 5 Cents a Gallon
1928

FLEET WING

A "BIRD" OF A
GASOLINE
There's a surging wave of power in every gallon

Buy at the Sign of FLEET-WING—It Pays!

DISTRIBUTED BY
SUTTON GASOLINE CO.
MONACA

1936

Burrell Oil Company – along the Ohio River, near the end of the P & LE railroad company bridge
1937

> A subsidiary of the Phillips Petroleum Corporation .   Had 250,000 gallon tank.
>
> Tank barges came to Monaca and electric pumps emptied the barges into the large tank.
>
> Then trucks conveyed the gasoline from here to Akron, Ohio and Coraopolis, the two main distributing plants.   There were no regular employees located at the Monaca plant in 1937.

***   ***   ***   ***   ***
***   ***   ***

HOTELS

and

INNS

HOTELS and INNS

While perusing the earlier census, the following names were found and had occupations that stated they were *Inn Keepers*, *Hotel Keepers*, or ran a *Boarding House*.   Researching did not resolve the mystery of where exactly many of these place were located or where these people lived and/or ran their businesses, but again, I felt it important to include them.

1841 Directory

George N. Fisher – hotel keeper

Peter Stupp - "76 Hotel" – hotel keeper

1850 Census

Christian Autrit – inn keeper

Charles Fiatkowski – inn keeper

Henry Metshan – inn keeper

Leopold Duva/Dura – boarding

Charles Schmallhousen – boarding house

1860 Census

Henry Brimbe – inn keeper

George Frank – inn keeper

1869 Directory

Adam Gress – hotel keeper

1870 Census

Amelia Bechtel –boarding

Sarine Durr – boarding

Mary Stewart – boarding

William Bickerstaff - hotel keeper

Cora Marcus – boarding

1880 Census

Alvin M. Bickerstaff – hotel keeper – Hanover Street (William's son)(Hanover became Fourth Street)

Lafayette Graham – tavern keeper – Hanover Street (hotel ???) (Hanover became Fourth Street)

John M. Shroder – tavern keeper – First Street (First Street became Atlantic Avenue)

Shroder's became the Point Breeze Hotel.

See further for additional information and pictures on Shroder's.

1910 Census

Jacob Elinic – Boarding House – unknown location

1920 Census

Mary Harlem – proprietor of hotel in the First Ward – unknown location

She resided in the 800 block of Washington Avenue

*** *** *** *** ***

Farmer's Hotel – about 5 lots in on left side of now Fourth Street (formerly named Hanover Street)
(across the street from the now Monacatootha Apartments)

1870s

Owned by Charles Johnston.

Today (2016), it would be estimated to have been located where #126 to #120 are
on Fourth Street.

Hotel of Cimotti   aka   Water Cure Hotel of Cimotti – 129 Fourth Street

1860s

129 Fourth Street was renamed and became known as Pennsylvania Avenue Ext.

This places it in the vicinity of the Orphan's School across from the German Lutheran Cemetery.

Was one of the buildings once known as Water Cure sanatorium which was then purchased by
Henry Cimotti who used the buildings for the hotel and as a pleasure resort.

His wife Elizabeth, their 6 children, and the domestic help also lived at the hotel.

1866 – it was purchased for Thiel College.

1871 - Property was bought by Charles Martin after the college moved to Greensville and it
became the Central Hotel.

Phillippsburg Summer Resort.

NOTICE to my friends and the public in
general, that the well-known Summer Resort of
H. W. CIMIOTTI'S, in Phillippsburg, Beaver county,
opposite Rochester, is now open for Visitors.

Application for Terms and Rooms, can be made at
my office, No. 100 corner of Fifth and Smithfield sts, or
at the Resort, at Phillippsburg.

je13:1w   F. W. CIMIOTTI.

Ad in Jun 1860 Pittsburgh newspaper.

Central Hotel – 129 Fourth Street (Pennsylvania Avenue)
1871, 1893, 1901, 1902, 1903, 1907, 1911, 1914, 1917

> By 1898, 129 Fourth Street was renamed and became known as Pennsylvania Avenue Ext.
>> This places it in the vicinity of the Orphan's School across from the German Lutheran Cemetery.
> Central Hotel was in business in Jan 1900.
> - Charles R. Martin, proprietor – 1871 to c. 1914.
> - 1892, 1893, 1898, 1903 James Markey was then the proprietor and ran the bar.
>   - James used to be in the shoe business.

There was a bar connected to the hotel.
Maggie Holl was the cook in 1902/03 – she resided in the hotel.
There was an ad for general housework girl in Aug 1907.
In 1911, 1912, Christopher C. Beeler was the proprietor.
The members of the "Little Red Star Band of American Indians" held many group meetings
in this hotel.   They were a group of prominent professional and businessmen, who
frequently donned their war paint and gathered in the Martin "wigwam" for a pow wow.

There was a terrible fire in the building 1917/1918.   The building was destroyed; one person
died in the fire and two people were injured.   An insurance journal stated there was
$20,000 in damages.   Another 1918 journal published on hotels stated that there was
$18,000 in damages done to the building.   C. Bielski was proprietor when it burned.   It
also stated the hotel was a landmark in this part of Pennsylvania and that the building
was used as hotel business for 40 years.   Actually, it was a hotel for closer to 50 years
when you consider when it was the Hotel of Cimotti.

Note - the pointer is showing the visible sign.

When In Monaca Stop at the

Central Hotel.

Best of Accommodations and Special
Rates to Regular Boarders.   The Utmost
Courtesy Extended to All.   Everything
Strictly Up-to-Date.

C R. Martin,   Proprietor.

CENTRAL HOTEL – formerly on Fourth Street, became known as Pennsylvania Avenue (was also former site of the Water Cure and Cimotti Hotel).

In the previous picture of the hotel, the view is from left to right, in the picture above, the view is from right to left. You will still see the same physical features of the building as well as note the sign for the hotel located below the tower structure of the building.

Colonial Inn aka Colona Hotel – 2565 Beaver Road
1935, 1940, 1947, 1969, 1989(?)

      Opened in 1935.

      John Pevek, proprietor in 1938

            (There were several big news items in 1938 regarding and stating that Mr. Pevek was arrested on blackmail charges, but I could not find any follow up stories as to his inocents or guilt.)

      1947 – Proprietor, Keith Ely.

      Mr. Ely and 8 others were arrested in an "alleged Monaca gambling house" raid at the inn.

      1969 owner/operator – Mildred Dravich of Hopewell.

            She was arrested in 1969 for gambling and related offenses in a raid

            (charged with lotteries, traffic in lotteries, and establishing a gambling place).

      Frank Kopecky (of *Frank's Place* on Beaver Avenue) was listed as an owner of this business at some point in time.

        Note: This appears to have been a different business than the Colonial Hotel / Imperial Hotel. This business was at 2565 Beaver Road, while the Imperial had the address of 2701 Beaver Avenue. The years of business varied also ?

New hotel...............(Unknow name)

In late Oct 1902, Chas. E. Garrard, of Hotel Monaca, announced that he was going to build a new hotel. He had purchased the land near the Opalite Tile Works, directly opposite the new proposed P & LE depot. He would use water from an excellent spring. The banquet hall would seat 250. Mr. Garrard was the proprietor of the Hotel Monaca at this time and was organizing a stock company for the erection of the new hotel. He stated that he would have the new hotel erected on special plans prepared by the best architects, and that a special feature would be the large seating in the banquet hall.

This would have placed his soon to be built hotel in the Colona area at that time. From the dates that were found for the Imperial Hotel / Hotel Imperial / Colonial Hotel, I strongly suspect this was the hotel that Chas. E. Garrard built. I found no other mention of any other hotels in the Colona area an that time period, nor any other mention of Mr. Garrard's name being associated with any hotel in that area, not even the Imperial Hotel.

I do know that H. T. Will was the owner of the Hotel Monaca after Apr 1, 1903 which tells me that Mr. Garrard had moved on to other employment.....hummm. He may have never followed through with the construction of the hotel   or   there just may have been nothing news worthy to report between 1902 and 1906 when Mr. Garrard may have been proprietor   or   he may have funded the building of this new hotel and then sold it as soon as it was completed -?-   I simply could find any thing more on this hotel.

Imperial Hotel / Hotel Imperial / Colonial Hotel - Colona – 2701 Beaver Street
1902, 1913, 1928
> Charles Coene was proprietor in May 1906.
>> (I believe "Coene" would have been Charles's last name, but I spelled it exactly
>> as it was in the information I found.)
> David Sunderland – barkeeper at the Imperial Hotel (lived at *Baker's Yards*).
> In business in Jan 1904, Feb 1913, Dec 1909, Dec 1928.
> J. C. Coene, proprietor in 1908. Mrs. J. C. (Olive Mae) Coene was the proprietor in 1910.
>> Olive also is listed as retail liquor handler (in the hotel).
> H. A. Neidergal, proprietor in 1909.
> Had a banquet area and many events were held there.
> Several articles in the news stated fights and stabbings too place there in Dec 1908 and 1909.
> It seems the Imperial Hotel was the scene of many fights and arguments. There were
>> stabbings, fights, shots fired, bricks and stones thrown, etc. In May 1906 there
>> was such a disturbance that Burgess Koehler quickly deputized members of council
>> and some citizens, forty persons in all, to go to the hotel and bring the huge fight
>> under control. This particular incident ended in the arrest of twenty-one
>> "foreigners" who were locked up. This is just one example of some of the problems and
>> occurrences that went on at this particular hotel over the years it was in business.

Hotel Monaca – corner of Ninth Street and Washington Avenue (300 Washington Avenue)
1898, 1902, 1912
> Let me start off with saying this was NOT the old Carey building, not what many people knew as the
> "Monaca Inn/Monaca Hotel," nor the current P Dubs. The building that housed/houses all these
> businesses is on the corner at Ninth Street and Pennsylvania Avenue.
>> The true *Hotel Monaca* building*, still standing in 2016, is the much larger building located on the
>> corner of Ninth Street and Washington Avenue.
>>> *MANY refer to this building as being the one Phoenix Glass owned if this helps clarify which
>>> building was the first/true *Hotel Monaca.*

The Hotel Monaca opened in 1898. There is still a visible keystone above the front door between the 2nd and 3rd storey windows.

Built by Paulus E. Koehler in 1898 and he was the proprietor for 2 years; then he sold it sometime in 1900 to 1902. In 1911, Paulus Koehler was a next door resident to the side of Hotel Monaca. (826 Washington Avenue).

The hotel had lofty rooms and offices. It was originally a four storey building, 86 x 46 feet in Dimension, and contained 50 large rooms.

The hotel would have been a very nice business in its day. There was a bar room accessible from Ninth Street. (That former entrance has been removed and replaced with a window.)

The hotel had its own dining area, cooks, and waitresses. Articles mention entertainment in the hotel ballroom. Chambermaids were employed to keep the rooms clean.

The interior appears to have been of the finest décor with architectural detailing (archways), rooms with transoms doors, large ornate wooden banisters on the stairways, and even linoleum floors in the hallways.

> *Fun Fact: In the early 1900s, linoleum for the floors was very much more costly in comparison to using marble.*

The rooms in the building on each floor that faced out over the corner of Ninth Street and Washington Avenue were noticeably larger than the others.   Articles on the hotel also indicate the guests had direct access to the theatre / opera building's area in the adjoining building.

Many local news articles indicated that numerous guests of the hotel did not just stay overnight, a weekend, or even an entire week, but were instead were usually long term residents of the Hotel Monaca and appeared to have stayed for months (possibly years) at a time.   There were many indications of business men/other proprietors who had their contact information directed to them with the "Hotel Monaca" as their place of residency.

> **I even found a few notices of natural deaths occurring while individuals were living at the hotel.   This would explain some of the "unusual" activity that has been reported occurring within the structure.*

William Peacock was the next proprietor of hostelry.   Due to William's ill health ……….

Charles C. Finch became proprietor on Jan 2, 1900.

J. F. Bixby, of Rochester, succeeded C.C. Finch as the proprietor of the Hotel Monaca as of about Feb 1900.   J. F. Bixby lived at the hotel while he was owner.

Feb 1902, Charles E. Garrard became the proprietor and lived at the hotel.   Charles E. purchased a site and began organizing a stock company for erection of a new hotel opposite the Opalite Tile works and directly opposite the proposed new Pittsburgh and Lake Erie Railroad depot (Colona area). This new hotel was to have 250 person banquet hall and drinking water from a nearby natural spring (which the town was once famed for—*Water Cure*). I found nothing else for this proposed hotel but there was a new Imperial Hotel built in Colona, this may have been Mr. Garrard's. (See previous information on the Imperial Hotel.)

H. T. Will was the owner of the Hotel Monaca after Apr 1, 1903.

- o   Modernly equipped, sanitary, plumbing throughout, everything new and clean.

Charles Javens, W. Bridgewater and A. F. Dietz, Pgh wholesale liquor dealer, owned the hotel.

Then W. H. Earn was proprietor for several years until Apr 1, 1910 when it went to Carl Herbert.

In 1912, there was an ad for a cook and another article stated Carl Herbert was proprietor.

Citizens National Bank was located in the Opera House block building, which when built, butted against the hotel building; there was direct access between the buildings for the convenience of the hotel guests. (The Citizens Nat'l. Bank building became the home of Campbell/Mayflower business; and today it houses the Ball Furniture business.)

Even when the Hotel Monaca was thriving in its business days, the newspapers made mistakes in its name. The error in the name was made when it was called *Monaca Hotel* in paper Nov 12, 1910. The article stated that it was located on the corner of Washington Avenue and Ninth Street and was sold from W.H. Hearn to Carl Herbert of Pittsburgh; this would definitely make it the "Hotel Monaca".

Again, I stress, the "Hotel Monaca" and "Monaca Hotel/Inn" were two different businesses and located on opposite corners (the *Monaca Hotel/Inn* was located on the opposite corner at 899 Pennsylvania Avenue).

J. T. Cashbaugh, proprietor in Mar 1917.

Phoenix Glass Co. purchased the Hotel Monaca property the first of Jan 1926 and planned to do improvements and move offices to the building. The former bar room was to be used as a lunch room.

In Feb 1983, Phoenix donated the now three-story* building, at the corner of Ninth Street and Washington, to the Borough of Monaca, who in turn sold it.

A fire destroyed the fourth storey of the building and it is now a "flat roof" structure.

Former Citizens' Nat'l. Bank / Campbell-Mayflower building on the left; Hotel Monaca on the right.
Both buildings are still standing, but due to a fire, the present day former
hotel building is missing the fourth floor and now has a flat roof.

This is a very poor picture of the Hotel Monaca, but it does show the fourth floor. Note all the striped awnings and the fourth floor.

c. 1910/1911

Modernly Equipped.   Sanitary Plumbing Throughout.

Hotel Monaca,
CHAS. B. GARRARD, Prop.

Everything New and Clean.   Monaca, Pa.

Feb 1902

Carl Herbert
Proprietor

HOTEL MONACA
Rates--$2.00 Per Day

Forty-Five Newly Furnished Rooms
With All Modern Conveniences

YOUR PATRONAGE IS SOLICITED
Both Phones

Sep 1911

This was from an old postcard - *Hotel Monaca*

The original post card was in color.   The front door was a nice wooden door.
There was a separate entrance to a bar area also (see pointer).
This post card also includes the now missing original fourth floor.
(Awnings on the front of the Citizen Bank Building (on the left of the picture) were bright red and white striped.)

Little Beaver Historical Society   Hotel Monaca, corner of Ninth Street /Washington Avenue

You cannot see the entry door to the bar area, it is out of the range of this picture, but it was on the left
of the window that has "BAR" on it.
The persons in the carriage are evidently quite affluent...... note their clothing and hats, the pipe, the blanket
over their lap, and the lady is holding a smaller dog, not to mention the fine horse and the carriage is
quite stylish also.

This is one of the still existing staircases of the hotel reflects the elegance
of hotel in its heyday.   The steps were of wood and the floors were covered
in Linoleum.

There were archways throughout the hallways.

This is a sample of one of the doorways to most of the rooms in the hotel. Note the transom window.

The transom windows in the Hotel Monaca were done in the style of the Victorian Era (1837-1901) which was reflected in the hardware attached for opening and closing.

Example of hardware that was used on the transom windows in the hotel.

This was the original safe used in the Hotel Monaca.

Hamilton Hotel - corner of Pennsylvania Avenue and Twelfth Street – 1199 Pennsylvania Avenue
1903, 1906, 1910, 1912, 1917-1919

     S. D. Hamilton, owner.

     Broke ground Dec/Jan 1903.   Opened Jul 4, 1903.   Earl Bros. of Monaca (architects)
         designed new hotel.

     There was a bar in the hotel.   Had basement wallpapered in Dec 1906.

     Was a licensed house continuously from 1903.

     S.D. Hamilton proprietor in Mar 1917.   He had been a painter in 1902/1903.

     Had a barber shop area in the basement.

     Was opposite Michael Leary's pool and billiard room.

     Referenced as Hamilton Hotel building in 1919 – had house beside it then.

     The building was no longer used as a hotel by or prior to Jul 10, 1919 because the Eagles
         purchased the building on that date for their club house/lodge.

         They evidently had a smaller building very close to the hotel building and wanted to have
         more space.   (There was an ad in May 1903 that stated the Monaca Aerie 4121, Fraternal
         Order of Eagles originally had their lodge "2 doors from Hamilton Hotel.")

     c. early 1900s   Photo courtesy BCHR&LF

The building has changed very little in appearance from 1903 and is still standing.
     Note the lettering on the left front window – *BAR*.   Also note the building to the left
     of the then Hamilton Hotel.   This building is no longer there, it is just an empty lot.

     facing Pennsylvania Avenue   2015   Twelfth St

_____?____ Hotel

I found several references to people staying or going to a hotel and restaurant at the corner of Eighth Street and Indiana Avenue.   But I could not find a name, owners, or other information for this hotel.   I suspect this may be references to the former George Lay Building but have nothing to justify that suspicion.

If in fact this unnamed hotel was actually the George Lay Building..............
>   It was owned and operated by George Lay.
>   George Lay came to Phillipsburg with Maximillian – he married Mary Baker.
>   The building was built by George Lay and would not have been used as a hotel for any length of time.   The Lay Building was used for many other purposes beginning at least by Nov 1903.

Monaca Inn often called Monaca Hotel
>   – 899 Pennsylvania Avenue (there in 1948 – still had guests in 1987)
>   NOTE – I know I keep repeating myself, but it is important to understand the differences ----- this was NOT the same as the "Hotel Monaca."
>   Both the "Hotel Monaca" and the Carey /Monaca Inn/Hotel buildings are still standing (2017).

This building was originally a grocery store and the site of the building was referenced for many years as Carey's corner.   It was by no means a true hotel although it did have sleeping rooms after the first floor became strictly a bar and grill area.

Changed name to *Monaca Inn* in 1972 – had a bar room in front corner of building and was renting rooms in 2001.   I did not speak to the current owners, but was told rooms are still available.

Although not a true hotel, after the building at 899 Pennsylvania Avenue (corner of Ninth Street and Pennsylvania Avenue) was no longer being used for a grocery business or a clothing business, nor had a family occupying it, the downstairs became more of a bar and grill with individual rooms on the 2nd floor being available to rent.

This building is now the P-Dub's Sports Bar business; very little change has occurred to the general outside appearance of this historic building.

>   (See Grocery section, as well as Restaurants and Bars section for a picture and more information on former businesses in this buiding.)

Shrode's Hotel – Phillipsburg
at least in 1870, 1876, 1880
    This hotel was built on the corner of First Street and Lacock Street.
                        (now Atlantic Avenue and Sixth Street)
    Was later best known as **Point Breeze Hotel** on Atlantic Avenue.

SRODE'S HOTEL. PHILLIPSBURGH. BEAVER CO. PA.
. P.O. WATER CURE, BEAVER CO. PROPRIETOR CAP'N JOHN. M. SRODES .

PUBLISHED BY
J. A. CALDWELL,
Condit, Ohio.
1876.

ENGRAVED, LITHOGRAPHED & PRINTED BY OTTO KREBS, PITTSBURGH, PA

Then became................

Point Breeze Hotel – corner of Atlantic Avenue and Sixth Street – 604 Atlantic Avenue
1883, 1893, 1902, 1903, 1904, 1912

> Two storey frame building.
> Built by John M. Srodes who was a river captain for many years.
> Mr. Srodes operated the hotel for many years and sold it to Tommy Lee in 1883 who
> sold it to Samuel Love in 1891.
> The Love family had a portion of the hotel that was their home. (1901)   (Mrs. Christina Love)
> Thomas C. Love was bartender in hotel in 1892, 1893 and then owned the hotel in 1902/03
> Thomas married Elizabeth__; they resided at the hotel.
> John Jacox was bartender 1902/03 – resided there.
> The license at the Point Breeze Hotel expired Mar 31, 1904 and Thomas Love, the proprietor
> did not apply for a renewal of license.
> Called "formerly Point Breeze Hotel" in Jul 28, 1910 when Miss Love's estate was being
> settled but……. in 1912 – ad for 17 yr old girl wanted to do housework in the hotel ???
> There was a fire in former hotel building in Mar 1981.
> It was being used as apartments and was heavily damaged by fire in Dec 2007.   The charred
> building was later torn down and now is just an empty lot.

Old Point Breeze Hotel, Monaca, Pa.

Valley View Hotel – Sylvan Crest (Center Township)
1953, 1958, 1971
> This hotel sat on the edge of Center Township and Monaca Borough, so I decided to include
>> limited information on it.   The building itself tied in to Monaca information since
>> the hotel was original the home built by the Welch family who owned and operated
>> the brick yard in Monaca, then after several other owners, was converted to a hotel.
> The building was still standing in Nov 1979; property owned by Louis Pappan since 1972.
> Sunday, Mar 30, 1981 – there was a horrible fire that destroyed the three storey brick building,
>> home of the former Valley View Hotel.   It was eventually razed and there are now
>> private homes on the property.

Photo – BCHR&LF
 These photos show views of the modified Welch house as it stood empty.   After James Welch, it was
owned by Mr. Tener, then Robert Garland as their summer homes, then several other owners and lastly was
modified to become the Valley View Hotel.   It commanded a wonderful view of the valley and the rivers being
situated on the edge of the hill at the top of the Sylvan Crest area; the structure could be seen from
Rochester and Beaver.

Kobuta Hotel – Rte. 18 (Potter Township)
1949 to 2013
> It sat along Frankfort Road (Route 18) in Potter Township.   Considered near Bellowsville, Kobuta
>> was its own small community and even had a post office for a period of time
> This establishment became most popular for the bar and grill area on first floor; eventually
>> had more of long term, lower income apartments on the second floor rather than a true
>> hotel.

1908 - David Fisher had a tenant house that was on the river bank at the old ferry boat landing. He moved it to
the top of the bank along Atlantic Avenue the beginning of Jun 1908.   I do not have a name or address or further
information.

N. Wurzel was report as having a hotel built on Pennsylvania Avenue – unknown address
1903   I did not find anything else on this hotel; plans may never have developed.
> N. Wurzel was also a real estate agent at this time. (He must have been a quite diverse
>> individual because in 1898 he was also listed under hardware dealer along with
>> several other enterprises.)

*** *** *** *** ***
*** *** ***

Jewelers

Insurance Agents, Real Estate Agents, Brokers

Travel Businesses

Attorneys at Law

Billiards / Pool Rooms / Arcades / Bowling

Newspapers and Newsstands and Printing

JEWELERS

Fred Patton – Sparling Building / corner of Sixth Street and Pennsylvania Avenue), then Keystone Block
Building on Pennsylvania Avenue in 1903

1900, 1901, 1902, 1903, 1906
   Opened a jewelry repair shop in the Wurzel Building on Pennsylvania Avenue
   Earlier in 1904 he redecorated the interior of his store.
   He disposed of his business in Dec 1906 when he secured a position of foreman at J & L steel.
   He had his store and residency in part of the Mateer Bros. Meat Market, but had moved out
       by Apr 5, 1907.
   He was listed as proprietor of a Jewelry Store and was a watchmaker.
   Fred married Vesta Baker of Monaca in the fall of 1904.
   Fred was the chief of the fire department in 1906.

_____

John A. Zarrillo – 1000 Pennsylvania Avenue (would have been where Municipal Bldg now sits-2016)
1949
   His business was in jewelry and watch repairing.

JIM'S RADIO
AND ELECTRIC REPAIR
John A. Zarrillo
JEWELRY — WATCH REPAIRING
LUCI'S STUDIO
YOUR PHOTOGRAPH AND SUPPLIES
Phone Rochester 2246-J
1000 Penna. Ave.   Monaca

Jul 1949

_____

Rupley's The Jeweler – 923 Pennsylvania Avenue
1908, 1909, 1912
   All ads stated "See our window."
       (Thad's Jewelry moved into the building.)

JEWELRY
Guaranteed as represented and
we back up that guarantee.

Watch and Clock Repairing
Guaranteed One Year.

FREE.
All goods sold engraved free.

See our window.

RUPLEY,
The Jeweler,
MONACA,   PA.

Cut Glass
Sterling Silver
Silver Plated Ware
Novelties—suitable
for card and other
parties
Clocks, Etc.

JEWELRY
Quality Style Price
must be considered when purchasing Jewelry. The RUPLEY Jewelry is moderately priced, has dis-
tinctive style, unusual quality.

S. M. RUPLEY
JEWELER
923 Penn Ave.   Monaca
Opposite the City Building.

A Full Line to
Choose from--

WATCHES
FOBS
BRACELETS
RINGS
LOCKETS & CHAINS
PENDANTS
CUFF LINKS
SCARF PINS
BROOCHES
BAR PINS
HAT PINS
SILVER PURSES
Etc.

1911

Thad's Jeweler's – 922 Pennsylvania Avenue - in the Penn Theatre Building (until at least 1957)
        – 1000 Pennsylvania Avenue in 1960   - then 923 Pennsylvania Avenue
1953 to 1998
        Opened in 1953.   Closed – Sep 30, 1998.
        Thad and Vera Konetsky, owners.

This is photo of his first store in 1953 on one side of the Penn Theatre building .   In 1953, the Penn Theatre building had Thad's on the left, the theatre marquee and entrance in the middle, and a dry cleaning shop on the right.   (Boro bldg would be on the left of this bldg.)

Later in the 1950s/early 1960s, his second store was located on the left of the municipal building --that building was torn down for parking lot so he had to purchase a new storeroom.

2nd location – note the boro building is on the right of his store location.

The building of Thad's 2nd location was torn down and the borough put in a municipal parking lot.   (Eventually the current municipal building was built on the site.)

By late 1961 or in 1962, his next business building was across the street and about
½ block down at 923 Pennsylvania Avenue.

This storeroom is now Clip and Cuddle.

From 1961 through the next few years, they added on to the rear of the building, little by little, and it now reaches the alley in the back. The new building's front appeared the same as it does today. Thad did intricate watch and jewelry repairs in the rear shop of the building.

1960

J. P. Johnston – ½ block from post office (which in 1906 would have been at the Keystone Building)
1906
J. P. was a jeweler and an optician.

_____

Dr. Herbert "Bert" Searight Malone - at 1218 Pennsylvania Avenue
- at 1108 or 1110 Pennsylvania Avenue by 1929
1902, 1903, 1930, 1931, 1934, 1943
On Pennsylvania Avenue in 1902/03
Bert was a jeweler, watchmaker, and repaired clocks; he also picked up and delivered.
A 1929 ad in a yearbook has him listed at 1110 Pennsylvania Avenue.
Bert owned and operated a jewelry store and he practiced optometry (was in business in 1933).
He lived at 1331 Indiana Avenue in 1912.
About 1934, he sold this jewelry business and it became McNees Jewelers (see further), but
Dr. Malone continued to practice optometry – eventually moving his business to Rochester.
In 1955, he received a plaque in recognition of 55 years' service as an optometrist from
the Beaver Valley Optometric Forum of the Pittsburgh Optometric Society.
In Jan 1919, H.S. Malone's jewelry store windows displayed a soldiers' art gallery and curio hall.
He had pictures of many of the Monaca and other Beaver County men who participated
in the great world war; it was principally of the "boys who went over there." Some were
finished in colors and encased in gilt frames. There were numerous relics of the war
that had been sent or brought over by the soldier boys as well as articles purchased by
them while they served in Paris and other European cities.
While in Monaca, Dr. Malone served on the School Board, was a member of the Knights of
Pythias, and Odd Fellows Lodge.

Former Malone & McNees building - 1108 Pennsylvania Ave.

1918 ad

_____

McNees Jewelry/ McNees Jewelers – 929 Pennsylvania Avenue
and 1108 Pennsylvania Avenue (at least by 1990)

1934, 1990, 1994
   Established in 1934.
   First owned by Herbert Malone from at least 1903 until 1930s.
   Owned by Glenn E. McNees until 1958, then Wilbur McNees, Sr.
       o G.E. McNees was jeweler and watchmaker.
   The building was located adjacent to what became best known as the Monaca Men and Boys
       store.
   As of 1994 McNees Jewelers had been in business 60 years.

McNEES
JEWELERS

Jewelers & Watchmaker
1108 Pennsylvania Ave.
Monaca
775-1879
"Family Owned Since 1934"

1990

BULOVA
AMERICA'S *Greatest* WATCH VALUE
Only $33⁵⁰
Quality Always

G. E. McNEES
Jeweler — Watchmaker
Penna. Ave.   Monaca

Jul 1949

1940

Original look of the front of the store.

***   ***   ***   ***   ***

INSURANCE and REAL ESTATE AGENTS

The majority of insurance agents in the 1800s and 1900s appear to have conducted their businesses from their homes; yet a few did have offices. Even as early as the mid 1800s, I found it interesting that they realized the need for insurance protection. Although I did not find listings for the costs of insurances, nor exactly what any particular policy would have covered, there were many mentions of "the insurance covering" the cost to replace merchandise or repairs from fires or other accidents. This tells me that the policies were most likely worthwhile for store and building owners to have purchased.

As with the insurance agents, the majority of the real estate agents in the 1800s and 1900s also appear to have conducted their businesses from their homes and still others had separate offices. As the demand for permanent residences and homes increased with the growth of Monaca, so did the real estate businesses. The real estate agents found an income in this type of business prospering for quite a period of years with all the supply and demand. It became much harder in the later years to have a solid business, so the number of agencies began to decline. Some of the businesses were combined to include real estate and insurances.

It is also logical that with all the mills and bigger businesses that settled in Monaca, these same men who were in the real estate and insurance businesses would have taken the opportunity to have a more steady source of income; this is when I believe the "thinning of the herds" occurred. It is also logical that many of the men would have most likely held on to their insurance and/or real estate business and conducted it during hours they were not working at another job. Another reason for the drop in individual real estate agents was due to their joining national franchise firms.

In Oct 1911, there were only 3 local real estate and insurance offices.
        Trumpeter and Malone, Henry Miksch, and H. L. Grimmell.
Also in 1911, the Monaca Council was renewing their fire insurance and decided to be fair, would be dividing it among all three of these businesses.

_____

Henry Cimotti – broker and insurance
1860

_____

O.H. Locke Agency – 1231 Pennsylvania Avenue
        O. H. Locke Agency was founded in 1898.

    Offut H. Locke – owner/operator
    1898 to 1955
        There were apartments above the business that the Locke family moved into in 1926 when
            they moved from Woodlawn and O. H. purchased H. L. Grimmell's business that was
            at this same location.

    John M. Paraniuk, owner /operator from 1955 to 1981.
    1955 to 1981   John acquired the agency from O.H. Locke and kept the name.

    Both Locke and Paraniuk conducted real estate, insurance, and notary business.

_____

John E. White – Insurance Agent – res Washington Avenue
1900
        John E. was the son of Arthur and Angelina White; he was living with them in 1900.
        In 1910 he was living on Pennsylvania Avenue; married Mary __; states his occupation
            as *laborer.*

_____

Frank L. Wilson & Co. – Pennsylvania Avenue
1902, 1903
>This business was listed as real estate and insurance dealers.
>
>1902/03 – F. L.'s wife was Anna E._; they lived on Pennsylvania Avenue (at the same address as the business).
>
>Moved from this building to G. A. Friebe's building (the barber).
>
>In 1903 – F. L. moved their offices to the 2nd floor of the Eckert building.

_____

John Taylor –real estate - unknown location
1900
>He lived on Pennsylvania Avenue.

_____

John M. Kirk – real estate office – Pennsylvania Avenue
1902/1903
>John's wife was Margaret M.; they lived on Atlantic Avenue.

_____

J. D. Anderson –Keystone Block building
1907
>He was an insurance agency and had a notary office.

_____

George Cooper – unknown address
1902, 1903
>George was an insurance agent; lived on Indiana Avenue.

_____

Edison Martine – unknown address
1930,
>Insurance agent; he resided at Indiana Avenue.

_____

John Sladic – Colona
1929
>Listed as an insurance agent.

_____

Felix Lay – unknown address
1892, 1893
>Listed as a real estate agent.

_____

Jas. M. Irons – Pennsylvania Avenue
1892, 1893, 1898. 1903
>He was also a dealer in carpets, wall paper and stationery items, as well as an insurance agent.

_____

The Monaca Realty Co. – 1231 Pennsylvania Avenue
1907, 1908

Sold real estate, rentals, fire insurance for homes.

This was a newly form organization comprised of all interested professional and business men of Monaca.

Their first meeting was at the Hotel Monaca the last week of Jul 1907; it was poorly attended due to short notice, so another meeting was scheduled for Aug 2, 1907.

The group of men who were interested in forming this organization planned for it to be one the most successful realty companies in the county.

It was decided that the stockholders in the company were limited to ten shares of stock which was the highest that any of them can hold.

Mr. Charles A. Dixon was one of the members/stockholders.

This organization was evidently short lived because H. L. Grimmell occupied the building by Sep 8, 1908.

_____

Howard L. Grimmell – 1231 Pennsylvania Avenue
1908, 1912, 1926

Was the successor to The Monaca Realty Company.

Howard was listed as an insurance agent.   He had his office newly painted in Sep 8, 1908.

In 1912, a directory stated his business and home address as being at 1219 Pennsylvania Avenue.   He was also listed as married to May __ in this same directory.

In 1926, he sold business to O. H. Locke and Mr. Locke continued the business at same location.

Everything in
Real Estate

I Sell, Exchange, Lease or Manage Real Estate

How about that property you have been trying to sell for years? I can find you a quick cash purchaser.
Or perhaps you have been looking for a nice home or a pleasant farm. My list is large and I can please you.

FIRE INSURANCE DEPARTMENT

An Insurance Agent is known by the Companies he keeps.

I offer for your selection the leading underwriters of the United States including the

Hartford Fire,   Royal,   Germania, Delaware,

Pittsburg Underwriters,

National Union,

Milwaukee Mechanics', and

Fidelity-Phoenix of New York.

Monaca Means Business.   Satisfactory Realty and Insurance Business Means

Howard L. Grimmell
MONACA.   Both 'Phones.

1911

_____

Trumpeter & Malone – unknown address
1911

Real estate agents.

_____

G. E./Gilbert Trumpeter – real estate and insurance business - 1236 Pennsylvania Avenue
1903, 1915, 1940, 1967
>In 1912 the address given was 1216 Pennsylvania Avenue, I thought this may have
just been a misprint, but then it was reported that he moved from another building
to the newly completed one at 1236 Pennsylvania Avenue the first of Jul 1922.
>Gilbert b 1869; married Lydia Barton and Marie Muller.
>In 1912 and 1920, Gilbert and Lydia lived on Atlantic Avenue.
>Gilbert (son of William and Mabel) worked in market gardening with his brothers until 1901 then
went into real estate and insurances which he did until his death – 1929.
>Gilbert b 1908; married Evelyn; they lived on Indiana Avenue.
>The building at 1236 Pennsylvania Avenue address also housed the CAMMAR financial institute.

ACRE FARMS FOR GARDENING PURPOSES.

Our acre farms are a good proposition, especially for the man who has industrious children. There are so many ways in which he can make an acre of land profitable, aside from leaving plenty of room for shrubbery and lawn. One of the ways we might suggest would be to raise flowers for sale. In this you would have practically no opposition, and you would soon have a large list of customers who would pay you good prices for a nice bouquet of flowers twice a week. A piece of ground 30 by 30 has been made to produce $30 in sweet peas alone. One girl, 14 years old, wanting to help a Monaca church and not having any money, sold $75 worth of flowers in three months, and what has been done by others can be done by you. There are so many ways one can make money when they have the land. Our acres are very reasonable in price and terms. For further information see the agent.

GILBERT TRUMPETER
Both Phones.   Monaca.

1913

––––––––

Nicholas Wurzel, Jr. – Real estate & insurance business - Pennsylvania Avenue (near Twelfth Street)
1901, 1907, 1910
>Prior to 1907, location of Wurzel's office is unknown, but in Jul of 1907 he moved into
his new office building on Pennsylvania Avenue.   He handled Hartford Fire Insurances.
>He was married to Theresa __; they resided at the same place as business in 1902/03.
>The name of Nicholas Wurzel was found connected to many different businesses.....
>Among these -- in 1898, a directory had him listed as a hardware dealer; in 1911
an article stated he was enlarging a pool room.

N. WURZEL,
Real Estate & Insurance.

$1,700—Lot corner of Pacific avenue and Fourteenth street, two alleys. A bargain on easy terms.

Pennsylvania Ave.,   MONACA, PA.

1903

––––––––

Western & Southern Agents
1965
        J. F. Berrigan, Manager in 1965.

_____

Burton D. Brubaker - Western & Southern Insurance Co. – 1555 Virginia Avenue
1934, 1965, 1990   Began in 1934.

_____

John Antoline –
1967 until 1984
        Began insurance business in 1967; handled National Life and Accident Insurance.
        John quit the insurance business to open a news stand business in 1984 – "Main Street News."

_____

William J. Miller Real Estate & Insurance – 907 Pennsylvania Avenue – then 203 Ninth Street (in 1953)
1929, 1930, 1945, 1953, 1954, 1967

1945

        This building was one of three razed for a new Dairy
    Queen at the corner of Ninth Street and Pennsylvania Avenue.

_____

Eberhardt Insurance Agency - 203 Ninth Street (1953)   - 316 Tenth Street (Dec 1956)
1951, 1956, 1970s   – 927 Pennsylvania Avenue
        William J. Eberhardt – proprietor; Geo. Gremer/broker.

1953 ad

_____

Mark Gudalis – 829 Pennsylvania Avenue
>Had his insurance business at this location for many years . The building was
>empty in 2015.

_____

Wm. H Heckerman Agency – 1009 Indiana Avenue
1955, 1960

_____

John C. Ramer – broker –Washington Avenue
1931

_____

Oscar W. Wolfe – 318 Ninth Avenue
1922, 1950, 1972, 1990
>Handled State Farm Insurances.

Like a good neighbor State Farm is there.
See me for car. life & health insurance
OSCAR W. WOLFE
318 Ninth Ave., Monaca
775-2531
State Farm Insurance Companies
Home Offices Bloomington Illinois

1990 ad

_____

Earle W. Timmons–broker – first on Indiana Avenue, then Penn Theatre Building at 922 Pennsylvania Avenue
1929, 1931

_____

Joseph Frank Insurance – 1012 Pennsylvania Avenue (Keystone Block Building)
>Insurance Agent – 2014.

_____

Bonnie Diamond – 1231 Pennsylvania Avenue
>Insurance agent – 2014.

_____

Rebecca Miller – 1206 Pennsylvania Avenue
Current
>Farmers insurance agency.
>(Ace Transportation, Inc. was or is in the rear 1206 Pennsylvania Avenue – 2014.)

_____

Nationwide – Center Insurance Agency – 1012 Pennsylvania Avenue (Keystone Block Building)
Current

_____

Paul Mandalakas Real Estate – corner Ninth Street and Washington Avenue
2011, Current
>His real estate agency is located in the old Hotel Monaca building.

_____

The Rossi Group – insurance agency - 318 Ninth Street
Current

_____

Joseph E. Smith Assoc. / JESA –1096 Pennsylvania Avenue (at 1018 Pennsylvania Avenue in 1990)
1983, Current
        Founded Oct 3, 1983.
        Marketing all lines of insurance.

_____

The York Agency Inc. – Insurance – 1231 Pennsylvania Avenue
1978, 2000, 2003, Current

2015

_____

Bechtel & Lindsay – 1036 Pennsylvania Avenue
1953, 1963

        Then........

Miksch Agency – 1036 Pennsylvania Avenue
1903, 1912, 1930, 1931, 1940
        Opened in 1903 by Henry Miksch and it was passed down through the family.
        Henry still had the business in 1912.   Henry also resided in the same building.
        He retired in Aug 1940.
                He was living at 111 Fourth Street in 1940.   He formerly was in the grocery
                business with his sister Mrs. Mary Bechtel but started in the real estate business.
                He was succeeded in business by his nephew William Bechtel, son of
                Fred and Mary Bechtel.
        Then ....

Bechtel Insurance Agency – 1036 Pennsylvania Avenue
1940, 1986, 2000s
        Was family owned business originally owned by Henry Miksch.
                1940 William and Vera Bechtel took over their uncle's business.
                1986 Hank Bechtel became the owner.
        Had insurance businesses in Monaca for over 60 years as of 2002.
        In 2002 it was run by Linda Hulme and Hank Bechtel.
        2014 – J. Kevin Kopac is listed here as an insurance agent.

        Then.......

Bechtel-Kopac Insurances – 1036 Pennsylvania Avenue
Current

_____

Branthoover Insurance – 298 Ninth Street
1979, Current
        Opened Dec 1979.   Owned by W. James Branthoover.   Nationwide Insurance business.

1990 ad

_____

This was most likely not a Real Estate Agent, but rather an individual who took out a large
ad to sell property he owned.

1906

***   ***   ***   ***   ***

TRAVEL BUSINESSES

Travel Unlimited – 1138 Pennsylvania Avenue
1974, 1977, 1985,
      Calvin Swink and Roy Winkler – owners 1975.
      Calvin Swink, Roy Winkler, and Daniel McPeek were the owners in 1976.
      Closed by 1988.

————

Centi Travel – 316 Tenth Street, then 1012 Pennsylvania Avenue
1984, 1990, 2011, current
      Located at the back section of building where Gnu Tubs is located (2016), former bank building.
      Started Oct 1984.   1988 owners were Arlene and Constance Centi.

*** *** *** *** ***

ATTORNEYS AT LAW

Phillip Grimm
1860

————

William J. Mellon – lawyer - 1529 Pennsylvania Avenue
1892, 1893, 1900, 1907, 1912
      He was the Borough Attorney in 1907.
      William married Ellen E., they resided on Pennsylvania Avenue and I believe he considered
            this his place of the business, too.
      By 1912, William had opened an office in Beaver; but still resided at Pennsylvania Avenue.

————

Charles R. Eckert – Attorney at Law
1906, 1907, 1912, 1916, 1920
      Had his office in Beaver under Eckert and Sohn but he continued to provide services to Monaca residents,
too,
            since Charles and Clara lived on Eckert Road in Monaca Heights.
      He was a former Congressman.
      Charles owned property/building(s) in the Monaca downtown area.

Charles R. Eckert

————

Squire W. W. Morgan – dispensed the law – Pennsylvania Avenue
1903, 1910
      Rented the office adjoining Mateer Bros. Meat Market.

————

Richard A. Alberti – Attorney at Law – 298 Ninth Street
1987, 1990, 2003

_____

William Butchko – attorney –
1994
      R. Eric Simon's successor.

_____

Robert E. McCreary and John Prather, Attorneys - 1026 Pennsylvania Avenue (2nd floor Batchelor Building)
1922, 1930, 1944
      Robert was the new District Attorney of Beaver County in Jan 1936.
      In Jul 1944, Robert was named by Governor Martin as judge of the court of common
            pleas of the Thirty-sixth Judicial District composed of Beaver County.   His term was
            through Jan 1946.
      Robert was b 1897 in Monaca; s/o Thomas McCreary; married Ellen Cain;
            lived at Pennsylvania Avenue.
            In 1922, his address was Seventeenth Street & Pennsylvania Avenue.

_____

R. Eric Simons, Attorney at Law – 1201 Pennsylvania Avenue
1950, 1990
      Opened office Jul 1950.
      Was first assistant to District Attorney Richard Steward in 1958.
            He served in that position from Feb 1953 and resigned in Dec 1958 to devote more
            time to his practice in Monaca.
      Eric was the borough solicitor in 1965, still in that position in 1975.

2015

_____

Law Offices.....
Joseph Askar, Attorney – 1016 Pennsylvania Avenue
Debra Genevie, Attorney – 1016 Pennsylvania Avenue
2002, 2015,
      In the Keystone Block Bldg.

***   ***   ***   ***   ***

BILLARDS   POOL ROOMS   ARCADES   BOWLING

Prof. J. E. Bittner's Billiard Parlors   aka
                    Bittner's Restaurant and Billiard Parlor –1311-1315* Pennsylvania Avenue
1898, 1907, 1910,
        John E. Bittner owner.
                *Beside Lindsay's store, which was at 1317 Pennsylvania Avenue in 1910.
        The restaurant was in front of building.   Pool and billiard room was in the rear.
        There were slot machines – one in both the lunch room and one in the billiard room.
        Hot and cold lunch served at all times – tables in first class condition.
        He used to be known for his turtle soup.
        He was also an avid organizer of community events.
        He had billiard and pool contests – in one there was a prize of $15 in gold.
        His business was fondly referred to as "Johnny's."
        Sep 30, 1908 - Plans for number of improvements to restaurant.
                John E. was married to Ida L. __; they had 3 children.
                1930 - John was living with daughter Beryl and her family.   Curiously, Ida was not
                        listed, but John was still marked as "married" (?).   He was also listed
                        as *chef* of the restaurant.
                John E. died earlier in 1944; Ida died in 1942.
                1939 and 1942 they lived at 932 Pennsylvania Avenue.
                Their daughter Beryl married Godfrey Miller.
                Another daughter, Elva B. married William Massey (former mayor of Monaca); Elva then
                        became Beaver County's first woman burgess when she succeeded her husband
                        in 1956.
        Also see Bittner's and Miller's under the Restaurant section.

        _____

Fred Leffert – pool room
1892, 1893
        Fred also was a dealer in fresh and smoked meats, poultry, and game in season.

        _____

Marsh Weigle – pool room – unknown location
1892, 1893

        _____

E. W. Nelson's Shooting Gallery & Bowling Alley – Sparling Building (corner of Sixth Street and
1904   Pennsylvania Avenue)

        _____

Michael Leary Pool Room – Pennsylvania Avenue – opposite the Hotel Hamilton – (1100 block)
1906
            He opened his pool and billiard room in the building opposite the Hotel Hamilton on
                Pennsylvania Avenue on Saturday, May 5, 1906.

        _____

Monaca Alleys   aka   National Billiard Parlor – 1142 Pennsylvania Avenue
1903, 1907, 1940, 1950
> Pool and billiards.
> Was renovated as of Sep 1940 – called National Bowling Alleys.
> There was a Monaca Bowling team who used the Monaca Alleys in 1906.
> There was a Duck Pin League in 1907.
> An ad in 1950 said"Monaca Bowling Alleys Opening Sept 15."   I have to presume this
> > was NOT the big bowling alleys on Pacific Avenue since that business did not
> > open until 1962.

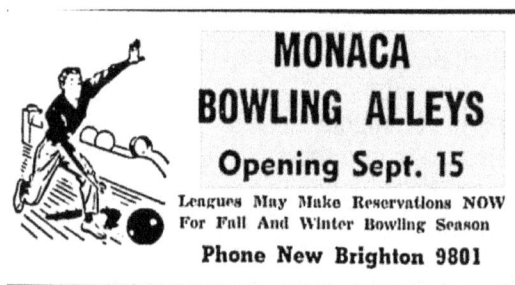

MONACA BOWLING ALLEYS
Opening Sept. 15
Leagues May Make Reservations NOW
For Fall And Winter Bowling Season
Phone New Brighton 9801

Aug 1950

————

E. Levy's "Owl Billiard Academy" – Pennsylvania Avenue
1902, 1904
> E. S. Levy was from Beaver Falls.
> Moved his pool tables and fixtures into the large store room in the Bartel Building to open
> > up a pool and billiard parlor – was closed the first of Jan 1904 and was no longer
> > there as of Feb 1904.
> (George Bartel moved in with his confectionery business Feb 1904.)

————

Wurzel's Arcade –   penny arcade business - Pennsylvania Avenue
1907, 1910, 1911
> G. N. Wurzel, Jr. – owner.
> He had a room in the rear of the arcade enlarged and a stage erected to accommodate moving
> > pictures and to run a vaudeville house –called *Nickelodeon and Family Theatre* (see
> > Theatre section).
> Mrs. A. Davis moved to Monaca from Darlington and as of Aug 2, 1907 was going to conduct a
> > restaurant in this penny arcade.
> In 1911 he again enlarged the pool room and added a table.

————

Dugan & Eikins – billiards – location unknown
1910

————

W. Reynolds – billiards, bowling, etc., - Colona
1910

————

Evidently the building at 912 Pennsylvania Avenue was a popular place for billiards, pool, and/or bowling alleys……….

Stoll Billiards – 912 Pennsylvania Avenue
1924

Frank "Ham" Rambo – on one half of the building at 912 Pennsylvania Avenue
1928, 1929, 1930
      He operated a billiards and pool business and had bowling alleys.
      The building was owned by Martin Mild of Center Township in 1929.
      The business and building suffered from water damage during a fire in Dec 28, 1929 of
            next door building at 910 Pennsylvania Avenue.

Mild Billiard Room – 912 Pennsylvania Avenue
1928, 1943

Mild Bowling Alleys - 912 Pennsylvania Avenue
1929, 1943
      Martin Mild was owner of the building.
      When I found references, some had Mr. Rambo as proprietor, others stated
            Martin Mild.   The reference of "Mild" may have come because he owned the
            building, but then he may have continued the businesses after Ham Rambo, too (?).

———————

Another popular place for billiards, pool, and/or bowling alleys was the basement area of the Block Building at 312 Ninth Street.   The basement area had a separate access/entrance from the street, so the operating hours of any business could be separate from those of any on the upper levels.

Zitzman's Pool Room – basement of the Citizen's Nat'l Bank Building – Ninth Street
1906   (??there was a George Zitzman who had a business on Ninth Street in 1901??)

Charles Sweet's pool room and restaurant – basement of the bank building (Citizen's)
1908, 1910
      Sept 1908 - He took charge of the pool and billiard parlor and lunch room in the basement of
            the Citizen's Bank Building. Was going to make a number of improvements – new side
            walls, room would be painted and decorated, the bowling alleys would be repaired, and
            everything put in first class shape.
      There were outside stairs to this business.
      In Mar 1909 he had it newly painted and decorated and added a large sign placed on the
            exterior of the place.
      By 1920, Charles was divorced and living in Pittsburgh.

Cable's Bowling - in the basement of the Citizen Bank Building – Ninth St
1902, 1904
      Conducted by John V. Cable.
      John married Elizabeth A; they resided at the same address as bowling alley (may have
            been in the hotel ?   (They were in Pittsburgh by 1910 where he owned a 5 & 10 store.)

George T. Bell's Pool Room – 312 Ninth Street
1912   George and Bertha lived on Monaca Heights.

———————

McClain Billiards & Bowling Parlors –1018 Pennsylvania Avenue - basement of Keystone Bldg
                                    -310-312 B Ninth Street - Citizen's Bank Building (Apr 1930)
1928, 1930, 1931, 1943
            Was also called "Marty's Place."
            John McClain was proprietor.   He was staying at the Hamilton Hotel in 1930.
      The basement area sustained damages from water and smoke due to a fire the
            end of Mar 1930.   John had the recreation room at that time.

ANNOUNCING THE OPENING
TODAY — of the

McClain Billiard & Bowling Parlors

IN THEIR NEW LOCATION

CITIZENS' BANK BLD'G - Monaca, Pa.

1930

Monaca Athletic Agency – 312 Ninth Street
1940, 1941

And yet one more "basement" area was used……………….

Pool Room – basement of Keystone Block Building
1910   W. H. Dunham of Rochester and Walter Eikins of Beaver owners.

Harry Davis Billiard Parlor– basement of post office (Keystone Building)
1924

On the 1940 census there was one man I have no further information on, nor even know if he had the
business in Monaca…….but since he lived on Pacific Avenue in Monaca, I wanted to list in this section. The article
stated: Louis Pacitti was a *partner* in "a recreational center."

Tony Persians Billiards and Restaurant – Pennsylvania Avenue
1920, 1922   He lived at 1743 Pennsylvania Avenue in 1920.

David L. Patton – billiard room – 1317 Pennsylvania Avenue
1928, 1943

————————

Harry Dinsmore – manager of a bowling alley – unknown location
1930   Harry was staying at 1213 Pennsylvania Avenue.

————————

A. C. Lackey – 2578 Beaver Street
1940, 1941

————————

Jos. Lopez Billiards – 1142 Pennsylvania Avenue
1940, 1956
        Billiards and pool business.

————————

Monaca Bowling Lanes   – 1221 Pacific Avenue
        Opened in Aug 1962.
        Had the formal grand opening on Aug 11, 1962.
        Closed - ?
        The Monaca Lanes Lounge opened in Aug 1965.
            Owned by Theofan and Eleanora Tselepis, Aliquippa and Thomas and Margaret Diaddigo,
                Aliquippa.

AMF

·16 AMF
LANES
·SNACKS
AIR CONDITIONED
COCKTAIL LOUNGE
AMPLE PARKING

Join A Summer League

MONACA
LANES
1221 PACIFIC AVE
774-3692

With bowling being another favorite activity of Monaca residents, there were many bowling alleys in Monaca, and clubs would often times various clubs would have their own set of two, three, or four alleys for club members and team games.   One of these clubs listed previous was the Monaca Cornet Band Room.   They had two very nice alleys in the back of the club, sponsoring adult and youth team competitions.   (I still have my bowling shirt that I wore while on a team at the Band Room from well over 50 years ago – white with blue embroidered lettering.) Matches were also held weekly in the Monaca Turn Verein.

St. John's Church had duck pin lanes in their recreation hall, too. The Monaca Lanes on Pacific Avenue, located by the former railroad station, was the only public place in Monaca that supported tenpin bowling by the mid 1900s; many other places still maintained the duck pin alleys.   (Center Lanes was opened in 1959 prior to the Monaca Lanes grand opening in 1962.)

The majority of the ones listed previously would have been for duck pins.   Bowling in general was a top recreational activity between the mid 1930s and about 1957.   In the later 1950s, duck pin bowling began to phase out.   This phase out was partially due to the fact that each owner of the place with the duck pin alleys depended on having people (mostly school kids) there to set pins; if they didn't show up for work, and a quick substitute found, then there was no bowling.   With duck pins, there was nothing automated, instead "human" pin setters had to be there to return the balls, clear the knocked down pins, and set/reset pins – no automated machines for those chores.   The introduction of ten pin bowling was probably the main reason for the phasing out of duck pin alleys.   By 1959, ten pin bowling was in full swing along with the convenience of automation involved with the ten pin alleys.

There were many teams in Monaca found over the years.   Listed below is a small sampling of their names and the years of participation to show the variety of teams.

Monaca Team – 1903	Indians Team– 1922
Manufacturers' League – 1940	Graters
Monaca High School duckpin leagues - 1954	Church and Club League - 1940
Monaca Junior Bowling League – 1940	(girls' and boys' teams)
Monaca Community Bowling League – 1940	Monaca Hardware
Monaca Nationals	Sons of Italy
Monaca Bowling League – 1941	Benny's Team – 1950s
Polish Club Team – 1950s	Eagles Team – 1950s
Monaca Hotel Team – 1950s	Armstrong's Team – 1950s
American Legion Team – 1950s	
Monaca Businessmen's and Club Bowling League – 1940	

Other teams over the years: Yanks, Giants, Redsox, Cubs, Pirates, Tigers, Bees, Reds, Athletics, Browns, Cubans, Nicks, Cubans, (and my favorite)- Unknowns (Yes, this was actually a name of a team.)

In my usual practice, I once again go off schedule and give miscellaneous information just for general purposes...............
        Did you know ....
    There were two kinds of duckpins – the Rubber band type and the Baltimore duckpins which had no rubber bands.   Rubber band duckpins originated in the 1920s in Western Pennsylvania.   A duck pin bowling ball was 4 ¾" to 5" in diameter (about the size of a grapefruit, slightly larger than a softball) and weighed 3 lb 6 oz to 3 lb 12 oz; having no finger holes. A duck pin ball is held in the palm of the hand when bowling.   A duck pin itself is shorter, smaller and lighter than a ten pin, about 2/3 the size.   Bowlers have three balls per frame (instead of two as in ten-pin bowling) to knock over a set of 10 pins.   If a bowler knocks down all 10 pins with their first roll in a frame, it is scored as a strike..   If all the pins are knocked down in two rolls, the bowler has made a spare.   If all the pins are knocked down in three rolls, it is scored as a straight ten (with no additional pins added next frame as in ten pins).
    A ten pin bowling ball has drilled holes for the fingers, is between 26.704" and 27.002" and weight can range from 6 to 16 lbs.   A ten pin is 4.75 inches wide; 15 inches tall; weighs from 3 lb 6 oz to 3 lb 10 oz.   In ten pins, there are only two throws of the ball per frame.

*** *** *** *** ***

NEWSPAPERS and NEWS STANDS and PRINTING

My research was aided considerably by articles and snippets of news in local publications. I found it interesting and wanted to share with you one woman who contributed much of the information to the newspaper (the *Daily Times* in particular). This was Mrs. Mae Perdew Gaertner. She was a veteran local newspaper woman with more than a quarter of a century of service as of 1937. She began her newspaper activity back in 1910 as a reporter for the old Beaver "*Star*" (Howard Bliss was the editor). Then she became an employee of the "*Tribune*" in Beaver Falls (John H. Telford editor). In 1916, Miss Mae Perdew married Elmer Gaertner of Monaca and became the mother of two daughters. Mae re-entered the newspaper field and was employed by *The Times*. Her husband died in 1936 and she not only tended to her family, but continued her work, publishing the happenings in the area. She lived at Indiana Avenue.

There were other representatives of *The Times* who report on Monaca news. One of those was.......
> Marshal R. Hall – *The Daily Times* – 1911, 1912
>> In 1912, Marshall was listed as the sporting editor of *The Daily Times*.
>> He lived at Pennsylvania Avenue in 1912.
> C. O. Denizer was a Representative – May 1917.

The Daily Times was first established Apr 2, 1874.
> *The Daily Times* was the only local daily newspaper circulated in Rochester – Monaca – Freedom - Beaver – Bridgewater – Conway – Vanport – Midland.

The Beaver Argus – one of the oldest newspapers in the country was established Nov 4, 1808.
> It consolidated with *The Times* Jul 1, 1930.
>> Published every evening except Sunday by the Daily Times Company. The Times Building was located at Third Avenue, Beaver; but the paper was a staple for all surrounding areas.

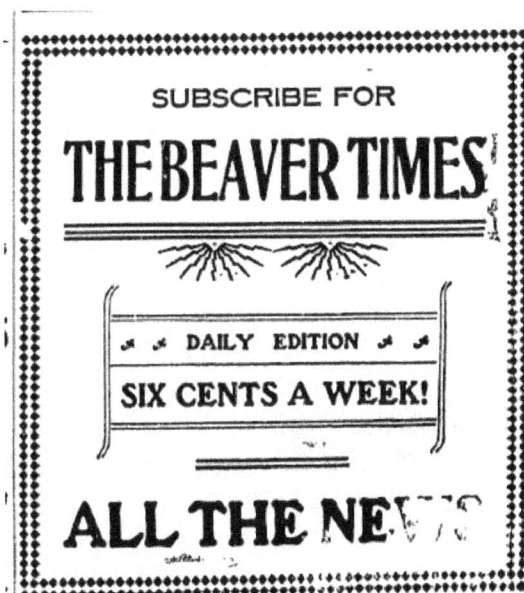

SUBSCRIBE FOR

THE BEAVER TIMES

DAILY EDITION

SIX CENTS A WEEK!

ALL THE NEWS

1906

Although not actually in the newspaper or printing business..............

Miss Cynthia Hood of Ninth Street took position of the *messenger* between Monaca and
       Pittsburgh and started late May 1903 – paper stated she was "well qualified for the position."

Harvey J. Taylor – was a *messenger* between Monaca and Pittsburgh
       In 1892, 1893 his profession was listed as *reporter.*
       Decided to discontinue the work as of Oct 1, 1903.

_____

Harry Neeley – printer (newspaper)
1900

_____

A. C. Antoline Advertising and Office Supply Co.– 1526 Washington Avenue
1945, 1989
       Owned by Albert C. Antoline in 1945; then by Richard S. in 1989 and Anna L. Antoline
          was office manager.
       They did not have a newspaper publication, but had office supply and advertising type of business
          in 1990.

_____

Office of *Monaca Herald* – Pennsylvania Avenue
1903, 1904
       The new weekly paper published at Monaca made its first appearance Friday, Nov 13, 1903
          and was called "*Monaca News*" – but name was changed by Nov 16, 1903
          to "*Monaca Herald*" because of a possible conflict that might occur between it and
          the *Beaver Valley News* which was published at New Brighton.
       The cylinder press arrived, was set up, and the paper was ready to be printed on
          Nov 19, 1903.
       George A. Jones – editor in Nov 1903.
       Cornelius Wurzel worked here in 1903.
       George A. Jones was the editor in 1904.
       Oliver Boyd entered the *Monaca Herald* office as an apprentice.
       Harry Patton was on the *Monaca Herald's* force in Mar 1904.

_____

Weber's News – (next to Roxy Theatre) – 924 Pennsylvania Avenue (1949)
1949, 1957, 1965   Moved to 1098 Pennsylvania Avenue (may have been #1018)
       Sold tobacco products.
       They sold all types of magazines, comic books, and coins. Had model airplanes for sale, too.

_____

J. A. Shaffer – was a news dealer on Pennsylvania Avenue
1903, 1904

_____

Monaca News Company – (1922) (Pennsylvania Avenue and Twelfth St)
                            – 1308 Pennsylvania Avenue   and 1317 Pennsylvania Avenue
1900, 1911, 1923, 1940, 1965, 1990

    At some point it was just known as...............

Mullen's News Depot
1902, 1929,
        George V. Mullen had this business for many years - a newspaper distributer.
                He married Minnie Lais (d/o George and wife #2 Alice Wilson Lais); they lived on
                Washington Avenue. He died in 1924; Minnie died in 1939.
        He conducted his news stand for many years and handled nearly 1500 papers
                by 1911 – both local and out of town papers. Upon George's death, his wife,
                Minnie and their daughter Ella ran the news stand; then sold it in Apr 1929
                to Charles Lindsay.   Minnie was listed on the Mercantile Tax List in 1928 and 1929.
        Was a "sub-station" for *The Daily Times* newspaper.
        These papers were either sold at the stand or distributed to subscribers by five
                newsboys in his employ.   The boys would deliver the early editions before they
                had to arrive or report to school; the afternoon issues were distributed
                shortly after school hours.
        Mr. Mullen was also known for being an agent for *The Daily Times* and was said
                to be instrumental in the large circulation of the paper in Monaca.
        In addition to selling the newspapers, Mr. Mullen carried a line of good cigars and candies;
                also sold fire crackers and fireworks.
        George was well known for his punctuality.
        He also served a number of years in the Borough Council.
        Through the census and directories, his occupation was listed as *News dealer/agency.*
        He had a large Hamilton lamp installed in front of his news agency on Jan 6, 1903.

As stated Charles Lindsay acquired the business in 1929.
        Operated by Charles K. Lindsay for more than 30 years.
        He distributed the *Daily Times* in Monaca.
        Charles also had a confectionery in town for many years.

    Then owned by........

Geo. J. Schmidt – Pennsylvania Avenue and Twelfth Street
        He was selling out at cost, dry goods, notions, shoes, tin and granite ware.

1937

FOR SALE—Soda fountain complete, A-1 condition, priced low for quick disposal. Monaca News Co., 1317 Pennsylvania avenue, Monaca.   8ı23-28 inc.

_____

Fisher's Store –   1001 Pennsylvania Avenue (corner of Pennsylvania and Tenth Street) beside
the Klingseisen bakery)

     See General Store Section for more details.

_____

Main Street News - 1206 Pennsylvania Avenue
1984, 1990, 1991
     Opened in 1986.
     Convenience store type business – John & Helen Antoline owners.
     Featured Herman's bakery products, magazines, newspapers, cigarettes, pop, milk,
         candy, crafts, Rosalind Candy, Stanley home products, and lottery tickets.
         The store also bought and sold baseball cards.
     It opened in 1986 and was remodeled inside and out, awning was added.
     John went on to become the Mayor of Monaca and also was a Beaver County
         commissioner in 1992.

_____

A more recent business that was found listed:
     Keystone Motorcycle Press – 1522 Atlantic Avenue – publishers

_____

Eshbaugh Printing Service – 421 Fifteenth Street
1977, 1978

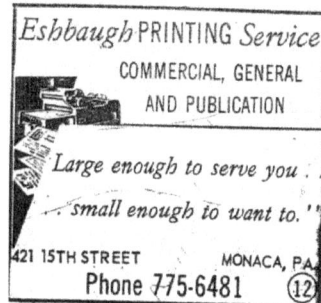

Eshbaugh PRINTING Service
COMMERCIAL, GENERAL
AND PUBLICATION

"Large enough to serve you . . .
. . . small enough to want to."

421 15TH STREET   MONACA, PA.
Phone 775-6481   ⑫

_____

Oscar L. Dixon Printing – 1135 Pennsylvania Avenue; in 1951 he was at 1531 Pennsylvania Avenue
1936, 1951

*** *** *** *** ***
*** *** ***

BIBLIOGRAPHY and/or REFERENCES are all listed at the end of Volume II.

Thus ends Volume I of this book, BUT ....

there is much more continued in Volume II.

VOLUME II   Table of Contents

RAILROAD DEPOTS / STATIONS
        Sixth Street Station   New Freight Station – Sixteenth Street
        Colona Depot   Monaca Passenger Depot / Station
RAILROAD COMPANIES
        Pittsburgh and Lake Erie Railroad / P & LE RR
        CSX Transportation
                CABOOSES
MONACA-BEAVER RAILROAD BRIDGES
MISCELLANEOUS RAILROAD INFORMATION
STREET CARS
        Beaver Valley Traction Company   Rochester Transit Corporation
        Monaca Heights Street Railway Company
MOTOR COACHES
        Mitchell Buss Company   Red Star Transit Company
        Rochester Motor Coach Company   Beaver Valley Motor Coach Company
CHURCHES (includes pictures and information on....)
        St. Peter's German Evangelical Lutheran Church   Lutheran Church of the Redeemer
        Slovak Lutheran   Emmanuel Baptist Church
        Colona United Presbyterian Church   McGuire Chapel
        First Presbyterian Church of Phillipsburg   First Presbyterian Church of Monaca
        Methodist Episcopal Church of Phillipsburg   Free Methodist Church
        Free Methodist Church of Sylvan Crest   Monaca Free Methodist Church
        Calvary Baptist Church   Emmanuel Gospel and Tract Mission
        St. John the Baptist   Other local churches serving Monaca residents
CEMETERIES (includes pictures and information on....)
        Baker Cemetery aka Baldwin Cemetery   Monaca German Lutheran Cemetery   aka
        Beaver County Poor Home Cemetery   St. Peter's Church Cemetery
        Fairview Cemetery   Union Cemetery
        McGuire Chapel Cemetery   St. John the Baptist Parish Cemetery
        North Branch Cemetery   Van Kirk Cemetery aka McCullough Cemetery
FINANCIAL INSTITUTES
    Includes pictures and information on past and recent banks, savings and loans, lending institutes.
MEDICAL
        Pharmacies / Drug Stores   Hospitals
        Doctors   Water Cure Sanitarium
        Beaver County Home aka County Poor Farm   Beaver County Tuberculosis Sanitarium
UNIONS
MILLS and INDUSTRY
ORGANIZATIONS
    Includes pictures and information on past, recent, present groups and organization.
ATHLETES and ATHLETICS
            Opalite Park   Colonial Steel Field / Colonial Field
            Clubs Teams   Noted Athletes of Monaca
FUN FACTS AND SNIPPETS OF INFORMATION
PEOPLE AND FAMILIES
ENTERTAINMENT and RECREATION
        NICKELODEONS and THEATRES
        LEISURE AND RECREATIONAL SITES
        AMUSEMENT and   PICNIC PARKS (includes pictures and information on many of the area parks)
        SWIMMING   Monaca Beaches   Monaca Swimming Pool
        GOLFING
        ROLLER SKATING
        ICE SKATING RINK
WEATHER EVENTS
ADS   INTERESTING ARTICLES   MISCELLANEOUS INFORMATION
    Includes information on a plane crash in the Ohio River.
HOUSE RESOLUTION – No. 406
1785 TO 1986 YEAR BY YEAR OF INTERESTING HAPPENINGS
BIBLIOGRAPHY and/or REFERENCES for both Volume I and Volume II.

www.ingramcontent.com/pod-product-compliance
Lightning Source LLC
Chambersburg PA
CBHW081646280326
41928CB00070B/3163